T0329626

AFTER CRISIS

CRISIS

Adjustment, Recovery and Fragility in East Asia

AFTER CRISIS

Adjustment, Recovery and Fragility in East Asia

Edited by
Jayati Ghosh and C.P. Chandrasekhar

 Tulika Books

Published by **Tulika Books**
35 A/1 (third floor), Shahpur Jat, New Delhi 110 049, India

First published in India 2009

ISBN: 978-81-89487-58-4

Typeset in Sabon and Univers at Tulika Print Communication Services,
New Delhi, and printed at Chaman Enterprises, 1603 Pataudi House,
Daryaganj, Delhi 110 002

Contents

.

Contributors   vii

Introduction JAYATI GHOSH & C.P. CHANDRASEKHAR   1

**The Changing Contours of Financial Crises
in Developing Countries**

Financial Crises, Reserve Accumulation and Capital Flows
PRABHAT PATNAIK   19

Continuity or Change?: Finance Capital in Developing Countries
a Decade after the Asian Crisis
C.P. CHANDRASEKHAR   32

Crisis and Its Aftermath in East and Southeast Asia

Adjustment, Recovery and Growth after Financial Crisis:
A Consideration of Five 'Crisis' Countries of East and
Southeast Asia
JAYATI GHOSH   55

Unchained Melody: Economic Performance after the Asian Crisis
EDSEL L. BEJA, JR.   69

Thai Capital after the Asian Crisis
PASUK PHONGPAICHIT & CHRISTOPHER BAKER   89

Ten Years after the Crisis: A Bright Future for Capitalism
in Thailand?
BRUNO JETIN   108

Monetarist and Neoliberal Solutions in Indonesia: Old Wine
in New Bottles?
RIZAL RAMLI & P. NURYADIN   120

The Role of Foreign Capital in the South Korean Financial
Crisis and Recovery
DOOWON LEE   142

The End of Developmental Citizenship?: Economic Restructuring
and Social Displacement in Post-Crisis South Korea
CHANG KYUNG-SUP   165

Financial Liberalization, Crises and the Role of Capital Controls:
The Malaysian Case
JOMO K.S.   180

The Philippines Ten Years after the Asian Crisis
JOSEPH ANTHONY LIM   191

**Economic Performance after Financial Crisis in
Other Emerging Markets**

Latin American Financial Crises and Recovery
JAN KREGEL   209

Patterns of Adjustment under the Age of Finance: The Case of
Turkey as a Peripheral Agent of Neoliberal Globalization
ERINC YELDAN   225

Recovery and Adjustment after the 1998 Russian Currency Crisis
VLADIMIR POPOV   245

Other Asian Experiences

China and Post-Crisis Globalization: Towards a New
Developmentalism?
DIC LO   273

Vietnam and the Experience of the Asian Crisis
PIETRO PAOLO MASINA   292

Index   309

Contributors

BRUNO JETIN is at the Research Institute for Development (IRD), France; and CEPN-University of Paris Nord, France.

C.P. CHANDRASEKHAR is Professor at the Centre for Economic Studies and Planning, School of Social Sciences, Jawaharlal Nehru University, New Delhi, India.

CHANG KYUNG-SUP is Professor of Sociology at Seoul National University, Seoul, South Korea.

CHRISTOPHER BAKER is an eminent historian and social scientist based in Bangkok, Thailand.

DIC LO is Professor of Economics at the School of Oriental and African Studies, University of London, UK; and at the School of Economics, Renmin University, Beijing, China.

DOOWON LEE is Professor at the School of Economics, Yonsei University, Seoul, South Korea.

EDSEL L. BEJA, JR. is Deputy Director of the Ateneo Center for Economic Research and Development, Philippines; and teaches economics and political economy at Ateneo de Manila University, Philippines.

ERINC YELDAN is Visiting Professor and Sheridan Barber Chair, University of Massachusetts, Amherst, USA; and Professor of Economics, Bilkent University, Ankara, Turkey.

JAN KREGEL is Professor of Economics at the Levy Economics Institute, Bard College, USA; Centre for Full Employment and Price Stability, University of Missouri, Kansas City, USA; and Tallinn University of Technology, Estonia.

JAYATI GHOSH is Professor at the Centre for Economic Studies and Planning, School of Social Sciences, Jawaharlal Nehru University, New Delhi, India.

JOMO K.S. is Assistant Secretary-General for Economic Affairs at UN-DESA, United Nations, New York. He was previously Professor of Economics at University of Malaya, Kuala Lumpur, Malaysia.

JOSEPH ANTHONY LIM is Professor of Economics at Ateneo de Manila University, Philippines.

P. NURYADIN is Senior Researcher at ECONIT Advisory Group, Jakarta, Indonesia.

PASUK PHONGPAICHIT is Emeritus Professor, Faculty of Economics, Chulalongkorn University, Bangkok, Thailand.

PIETRO PAOLO MASINA is Associate Professor of International Political Economy, University of Naples 'L'Orientale', Italy.

PRABHAT PATNAIK is Professor at the Centre for Economic Studies and Planning, School of Social Sciences, Jawaharlal Nehru University, New Delhi, India; and Vice-Chairman of the State Planning Board, Government of Kerala, India.

RIZAL RAMLI is the former Coordinating Minister of Economics in Indonesia; and current Chairman of the Board of ECONIT Advisory Group, Jakarta, Indonesia.

VLADIMIR POPOV is Professor at the New Economic School, Moscow, Russia; and at the Institute of European and Russian Studies (EURUS), Carleton University, Ottawa, Canada.

Introduction

Jayati Ghosh & C.P. Chandrasekhar

The global financial crisis that exploded around September 2008 was just one more in a series of crises that have affected more than sixty countries in the era of globalization and financial liberalization. Of course the latest crisis is particularly significant in a number of ways: it originated in the core of capitalism, in the world's largest and most powerful economy, the United States; it has spread dramatically across the world, through financial contagion and the effects on the real economy, even to countries that earlier seemed to be relatively secure; it is calling into question many of the mainstream economic dogmas that have dominated economic policy-making for more than two decades. Yet in some other significant ways, this crisis is not very different from those that have preceded it in the recent past, since it reflects many of the consequences of unregulated finance and the imbalanced development of capitalism. So any analysis of previous crises, and particularly of the implications of different strategies of adjustment and recovery after such crises, still has much relevance for the current situation.

July 2007 marked the completion of a decade since the onset of financial crises in several East and Southeast Asian countries. The crisis of 1997, whose effects are still visible, focused attention on the dangers associated with a world dominated by fluid finance. It brought home the fact that financial liberalization can result in crises even in so-called 'miracle economies'. Prior to the crisis, the pace and pattern of growth in many countries in that region were challenging the dominance of the original capitalist powers over the global economy. In fact the crisis marked the waning of the 'East Asian miracle', which could be described as the third major process in the post-war period (after the initial success of import-substituting growth in many developing countries and the oil price hikes of the 1970s) that sought to alter significantly the distribution of income across the world in favour of some developing nations. The 1997 crisis set back that process, and even after a decade many of these countries have not been able to recover their pre-crisis dynamism.

The Asian crisis ensured this turn of events through a number of routes. In hindsight, it is clear that currency and financial crises have devastating effects on the real economy. Even when crises are essentially financial in origin and in their unfolding, their effects do not remain confined to the realm of finance. The ensuing liquidity crunch and wave of bankruptcies result in severe deflation, with attendant consequences for employment and the standard of living. The adoption, post-crisis, of conventional IMF (International Monetary Fund) stabiliza-tion strategies tends to worsen the situation. Thereafter, governments become so sensitive to the possibility of future crises that they continue to adopt very restrictive macroeconomic policies and restrain public expenditure even in crucial social sectors. Finally, asset-price deflation and devaluation pave the way for foreign capital inflows that finance a transfer of ownership of assets from domestic to foreign investors, thereby enabling a conquest by international capital of important domestic assets and resources.

This book is concerned with delineating the alternative trajectories of post-crisis development in different economies, the lessons they offer and the implications they have for alternative policies. The initial adjustment to the crisis varied significantly across countries, from an acceleration of liberalization in some (South Korea and Thailand) to greater intervention in others (Malaysia). In some ways, all these economies have recovered. But the recovery has not meant a return to 'miracle' status. Instead, it has been accompanied by significant acquisition, at deflated prices, of productive assets in these economies by foreign firms. It has involved a substantial restructuring of the financial sector. It has altered the nature of engagement of the world system by these economies. And it has involved a setback to achievements on the human development front.

Clearly, therefore, it is important to take stock of these processes of adjustment and restructuring, their impact in terms of recovery and growth, the degree to which the problem of fragility has been addressed and the fallout for progress on human development. This is important not only for understanding the experience of the 'crisis economies' of East and Southeast Asia *per se*, but also because it is now becoming evident, a decade after the crisis, that the inter-national financial system has still not evolved effective ways of preventing such crises among emerging economies and of reducing their damaging effects. Indeed, an examination of the post-crisis experience of countries outside the East Asian region reveals important similarities (as well some notable differences) that have implications for all developing countries that have undergone a significant degree of global economic integration.

This book therefore has a wider focus than the East Asian 'crisis econo-mies' alone, in that it tries to situate post-crisis developments in a broader analysis of the recent political economy of international capitalism, in particular, the role of mobile finance. It also offers comparative perspectives on post-crisis restructuring in other important developing countries that have experienced crisis, such as Russia, Turkey, Argentina, Brazil and Mexico; as well as on the experience of other countries in Asia that were affected by, but did not experience the financial crisis. While the essays in this book were originally written in 2007, they still remain extraordinarily relevant to the present times, not least because they anticipated the processes that led to the global financial meltdown in 2008. A key insight of much of the analysis in this book is how market-oriented strategies to cope with the crisis created further financial fragility in many post-crisis economies, thereby rendering them extremely vulnerable to future contagion and volatility, exactly in the manner that has been experienced in 2008 and 2009. To that extent, many of these papers effectively predict the severe impact on both the financial variables and the real economy that the global crisis is currently having upon developing countries in particular.

Of course, several of the papers do focus directly on the experience of adjustment and recovery in East and Southeast Asia. Two questions dominate in these discussions. First, how the particular choices made after the crisis influenced the differential dependence on and the impact of new forms of finance in different countries, and the transformation of the nature and role of the financial sector. Second, how this affected development trajectories and outcomes in the countries concerned, in particular with respect to the substantial dilution of the developmental role of the state, the growing presence of foreign firms and the increase in consolidation and concentration in the real sectors, and the impact all this has had on employment, social indicators and the environment.

The first section of the book is devoted to papers that analyse the implications of recent developments in what is now very clearly the *world* of finance, for the potential for financial stability and crisis, and for real economies in the developing world. They provide both theoretical arguments and empirical analyses with regard to the effects of the mobility of finance on economic volatility and real economic processes in affected countries.

The starting point for Prabhat Patnaik's analysis is the recognition that financial liberalization has had the important effect of bringing third world assets into the ambit of portfolio decisions of first world wealth-holders. His important insight is that for a developing country under financial openness, a stock equilibrium cannot exist without inelastic expectations regarding the value of that country's currency with respect to the dollar (or reserve currency). The stock equilibrium is determined by the behaviour of financial asset markets, which determines the exchange rate. When this entails a rise in the exchange rate (because the country concerned is found attractive by international investors), income and employment must shrink. Such a rise can be prevented if the central bank intervenes to stabilize the exchange rate by holding more foreign currency reserves, which therefore becomes necessary not only as a precaution against future financial crisis, but also for preventing a drop in the level of employment and income in the economy.

However, this attempt to stabilize the economy also means that the stock equilibrium cannot be achieved. Furthermore, even with the disequilibrium, the central bank cannot prevent the occurrence of financial crises – all it can do is to prevent domestic financial crises from spilling over into foreign exchange crises. But even that is achieved at the cost of compounding the problem of instability over time. This is not an argument against central bank intervention but, rather, that such intervention should be transcended, essentially through the imposition of capital controls.

C.P. Chandrasekhar analyses the global trends in financial markets as well as the changes in financial structures that have occurred since the Asian crisis. He notes that the recent period has been marked by an unprecedented increase in liquidity in the international financial system, which has led both bank and non-bank financial institutions to search for new avenues of financial investment globally. This has led to an acceleration of mainly private financial flows to developing countries precisely during the years when, as a group, they have been characterized by rising surpluses on their current account. However, the high degree of concentration of such flows has implied excess exposure in a few 'chosen' countries. Meanwhile risk assessments are pro-cyclical, underestimating risk when investments are booming and overestimating risks when markets turn downwards. This has been associated with the herding of investors in developing country markets and their willingness to invest a larger volume of money in risky, unrated instruments. So he argues that in the decade after the Asian crisis, structural changes in the global financial system have been such that risk, including systemic risk, has only increased.

Financial liberalization has been critical to the process of financial consolidation and the proliferation of new institutions and instruments, which has contributed to the greater prevalence of systemic risk. The core of this system is unregulated entities making huge profits on highly speculative investments, specifically hedge funds and private equity firms. The proliferation of these new kinds of cross-border institutions, new instruments and new business practices creates new vulnerabilities that are reflected in financial booms that bear little relationship to 'fundamentals', as well as in crises. The impact is further complicated by the entanglement between institutions that financial liberalization allows, such that any downturn in one specific market spreads the effects into markets where these institutions have made unrelated investments. This is exemplified by the behaviour of financial markets in the wake of the 'sub-prime' lending crisis in the US.

So, notwithstanding perceptions that 'the world has changed', Chandrasekhar's paper points to an important continuity, in terms of both persisting and new forms of financial fragility that can lead to further financial crisis. He notes that self-regulation in financial markets clearly does not work, and so new measures to govern finance are essential.

The second part of the book is devoted to analyses of the processes of adjustment and recovery in the five East and Southeast Asian economies that were directly affected by the financial crisis of 1997–98: Thailand, South Korea, Indonesia, Malaysia and the Philippines. Two papers deal with these countries as a group, while others take up aspects of the particular experience of each of these countries.

Jayati Ghosh notes that because these economies appear to have recovered quite substantially, in current mainstream discussion the Asian crisis is often discussed not in terms of its negative impacts, but rather presented as an example of how economies can recover relatively quickly from crisis and continue on a favourable growth trajectory. However, a closer examination of the data suggests that while output and export growth have recovered to varying degrees, there have been significant changes in the pattern of growth, investment and employment generation. The most startling change is the divergence between savings and investment rates. Savings rates in these five countries increased from their already very high levels of 30–45 per cent, but investment rates plummeted, in some cases to only half the earlier level.

So, after 1998, although all these countries became more 'open' in terms of trade, finance and industrial policies, they stopped being net recipients of foreign savings. Instead, they have shown the opposite tendency of net resource outflow, as domestic savings have been higher than investment. The net savings were exported, either through private capital outflows or by adding to the external reserves of the central banks, which are typically held in very safe assets abroad (such as US Treasury Bills). This has happened even though the development project is not complete in these countries and the need for more domestic investment persists. Ghosh points out that in addition to monetary and financial policies, a large role in the reduction of investment rates was played by deflationary fiscal policies. This, in turn, has made aggregate employment growth much slower than before. So the effects of financial crises have gone beyond temporary economic shocks, since they have altered longer-term economic trajectories in less desirable ways.

Edsel Beja considers recent economic performance in the crisis-affected economies in terms of output foregone because of the crisis, and subsequent growth compared to previous growth. He argues that the growth performance after the crisis has actually been inferior when compared to pre-crisis performance. While there was robust economic growth in the immediate years after the crisis that resulted in some reductions in the costs, subsequent sluggish economic expansion meant that further cuts in the costs were not realized, and so the costs increased as a result. So the crisis-affected economies have not recouped the losses of 1997. While stronger economic performance is needed to reclaim the lost opportunities, Beja argues that unless economic policies in these economies move in a positive direction – reviving some of the strategies that proved useful in the past while also introducing new components to meet current challenges – future economic progress is likely to be limited and punctuated by crises. In particular, complacency with a seemingly stable economic environment is misplaced as long as the international financial system is characterized by massive and volatile financial flows, but economies remain ill-equipped to deal with the challenges produced by such flows.

These more general analyses of the recovery in the crisis-affected economies are confirmed by the specific consideration of particular country experiences. Thailand was the country in which the Asian financial crisis first 'broke', and the subsequent contagion affected other countries in the region. Pasuk Phongpaichit and Chris Baker provide a comprehensive assessment of the impact on Thai capital of both the crisis and the recovery. They note that after the crisis the Thai economy became significantly more open, more integrated into global markets, and more dependent on foreign investment and foreign demand. The most critical point that emerges from the paper relates to the significantly increased concentration of capital in Thailand after the crisis. One process was internal, as the crisis created a large number of losers among local business groups and a much smaller number of winners who expanded into the space created by the collapse of their rivals. However, the more significant process was the intrusion of multinationals, which began with the post-crisis government-sponsored fire-sale of distressed Thai companies, and continued into the following decade. Phongpaichit and Baker provide detailed examples of the retail market (where three multinational chains displaced tens of thousands of smaller stores), the automotive industry and the downstream steel industry. Even in the mobile phone market, which had substantial political support, two multinationals acquired a dominant position.

While the multinational-dominated export-oriented segment of the Thai economy boomed in the decade following the crisis, domestic investment recovered only partially. As a result, the pattern of high investment and savings rates that had characterized the pre-crisis period was broken, as both fell sharply. (Subsequently, there was a recovery of investment even if not to pre-crisis levels, because of the slightly different reconstruction strategy of the Thaksin government.) Investment rates fell because of declining rates of public investment as well as the shift away from a bank-based system to the Anglo-Saxon model of financing investment. Thus the crisis induced a fundamental change in the nature of Thai capital's involvement in the economy. Over the second half of the twentieth century, domestic capital had played a key role in expanding the productive potential of the Thai economy. However, after the 1997 crisis, it has been confined mostly to a rentier and service role in an economy dominated by multinational firms.

Bruno Jetin also considers the Thai experience, this time from the perspective of functional distribution of income and the returns to capital and labour. He argues that, while the financial crisis played a proximate role, the deeper origins of the crisis lay in the productive sphere, in the over-accumulation that had characterized Thai capitalism especially in the preceding decade. After the crisis the profit rate recovered rather quickly, and thereafter has remained high. This reflects the ability of employers to capture the major part of labour productivity at the expense of workers' compensation. However, the rate of accumulation, which had moved in line with the profit rate in the past, seems now to be disconnected from profit and has been decelerating, and this may affect the ability to increase productivity in future. This factor, combined with recent tendencies of the exchange rate, may combine to erode external competitiveness of Thai production and put further downward pressure on workers' income shares. Jetin therefore concludes that, despite the near-eradication of absolute poverty, Thai capitalism is unable to combine long-term growth and social progress, and is indeed dependent on the permanent repression of labour incomes.

The next paper deals with Indonesia, the country in which the crisis may have had the most significant political and economic impact, creating not only a major economic depression but also the conditions in which the authoritarian Soeharto regime collapsed. Rizal Ramli and P. Nuryadin show that the implementation of the IMF-inspired adjustment programme was the chief reason for Indonesia's slow recovery from the crisis, as compared to the other crisis-hit countries. In the immediate aftermath of the crisis, IMF recommendations – pushed also by the domestic 'Berkeley mafia' that controlled economic policy – created financial instability and mass bankruptcies by emphasizing a super-tight monetary policy. Then the IMF encouraged the transformation of private debt into public debt, thereby putting a huge burden on the state exchequer and precluding the possibility of an expansionary fiscal stance to aid recovery. In consequence, Indonesia's external debt doubled in the four years after the crisis, amounting to more than the GDP (gross domestic product) in 2001. The size of the domestic debt has been closely connected to Bank Indonesia's monetary policy, which kept interest rates high. The high levels of public debt and repayment requirements have led to reduced public expenditure, higher user charges on public services and privatization of state assets. The Indonesian government's recovery policies, supported by the IMF, relied on debt rather than investment for development and thus drove the economy into a deeper debt trap.

According to Ramli and Nuryaddin, efforts to stabilize financial indicators in Indonesia after the crisis have too often sacrificed the performance of the real sector, resulting in increases in poverty and unemployment. The obsession with very conservative monetary and fiscal targets has led to economic performance well below the potential in the period 2002–06, which may even point to the beginning of a process of deindustrialization. Despite this, the financial sector has boomed, in the form of unsustainable asset bubbles driven by hot money or the inflow of speculative finance from abroad. The authors suggest that this is creating conditions for a re-enactment of the financial crisis more than a decade after the first one. They conclude that any internal or external shock could precipitate such a crisis once again.

Doowon Lee's analysis of the role of foreign capital in the financial crisis and recovery in South Korea presents a somewhat different perspective. Lee argues that foreign capital was associated with the crisis because two types of mismanagement of foreign loans triggered the South Korean financial crisis in 1997: a mismatch of maturity, as South Korean financial institutions borrowed short-term foreign loans and lent long-term to South Korean firms; and miscalculation of the amount of usable foreign exchange reserves. But the recovery from the crisis was faster than expected, to some extent because of the role played by foreign capital (this time largely in the form of acquisitive foreign direct investment) in stabilizing the exchange rate and injecting liquidity into the system. The inflow of foreign capital also greatly altered the system of corporate governance in South Korea.

Foreign capital inflow further meant that the ownership structure of commercial banks in South Korea greatly changed, as it transferred a substantial part of the banking system to foreign owners and generally encouraged a process of consolidation. This was associated with improved bank profitability, but also with growing speculative investment with a short time-horizon. Most notably, several foreign private equity funds took over South Korean financial and real estate assets at discounted prices after the crisis, and sold them at much higher prices with windfall profits. It has been argued that foreign investors have also been responsible for depressing the investment spirit of South Korean firms by demanding very high dividend payments and imposing threats of hostile takeover. After the crisis, both foreign and domestic banks have focused on household loans without providing sufficient amounts of corporate loans, further adding to the deteriorating investment potential of South Korean firms. Lee concludes that foreign capital can be 'a double-edged sword' and that therefore it is necessary to be cautious in sequencing capital account liberalization policies, as well as to distinguish short-term speculative investors from long-term strategic investors.

Chang Kyung-Sup provides a comprehensive analysis of another aspect of the effects of the South Korean crisis: the end of the 'developmental citizenship' offered by the authoritarian developmentalist state of the previous decades, which had guaranteed the entitlement to work even if not other democratic rights. This developmental politics turned out to be untenable by late 1997 as too many South Korean workers found themselves without any meaningful public or private mechanisms for weathering the sudden economic crisis. The post-crisis recovery involved 'structural adjustments' of export-oriented firms and banks with radical changes in labour relations (including, of course, massive layoffs), as well as organizational transitions in ownership and management. Post-crisis industrial restructuring above all implied jobless growth. As a result, the spectacular growth of corporate incomes in the first few years of the new millennium had no positive impact whatsoever on worker incomes, with a majority of the workers actually experiencing income declines.

According to Chang, therefore, the post-crisis South Korean economy has fundamentally disenfranchised the worker population, whether they actually work or not. Labour relations have undergone major change as most new jobs are based on non-regular temporary contracts. In consequence, poverty is no more an exclusive condition of joblessness, as the working poor become more prevalent in South Korea. Chang interprets the recent more active stance of the South Korean state with respect to social policy as a necessary fallout consistent with the neoliberal attack on grassroots livelihood. By making the conditions of work so much more precarious for the bulk of workers, the neoliberal labour regime in South Korea has also successfully incapacitated organized labour's public legitimacy in the post-crisis context.

Jomo K.S. analyses the crisis and immediate post-crisis economic perform-ance in Malaysia, with special reference to the role of capital controls. He points out that the nature of Malaysia's external liabilities at the beginning of the crisis was quite different from that of the other crisis-stricken East Asian economies, since a greater proportion of Malaysia's external liabilities consisted of equity rather than debt. In a way, this actually meant greater vulnerability because of greater reliance on the capital market, and Malaysia paid a heavy price when portfolio divestment accelerated in late 1997. However, the recovery in Malaysia was faster and stronger than in other countries in the region with the exception of South Korea. Jomo attributes this to the stronger efforts at fiscal reflation in both Malaysia and South Korea, rather than to the temporary capital controls introduced by the Malaysian government fourteen months after the crisis broke. He argues that, while these capital controls did not have any of the disastrous effects predicted by neoliberal economists at the time, the one-year lock-in of foreign funds into Malaysia came too late to avert the crisis or even to help retain the bulk of foreign funds that had fled earlier, and the actual effects of the capital controls instituted for a few months between September 1998 and February 1999 remain ambiguous.

The recovery in Malaysia was the product of a combination of other forces: the quick recourse to extensive countercyclical public spending; measures to restore bank liquidity by public takeover of major non-performing loans and bank recapitalization; and the impact of the changes in the exchange rate which effectively meant that the currency was undervalued enough to encourage exports in the immediate aftermath of the crisis, even as domestic recovery was pursued through fiscal means. However, Jomo notes the costs of maintaining an undervalued *ringgit*, especially in the context of an economic upturn of what is still a very open economy. He is critical of the specific capital control measures instituted by the Mahathir government, which he sees as 'compromised by political bias, vested interests and inappropriate policy instruments'. However, he notes that such unorthodox crisis management measures remain both potent and desirable in situations when such problems cannot be overcome by other means, and therefore the case for capital controls in specific situations remains a strong one despite the flawed Malaysian experience.

Joseph Lim's study of the Philippine experience highlights the low quality of economic growth in the Philippines both before and after the Asian crisis. The 1997 crisis was just one in a long series of boom–bust cycles that the Philippine economy has undergone over more than three decades. While the last five years have shown signs of 'boom' once again, Lim points out that recent economic growth has been marred by a number of adverse features: falling investment rates, a stagnant industrial and particularly manufacturing base, inadequate structural change, and poor employment generation.

In the past, balance of payments crises in the Philippines were triggered by current account deficits that triggered capital flight. These led to sharp devaluations that pushed the current account back towards balance, although usually through domestic recession. The recent period has been different because relatively high growth has been accompanied by current account surplus, largely because of remittances from Filipino workers abroad. However, in this period the open capital account has generated balance of payments volatility because of very large inflows and outflows of capital often generated by external forces. The most recent volatility in 2007, caused by large capital inflows until the middle of the year followed by panic outflows in the wake of the US sub-prime loan crisis, suggests that financial crises are still very possible. This possibility is exacerbated by domestic factors such as the fiscal crisis, continuing weakness of the banking system and political uncertainties, causing Lim to suggest that a 1997-style crisis may be replayed in the near future.

To counter this, Lim suggests a package of alternative economic and social policies that move away from the neoliberal orthodoxy that has guided economic policy-making in the Philippines for several decades. This includes policies such as maintaining an undervalued currency using market-based capital controls whenever necessary; reducing fiscal tightness; concentrating tax collection on large corporations and rich households, a more progressive industrial policy; a different approach to banking and finance involving a shift from restrictive inflation-targeting and financial liberalization; and social policies for poor and vulnerable groups. He argues that this would address the problem of low-quality growth as well as the extreme vulnerability of the Philippines economy to external shocks and contagion.

This set of essays on the post-crisis growth trajectories of the countries hit by the Asian crisis provides evidence of some variation in strategy and experience, but also some disturbing similarities. In general, the return to growth has been associated with much less buoyancy in employment generation, lower investment rates and greater volatility in financial markets, rendering the economies more fragile and more externally dependent than they were before the crisis. And, in several of the countries, conditions similar to those that prevailed just before the 1997 crisis were apparent once again in late 2007, even as international financial entanglements had grown more complex.

Is this an inevitable consequence of the kind of financial crisis that hit these economies in 1997, or a more regionally specific reflection of the particular adjustment that were followed? Such a question cannot be answered without a comparative look at other country experiences: both those of economies outside the region that have been affected by financial crisis and of economies within the Asian region that did not suffer from such crises. To this end, the next two sections of this volume take up such experiences. The third section contains analyses of economic performance after financial crisis in the developing economies of Latin America, Turkey and Russia. The fourth section turns to an examination of the experiences of China and Vietnam to consider how they weathered the financial crisis in their neighbourhood in 1997–98, and their subsequent growth experience.

Jan Kregel considers the adjustment strategies and subsequent growth experience of crisis-hit countries in Latin America. He notes that although the financial crises that struck emerging market developing countries in the 1990s were all characterized by large and abrupt capital reversals, the causes of the conditions that first generated the capital inflows and then triggered the capital reversals were very different in Latin America compared to Asia. In Latin America, on the other hand, savings and investment rates had been persistently low, with chronic fiscal and external disequilibrium associated with hyperinflation and high exchange rate volatility.

The post-crisis adjustment strategies followed in Latin America undermined the stability of the macroeconomic fundamentals and the adjustment of the production structure through five routes: the overvaluation of the exchange rate, resulting from the resumption of capital inflows after further financial deregulation; the monetary tightening associated with high levels of real interest rates; the composition of the fiscal budget with an increasing component of interest expenditure; the composition of the external account, which involved greater outflows on account of debt repayment and payments for factor services; and the failure of adjustment of the industrial production structure to reduce the dependence of increased investment and increased export capacity on imported inputs.

Kregel shows that while Mexico, Brazil and Argentina all managed to tame high or hyperinflation and enjoyed exchange rate stability, booming financial markets and rising foreign investment, by the middle of the 1990s they were also experiencing rising external and fiscal deficits, increasing external indebtedness and faltering growth performance. The crisis of the mid to late 1990s forced all three countries to abandon their rigid exchange rate policies, and this provided an opening for recovery and higher growth that was experienced in all of them. However, after the crisis, both Brazil and Mexico took measures to restore their prior policy stance, although with nominally flexible exchange rates. Their expansions were thus short-lived and they were soon experiencing a return of capital inflows and exchange rate overvaluation in conditions of low trend growth. Argentina, on the other hand, explicitly rejected a return to externally financed growth and introduced policies to keep interest rates low and a policy of stabilization of the real exchange rate. It has consequently experienced higher than trend growth on a sustained basis since the recovery began in mid-2002.

Erinc Yeldan discusses the case of Turkey, which experienced severe political, financial and economic crises in November 2000 and again in February 2001. The IMF was involved with the macro management of the Turkish economy both prior to and after the crises, and it encouraged the Turkish government to implement an orthodox stabilization and adjustment strategy. This involved raising interest rates and maintaining an overvalued exchange rate, as well as a contractionary fiscal policy with a large primary budget surplus achieved through the privatization of public assets, reduced subsidies to agriculture and reduced public spending on social sectors. The end result in Turkey was the shrinkage of the public sector, deteriorating education and health infrastructure, and failure to provide basic social services to the middle class and the poor. Furthermore, as domestic industry intensified its import dependence, it was forced to adopt increasingly capital-intensive foreign technologies with adverse consequences on domestic employment. In the meantime, Yeldan argues, transnational companies and the international finance institutions have become the real governors of the country, with implicit veto power over any domestic economic and/or political decision that is likely to act against the interests of global capital.

The Russian economy recovered from the 1998 financial crisis much more rapidly than the countries of East Asia, as elaborated by Vladimir Popov. One month after the August 1998 currency crisis, the Russian economy started growing at about 7 per cent a year (after nearly nine years of output falls during the transformational recession of 1989–98) ; investment increased; and the inflow of foreign investment as well as the share of government spending in GDP (that had both fallen dramatically during 1989–98) started to rise. The growth of oil revenues forms only part of the explanation for this, especially as the Russian economy started to recover in October 1998, immediately after the devaluation and half a year before the turnaround in oil prices. Popov argues that the more important factors that contributed to the restoration of growth were the end of the transformational recession and the devaluation of the previously overvalued exchange rate. In both Russia (1995–98) and Argentina (1991–2002), the attempts to maintain an overvalued exchange rate led to the reduction of output, whereas devaluation effectively triggered the growth of output.

Therefore, Popov argues, the nature of the Russian 1998 currency crisis was very different from that of the East Asian currency collapses of 1997. As a result, the consequences of the currency crisis in Russia were also different from those in East Asia, inasmuch as in Russia the crisis largely discredited the neoliberal economic model of the 1990s, whereas in East Asia the backlash of the currency crises was misguidedly directed against the developmental state model. The reforms that were favoured and introduced after the crisis in Russia were mostly of the *dirigiste* type: strengthening the state fiscal and administrative capacity, creation of a stabilization fund and accumulation of reserves, some re-nationalization in the oil industry and restraints on the political influence of the 'oligarchs'. However, these reforms were not consistent enough: the real exchange rate continued to increase and the institutional capacity of the state was not restored to the pre-transition level. Also, they were sometimes accompanied by measures in the opposite, pro-market direction, such as cuts in taxes and elimination of capital account control. Thus, despite some modest progress in recent years, in particular growth of output and income caused mostly by high oil prices, Russia once again developed a Dutch disease (expressed in the overvaluation of the rouble), and did not manage to use the favourable terms of trade for repairing the damage inflicted in the 1990s to public consumption and to manufacturing industries.

There are analysts who have argued that the export slowdown that preceded the financial crisis in East Asia was caused at least partially by the devaluation of the Chinese *renminbi* in 1994. Others have pointed out that the restraint showed by China during and after the crisis, in not engaging in another competitive devaluation, was instrumental in allowing the crisis-affected economies to recover through exports. While these may still be debated, it is certainly true that China and Vietnam managed to withstand the adverse effects of this crisis to a significant extent, and therefore their experience over this period deserves greater attention.

Of course the Chinese economy deserves to be studied in this context for other reasons as well. China continues to attract international attention because of the size of its rapidly growing economy, which continues to expand at one of the fastest rates in the world. Dic Lo considers the nature of this growth and argues that, because of its significant and rising position in the world economy, China's attempt to construct an alternative model of development is bound to have a systemic impact on the future direction of globalization.

Dic Lo notes that over much of the post-1979 reform era, especially the first half, China's economic growth was largely a labour-intensive one, propelled by the absorption of new entrants to employment, and reflecting a massive process of transfer of labour from the rural agricultural sector to higher-productivity industry and services. Starting from the early 1990s, however, economic growth became more capital-deepening and, as a result, the ability of economic growth to generate new employment diminished. Despite very rapid output growth, expansion in employment has tended to lag behind that of the labour force, quite in contrast to the situation prior to the mid-1990s. This was associated with another economic shift. The labour-intensive growth path that prevailed in the first half of the reform era was associated with a rapid expansion in consumption demand, which was in turn underpinned by an egalitarian pattern of income distribution. With the progress of market reforms and growing income inequalities, consumption expansion slowed down substantially and the economy switched from being supply-constrained to becoming demand-constrained. Therefore, from the mid-1990s onwards, insufficient aggregate demand prevailed in the economy and investment replaced consumption as the main driving force behind the expansion in aggregate demand. The capital-deepening growth path generated rapid productivity improvement, but only at the cost of allowing less and less of the expanding labour force to be absorbed into employment. In addition, the privatization and downsizing of state-owned enterprises (SOEs) in 1995–97 resulted in mass unemployment, while the complete commercialization of state banks resulted in their behaviour switching from excessive lending to excessively cautious lending.

So China's economy was already on a downturn trend on the eve of the East Asian crisis, with demand deficiency as the central issue. In the face of the worsening external environment caused by the East Asian crisis, the Chinese state leadership adopted four major types of anti-crisis policies between 1998 and 2002. First, there were several Keynesian-type fiscal packages for expanding investment demand, which were financed by debt issues of unprecedented scales. Second, a range of welfare state policies, which included increasing the benefits for retired or unemployed workers, raising the remuneration of public sector employees, and lengthening the paid holidays of workers – all aimed at reversing the trend of stagnant consumption. Third, policy measures were undertaken to revitalize the state sector, including the setting up of four state asset management companies responsible for taking over a substantial share of non-performing loans from state banks and for a programme of debt-equity swaps, which were aimed at improving the financial conditions of state-owned enterprises and the balance sheets of state banks. Finally, the East Asian crisis led to a more cautious approach to reforming the regime of external transactions – in particular, the leadership in effect shelved the target of liberalizing the country's capital account.

According to Lo, these policies represent a retreat from the previous stance of pursuing a unidirectional movement towards the idealized, canonical market economy. Thus, while they were designed to be short-term anti-crisis policies, they turned out to be very powerful in shaping the long-term path of economic development. Together with other related policies (such as the increased protection of labour rights, the enforcement of minimum wage legislation, the emphasis on income redistribution to avoid further worsening social polarization, the expansion in social welfare provision, as well as the ongoing attempts to re-construct a government-funded health-care system), these policies are all conducive to the pursuit of compensation-enhancing employment.

They are also consistent with, if not also conducive to, the prevailing capital-deepening path of economic growth. So, Lo notes, the sustainability of the prevailing pattern of Chinese economic growth and employment expansion depends on whether the fast productivity gains in industry can be effectively channelled to the development of the labour-absorption capability of services.

While China's size allowed it to adopt its own strategy for dealing with the external impact of the Asian crisis, smaller open economies in the region were necessarily more constrained. In this context, the resilience of the economy of Vietnam is worth noting. Pietro Paolo Masina describes how by the early 1990s, Vietnam had become one of the most dynamic economies of East Asia, although starting from very low levels of GDP per capita, and had also achieved significant poverty reduction. In the first part of the 1990s, before the outbreak of the regional economic crisis, economic growth was consistently between 8 and 9 per cent per year. Although Vietnam did pay a price for the regional crisis with a deceleration of growth, it was much less affected than the other countries of the region. Recovery was also faster and more balanced than in the rest of East Asia, and by the mid-2000s the economy was growing once again at more than 8 per cent per year.

This resilience to the regional crisis was largely policy-determined. Since the *dong* was not convertible, the country was protected from speculative attacks against the national currency. Financial contagion could not enter via unregulated short-term financial flows because they were strictly controlled. The government set strict controls on trade flows and succeeded in balancing imports and exports to avoid creating a condition of external vulnerability. Unlike China, Vietnam could not afford to launch an anti-cyclical economic policy through state invest-ment in infrastructure to keep the economy growing fast, despite the regional depression. There was only one area in which the Vietnamese state was able to channel resources and eventually create an anti-cyclical stimulus to the economy, but it was a crucial one: agriculture and rural development. This produced two positive results. First, while the regional crisis led to a sharp deceleration of growth in industry and services, agricultural growth accelerated in the period 1997–2001, contributing to more resilient GDP growth. Second, this strength of the agricultural sector sheltered a part of the population that was temporarily prevented from finding job opportunities in the industrial sector. This counter-cyclical role played by agriculture made it possible to continue reducing poverty rates in Vietnam even through the period of regional crisis.

These widely varying experiences point to the crucial role played by economic policies in determining the degree of susceptibility of financial crisis; the extent to which such crises are translated into wider economic crises; the nature of the recovery; and the extent to which subsequent growth trajectories provide adequate employment generation, better livelihood opportunities and improved conditions of life. They point to the crucial lesson that the experience of globalization is not, and need not be, uniform across countries, but is fundamentally shaped by macroeconomic and financial policy stances.

No country is immune from the adverse effects of globalization. But the variation in policies and outcomes points to elements that can help design context-specific policy packages that reduce the vulnerability of developing countries to crises that are often not of their making. Appropriate policies can also influence the process of growth in ways that render it more sustainable as well as make it more employment-intensive, broad-based and egalitarian. These lessons are particularly important in the current international context, when many, if not most, developing countries are confronted with very similar policy choices in terms of coping with the effects of the crisis and striving for rapid and sustainable recovery. These recent experiences therefore provide a useful guide to what can be done, and also what not to do, in the face of a financial crisis.

The Changing Contours of Financial Crises in Developing Countries

Financial Crises, Reserve Accumulation and Capital Flows

Prabhat Patnaik

I

The end of the *dirigiste* era has brought in its wake a process of liberalization of financial flows into and out of most third world economies. This process began early in some parts and later in others; and it has proceeded to different extents in different countries. Nonetheless, it is a fact of life in much of the third world. Any such liberalization brings third world assets into the ambit of portfolio decisions of first world wealth-holders. This has certain implications, one of which is the unleashing of financial crises in the third world. Let us first look at a simplified picture of the financial crisis.

The introduction into the portfolios of first world wealth-holders of some of these assets that were hitherto inaccessible to them, is likely to entail an improvement in these portfolios. Hence their demand for these assets will go up, through an *ex ante* reduction partly in their demand for money and partly in their demand for other non-money assets. This will have an impact on the prices of the third world assets and a new stock equilibrium will be established where, under standard assumptions, the returns at the margin, or what Kaldor (1964) called the 'own rates of money interest', from each of the assets belonging to this augmented universe and entering into the wealth-holder's portfolio are equalized for each wealth-holder.

A sufficient condition for such a new equilibrium to come about, if we follow Keynes, is that the elasticity of price expectation must be less than unity for all assets for all wealth-holders, even though the expectations themselves may be divergent among them. This divergence of expectations played a crucial role in Keynes' analysis. It meant a division of the wealth-holders into 'bulls' and 'bears', which explained both how asset transactions actually took place and how equilibrium was established, through a shifting of the line demarcating the two. But it precluded any notion of a 'representative wealth-holder', such as was invoked in the analyses of Kalecki (1954), Kaldor (1964) and Hicks (1946). In what follows, however, since our concern will be with examining equilibrium conditions and not with the process through which equilibrium is arrived at, we shall invoke the notion of a 'representative wealth-holder' which, as Kahn (1972) had pointed out, assumes a 'dense concentration at the margin'. But we shall distinguish between the 'representative wealth-holder' from the first world and the 'representative wealth-holder' from the third world.

While inelasticity of price expectations in the asset market is a sufficient condition for equilibrium, it is obviously not a necessary condition. Even with unit elastic price expectations, equilibrium can still come about through what Keynes called the 'minor influence' of variations in the 'own rates of own interest'.[1] Likewise, the principle of increasing risk (Kalecki 1954) may be invoked as an equilibrating mechanism, since it works in favour of a diversified portfolio. But these other equilibrating forces, in the absence of inelastic price expectations, are likely to be too weak in practice to bring about a meaningful stock equilibrium. We can therefore, without much violence to reality, ignore the fact of inelastic price expectations not being a necessary condition in the analysis that follows. Of course, when we say elasticity of price expectations, we refer, in the case of first world wealth-holders, to the elasticity of *dollar price expectations*, i.e. we aggregate the price expectations in the foreign exchange market as well as in the asset markets.

While inelastic price expectations ensure a stock equilibrium, there is no reason why the sequence of stock equilibria should exhibit a pattern that includes a financial crisis. To understand the occurrence of a financial crisis *as a systemic phenomenon*, rather than just a massive erratic shock, we have to go beyond the mere existence of stock equilibria. Thus, in the absence of inelastic expectations, we have no stock equilibrium; but in the presence of inelastic price expectations, while we have stock equilibria, we have no systemic explanation as yet for a financial crisis.

The matter can be put differently. One can understand a financial crisis arising from *elastic price expectations*, i.e. as an expression of the fact that no equilibrium exists and the economy hurtles in a particular direction; but to understand a financial crisis in the context of a sequence of stock equilibria, which are ensured by inelastic expectations, requires additional theoretical construction. A possible construction is the following one.

We can visualize each wealth-holder revising expectations (or, alternatively, acting upon revised expectations) only at discrete intervals. The gap between two successive dates when the wealth-holder revises expectations is our 'period', and we can assume for convenience that all wealth-holders behave identically in this respect. We can imagine all wealth-holders making their portfolio choices at the beginning of each period, on the basis of a given expected price that each wealth-holder has for the end of the period. No matter what the actual asset prices that emerge from their choices, this end-of-period expected price remains unchanged for each. But the expected price *for the end of the next period* is influenced by the actual asset prices ruling in the stock equilibrium of the current period. We thus have inelastic (in fact, zero-elastic) asset price expectations *during the period* which ensures a stock equilibrium. But we have the feedback effect of the current equilibrium price on the next period's expected price, which makes possible a dynamic sequence of stock equilibria.

This construction is by no means far-fetched or unrealistic. It merely presumes that people take time to adjust their expectations in response to actual price movements, that they want to 'wait and watch' and 'look around' before revising their expectations about the future. On the basis of this premise, we can understand financial crises arising in the context of a sequence of stock equilibria in the following manner.

When wealth-holders do revise their expectations, there are two different considerations they reckon with: if prices are rising, then they normally expect this momentum to continue for some more time; as against this, when prices have gone 'too high' or 'too low', they expect some rectification to occur in the form of counteracting price declines or increases. Denoting the expected price at the end of period t by p^e_t and the actual price during period t by p_t, the price expectation formation rule can be given simply as:

$$p^e_{t+1} = p_t . (a.p_t / p_{t-1} - b.p_t / p^*) \qquad \text{(E)}$$

where p^* is the 'normal price' according to the conception of a particular wealth-holder (it may differ across wealth-holders but, being based on historical experience, is not too dissimilar across them, which fits in with the 'representative wealth-holder' assumption), relative to which the asset price in any period is considered 'too high' or 'too low'.

For depicting stock equilibrium, let us make the most simple assumption that there is only one asset in the third world economy which has a perpetual life, so that its rate of return is simply its nominal earning e (assumed to be constant over its lifetime) divided by its price. And that first world wealth-holders compare this asset to some representative first world asset with a rate of return r^*. The equilibrium condition for a representative first world wealth-holder then can be written as:

$$r^* = e / p_t + p^e t / pt - 1 - \rho \qquad \text{(F)}$$

where ρ is the marginal risk premium required to compensate the wealth-holder for holding the third world asset as compared to the first world asset.

Now the anatomy of a financial crisis according to the above conception can be understood as follows. Let us start from a situation where, for simplicity, the expected and actual prices of the third world asset are equal and hence equal p^*. Starting from this situation, if first world wealth-holders get access to this asset, then its price increases, and we have a series of stock equilibria through which its price keeps rising. But as long as $a > b$, a time will come when the expected price for the asset will be such that it no longer appears attractive relative to the first world asset. Its price increase will first slow down and then come to a stop. But, by the time that happens, the rate of return it earns has become lower than r^* (provided a is sufficiently larger than b), and hence there will be a reverse shift away from the third world to the first world asset (this shift in fact will begin much earlier), which will bring down the price of the former and start a downward price spiral that constitutes the essence of a financial crisis.

All this can be refined. The idea of an automaticity about the crisis coming to an end, which the above model implicitly suggests, can be abandoned. The downward price movement can be made, as indeed it should be, sudden, sharp and without any obvious restraints (since expectations are likely to turn elastic over a whole range of prices when the prices are declining). But this model can illustrate the argument I wish to make.

II

The rise in the dollar prices of the third world assets consists of two parts: a rise in the dollar value of the local currency and a rise in the local currency value of the assets. Before the economy opened itself up to financial flows, the first of these considerations did not figure in anyone's calculations. There was a stock equilibrium in the economy with the 'own rates of money interest' being equal (calculated in local currency) across all assets for the representative domestic wealth-holder. If one of these, say the deposit rate, is fixed, then all the others must adjust to it in equilibrium. Now, suppose after the economy has got 'opened up', banks continue to accept any amount of deposits at the same (fixed) interest rate. Then, the same own rates of money interest in local currency must prevail in a stock equilibrium after the 'opening up' as the ones that prevailed before. But for this new stock equilibrium to prevail, it is necessary not only that there should be inelastic price expectations in the markets for local currency assets, but also that there should be inelastic price expectation in the foreign exchange market. If price expectations are elastic with regard to the local currency price of the asset, then there would be no equilibrium to start with, even prior to the opening of the economy to financial flows. But, in addition, after the economy is 'opened up', a stock equilibrium cannot exist in the absence of inelastic price expectations in the foreign exchange market. *Thus, inelastic expectations with regard to the dollar value of the third world currency is a condition for the existence of a stock equilibrium in a third world economy 'opened up' to financial flows.*

Now, suppose the government wants to avoid financial crises. The most obvious way in which it can intervene is by stabilizing the dollar value of the local currency. This is because, unlike other assets, the supply of local currency is within the powers of the central bank, and hence (whether directly or indirectly) of the government, and can be augmented at will. The central bank can simply buy dollars at the going exchange rate and hold them as foreign exchange reserves when the demand for local assets by first world wealth-holders increases.

Let us look at the implications of this. If we denote the 'own rates of money interest' (in local currency) on local currency assets before and after 'opening up' by ε (which does not change for reasons just discussed), then, with the exchange rate remaining unchanged through central bank intervention, the condition for a new stock equilibrium will be

$$r^* = \varepsilon - \rho \, ... \qquad\qquad\qquad\qquad (G)$$

But, *ex hypothesi* the reason why first world wealth-holders wanted to move into the third world economy's asset in the first place was that the *r.h.s.* in (G) exceeded the *l.h.s.* An equilibrium can be reached only if this inequality is converted into an equality by the very process of the increase in the *ex ante* demand for the third world economy's asset. But the only equilibrating factor in (G) is ρ, the marginal risk premium, which represents compensation for foreigners against two kinds of risk: the foreign exchange risk and the risk associated with the asset market (compared to the risk of holding the first world asset).

The very stabilization of the exchange rate, however, *actually reduces* the first kind of risk, while the second kind of risk remains unchanged. (As for the principle of increasing risk, it becomes relevant in the present context only if there are substantial increases in the actual holding of local currency assets by foreigners. With ε remaining unchanged, there is no reason why such substantial transfers of local currency assets should occur at all from domestic to foreign owners.) Hence central bank intervention reduces the value of ρ, if anything, and allows little scope for ρ to increase as the foreigners' demand for local assets increases. *The attempt to eliminate financial crises therefore prevents the existence of a stock equilibrium altogether.* Looking at it differently, inelastic price expectations are a condition for stock equilibrium only when *prices are allowed to move around.* If there is a restriction on price movements, even though this may itself ensure inelastic expectations, it cannot ensure the existence of a stock equilibrium.

The prevention of crises through government intervention, in short, entails that no mechanism to arrest the rising demand for the local asset remains. True, we have assumed so far that the asset that 'rules the roost' among local currency assets, and to whose rate all other rates are tethered, sees no shift in its rate of return.[2] If this asset happens to be bank deposits, then it may appear that this assumption loses its rationale, and that variations in the deposit rate can be a policy instrument for achieving a stock equilibrium. But, even assuming that the correct deposit rate for bringing about an equilibrium can be accurately estimated, monetary policy is not free to fix the deposit rate anywhere it likes, since it must *inter alia* cover the minimum lenders' risk.[3] In other words, the deposit rate may be ostensibly what 'rules the roost' (if it does), but underlying it will be something more solid. The conclusion that government efforts to overcome financial crises negate the possibility of a stock equilibrium itself, therefore, remains valid.

Crises, Marx said, are a way of resolving, forcibly and temporarily, the contradictions of capitalism. Of course, Marx often tended to look at crises in purely cyclical terms, i.e. he assumed an automaticity about recovery from the downturn, much the way we have assumed above. There is in fact no such automaticity. Even so, a crisis is a way of rectifying, no doubt in a most explosive and painful manner, the unrestrained movements of the economy, or of particular markets, in particular directions. In the simple model sketched above, a financial crisis was the mechanism for preventing an unrestricted explosion of the demand for the third world economy's asset. In the absence of crises, there is nothing to prevent such an unrestricted explosion of demand.

The fact that the above model holds the occurrence of financial crises as the factor responsible for arresting the unrestricted explosion of demand for financial assets may not be obvious at first sight. It may appear as if the restraint on demand for the asset arises *spontaneously* because its price at some point begins to look as if it is 'too high'. *But the reason that wealth-holders get panicky when they think that the price has become 'too high' is their fear of an impending financial crisis.* In other words, it is the fact of financial crises that acts as an equilibrating mechanism.[4] It ensures that the 'across-periods' elasticity of price expectations ultimately comes down to levels where demand tapers off. This in turn produces an actual financial crisis, which again keeps the fear of financial crises alive in the minds of the wealth-holders. *In short, a crisis-free capitalism, including a financial crisis-free capitalism, is a chimera.* But the fact that capitalism cannot be made crisis-free is not an argument for living with crises, or for tolerating or welcoming them; it is an argument for going beyond the existing capitalism.

III

The building up of foreign exchange reserves is not just for preventing financial crises. It is also a measure for preventing the unemployment and immiserization that would follow the inflow of foreign currency into a third world economy for asset acquisition, if its currency price were perfectly flexible. When third world assets are opened up to first world wealth-holders, if the *l.h.s.* of (F) above is lower than the *r.h.s.* for some wealth-holders in the initial situation, then the demand for such assets will increase. This, *in the absence of government intervention*, will raise their price until, with inelastic (or zero-elastic, as we have been assuming) expectations, the *r.h.s.* gets lowered to establish equilibrium. Since, in the case of local currency-denominated bank deposits, there is no increase in the local currency price of the asset, the rise occurs in the price of the local currency itself in terms of foreign exchange.

But here we come to a striking conclusion. *While the condition for stock equilibrium remains unchanged, the process of attaining stock equilibrium, involving fixed-rate local currency assets, necessarily impinges on flow magnitudes as well, as in the case of Keynes' bond market.* In other words, this process of impinging on flow magnitudes does not alter the conditions for stock equilibrium, but it occurs nevertheless. The rise in the price of the local currency (in terms of foreign exchange), which must occur for stock equilibrium, simultaneously results in imports out-competing domestic production both in the domestic and the international market. In sectors like industry which are prone to output adjustment, this gives rise to reduced output along with reduced price, and hence unemployment. In sectors like agriculture where short-period output adjustment does not occur, it results in reduced price and hence increased immiserization of the peasants. Currency appreciation, in short, brings hardships in the form of unemployment and immiserization, to prevent which the central bank intervenes by holding foreign exchange reserves at a particular exchange rate.

Approaching the issue from another angle, we can distinguish between four different notions of 'equilibrium exchange rate': that exchange rate which best serves the employment objective (i.e. makes the economy 'competitive' without inviting retaliation); that exchange rate which best serves the objective of inflation control (the NAIRE or non-accelerating inflation rate of exchange rate[5]); that exchange rate which clears the foreign exchange market; and that exchange rate which attains stock equilibrium.

The third of these, which is the most common meaning given to the term 'equilibrium exchange rate', is actually meaningless. The concept of an exchange rate that 'clears' the foreign exchange market has no meaning, exactly for the same reason that the concept of an interest rate that equalizes 'savings' with 'investment' has no meaning, namely, that it presupposes some given level of income. For every level of income there is a separate 'equilibrium' exchange rate in this sense. Let us therefore look at the other three concepts. The economy can be in equilibrium in the sense of being in a state of rest, without either inviting retaliation from rivals or experiencing accelerating inflation, only when the 'stock equilibrium exchange rate' exceeds the other two, and prevails. The state of equilibrium of the economy can then be captured by

$$r^* = \varepsilon + (p^e / p) - 1 - \rho \ldots \qquad \qquad \text{(H)}$$
$$Y = f^{-1}(p)$$

where ε refers to the rate of return on the fixed rate local currency asset (such as bank deposits), p is the price of the local currency in terms of foreign exchange, ρ the differential marginal risk premium associated with holding the fixed-rate local currency asset as compared to the foreign asset, and Y the level of income. *What this shows is that the exchange rate is determined by the stock equilibrium, while the foreign exchange market is 'cleared' at this exchange rate through income (and hence employment) adjustment (with given levels of domestic investment, and given ratios of consumption, tax revenue and fiscal deficit to income).*

It follows from this that when the stock equilibrium entails a rise in the exchange rate, income and employment must shrink. This rise can be prevented if the central bank intervenes to stabilize the exchange rate by holding reserves. The holding of reserves therefore becomes necessary not just for preventing a future financial crisis of the sort we have been discussing so far, but also for preventing a drop in the level of employment in the economy and in the levels of income of the peasants.

The problem with stabilizing the exchange rate and the associated measure of holding reserves, however, is that *it makes things worse over time*. Since ε in (H) is given, and since the stock equilibrium before 'opening up' must have ensured that the 'own rate of money interest' on all assets equalled ε, the fact that foreigners wish to hold local currency assets after 'opening up' implies that ε

exceeds $(r^* + \rho)$. Under these conditions, however, exchange rate stabilization makes it impossible to attain a stock equilibrium after 'opening up', since no equilibrating mechanism now exists. *It follows, then, that exchange rate stabilization makes it impossible to achieve a stock equilibrium.*

We have till now not discussed either the disequilibrium behaviour of the system or the process through which equilibrium is reached. We have talked of foreigners' demand for local assets raising their prices, but we have said nothing about the actual financial flows. Strictly speaking, from an examination of equilibrium conditions we cannot jump to any theoretical conclusions about the magnitude of actual financial flows. But it is plausible to assume that the magnitude of financial flows into an economy will be linked to the magnitude of the foreigners' demand for its assets. It follows that since the excess demand for the economy's assets is not eliminated in this case, foreign exchange reserves keep piling up. And since, with the piling up of reserves, the marginal risk premium associated with holding the local currency declines further from the already low level to which the stabilization of the exchange rate had brought it down, the excess demand for the local currency asset will keep increasing and reserves will keep piling up over time even faster.

Let us look at this disequilibrium behaviour briefly. The fact that the economy does not 'explode' in a situation of perennial excess demand for domestic assets is because, in practice, only a certain finite amount of financial inflows occurs in any period, notwithstanding this excess demand, which affects domestic asset prices but keeps them within bounds. Even within this overall disequilibrium, however, portfolio adjustments made by *domestic wealth-holders will ensure that all 'own rates of money interest' in local currency terms equal ε.* This will happen through an increase in their prices relative to their expected prices. The sequence of such states of rest across periods (they cannot strictly be called 'stock equilibria') can still generate a domestic financial crisis, in the form of a sharp drop in the price of some local currency assets, for exactly the same reasons discussed earlier.

When such a drop occurs, foreigners will not be unaffected by it. In other words, it will also entail a reduction in demand for the local currency itself. But even if there is no foreign exchange crisis, because the reduced demand for the local currency is handled through the decumulation of foreign exchange reserves, the collapse of the price of some local currency assets will have serious adverse consequences.

Central bank intervention in the form of holding foreign exchange reserves to prevent financial crises, in a world with free financial flows, therefore, is ineffective in two senses. It prevents, first of all, the achievement of a stock equilibrium altogether. Second, even within this overall disequilibrium, it still cannot prevent the occurrence of financial crises. *The most it can do is to prevent domestic financial crises from spilling over into foreign exchange crises,* but even that is achieved at the cost of compounding the problem of instability over time. Of course, this does not mean asking for a removal of central bank intervention. On the contrary, such intervention is essential in a regime of free financial flows for preventing increased unemployment and immiserization. *But it is this regime itself that needs transcending.* One can go further. Since this regime represents the latest phase of existing capitalism, transcending it means transcending existing capitalism.

Putting it differently, crises, though painful, play a certain role under capitalism. The prevention of crises by foreclosing this role creates instability in a different way, by undermining the *modus operandi* of the system. To say this, echoing Marx, is not to plead for an acceptance of crises; it is to plead against the acceptance of capitalism as we have known it, since this knowledge has shown that 'crisis-free capitalism' is a chimera. This does not of course mean that we should not demand intervention against crises, but we should do so without any illusions, and only as part of a process of going beyond existing capitalism.

IV

The accumulation of reserves by several third world economies is often seen as a factor reducing global demand.[6] This is not true. A distinction must be drawn here between reserve accumulation that is accompanied by a current account surplus, and reserve accumulation that is unaccompanied by such a surplus. The cases of China and India belong respectively to these two categories. *In the case of the latter, reserve accumulation, as already discussed, has an expansionary consequence on the level of aggregate demand of the reserve-accumulating economy,* for in its absence there would be a currency appreciation causing domestic unemployment. But since such an appreciation would be accompanied by a corresponding increase in the aggregate demand of those countries whose currencies have depreciated relatively, the level of world aggregate demand would remain unchanged. In short, the level of world aggregate demand is unaffected whether or not there is reserve accumulation of this sort.

Even in the case of the former, reserve accumulation *per se* cannot be said to have caused a decline in world aggregate demand. If China, for instance, decided not to accumulate reserves but to let her currency appreciate, there will be a decline in the level of aggregate demand in China which will be accompanied by an increase in the aggregate demand of countries currently out-competed by China, notably the US. In principle, there is no reason to believe that the level of world aggregate demand will change on account of China's reserve decumulation. It is only if reserve decumulation in China is accompanied by a corresponding increase in some other item of aggregate demand that we can expect an increase in the level of world aggregate demand. If, for instance, the Chinese economy, instead of running current account surpluses, decides to enlarge domestic absorption through enlarged government expenditure while keeping the exchange rate unchanged, there will be an increase in world aggregate demand. But then, this has nothing to do with reserve decumulation *per se*: all it says is that the level of world aggregate demand goes up if the domestic absorption of one particular country goes up without that of any other country reducing, which is but a truism.

The conclusion in both cases, that the level of world aggregate demand remains unchanged in the event of a decumulation of reserves through an appreciation of the exchange rate, assumes that the economy whose currency has depreciated relatively and which experiences an increase in aggregate demand as a consequence, is unconcerned with the associated increase in its domestic prices. If the price effects of an expansion of its aggregate demand entail high social resistance, as might be expected in the case of the US perhaps, which has a restraining effect on the magnitude of its demand expansion, then *reserve decumulation on the part of the 'emerging market economies' through an appreciation of the exchange rate has a contractionary effect on world aggregate demand*. It follows that the accumulation of reserves through central bank intervention in keeping the exchange rate fixed makes the level of world aggregate demand no lower than it otherwise would have been; but it invariably has a net expansionary effect on the level of aggregate demand of the reserve-accumulating economy itself, compared to what it would be if reserves did not accumulate and the exchange rate was allowed to appreciate.

The concern with the accumulation of reserves represents, however, a refracted perception of something altogether different. While such accumulation has no effect *per se* on the level of world aggregate demand (except for the fact that its substitution by larger domestic absorption would be beneficial for all, which is a very different proposition), it does undermine the position of the leading capitalist economy, by accumulating claims against it. Throughout the history of capitalism, the diffusion of industrial capitalism from the core to 'newly industrializing countries' has been accompanied by the leading capitalist power of the time running a current account deficit vis-à-vis the 'newly industrializing economies', thus offering them space in its domestic market. But this never caused any net accumulation of claims against the leading capitalist power, because it always had access to a drain of surplus from colonies in addition to having the colonial ·markets 'on tap', which more than paid for its current account deficits vis-à-vis the 'newly industrializing countries'. Its currency, therefore, was never under pressure, even as it ran current account deficits against the newly industrializing countries of the time. The fact that the leading capitalist power of today finds its currency under pressure and itself becoming a heavily indebted nation, is because the possibilities of colonial drain no longer exist, though misadventures for resurrecting the system of colonial drain, especially from oil-rich third world countries, have not been given up.[7]

V

The proposition advanced above, that central bank intervention for stabilizing the exchange rate, in order to prevent unemployment through exchange rate appreciation and future financial crises, has the effect of making things worse over time, is borne out by the Indian experience. It was argued earlier (in section III of this paper) that even within the overall stock disequilibrium that characterizes a situation of central bank intervention to stabilize the exchange rate, the 'own rates of money interest' in local currency (in Kaldor's terminology) will be equal to ε and to each other. Since this comes about through movements of actual asset prices relative to their expected prices, and hence entails significant movements in actual asset prices, it does not prevent financial crises. (In India's case, it is the stockmarket crisis that is pertinent.) Government intervention in India, therefore, has taken the form of *both* stabilizing the exchange rate *and* keeping the stockmarket boom going, through selective interventions by way of 'liberalization' and fiscal incentives.

But the very logic of a combination of a stockmarket boom and stabilized exchange rate has meant a continuous shift of foreign demand towards the local currency assets, and hence towards the local currency as well. This has saddled the Reserve Bank of India with burgeoning reserves, which have, in the course of three years, climbed to $200 billion. And precisely because such large reserves make the rupee less vulnerable to collapse, the marginal risk premium associated with holding the rupee has gone down, thereby further stimulating financial inflows and hence adding to reserves.

This situation of disequilibrium would not matter, except for the fact that there is a massive difference between the rate of return earned by those who are bringing in financial inflows and the rate of return earned on the reserves. If a minimum of 20 per cent is taken as the rate of return, inclusive of asset price appreciation, for those who bring in financial inflows, then, given the fact that the reserves earn no more than about 1.5 per cent on average, the annual loss owing to this difference comes to about 6 per cent of the GDP (gross domestic product) of the country. In other words, the country, as it were, is borrowing dear to lend cheap, to an extent where its annual loss at present amounts to 6 per cent of the GDP. This is not to say that 6 per cent of the GDP is being actually drained out of the country every year. But the fact that it is not being actually drained out now only implies that the size of the drain will be even larger in future.

The so-called 'sterilization' operations, meant ostensibly to control money supply, are really a means of preventing damage to the banking system under the weight of this loss. Precisely because we are in a disequilibrium situation where financial inflows continue to occur, and foreign exchange reserves continue to get built up, the magnitude of reserve money increases sharply which finds its way into the banks and far outstrips the demand for credit from 'worthwhile borrowers'. Banks' profits are threatened by this discrepancy, and the Reserve Bank steps in to shore up these profits by putting income-earning government securities into the banks' portfolio. The Reserve Bank's doing so, however, means a substitution of foreign exchange reserves for government securities in its own asset portfolio, with the former earning much lower rates of return than the latter. This therefore lowers the Reserve Bank's profitability and hence reduces a whole range of development finance activities that it promotes using its profits. In short, the Reserve Bank is taking upon itself the losses that the commercial banks would otherwise have incurred owing to this disequilibrium situation.

Many in India, in a throwback to mercantilism, have applauded the accumulation of reserves, deeming it to be a great success for the neoliberal policies. For reasons just discussed, nothing could be farther from the truth. Very recently, the Reserve Bank has allowed an increase in the dollar price of the rupee (partly, perhaps, to control incipient inflationary pressures), but the effects of this move are already apparent in the form of lower export prices for the already hard-pressed peasants.

What the Indian case clearly demonstrates is that measures aimed at avoiding financial crises push the economy into a perennial disequilibrium. This choice between the devil and the deep sea may well be avoided in the first instance through the imposition of capital controls. Such controls will bring in their train a whole range of further developments, the cumulative impact of which will be a shift in the balance of class forces that underlies contemporary Indian capitalism. But this shift can occur only if there is no sudden panic-stricken or externally imposed change in between, of course, entailing an abandonment of controls.

Notes

[1] For a discussion of 'own rates of own interest', see Kaldor (1964).

[2] Kaldor (1964) had raised the whole question of why money 'ruled the roost' among all the assets, in the sense that the yield on money determined the vector of own rates of money interest on all other assets.

[3] The question may be asked: if the opening up of third world assets to first world wealth-holders makes them demand these assets, and if among assets in each place the one that 'rules the roost' is tethered to the minimum lending risk, then this must pre-suppose that the lending risks are higher in the third than in the first world. This is an entirely plausible supposition, since the higher level of development of the institutions of capitalism will normally be associated with lower lenders' risk.

[4] One is reminded here of Dennis Robertson's (1937) remark about 'the dying embers of liquidity preference' having to be periodically stoked through falls in bond prices. Likewise, the runaway demand for third world financial assets has to be periodically curbed through falls in the prices of these assets. The difference between the two cases, however, consists in this: the memory of these falls produces actual falls, *which in turn perpetuate this memory.*

[5] The concept of a non-accelerating inflation rate of exchange is discussed in Patnaik and Rawal (2005).

[6] Ocampo, Kregel and Griffith-Jones (2007: 156) write: 'Irrespective of the exchange rate regime adopted to insure themselves against sudden shifts in market sentiment, most emerging economies have kept increasingly high stocks of international reserves. This "self-insurance" option entails significant costs and could constrain global growth as it reduces global aggregate demand.'

[7] The arguments of this paragraph have been developed at length in Patnaik (2005).

References

Hicks J.R. (1946), *Value and Capital*, Oxford: Clarendon Press.

Kahn, R.F. (1972), 'Notes on Liquidity Preference', in *Selected Essays on Employment and Growth*, Cambridge: Cambridge University Press.

Kaldor, N. (1964), 'Own Rates of Interest', in *Essays on Economic Stability and Growth*, London: Duckworth.

Kalecki, M. (1954), *The Theory of Economic Dynamics*, London: Allen and Unwin.

Ocampo, Jose Antonio, Jan Kregel and Stephanie Griffith-Jones, eds. (2007), *International Finance and Development*, Hyderabad: Orient Longman.

Patnaik, P. (2005), 'Contemporary Capitalism and the Diffusion of Activity', Inaugural Lecture for the Sukhamoy Chakravarty Chair, *Economic and Political Weekly*.

Patnaik, P. and V. Rawal (2005), 'The Level of Activity in an Economy with Free Capital Mobility', *Economic and Political Weekly*, Vol. 40, No. 14, April.

Robertson, D.H. (1937), 'Mr. Keynes and the Rate of Interest', *Economic Journal*.

Continuity or Change?

Finance Capital in Developing Countries a Decade after the Asian Crisis

C.P. Chandrasekhar

The crises in East Asia and in many other developing countries have focused attention on a number of dangers associated with a world dominated by fluid finance. In particular, they have sent out the message that if countries choose to liberalize their financial policies to attract financial investors to their markets, they are prone to boom–bust cycles, with adverse implications for the real economy.

Underlying these financial cycles are speculative tendencies fostered by financial liberalization and globalization. These tendencies have rendered global financial institutions prone to overexposure in individual markets, often as a result of unsound financial practices. A combination of several factors – the competitive thrust for speculative gains on funds garnered from profit-hungry investors, the herd instinct characteristic of financial investors, and the moral hazard generated by an implicit guarantee from the state that the financial system will be bailed out in periods of crisis – resulted in a situation where lending to and financial investments in particular countries continued well after there was evidence that high-risk exposure had exceeded warranted limits. The corollary of this was that supply-side factors were likely to result in boom–bust cycles in financial flows to developing countries, with a surge in such flows followed, in all likelihood, by their sudden collapse.

The capital that drives this supply-side push originates in the transformation of capitalism that has occurred under the sway of neoliberal and neoconservative ideologies. The growing inequality that characterizes an unregulated capitalism, in which wages stagnate while productivity and profits rise, has resulted in the accumulation of vast sums of capital in the hands of a few investors in the metropolitan centres of global capitalism.[1] These gains are lightly taxed by governments that are not committed to appropriating a part of the surpluses of the rich to improve the welfare of the poor. Lower down the ladder, investment capital accumulates with mutual and pension funds in which less protected populations deposit the savings they set aside to insure their future. The lack of state-funded welfare in today's more liberalized and open capitalism is forcing the middle classes in the developed countries to save by subscribing to these funds, which have become important sources of financial capital. Financial firms in the developed countries leverage capital from these sources by borrowing huge sums, and use the resulting corpus to indulge in financial speculation.

The problem is that the crises resulting from this process do not remain restricted to the financial sector. When the surge in capital flows is reversed, a massive liquidity crunch and a wave of bankruptcies follow. This results in severe deflation, with attendant consequences for employment and the standard of living. Asset prices collapse and pave the way for international acquisitions of domestic firms at low prices, denominated in currencies that have substantially depreciated. A crisis triggered by finance capital becomes the prelude to a conquest by international capital in general, with substantial changes in the ownership structure of domestic assets without much greenfield investment.

These messages driven home by the crisis triggered a debate on the policies that needed to be pursued at national and international levels to prevent the recurrence of boom–bust cycles of this kind. The intent here is not to track the efforts at fashioning a 'new international financial architecture', or to list the policies that were adopted in individual countries in response to financial crises. The question is, a decade after, are we in a world where unbridled capital flows are not inimical to stable growth, where vulnerability is reduced because of the prudence built into the financial system, and where the probability of financial crisis that can set back decades of advances in social welfare, are significantly lower?

The Burgeoning of Finance

In terms of magnitude, finance capital has expanded massively during the last decade. Measuring the absolute size of globally dispersed finance capital is indeed a difficult proposition. Given the diversity of agents, instruments and markets, and the lack of transparency in certain over-the-counter markets, it is extremely difficult to gauge the size of the corpus that functions as financial capital. But the available figures do point to a galloping growth in the global operations of financial firms.

One obvious form it has taken ever since the international lending boom of the late 1970s and after, was the expansion of banks in the developed industrial countries into less developed countries, especially into the so-called 'emerging markets'. The net result was an increase in the international assets of the big banks of the developed world. This trend has only gained strength in recent years. At the time of the East Asian crisis, at the end of June 1997, twenty-three countries reporting to the Bank of International Settlements (BIS) reported that the international asset position of banks resident in those countries stood at $9.95 trillion, involving $8.6 trillion in external assets after adjusting for local assets in international currencies (Bank of International Settlements 1997). By December 2006, when forty countries were reporting, this had risen to $32.14 trillion, with external assets totalling $28.48 trillion (Bank of International Settlements 2007a). This expansion in international asset position was not only the result of an increase in the number of countries reporting. The trend was visible in countries that reported on both dates as well. Thus the international assets of UK-based banks had increased from $1.5 trillion to $5.8 trillion, and that of US banks from $0.74 trillion to $2.6 trillion.

But this is not all. Increasingly, non-bank financial firms – pension funds, insurance companies and mutual funds – have emerged as important intermediaries between savers and investors. According to a BIS study (Committee on the Global Financial System 2007: 5), the total financial assets of institutional investors stood at $46 trillion in 2005. Of this, insurance firms accounted for close to $17 trillion, pension funds for $12.8 trillion and mutual funds for $16.2 trillion. The United States dominated, accounting for as much as $21.8 trillion of institutional investors' assets, while the United Kingdom was far behind at just $4 trillion. Here too, growth has been rapid, with total assets more than doubling between 1995 and 2005: from $10.5 trillion in the US and $1.8 trillion in the case of the UK. The assets of autonomous pension funds in the US, for example, rose from $786 billion in 1980 to $1.8 trillion in 1985, $2.7 trillion in 1990, $4.8 trillion in 1995, $7.4 trillion in 2000 and $8 trillion in 2004 (Organization for Economic Cooperation and Development 2001, 2003).

Besides these institutions, there are other less regulated and opaque institutions, particularly highly leveraged institutions like the hedge funds and private equity firms, which directly manage financial assets for high net-worth individuals, besides the institutional investors themselves. Assets managed by around 9,000 surviving hedge funds are now placed at around $1.6 trillion (Financial Stability Forum 2007). And, according to one study, private equity assets under management are nearing $400 billion in the United States and just under $200 billion in Europe. Private equity expansion is also reportedly strong, with aggregate deal value growing at 51 per cent annually from 2001 to 2005 in North America.[2]

Transactions other than in debt and equity by these entities have also risen rapidly. In 1992, the daily volume of foreign exchange transactions in international financial markets stood at $820 billion, compared to the annual world merchandise exports of $3.8 trillion or a daily value of world merchandise trade of $10.3 billion. According to a recent BIS report (Bank of International Settlements 2007b: 5), the average *daily* turnover (adjusted for double-counting) in foreign exchange markets rose from $800 billion in 1992 to $1.5 trillion in 1998, before declining to $1.2 trillion in 2001. It then rose to $1.9 trillion in 2004 and sharply further to $3.2 trillion in 2007. With the average gross domestic product (GDP) generated globally in a day at close to $100 trillion in 2003, this may appear to be a small 3 per cent relative to real economic activity across the globe. But the sum involved is huge relative to the daily value of world trade. In 2006, the annual value of world merchandise exports touched $11.8 trillion, while that of commercial services trade rose to $2.7 trillion. Thus the daily volume of transactions in foreign exchange markets exceeded the annual value of trade in commercial services, and was close to a third of the annual merchandise trade.

More significant is the trade in derivatives. The BIS estimates (Bank of International Settlements 2007b: 10) that the average daily turnover of exchange-traded derivatives amounted to $6.2 trillion in April 2007, as compared with $4.5 trillion in 2004, $2.2 trillion in 2001 and $1.4 trillion in 1998. In the over-the-counter (OTC) derivatives market, average daily turnover amounted to another $2 trillion in 2007 at current exchange rates (as compared with $1.2 trillion, $575 billion and $375 billion, respectively, in 2004, 2001 and 1998). Thus total derivatives trading stood at $8.2 trillion a day, which, together with the $3.2 trillion daily turnover in foreign exchange markets, adds up to $11.4 trillion. This almost equals the annual value of global merchandise exports in 2006.

All of this has meant liquidity at unprecedented levels in the international financial system, ensuring that the pressure to push funds into emerging markets that prevailed at the time of the debt crisis in the 1980s and the East Asian crisis in 1997 has only intensified. The massive increase in international liquidity has found banks and non-bank financial institutions desperately searching for means to keep their capital moving.

One consequence of these developments is that at different points in time, one or another group of developing countries has been discovered as a 'favourable' destination for foreign financial investors. Increased competition and falling returns in the developed countries are also encouraging financial firms to seek out new opportunities in emerging markets. This supply-side push can translate into an actual flow only when the developing countries as a group, and the so-called emerging markets among them, relax controls on the inflow of capital and the repatriation of profits and investment, as well as liberalize their financial systems to accommodate international players and their operating strategies. In practice, despite the East Asian crisis and similar crises that have followed it in other parts of the world, and the evidence that such crises result from more open capital accounts, the developing countries have competed with each other to attract these inflows.

Capital Flows to Developing Countries: New Trends

Overall, the willingness to accommodate supply-side pressures has had rather dramatic implications for capital flows to developing countries. The first of these is an acceleration of financial flows to developing countries precisely during the years when, as a group, they have been characterized by rising surpluses on their current account. Total flows touched a record $571 billion in 2006, having risen by 19 per cent on top of an average growth of 40 per cent during the three previous years. Relative to the GDP of these countries, total flows, at 5.1 per cent, are at levels they reached at the time of the East Asian financial crisis in 1997. (The figures in this section are from World Bank 2007.)

A second feature is acceleration of the long-term tendency for private flows to dominate over official (bilateral and multilateral) flows. Private debt and equity inflows, which had risen by 50 per cent a year over the three years ending 2005, increased a further 17 per cent in 2006 to touch a record $647 billion. On the other hand, net official lending has declined over the last two years, partly because some of the developing countries chose to make advance repayments of debt owed to official creditors, especially the IMF and the World Bank.

Third, in recent years, following the period immediately after the 1997 crisis when debt flows had almost dried up, both equity and debt flows to developing countries have risen rapidly. Net private debt and equity flows to developing countries have risen from a little less that $170 billion in 2002 to close to $647 billion in 2006, an almost four-fold increase over four years. While net private equity flows, which rose from $163 billion to $419 billion, dominated the surge, net private debt flows too increased rapidly. Bond issues rose from $10.4 billion to $49.3 billion, and borrowings from international banks from $2.3 billion to a huge $112.2 billion. What is more, net short-term debt, outflows of which tend to trigger financial crises, rose from around half a billion in 2002 to $72 billion in 2006.

The fourth feature, which is a corollary of these developments, is a high degree of concentration of flows to developing countries, implying excess exposure in a few countries. Ten countries out of 135 accounted for 60 per cent of all borrowings during 2002–04, and that proportion rose subsequently to touch three-fourths in 2006. In the portfolio equity market, flows to developing countries were directed at acquiring a share in equity either through the secondary market or by buying into initial public offers (IPOs). IPOs dominated in 2006, accounting for $53 billion of the $96 billion inflow. But here too there were signs of concentration. Four of the ten largest IPOs were by Chinese companies, accounting for two-thirds of total IPO value. Another three of these ten were by Russian companies, accounting for an additional 22 per cent of IPO value.

Finally, despite the rapid rise in developing country exposure, with that exposure being excessively concentrated in a few countries, the market is still overtly optimistic. Ratings upgrades dominate downgrades in the bond market. And bond market spreads are at unusual lows. This optimism indicates that risk assessments are pro-cyclical, underestimating risk when investments are booming and overestimating risks when markets turn downwards. Two consequences are the herding of investors in developing country markets, and their willingness to invest a larger volume of money in risky, unrated instruments.

In sum, we are now witnessing a return to a period when large and rising inflows, herd behaviour and overexposure characterized capital flows from the North to the South. Is there reason to believe, as some would suggest, that this time round these developments are benign, or even positive, from the point of view of the developing countries? Besides the many crises that have occurred across the developing world, including in Argentina and Turkey, during the decade since 1997, structural changes in the global financial system suggest that risk, including systemic risk, has only increased.

Structural Transformation of Global Finance

Associated with the rapid rise of capital flows to developing countries is the institutional globalization of international finance. During the 1990s, the three-decade-long process of proliferation and rise to dominance of finance in the global economy reached a new phase. This phase was characterized by a growing process of financial consolidation that concentrated financial activity and financial decision-making in a few economic organizations, and integrated hitherto demarcated areas of financial activity that had been dissociated from each other to ensure transparency and discourage unsound financial practices.

A study of financial consolidation commissioned by finance ministers and central bank governors of the Group of 10 (2001)[3] found, as expected, that there had been a high level of merger and acquisition (M&A) activity in the study countries during the 1990s, with an acceleration of such activity especially in the last three years of the decade. The number of acquisitions by financial firms from the survey countries increased from around 337 in 1990 to between 900 and 1000 by the end of the decade. Further, the average value of each of these acquisitions increased from $224 million in 1990 to $649 billion in 1999. Clearly, M&A in the financial sector was creating large and complex financial organizations in the international financial system.

Further, while the evidence for the 1990s as a whole seemed to indicate that M&A activity was largely industry-specific, with banking firms tending to merge dominantly with other banks, the pattern was changing over time. In 1994 there was one instance of cross-industry M&A for every five instances of intra-industry mergers, and the ratio had come down to one in every three by 1999. The merger and acquisition drive within the financial sector was not to merely create large and excessively powerful organizations, but firms that straddled the financial sector. Exploiting the process of financial liberalization, these firms were breaking down the Chinese walls that had been built between different segments of the financial sector.

Given the wave of financial liberalization in the developing world, it was inevitable that this process would affect them as well. According to a Committee on the Global Financial System study (2004), there was a surge in foreign direct investment in the financial sectors of developing countries. Using cross-border M&As targeting banks in emerging market economies (EMEs), the study found that cross-border deals involving financial institutions from EMEs as targets, which accounted for 18 per cent of such M&A deals worldwide during 1990–96, rose to 30 per cent during 1997–2000. The value of financial sector foreign direct investment (FDI) rose from about $6 billion during 1990–96 to $50 billion during the next four years. Such FDI peaked at $20 billion in 2001, declined sharply in 2002, but stabilized in 2003. The net result is a clear shift in the ownership structure of the financial sector (see Table 1). Anecdotal evidence indicates that this figure would have risen sharply since then.

Turning to Asia, the study found that:

> The proportion of cross-border M&As in East Asia's financial sector initially was small compared with other regions. The value of cross-border M&As targeting non-Japan Asian countries was $14 billion or 17 per cent of the total during 1990–2003. Asia, however, has been one of the fastest growing target

TABLE 1   *Ownership Structure in the Banking Systems of Emerging Market Economies* [1]

Country	1990			2002 [2]		
	Domestic		Foreign	Domestic		Foreign
	Private[3]	Government		Private	Government	
Asia						
China	0	100	0	98		2 [4]
Hong Kong SAR	11	0	89	28		72
Indonesia	–	–	4	37	51	13
India	4	91	5	12	80	8
Korea	75	21	4	62	30	8
Malaysia	–	–	–	72		18
Philippines	84	7	9	70	12	18
Singapore	11	0	89	24	0	76
Thailand	82	13	5	51	31	18
Latin America						
Argentina	–	36 [5]	10 [6]	19	33	48
Brazil	30	64	6	27	46	27
Chile	62	19	19	46	13	42
Mexico	1	97	2	18	0	82
Peru	41	55	4	43	11	46
Venezuela	93	6 [7]	1 [7]	39	27	34
Central and Eastern Europe						
Bulgaria	–	–	0	20	13	67
Czech Republic	12 [5]	78 [5]	10 [5]	14	4	82
Estonia	–	–	–	1	0	99
Hungary	9	81	10	11	27	62
Poland	17 [7]	80 [7]	3 [7]	10	17	63
Russia	–	–	6	23	68	9
Slovakia	–	–	0	9	5	85

Notes: [1] Percentage share of total bank assets. 2002 figures for Central and Eastern Europe: percentage share of regulatory capital.
[2] Data are shown for the latest year available, which is mainly 2002.
[3] Calculated as residual.
[4] 1999.
[5] 1994.
[6] Average of 1988–93.
[7] 1993.

Source: Committee on the Global Financial System (2004).

regions for M&A, with a sizeable jump in cross-border M&A activity occurring in Korea and Thailand. In addition, there has been a large number of small-value cross-border M&A transactions in the finance sector between East Asian economies. In 2003, Asia received the largest share of FSFDI inflows.

While liberalization and the high returns offered by hitherto protected financial markets offered new opportunities, financial crises favoured globalization. As the study of the Committee on the Global Financial System (CGFS) notes: 'A standard response to crises by EME governments, encouraged by the international financial institutions, was to accelerate financial liberalization and to recapitalize banks with the help of foreign investors. This was the case in Latin America in the years following the 1994 Mexican crisis.' In Asia also governments liberalized the terms of foreign entry and ownership after the crisis, but because of the major role played by governments in the recapitalization of banks, the expansion of foreign presence came with a delay.

Thus the global financial system is obviously characterized by a high degree of centralization. With US financial institutions intermediating global capital flows, the investment decisions of a few individuals in a few institutions virtually determine the nature of the 'exposure' of the global financial system. The growing presence of a few international players in the developing countries and their consolidation had implications for the accumulation of risk in markets where agents tend to herd. Unfortunately, unregulated entities making huge profits on highly speculative investments are at the core of that system.

The Role of New Institutions: Hedge Funds and Private Equity Firms

Liberalization has not just increased consolidation and global integration of the banking industry in developing countries. Many of these countries are now home to the activities of institutions like hedge funds and private equity firms that are loosely regulated in the developed countries, are highly leveraged, and pursue unconventional, speculative and risky investment strategies in relatively illiquid assets aimed at exploiting mispricing and arbitrage opportunities to ensure high returns for their investors. With investment banks and fund managers adopting similar practices, the distinction between these and other financial institutions is blurring at the level of activity, excepting perhaps for the concentration of the activities of these entities on specific kinds of trades.

Many years back the Group of 30 had cautioned governments that these funds were a source of concern because they were prone to 'undercapitalization, faulty systems, inadequate supervision and human error'. While controversial for long, hedge funds gained notoriety in 1992 when George Soros' Quantum Fund was held responsible for the speculative attack on the British pound, and in the late 1990s with the collapse of the much-publicized Long Term Capital Management with its star traders, Nobel-winning economists and high-return track record. For developing countries, their notoriety was linked to the role they are alleged to have played in the currency speculation that precipitated the 1997 crisis.

Yet, hedge fund activity in developing countries has increased substantially in recent years, including in Asia. Encouraged by liberalization that ensures not only the entry but the proliferation of instruments, the growth of derivatives markets, the emergence of futures and the increase in shorting possibilities, these firms have devoted much attention to these markets. According to one estimate quoted by the Financial Stability Forum (2007), the share of hedge fund assets managed in Asia rose from 5 per cent in 2002 to 8 per cent in 2006. These increases have been at the expense of the US, which, while recording a significant increase in hedge fund activity in absolute terms, has seen a decline in share of the global total, from more than 80 per cent in 2002 to about 65 per cent in 2006.

Besides hedge funds, over the last quarter of a century, portfolio diversification by financial investors in developed countries seeking new targets, higher returns and/or a hedge has seen a revival of private equity firms. Private equity, as originally broadly defined, involves investment in equity linked to an asset that is not listed and therefore not publicly traded in stockmarkets. Given this definition, a range of transactions and/or assets fall under its purview, including venture capital investments, leveraged buyouts and mezzanine debt-financing, where the creditor expects to gain from the appreciation in equity value by exploiting conversion features such as rights, warrants or options.

While private equity has been growing rapidly, its activities in the developed countries is being curbed by the growing opposition to these firms and their activities. A major criticism of private equity firms is their lack of transparency. Besides, they are accused of yielding the hatchet against workers or breaking up companies when firms are being restructured.

One result of all this is that private equity firms are finding it harder to conduct their business in the US and Europe. Not surprisingly, there are signs that their business is increasingly moving overseas, especially to emerging market countries where markets are booming because of foreign institutional investment (FII) inflows.

According to the Emerging Markets Private Equity Association, fundraising for emerging market private equity surged in 2005 and 2006. Estimated at $3.4 billion and $5.8 billion in 2003 and 2004, respectively, the figure shot up to 22.1 billion in 2004 and $21.9 billion in the period up to 1 November in 2006. Asia (excluding Japan, Australia and New Zealand) dominated the surge, with the figure rising from $2.2 and $2.8 billion in 2003 and 2004, to $15.4 billion in 2005 and $14.5 billion during the first ten months of 2006.[4]

Deal-making in the region has also gained momentum. Dealogic estimates that the value of private equity deals in the Asia Pacific, excluding Japan, more than tripled, to $26 billion in 2006 from $7 billion in 2005.[5] Private equity buyouts have accounted for 7 per cent of regional M&A volume in 2006, up from 3 per cent in 2005 but still below the global figure of 17 per cent. Though Australia accounted for $11.7 billion in activity, deals in the Indian subcontinent jumped to $3.1 billion in 2006 from $764 million in 2005, with Kohlberg Kravis Roberts & Co.'s $900 million purchase of Flextronics Software Systems – India's largest deal. North Asia deals totalled $10.4 billion, led by Goldman Sachs' $2.6 billion investment in Industrial & Commercial Bank of China – the year's biggest regional deal. Investment banks have raked in $304 million in net revenue from private equity investors thus far in 2006, compared with $239 million in 2005.

The Transformation of the Financial Sector

The evidence of a rising foreign presence in the financial sector in developing countries suggests that the flow of capital is accompanied by a movement of firms and institutions from developed to developing countries. Countries wanting to attract financial investments have to accommodate financial investors as well. Further, when these entities are permitted to enter the developing country markets, they would be interested in the replication of their trading practices in the new environment. Policies of financial liberalization are *inter alia* meant to meet these requirements of finance capital in countries seeking to attract financial investments. Financial liberalization therefore: (i) opens the country to new forms and larger volumes of international financial flows; (ii) allows the entry of foreign financial entities, varying from banks to private equity firms, into the country; and (iii) dilutes or dismantles regulation and control that do not permit or curb the operation of the entities and their pursuit of preferred practices. A consequence of such liberalization is financial consolidation and the proliferation of new institutions and instruments.

It has been argued for some time now, and especially since the East Asian crisis, that the first of the above features of financial liberalization, involving liberalization of controls on inflows and outflows of capital, respectively, has resulted in an increase in financial fragility in the developing countries, making them prone to periodic financial and currency crises.

Analyses of individual instances of crisis have tended to conclude that the nature and timing of these crises had much to do with the shift to a more liberal and open financial regime. What is less emphasized is the vulnerability that stems from the proliferation of new kinds of foreign institutions, new instruments and new business practices in the wake of liberalization. As we have seen, the increase in the extent and width of liberalization over the last decade has not only led to a surge in capital flows in recent years, but also encouraged the entry of speculative investors adopting unusual lending and investment practices in environments that are even less regulated than the US, for example. This would therefore have substantially increased, rather than reduced, financial vulnerability over the last decade.

Signs of Vulnerability

One obvious instance of increased vulnerability is the massive 'boom' in stockmarkets that emerging markets across the Asian region are experiencing (see Charts at the end of this paper). Market observers, the financial media and a range of analysts agree that foreign investments have been an important force, even if not always the only one, driving markets to unprecedented highs. There

TABLE 2   *The Structure of Private Credit to Developing Countries* ($ bn)

	Bonds	Banks	Others	Short-term	Total
1998	38.8	49.4	-5.3	-65.3	17.6
1999	30.1	-5.3	-1.5	-17.3	6.0
2000	20.9	-3.8	-3.7	-6.3	7.1
2001	10.3	7.8	-6.5	-23.7	-12.1
2002	10.4	2.3	-6.9	0.5	6.3
2003	24.7	14.5	-4.4	55.0	89.8
2004	39.8	50.6	-4.0	68.4	154.8
2005	55.1	86.0	-4.9	67.7	203.9
2006	49.3	112.2	-5.5	72.0	228.0

Source: World Bank (2007).

are a number of reasons why this trend points to vulnerability. To start with, the spike in stock prices is extremely sharp. Second, this boom is generalized and occurs independent of the relative economic performance of the country concerned. This not only implies that fundamentals do not have a prime role in determining the behaviour of markets, it also means that the danger of contagion is real. Third, this occurs both in countries where investors have burnt their fingers in 1997 and in those they have not.

Another indicator of vulnerability is the revival of the credit spiral that underlay the East Asian crisis. It is no doubt true that in the years immediately following the crisis, the flow of private non-guaranteed debt to developing countries as a group fell till 2000 and registered a marginal decline in the subsequent two years up to 2002 (Table 2). With governments wanting to discourage debt-dependence and creditors wary of lending any further, even public and publicly guaranteed debt from private creditors registered a sharp decline during those years. But matters seem to have changed dramatically over the last four years. The flow of non-guaranteed debt from private sources into developing countries increased by 250 per cent over the four years ending 2006, or at a scorching pace of 28 per cent compound per annum. Simultaneously, governments too seem to have overcome their fear of debt, with public or publicly guaranteed debt from private creditors having risen by more than 150 per cent or growing at a compound rate of around 11 per cent annum. In sum, creditors appear willing to lend and debtors willing to borrow, resulting in an aggregate scenario that spells debt-dependence of a much larger magnitude than preceded the 1997 crisis.

There has been some change in composition by source as well. While, in the immediate aftermath of the 1997 crisis, the relatively small inflow of debt was on account of bond issues by developing countries, with bank credit collapsing and turning negative, more recently there has been a revival of bank credit. In terms of target, as happened at the time of the crisis, there has been a sharp shift in borrowing away from the public to the private sector. The corporate share of external debt has risen from less than one-fifth of the total in the late 1990s to more than one-half in 2006.

What is disturbing is the extreme concentration of these flows, with a growing and now substantial share of it flowing to Europe and Central Asia. In 2006, 57 per cent of flows of private non-guaranteed debt went to this region, while East Asia and the Pacific received 14 per cent, and Latin America and the Caribbean 19 per cent. Just ten countries accounted for thee-fourths of all borrowing in 2006, a sharp increase from the already high 60 per cent average during 2002–04. What is more, the evidence points to a growing share of lending to banks in developing countries, who are interested in exploiting the lower interest rates in international markets as opposed to domestic markets. Loan commitments to the banking sector totalled $32 billion in 2006, which exceeded commitments to the oil and gas sector, a traditional leader.

Finally, the World Bank's report on *Global Development Finance 2007* suggests that there has been a decline in credit quality accompanying these developments.

> As private debt flows swell, riskier borrowers may be taking a larger share of the market. The share of bonds issued by unrated (sovereign and corporate) borrowers rose from 10 per cent in 2000 to 37 per cent in 2006, and the share of unsecured loans in total bank lending rose from 50 per cent in 2002 to almost 80 per cent in 2006. (World Bank 2007: 47)

The point to note, however, is that despite these disconcerting trends, creditor confidence is at a high. The average spread between interest rates charged on developing country loan commitments and the benchmark LIBOR fell from more than 200 basis points in 2002 to 125 in 2006, and the average loan maturities have become longer.

The inevitable conclusion from this evidence, that creditors are not pricing risk adequately and taking it into account when determining exposures, needs explaining. One explanation could be that creditor profiles have changed significantly with the entry of intermediaries such as hedge funds and other less risk-averse entities into the credit market. Another could be the growing role of credit derivatives, which allows for the pooling of risk and the transfer of risk to entities that are less capable of assessing them.

According to figures reported in the *Financial Times*:

> The outstanding notional volume of credit derivatives contracts has doubled every year since the start of this decade to reach $26,000bn in the middle of last year. This has led many traditional credit investors to rethink their strategies. But above all, it has triggered a sharp increase in the number and scale of credit-focused hedge funds. In 1990, according to Hedge Fund Research, hedge funds focused on fixed income strategies accounted for just over 3 per cent of the $39bn of assets under management in the industry. By the end of last year, a more varied array of credit-related strategies accounted for almost 7.5 per cent of a $1,400bn industry – and that does not include convertible bond arbitrage. Similarly, the volume of assets under management in fixed-income arbitrage

strategies alone, which seek to exploit price differences between related bonds
and rely heavily on derivatives, has leapt from $5.8bn in 2001 to $41bn at the
end of 2006, according to HFR. (Davies and Beales 2007)

Since these developments are also taking place in the emerging markets, hedge
funds are looking for a role there as well.

These two aspects are indeed related. The emergence of credit derivatives
has rendered credit assets tradeable. This allows those looking for quick or early
profits to operate in this area. But even here, financial innovation has played a
role. Till recently, other than banks, the major players in the credit business were
pension funds and insurers. But with equities proving to be inadequately remunerat-
ive investments, banks increasingly geared to creating new instruments based on
debt and credit derivatives offering liquid credit instruments, new players – hedge
funds and pension funds, have emerged as investors, and new operators – specialized credit funds and managers of collateralized debt obligations, have emerged
as providers of instruments.

Financial Entanglement and Emerging Markets

Just as the world was recalling the 1997 Asian financial crisis on its
tenth anniversary, the dangers associated with the accumulation of risk in emerging
markets was driven home by the simultaneous collapse of stock indices in the
world's leading financial markets on Friday, 27 July, including those in so-called
'emerging markets' in developing countries. What is disconcerting is that this
synchronized collapse of markets was not the result of developments in each of
the countries where these markets were located. Rather, the source of the problem
was a crisis brewing in the housing finance market in the US, the ripple effects of
which encouraged investors to pull out of markets globally. Since then, with the
central banks of the developed countries moving in to reduce interest rates and
inject liquidity into markets, the latter have recovered. But they remain volatile
and prone to a downturn.

Underlying these ripple effects is the financial entanglement which results
from the layered financial structure, the 'innovative' financial products and the
inadequate financial regulation associated with the increasingly liberalized and
globalized financial system in most countries. Few deny that the sub-prime housing
loan market in the US – consisting of loans to borrowers with a poor credit
record – is faced with a crisis, reflected in payment defaults and foreclosures.
The problem lies in the way in which the preceding boom was triggered and kept
going. Housing demand grew rapidly because of easy access to credit, with even
borrowers with low creditworthiness scores, who would otherwise be considered
incapable of servicing debt, being drawn into the credit net. These sub-prime
borrowers were offered credit at higher rates of interest, which were sweetened
by special treatment and unusual financing arrangements – little documentation
or mere self-certification of income, no or little down payment, extended repayment
periods, and structured payment schedules involving low interest rates in the

initial phases which were 'adjustable' and moved sharply upwards when they are 'reset' to reflect premia on market interest rates. All of these encouraged or even tempted high-risk borrowers to take on loans they could ill afford, either because they had not fully understood the repayment burden they were taking on, or because they chose to conceal their actual incomes and take a bet on building wealth with debt in a market that was booming.

What needs to be understood is that the problem is largely a supply-side creation driven by factors such as easy liquidity and lower interest rates. Utilizing these circumstances, mortgage brokers attracted clients by relaxing income documentation requirements or by offering grace periods with lower interest rates, on the completion of which higher rates kick in. As a result, the share of such sub-prime loans in all mortgages rose sharply. Estimates vary, but according to one by Inside Mortgage Finance quoted by the *New York Times* (Creswell and Bajaj 2007), sub-prime loans touched $600 billion in 2006, or 20 per cent of the mortgage loan total, as compared with just 5 per cent in 2001.

The increase in this type of credit occurred because of the complex nature of current-day finance that allows an array of agents to earn lucrative returns even while transferring the risk associated with the investments that offer those returns. Mortgage brokers seek out and find willing borrowers for a fee, taking on excess risk in search of volumes. Mortgage lenders finance these mortgages, not with the intention of garnering the interest and amortization flows associated with such lending, but because they can sell these mortgages to Wall Street banks. The Wall Street banks buy the mortgages because they can bundle assets with varying returns to create securities or collateralized debt obligations, involving tranches with differing probabilities of default and differential protection against losses. They charge hefty fees for structuring these products and valuing them with complex mathematical models before selling them to a range of investors such as banks, mutual funds, pension funds and insurance companies. These entities in turn can create a portfolio involving varying degrees of risk and different streams of future cash flows linked to the original mortgage. To boot, there are firms like the unregulated hedge funds which make speculative investments in derivatives of various kinds in search of high returns for their high net-worth investors. Needless to say, institutions at every level are not fully rid of risks, but the risks are shared and rest in large measure with the final investors in the chain.

This structure is relatively stable so long as defaults are a small proportion of the total. But if as the share of sub-prime mortgages in the total rises the proportion of defaults increases, the bottom of the barrel gives and all assets turn illiquid. Rising foreclosures affect property prices and saleability adversely as foreclosed assets are put up for sale at a time when credit is squeezed, because lenders turn wary. And securities built on these mortgages turn illiquid because there are few buyers for assets whose values are opaque since there is no ready market for them. The net result is a situation of a kind where a leading Wall Street bank like Bear Stearns has to declare that the investments in two funds it created linked to mortgage-backed securities were worthless. The investors themselves have to sell off other assets to rebalance their portfolios, sending ripples into markets such as those in developing countries that have little to do with the US sub-prime market.

The problem is not restricted to the Wall Street banks. In early August, the French bank BNP Paribas suspended withdrawals from three of its funds exposed to the mortgage-backed securities market. The bank reportedly attributed its decision to 'the complete evaporation of liquidity in certain market segments' which constrained it from meeting withdrawal demands that could have turned into a run on the fund. In some cases a bail-out becomes necessary, as was true of the Dusseldorf-based IKB bank, which, through an offshore front company Rhineland Funding, had invested as much as $17.5 billion in asset-backed securities. As the value of its assets fell, Rhineland had to call on a 12 billion Euro line of credit that it had negotiated with a group of banks, including Deutsche Bank, besides IKB itself. Deutsche Bank decided to opt out of its promise to lend, and the result was the discovery that the Fund had suffered huge losses and needed a bail-out led by the state-owned KfW. In the UK, Northern Rock, a top mortgage lender that is a bank and which began as a housing society, incurred losses in the sub-prime market and became the target of a bank run. Worried depositors began pulling out their money, forcing the Bank of England to intervene because of fears that the disease may spread to other banks. The Bank of England offered Northern Rock funds to tide over the crisis and depositors a guarantee that their deposits were safe. In sum, the effects of the sub-prime crisis are weakening distant segments of the global financial system, as a result of financial entanglement.

Entanglement also makes nonsense of the theory that a complex financial system with multiple institutions, securitization, proliferating instruments and global reach is safer because it spreads risk. This was illustrated by the example of IKB referred to above. Banks wanting to reduce the risk they carry resort to securitization to transfer this risk. But institutions created by the banks themselves, linked to them in today's more universalized banking system or leveraged with bank finance, often buy these instruments created to transfer risk. In the event, as *The Economist* ('Prime Movers', 11 August 2007) put it, 'banks [that] have shown risk out of the front door by selling loans, only . . . let it return through the back door'. This, it noted, is what exactly transpires in the relationship between the three major firms – Goldman Sachs, Morgan Stanley and Bear Sterns – that offer prime-brokering services, including loans, to highly leveraged institutions like hedge funds. The bail-out of Long Term Capital Management in 1998 was necessitated because of entanglement of this kind involving all the leading merchant banks.

Investments by banks, pension funds and mutual funds are driven by the search for high and quick returns in a world of excess liquidity. In deciding to make investments on structured products intermediated at different levels, these institutions, ill-equipped to judge the true value and riskiness of these assets, rely on rating agencies. But these ratings have turned out to be unreliable and pro-cyclical, serving as erroneous and belatedly corrected signals. Noting that 'in a matter of weeks thousands of portions of subprime debt issued as recently as 2005 and 2006 have had their ratings slashed', *The Economist* ('Sold down the river Rhine', 11 August 2007) has argued that investors should not have trusted the original ratings because 'the rating agencies were earning huge fees for providing favourable judgments'. What is more, even when there is no deception involved, the rating agencies are not equipped to assess these products themselves, and rely on information and models provided by the creators of the products themselves. Once an asset is rated, there is much reluctance to downgrade it, because it would raise doubts about related ratings as well as trigger a sell-off that affects prices of related securities, which may warrant further downgrades.

The problem is that if these factors result in the accumulation of doubtful assets by investors such as banks, pension funds and mutual funds, any downturn spreads the effects into markets where these institutions have made unrelated investments. In fact, institutions overexposed to complex structured products whose valuation is difficult are saddled with relatively illiquid assets. If any development leads to liquidity problems, they are forced to sell off their most liquid assets, such as shares bought in booming emerging markets. The effect that this can have on those markets would be all the greater, the larger the exposure of these institutions in them. This is precisely what happened in July in most emerging markets, including those in Asia.

In sum, a decade after the 1997 crisis, we are witnessing trends that imply an increase in financial fragility which can lead to further financial crises, with extremely adverse implications for growth, stability, employment and social welfare. This is the element of continuity in a world that is seen as having changed substantially. Clearly, self-regulation does not help. New measures to govern finance and financial flows are a necessity.

There are many lessons that are once again being driven home by recent developments, which are of particular significance for developing countries that are rapidly liberalizing their financial systems. First, excess liquidity in a loosely controlled financial system which encourages the flow of capital to developing countries also provides the basis for speculative and unsound financial practices, such as excessive sub-prime lending, that increase fragility. Second, such practices are encouraged by the 'financial innovation' that liberalization triggers, which increases the layers of intermediation and allows firms to transfer risk. As a result, those who create risky 'products' in the first instance are less worried about the risk involved than they should be. Third, as the product moves up the financial chain, investors are less sure about its risk and value than they should be, rendering even low-risk, first-stage tranches prone to value loss. Fourth, this inadequate knowledge appears to be true even of the rating agencies on whose ratings investors rely, resulting in erroneous ratings and belated rating downgrades. This implies that as and when a rating downgrade does occur, the asset turns worthless, since there is nobody willing to buy into the asset. Fifth, new forms of self-regulation appear to be poor substitutes for more rigorous control, since the current crisis originates in a country whose financial sector is considered the most sophisticated, well-regulated and transparent, and serves as a model for others reforming their financial sectors. Finally, financial globalization and entanglement imply that countries with more open and integrated financial systems are prone to contagion effects even if the virus originates in remote locations and markets. These are lessons that must inform policy in these so-called emerging markets.

Notes

[1] For example, the wealthiest 1 per cent of Americans reportedly earned 21.2 per cent of all income in 2005, according to data from the Internal Revenue Service. This was an increase in share relative to the 19 per cent recorded in 2004, and exceeded the previous high of 20.8 per cent set in 2000, at the peak of the previous bull market in stocks. As compared with this, the bottom 50 per cent earned 12.8 per cent of all income, which was less than the 13.4 per cent and 13 per cent recorded in 2004 and 2000, respectively. See Ip (2007).

[2] Figures from *Venture Economics, Private Equity* and *Buyouts Magazine,* quoted in Bloomberg and Schumer (2006).

[3] The study covered, besides the eleven G-10 countries (US, Canada, Japan, Belgium, France, Germany, Italy, Netherlands, Sweden, Switzerland and UK), Spain and Australia.

[4] 'Emerging Markets Private Equity: The current landscape and the road ahead', *EM PE Quarterly Review,* Volume II, Issue 4, Q4, 2006, available at www.empea.net/docs/newsletters/EMPE_QuarterlyReview_Vol2_Issue4.pdf, accessed 2 February 2007.

[5] Metrics 2.0, 'Asia Pacific Private Equity Deals Tripled in 2006', http://www.metrics2.com/blog/2006/12/13/asia_pacific_private_equity_deals_tripled_ in_2006.html, accessed 27 February 2007.

References

Bank of International Settlements (1997), 'BIS Reporting Banks: Summary of International Positions', *BIS Quarterly Review: International Banking and Financial Market Developments,* November: A1–A2.

———— (2007a), 'BIS Reporting Banks: Summary of International Positions', *BIS Quarterly Review: International Banking and Financial Market Developments,* September: A7–A8.

———— (2007b), *Triennial Central Bank Survey of Foreign Exchange and Derivatives Market Activity in April 2007,* Basel: Monetary and Economic Department, Bank of International Settlements.

Bloomberg, M.R. and C.E. Schumer (2006), *Sustaining New York's and the US' Global Financial Services Leadership* (New York: Office of the Mayor, City of New York and United States Senate).

Committee on the Global Financial System (2004), *Foreign Direct Investment in the Financial Sector of Emerging Market Economies* (Basel: Bank for International Settlements).

———— (2007), *Institutional Investors, Global Savinga and Asset Allocations: Report submitted by Working Group* (Basel: Bank of International Settlements).

Creswell, J. and V. Bajaj (2007), 'A Mortgage Crisis Begins to Spiral, and the Casualties Mount', *The New York Times,* 5 March.

Davies, P.J. and R. Beales (2007), 'Introduction: New players join the credit game', *The Financial Times,* 13 March.

Financial Stability Forum (2007), *Update of the FSF's 2000 Report on Highly Leveraged Institutions,* 18 May, at http://www.fsforum.org/publications/HLI_Update-finalwithout embargo19May07.pdf, accessed 15 June 2007.

Group of 10 (2001), *Report on Consolidation in the Financial Sector,* 25 January, at http://www.imf.org/external/np/g10/2001/01/Eng/index.htm, accessed 15 May 2002.

Ip, G. (2007), 'Income Inequality Widens', *The Wall Street Journal*, 12 October.

Organization for Economic Cooperation and Development (2003), *Institutional Investors Statistical Year Book 1992–2001* (Paris: OECD).

——— (2001), *Institutional Investors Statistical Year Book* (Paris: OECD).

World Bank (2007), *Global Development Finance 2007: The Globalization of Corporate Finance in Developing Countries* (Washington DC: World Bank).

CHART 1   *Movements in the Indian Composite Stock Index (Sensex)*
         (base 1978–79 = 100)

Source: www.globalfinancialdata.com.

CHART 2   *Movements in the Jakarta Stock Exchange Composite Index*
         (base 14 August 1991 = 100)

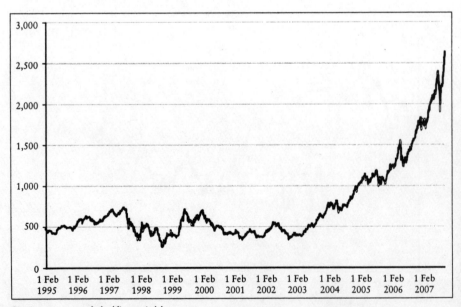

Source: www.globalfinancialdata.com.

CHART 3 *Movements in the Korea Stock Exchange Stock Price Index*
(base 4 January 1980 = 100)

Source: www.globalfinancialdata.com.

CHART 4 *Movements in the Kuala Lumpur Stock Exchange Composite Index*
(base 3 January 1974 = 100)

Source: www.globalfinancialdata.com.

CHART 5 *Movements in the Manila Stock Exchange Composite Index*
         (base 30 September 1994 = 2922.21)

Source: www.globalfinancialdata.com.

CHART 6 *Movement in the Thailand SET General Index*
         (base 1 August 1975 = 100)

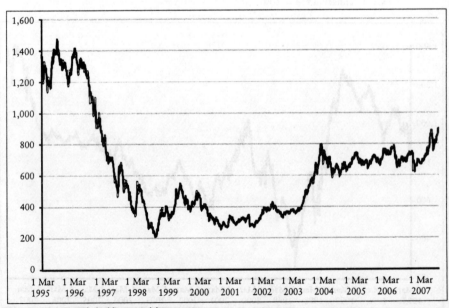

Source: www.globalfinancialdata.com.

Crisis and its Aftermath
in East and Southeast Asia

Adjustment, Recovery and Growth after Financial Crisis

A Consideration of Five 'Crisis' Countries of East and Southeast Asia

Jayati Ghosh

The East Asian financial crisis a decade ago was a sharp shock, which rocked financial markets globally for a short time. It was one of the more glaring examples of 'contagion effects' in financial markets, spreading rapidly from Thailand to other countries in the region even when the economies concerned appeared to have different characteristics. It created huge disruptions in the economies and societies of the region, causing large increases in unemployment, sharp increases in poverty and, in some cases, major political changes. It also presaged the other financial crises that have hit various parts of the developing world (Russia, Turkey, Argentina) since then.

At the time, during and just after the financial crisis in 1997 and 1998, there was surprise and some amount of consternation in international policy-making circles as well as in the mainstream financial press. The East and Southeast Asian economies that were hit by the crisis were, after all, some of the best performers among developing countries in terms of both GDP (gross domestic product) growth and exporting ability. Their governments had embraced globalization in all its aspects, not only in terms of export orientation but very extensive trade liberalization and, more recently, financial liberalization. The five countries that were particularly affected by financial crisis – Thailand, South Korea, Indonesia, Malaysia and the Philippines – had all been characterized by rapid export growth, especially in 'sunrise' manufacturing industries, and were substantial recipients of private foreign capital. In general they were characterized by 'prudent' macro-economic policies – three of them were running government budget surpluses and the other two had budget deficits that could be considered as moderate rather than excessive. They were regularly lauded by the Bretton Woods institutions as positive examples for other developing countries to follow, and cited as success stories of global integration.

Therefore, when the crisis struck the attempt was made, especially in mainstream policy discussions, to find causes for it that were outside the pattern of economic integration and liberalization that had been so favourably cited (Corsetti *et al.* 1999; Radelet *et al.* 1998; Johnson *et al.* 2000). 'Crony capitalism' and opaque financial systems that distorted the pattern of investment; exchange rate rigidity because of the practice of pegging exchange rates to the appreciating US dollar that adversely affected export competitiveness – these and other such factors were routinely evoked to explain away the crisis in what were otherwise apparently still model economies. The more plausible reasons for the crisis were rarely discussed or all too quickly swept away in the mainstream discussion. Thus the more structural problem of fallacy of composition that made the excessive focus on exports as the engine of growth more difficult as competing developing country exporters entered the scene was ignored in favour of blaming fixed exchange rates *per se*. The more proximate impact of external financial liberalization – in terms of allowing inflows of capital that enabled short-term borrowing for long-term projects, breaking the link between the ability to access foreign exchange and the need to earn it, and causing appreciation of the real exchange rate that shifted incentives within the economy from tradeables to non-tradeables – was also underplayed. Yet, of course, these were primary instrumental factors in causing the crisis (as elaborated in Jomo, ed. 1998; Johnson 1998; Ghosh and Chandrasekhar 2001), and the failure to recognize these as potentially destabilizing economic strategies was part of the problem in subsequent crises in Turkey, Argentina and elsewhere.

Similarly, the subsequent economic recovery in the crisis-ridden countries of Southeast Asia has also been subject to multiple interpretations. Some have argued that the quick and brutal policy response of fiscal and monetary tightening enabled the economic stabilization and generation of current account surpluses that followed relatively quickly. But there is no question that the IMF (International Monetary Fund)-inspired strategy of high interest rates, tight monetary policy and fiscal compression actually made things worse in terms of deepening the crisis into a downward spiral especially over 1998, most notably in Thailand, Indonesia and the Philippines. The subsequent recovery, when it did occur, was essentially led by fiscal expansion – first in Malaysia where the use of expansionary fiscal policy began as early as 1998, and subsequently in South Korea, facilitated by external resources through the Miyazawa Initiative from Japan. Even so, the recovery too has been treated rather differently in some analyses, which have argued that the period of the crisis was simply a minor blip in an otherwise healthy and sustainable growth process driven by reliance on market-based reforms, foreign investment and export orientation.

This interpretation has been further fuelled by the fact that ten years after the East Asian financial crisis broke out, the economies of the region appear to have recovered quite substantially. Indeed by now, in mainstream discussion, the Asian crisis is often discussed not in terms of its negative impacts, but rather presented as an example of how economies can recover relatively quickly from crisis and continue on a favourable growth trajectory. There are even those who argue that the Asian financial crisis was in general a good thing, since it did not destroy the basic economic growth trajectory of the region and forced the economies in question to intensify liberalizing reforms, especially in the financial sector, and thereby reduce 'crony capitalism'. In addition, the reduction of monopoly

power through the break up of some of the large South Korean industrial conglomerates (or '*chaebols*') and the political collapse of the Suharto dictatorship in
Indonesia are cited as some of the positive by-products of the crisis.

This view is current not only in international financial circles but even
among some Indian policy makers. This is of especial concern, since it suggests
that policy makers in India (and other developing countries) may not be sufficiently
worried about a potential financial crisis as to take adequate precautionary
measures to avoid it. Given the large capital inflows because of financial markets'
fascination with India as a hot destination even with the increasing volatility in
this and other markets, the continuing policy moves towards external financial
liberalization and the recently increased reliance on exports as a growth engine,
there are certainly at least some similarities of current economic conditions in
India with the situation of pre-crisis Southeast Asian countries.

That is why it is particularly important to evaluate the subsequent performance of those economies that were particularly affected by the 1997 financial
crisis. Of course, a decade is in any case a useful time to take stock, especially as
it is considered sufficiently long for the basic tendencies in the economy to have
emerged. In this paper, the post-crisis experience of the five economies of Thailand,
South Korea, Malaysia, Indonesia and the Philippines is considered. It is found
that while output growth has recovered to varying degrees, in all these countries
there has been a significant change in the pattern of growth and investment,
which has meant that the subsequent growth has had very different implications
for employment generation compared to the previous period.

It is essential to examine export performance, if only because for some
time now it has been considered as central to how the economies have performed
overall. Export growth was seen as the key to the success of these five economies
in the late 1980s and the first half of the 1990s, and it is routinely cited as the best
indication of the recovery as well. Export growth in the region was very high in
the pre-crisis years, with these countries showing among the most rapid rates of
export expansion in the world, between 10 and 20 per cent per year in US dollar
terms. The deceleration of export growth in 1996 is widely recognized as one of
the proximate causes of the crisis. This is evident from Chart 1. The slump in
exports that began from the middle of 1996 continued well into the crisis years of
1997 and 1998; however, exports recovered fairly quickly in these countries
immediately thereafter, aided by the very major depreciations of currency that
were induced by the crisis. As is evident from Chart 1, by 2000 all these five
countries were showing sharp increases in rates of export growth of more than 10
per cent, and in Indonesia it was even more than 30 per cent.

Subsequently, however, export growth has been very volatile in all five
countries. There was a dramatic collapse (associated with absolute declines in
US dollar terms) in 2001. This was also the period when world trade values fell.
The apparent synchronicity of export behaviour in these five countries, despite
rather different domestic economic strategies, suggests that export performance
from the late 1990s, but especially after 2000, has been strongly influenced by

CHART 1 *Export Growth Rates* (per cent per year in current US dollar terms)

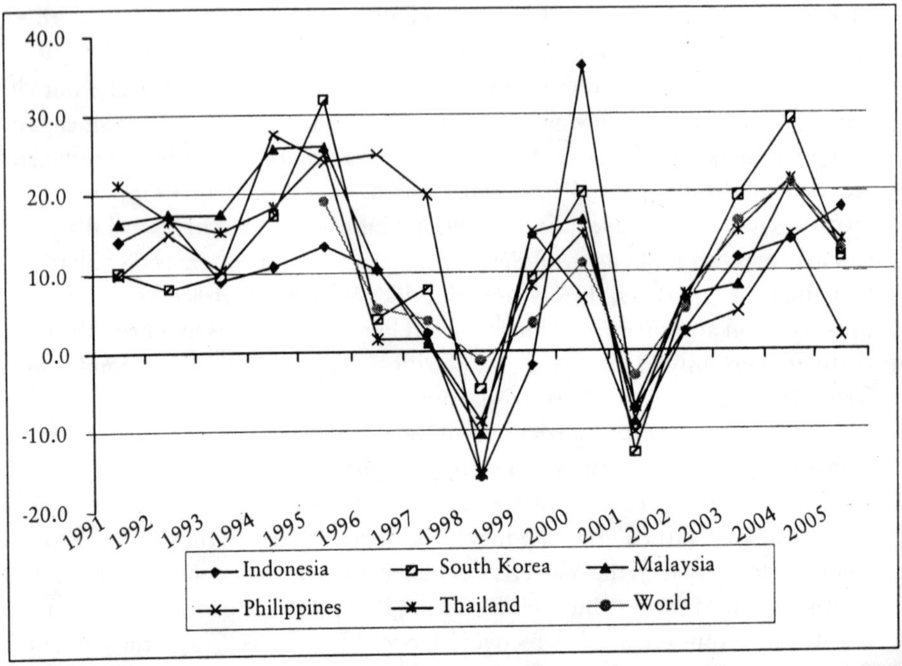

Source: World Bank World Development Indicators online for five Asian countries and IMF Balance of Payments Statistics online for world.

global developments. This is also evident from Chart 1, which shows that the cyclical pattern of world exports is reflected in the export performance of these five countries. Thus the period 2003–05 has been one of global export boom, with both primary producers and manufactured goods exporters in the developing world posting high rates of growth.[1] So Asian export performance has generally tracked global exports. The difference is that before the crisis, export growth in these countries was generally higher than the world average (with the exception of South Korea, where it was only slightly lower). However, from 2002 onwards, exports in these countries (again except for South Korea) have grown at a lower rate than the world average. Also, the rates of export growth in the most recent three-year period, which is seen as the period of export boom, are below the rates of increase achieved in the period 1992–95, just before the crisis.

One difference, which may become more significant in future, is that a higher proportion of exports from these countries is now directed towards other countries in Asia, reflecting the new patterns of trade created by relocative capital and the crucial role of processing. The now dominant role of processing exports in China has made that country a huge and growing market for manufactured goods from these five countries as well as other Asian countries, these imports being further processed for re-export. In that sense the US and European Union still remain the main drivers of export demand for the region as a whole.

In terms of other variables which may be more indicative of the actual health of these economies, the evidence is more mixed. Both aggregate GDP growth and industrial growth are still substantially below the average rates achieved in the period before the crisis. They have also been more volatile and fluctuating. Charts 2 to 6 provide information on trends in annual real GDP growth rates, savings and investment rates in these five countries.

One striking feature of the growth experience of all these five economies, as evident from Charts 2 to 6, is how dramatic the shock of 1998 was in terms of absolute declines in aggregate income. Subsequently GDP growth did recover, but in general this involved growth rates that have been slightly lower, and definitely more volatile, than the growth rates of the previous period.

But the most startling change that has occurred in these countries is the broad macroeconomic shift in terms of a large divergence between savings and investment rates. The East and Southeast Asian region has generally had very high savings rates – between 30 and 45 per cent in these five countries – for some time now. But the period subsequent to the financial crisis has seen an increase in these already high rates, especially in the 'crisis' countries. However, investment rates (that is, the share of investment in GDP) have plummeted in all these countries.

Thus, in South Korea the savings rate increased from just under 40 per cent in the three years before the crisis to more than 42 per cent in 2003–05 (Chart 2). But the investment rate collapsed by almost half over the same period, from 42 per cent to 21 per cent. An almost identical pattern is evident for Malaysia, where investment rates halved from 42 per cent to 21 per cent, but domestic

CHART 2 *GDP Growth, Savings and Investment Rates in South Korea*

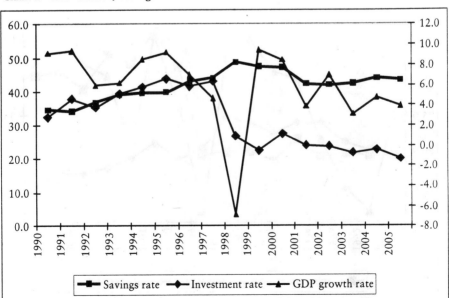

Source: World Bank World Development Indicators online.

CHART 3 *GDP Growth, Savings and Investment Rates in Malaysia*

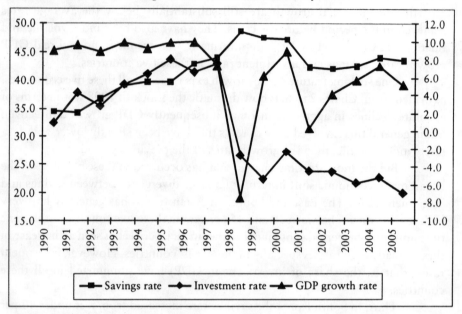

Source: World Bank World Development Indicators online.

CHART 4 *GDP Growth, Savings and Investment Rates in the Philippines*

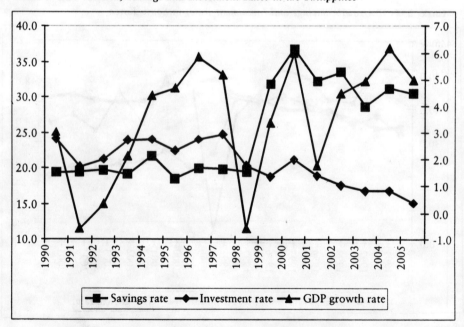

Source: World Bank World Development Indicators online.

CHART 5 *GDP Growth, Savings and Investment Rates in Indonesia*

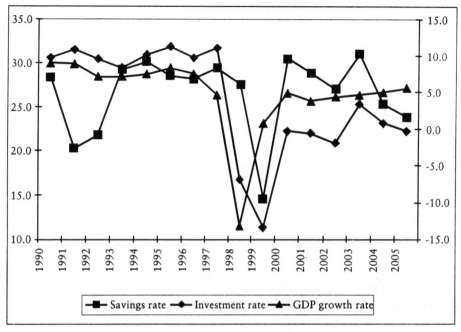

Source: World Bank World Development Indicators online.

CHART 6 *GDP Growth, Savings and Investment Rates in Thailand*

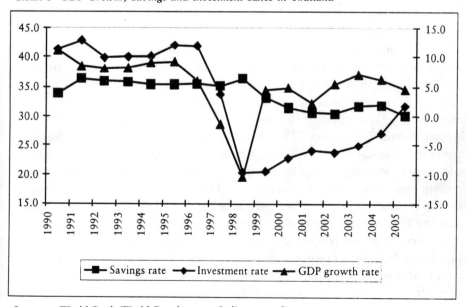

Source: World Bank World Development Indicators online.

savings rates increased from an already high 41 per cent to more than 43 per cent between the same two years (Chart 3). In the Philippines, over the same years, the savings rate went up from 26 per cent to 30 per cent, but the investment rate fell from 24 per cent to only 16 per cent (Chart 4).

In Indonesia, the savings rate has remained unchanged at around 29 per cent but the investment rate has fallen from 31 per cent to 23 per cent (Chart 5). Only Thailand shows a different recent trajectory: while the investment rate fell sharply after the crisis, it has recovered somewhat in recent times, although it is still only 28 per cent in the latest three-year period compared to 41 per cent in the pre-crisis period (Chart 6). The savings rate has also shown a different trend from the other countries: it has actually declined somewhat from 35 per cent average for 1994–96 to 31 per cent in 2003–05. This different pattern has also resulted in a different employment pattern in the recent past, as is described in the following section. However, even in Thailand, the pre-crisis period was generally character-ized by investment rates that were higher than savings rates, whereas the post-crisis period has generally been one in which savings rates have been higher than investment rates.

The recovery in output growth (even if not to the rates achieved in the pre-crisis years) along with the decline in investment rates in these countries suggests that ICORs (incremental capital–output ratios) would have been increas-ing in the recent period. Obviously this requires further investigation, but it is clearly the case that the recent period has been marked by productivity increases, especially in manufacturing. This certainly reflects the impact of external competi-tion in both exporting and import-substituting activities, as producers find it necessary to adopt the most recent and cost-reducing technological changes. While increasing aggregate ICORs are clearly to be desired, they also point to greater losses of possible output expansion because of investment rates below the potential offered by the higher domestic savings rates.

Therefore, in all these five countries, the crisis years of 1997 and 1998 mark a clear break from the earlier trend, when typically domestic investment rates were higher than saving rates, and the balance was met by an inflow of for-eign capital. The latter is in fact what one would expect in a developing country, since it is generally supposed that developing countries are characterized by a shortage of investible resources. Therefore economic openness, especially to foreign investment, is designed to allow foreign resources to add to domestic savings in order to generate a higher rate of investment than would be possible using only domestic resources. After the crisis, from 1998 onwards, these five economies actually became *more* 'open' in policy terms, especially with respect to rules regarding foreign investment. Nevertheless, after 1998 all these five countries have stopped being net recipients of foreign savings and instead have shown the opposite tendency of net resource outflow, as domestic savings have been higher than investment. This has meant that there has been a process of squeezing out savings from the population as a whole but not investing it within the economy to ensure future growth. Instead, these savings have effectively been exported, either through capital outflows or by adding to the external reserves of the central banks, which are typically held in very safe assets abroad (such as US Treasury Bills). This has happened even though the need for more investment within these countries is still very great. Indeed the development project is still not complete in these countries, and especially not in Indonesia, Thailand and the Philippines, where poverty and backwardness remain substantial.

This rather paradoxical situation, which is reflective of a broader international tendency whereby developing countries have been providing their resources to the developed world, and in particular to the United States, has been described by some American commentators as a 'savings glut' (Bernanke 2005). Quite apart from the many problems with such an argument, it is immediately apparent from Charts 2 to 6 that the problem in these countries has not been the rise in savings so much as the collapse in investment. True, saving rates have increased, affected also by crisis-induced shifts in income distribution that have reduced workers' consumption and transferred more income to those in a better position to save. But the sharp collapse in investment rates that has been noted above has come about because of other factors that have led to the emergence of this 'savings surplus'.

Thus the growing savings surplus is partly – but only partly – the result of the decisions of private agents in these countries. And even these private decisions have been strongly affected by official economic policies. For example, stringent monetary conditions, increasing real interest rates and an excess of very rigid and inflexible forms of prudential regulation have caused bank credit to be less easily available for investment. A range of other post-crisis measures dampened private investment by directly and indirectly raising the costs of finance and reducing access to it. This has obviously reduced investment by large corporate entities, but it has had even stronger detrimental effects upon small enterprises which have found it more difficult to access credit. It is worth noting that the only economy that has shown a different pattern in savings and investment – that of Thailand – is one where the government of Thaksin Shinawatra systematically made greater access to institutional credit by small enterprises and farmers a major plank of the post-crisis reconstruction strategy.

But monetary and financial policies are only one part of the story. A very large role in the reduction of aggregate investment was played by fiscal policies of governments in these countries, who increased their own savings and cut down on fiscal deficits or increased fiscal surpluses across the region. Even though the financial crisis in these countries was essentially brought on by private profligacy in a financially liberalized environment, the aftermath of the financial crises has created an environment of excessive caution on the part of governments. The pressure on government has been to keep government budget deficits under control by reducing their spending. This in turn means that governments in these countries have not spent as much as could be easily sustained by the economy, to ensure better conditions for the people or to encourage more sustainable growth and generate more employment. This is evident from Chart 7, which shows how

CHART 7   *Fiscal Deficits as per cent of GDP*

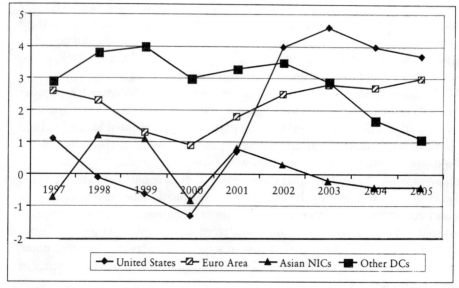

Source: IMF World Economic Outlook 2007.

the Asian newly industrializing countries (NICs, a group which is dominated by the five countries being considered in this paper) have not only run very low budget deficits (around or less than 1 per cent of GDP since the late 1990s), but also have been running budget surpluses for the past few years. All other developing countries have still been running budget deficits, even though these are small and getting smaller.

It is worth noting that the developed countries have not been so circumspect: the United States moved from budget surplus to growing budget deficit after 2001, and the US deficits are now once again the highest in the world in absolute terms and also high as a share of GDP. Even the Euro area has shown higher budget deficits in the recent past.

So the major cause for this apparent excess of capital which is then being exported to the US and other developed countries is deflationary policies on the part of these governments, which suppress domestic consumption and investment. This obviously has effects on current levels of economic activity, but it also negatively affects future growth prospects because of the long-term potential losses of inadequate infrastructure investment, etc.

Why are governments in these countries pursuing such an apparently counterproductive policy which runs against the interests of their own current and future economic growth? One obvious reason is the fear of a repeat of the large and destabilizing movements of speculative capital which were such a strong feature of the financial crisis of 1997–98. The idea is to guard against the possibility of such potentially damaging capital flight by building up substantial foreign exchange reserves, even when these may involve large fiscal losses. But this is only one reason. The other reason is that the current economic strategy in these countries is still centred around the obsession with exports as the engine of growth, which are combined with deflationary domestic policies that keep levels of aggregate domestic investment lower than savings. This causes an 'excess supply' of foreign exchange in the currency market, which would in turn involve an appreciation of currencies, thereby adversely affecting exports! In a world of liberalized trade where exchange rates cannot be easily controlled, this means that currencies have to be kept at 'competitive' levels through market-based means. And this in turn means that foreign currency inflows – whether through more exports or remittances or through capital flows – must be counteracted by central bank market intervention to purchase foreign currency, to prevent un-desired appreciation of the currency. The macroeconomic counterpart – and cause – of the rising foreign exchange reserves held by the central banks of all these countries is therefore the excess of domestic savings over investment, which is actually a huge potential wasted for these economies. So financial liberalization forces a deflationary strategy on governments that in turn contributes to the accumulation of unutilized foreign exchange, thereby threatening currency appreciation. The deflationary effect of this economic strategy is reflected in lower levels of economic activity than could have been potentially achieved, as well as higher levels of unemployment. This in turn helps us to understand why growth rates are in general lower, why employment generation has been inade-quate and unemployment rates are rising, and why conditions of a large section of the poor do not improve in these countries, despite the apparent aggregate eco-nomic 'recovery'.

Thus aggregate employment growth is also much slower than before. This has in turn been reflected in a drop – substantial in some of these countries – in worker population rates. This is evident from Table 1, which shows that both male and female work participation rates have tended to decline, although they have shown somewhat divergent trends in the different countries. In Indonesia, male worker population rates have fallen from an average of 79 per cent in the three years preceding the crisis to 77 per cent over 2003–05, though of course that is still a high rate. For women, the decline has been from 47 per cent to 45 per cent. For South Korea, the decline is not so marked between the two periods – there was a very sharp drop for both men and women in the period just after the crisis, but a recovery thereafter. Male work participation rates in the most recent three-year period at 71 per cent were still below the pre-crisis rate of 73 per cent; however, for females the rate actually increased between these two periods by 1 percentage point, to 48.6 per cent. There is evidence that for women, more of this is part-time work. In Malaysia, aggregate worker population rates show no change, but this reflects a decline for men and an increase for women (both by 2 percentage points). In Thailand female rates have remained broadly unchanged at 65 per cent, but male rates have fallen substantially, from 83.5 per cent to 79.8 per cent, between the two periods. The Philippines is the clear outlier in this case – aggregate worker population rates have actually increased between the two

TABLE 1   *Worker Population Rates* (per cent)

	Indonesia		South Korea		Malaysia		Philippines		Thailand	
	Male	*Female*	*Male*	*Female*	*Male*	*Female*	*Male*	*Female*	*Male*	*Female*
1991	78.9	47.4	72.0	46.2	78.9	42.6	76.2	42.0	84.7	70.4
1992	79.8	47.1	72.3	46.1	78.7	42.3	76.5	43.0	85.1	68.9
1993	78.9	47.1	71.8	46.0	79.4	42.6	75.7	42.8	84.3	66.4
1994	78.1	46.9	72.8	46.9	79.4	42.5	76.3	42.8	83.9	63.7
1995	78.5	46.7	73.4	47.7	79.4	42.4	76.8	44.4	83.6	65.3
1996	80.1	47.0	73.5	48.4	79.9	42.5	77.6	44.9	83.0	66.5
1997	79.8	46.6	73.0	49.0	79.9	42.4	76.8	44.7	82.9	66.8
1998	79.1	46.6	68.3	44.7	79.4	41.9	75.9	44.5	80.4	63.9
1999	79.9	47.2	68.2	45.5	78.6	42.2	75.1	45.3	79.6	63.0
2000	80.1	47.1	69.4	46.9	79.2	44.1	73.3	43.6	80.1	63.9
2001	78.7	46.1	69.5	47.5	79.0	43.9	75.4	46.8	80.4	63.4
2002	77.8	45.5	70.6	48.2	78.9	43.8	74.9	46.8	80.7	63.7
2003	77.5	45.2	70.3	47.1	78.6	43.6	74.7	46.8	80.5	63.7
2004	77.1	45.1	71.0	48.5	78.7	44.4	74.4	47.5	80.0	64.8
2005	77.7	44.3	70.9	48.6	78.6	44.8	76.9	50.7	79.9	65.0

Source: ILO Key Indicators of Labour Markets, fifth edition, 2007.

periods, and this is even though male rates have remained unchanged, but female rates have moved sharply up from a pre-crisis average of 44 per cent to 50 per cent in the most recent period. Once again, in the Philippines there is other qualitative evidence suggesting that much of the new work is in the form of part-time and less formal employment.

Even in the sectors where export growth has been buoyant, such as manufacturing, employment has not picked up, and in South Korea and Malaysia manufacturing employment has actually fallen in absolute numbers compared to the pre-crisis years. Overall, survey and other micro evidence suggests that even where employment has not fallen or has even increased, the quality of employment has deteriorated in that there is a greater proportion of insecure casual contracts, low-grade self-employment and part-time work in total employment, especially for women workers.

Further, unemployment rates are on the rise, even in the countries where there has been an increase in worker population rates. Table 2 shows that there has been an increase in open unemployment rates in these countries, even though, except for South Korea, none of them has any unemployment benefit or social security system worth the name. Open unemployment rates in Indonesia have increased from an average of 3.6 per cent in the three years before the crisis to 10 per cent in 2003–05. Open unemployment rates for Indonesian women were as high as 14 per cent in 2005. In South Korea the increase in unemployment has been from 2.2 to 3.7 per cent of the labour force. Malaysia experienced the least decline in employment and the most rapid recovery from the crisis, yet even here

TABLE 2   *Unemployment Rates* (per cent of labour force)

	Indonesia	South Korea	Malaysia	Philippines	Thailand
1990			4.7	8.1	2.2
1991		2.4		9	2.7
1992	2.8	2.5	3.7	8.6	1.4
1993		2.9	3	8.9	1.5
1994	4.4	2.5		8.4	1.4
1995		2.1	3.1	8.4	1.1
1996	5.5	2	2.5	7.4	1.1
1997		2.6	2.5	7.9	0.9
1998	6.3	7	3.2	9.6	3.4
1999	6.1	6.3	3.4	9.2	3
2000	8.1	4.4	3	10.1	2.4
2001	9.1	4	3.5	9.8	2.6
2002	9.5	3.3	3.5	10.2	1.8
2003	9.9	3.6	3.6	10.2	1.5
2004	10.3	3.7		10.9	1.5
2005		3.7			1.3

Source: ILO Key Indicators of the Labour Market, fifth edition, 2007.

the average unemployment rates increased from the pre-crisis 2.7 per cent to 3.5 per cent of the labour force in the most recent three-year period. In the Philippines it increased from 7.6 per cent to 10.6 per cent of the labour force. Overall, for these four countries, these higher open unemployment rates have been associated with declining rates of labour force participation, indicating more and more 'discouraged workers', especially among women. Thailand is the only country where, after an initial post-crisis increase, unemployment rates are down to the relatively low pre-crisis levels. And it has already been noted that Thailand has been something of an exception in avoiding the most extreme deflationary policies, and has therefore experienced higher investment rates and output growth recovery than the other countries.

Most crucially, one important fallout of the financial crisis has been that the project of the developmental state, which was such an essential feature of economic progress in the region in the past, has effectively been abandoned. So financial crises do more than simply create sharp and painful economic shocks for the residents of the country – they also alter longer-term economic trajectories in unfortunate ways.

Note

[1] The rates of growth described in Chart 1, in US dollar terms, would slightly over-estimate the real rate of export expansion in this most recent period because this is also the period when the US dollar's value had been falling in international currency markets.

References

Bernanke, Ben (2005), 'The global saving glut and the US current account deficit', at http://www.federalreserve.gov/boarddocs/speeches/2005/200503102/default.htm.

Corsetti, Giancarlo, Paolo Pesenti and Nouriel Roubini (1999), 'What caused the Asian currency and financial crisis?', *Japan and the World Economy*, Vol. 11, No. 3: 305–73.

Johnson, Chalmers (1998), 'Economic crisis in East Asia: The clash of capitalisms', *Cambridge Journal of Economics*, Vol. 22, No. 6: 653–61.

Ghosh, Jayati and C.P. Chandrasekhar (2001), *Crisis as Conquest: Learning from East Asia*, New Delhi: Orient Longman.

Johnson, S., P. Boone, A. Breach, E. Friedman (2000), 'Corporate governance in the Asian financial crisis', *Journal of Financial Economics*, Vol. 58: 141–86.

Jomo, K.S., ed. (1998), *Tigers in trouble: Financial governance, liberalization and crises in East Asia*, London: Zed Books.

Radelet, Steven, Jeffrey D. Sachs, Richard N. Cooper, Barry P. Bosworth (1998), 'The East Asian Financial Crisis: Diagnosis, Remedies, Prospects', *Brookings Papers on Economic Activity*, No. 1: 1–90.

Unchained Melody

Economic Performance after the Asian Crisis

Edsel L. Beja, Jr.

Introduction

This paper raises three issues that have been underplayed thus far in the ongoing retrospection on the 1997 Asian crisis (see ADB 2007; Burton and Zanello 2007; World Bank 2007; Ito *et al.* 2007; UNESCAP 2007). The first is that recent economic performance in Indonesia, Malaysia, Philippines, South Korea and Thailand (henceforth, crisis-affected economies) has actually been inferior when compared to pre-crisis performance. This is related to the second point: that the crisis-affected economies have not recouped the losses of 1997, and stronger economic performance is needed to reclaim the lost opportunities. Third, it is argued that unless economic policies in these economies move in a positive direction – reviving some strategies that proved useful in the past and also putting in new components to meet current challenges – future economic progress is likely to be limited and punctuated by crises. Complacency about a seemingly stable economic environment is misplaced as long as the international financial system is characterized by massive and volatile financial flows, but economies remain ill-equipped to deal with the challenges produced by such flows. If the international financial system is the culprit in creating and propagating crises, policies are needed to address these threats. The effectiveness of such policies will largely depend on the political willingness to go in for unpopular measures, as well as the skilfulness of policy makers in forging international cooperative arrangements that lead to coordinated actions.

There are different ways to analyse the relationship between economic performance and crisis. One view is that an economy is able to bounce back quickly after being hit by a crisis. As such, if there is a strong crisis, there is also a strong recovery. A crisis becomes a mechanism that pushes a government to undertake serious adjustments to achieve robust economic performance. Thus a crisis is seen as transitory because no economic derailment or loss in economic momentum is expected. Moreover, the cost of a crisis is quickly recouped. In fact, it has even been argued that because of the reforms brought about by the crisis, the economy is thrust on to a higher economic growth trajectory.

The alternative view suggests that an economy cannot completely bounce back after being hit by a crisis. In fact it faces difficulties in terms of recovery and recouping the costs of the crisis. This situation occurs because domestic institutions are weak or were damaged by the crisis, or are not designed to respond to it, especially when the nature of crises is changing and intensifying. Of course, repeated crises undermine institutions, pushing the economy to a lower growth trajectory. The costs of a crisis linger because the restorative capacities of the economy are compromised. There are therefore serious economic implications of a crisis. Arguing that an economy is unharmed because of what appears to be strong recovery in the post-crisis period is misguided. Thus the resulting lower growth trajectory means that a one-shot adjustment is not enough to recoup the losses. Constant adjustment of policies is important not only to bring the economy to a superior growth trajectory, but also to sustain robust economic expansion.

Of course, there are many sources of economic perturbations. Some of them can cause the economy to achieve stronger economic expansion. There are also non-transitory effects, but they are positive in such cases. For instance, the discovery of oil deposits brings commercial benefits to relieve an economy of foreign exchange constraints, enabling it to finance economic growth and development projects. It is true that if the earnings are squandered or not well utilized, a Dutch disease can occur in due course, thereby reversing the gains with economic stagnation. Similarly, capital inflows brought in by the reorganization of the global manufacturing system and finance can lead to stronger economic expansion. Again, if the opportunities are not capitalized to bring about human capital formation, technology adaptation and industrial deepening, etc., bottlenecks soon materialize to produce vulnerabilities that are destabilizing in the long term and put the economy at risk. If economic stagnation, economic mismatches, institutional rigidities and so on corrode institutional capacities, the economy can be easily pushed down to a lower economic growth trajectory when it is hit by a crisis.

In the next section, this framework is used to analyse how economic performance was affected in the crisis-hit countries. The third section presents some attempts at 'costing' the crises. Policy issues are discussed in the fourth section, and the last section concludes.

Post-Crisis Growth Performance[1]

The framework given above is used to analyse the economic performance of the crisis-affected countries. Data on GDP (gross domestic product) per capita (in 2000 prices) are taken from the *Asian Development Outlook 2007* and *World Development Indicators 2007* for the period 1987–2007. The data are normalized to 1996 to distinguish the trends before and after the crisis.

Chart 1 illustrates that by the mid-2000s, the crises-affected economies exceeded their 1996 GDP per capita, albeit at different speeds. Indonesia took the longest to regain its 1996 GDP per capita, which was reached by 2004. Thailand had a comparable experience, regaining its 1996 GDP per capita level in 2003. In the case of Malaysia, 1996 GDP per capita was regained in 2000. Both the

CHART 1   *GDP per capita in the Crisis Countries* (normalized to 1996)

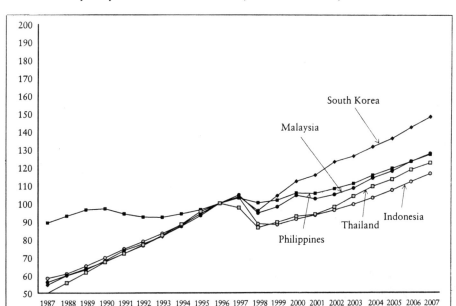

Source: Asian Development Outlook 2007 and World Development Indicators 2007.

Philippines and South Korea bounced back quickly from the contractions in 1998, exceeding the 1996 GDP per capita by 1999.

What is more interesting in Chart 1 is that between 1987 and 1996, Indonesia, Malaysia, South Korea and Thailand had a tight pattern of economic expansion, especially during the first half of the 1990s, as if increasingly chained to one another with sustained robust economic growth. If the time-frame is stretched back to include earlier periods, 1987–96 becomes an exceptional period for the four economies. Arguably, the decade before the crisis was a period of economic convergence among these economies that is not found in the performance of the other economies in the region.[2]

Thailand diverged from the group in 1997, when GDP per capita contracted by 2.4 per cent. The other four economies experienced contractions the following year: Indonesia by 14.3 per cent, Malaysia by 9.6 per cent, South Korea by 7.5 per cent and the Philippines by 2.5 per cent. From 1998, economic performance of the crisis-affected countries became increasingly disparate. As Chart 1 shows, Indonesia dropped the farthest relative to South Korea, and Malaysia, the Philippines and Thailand were between the two economies. These trends are expected to continue in the coming years. It can therefore be concluded that the crisis resulted in a divergence in economic expansion in the region.

Further analysis can be had if the information in Chart 1 is transformed by applying rotational analysis. Note that because the Philippines has a different

CHART 2 *GDP per capita at 2000 Prices, Rotated at 1996*

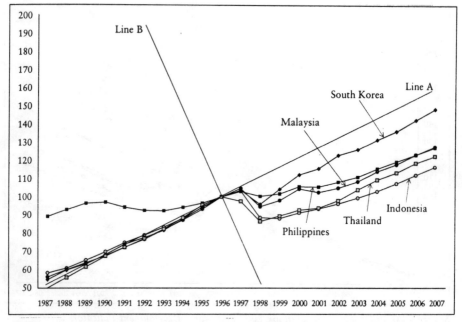

Source: Asian Development Outlook 2007 and World Development Indicators 2007.

trend, the trends of the other economies are used as control trend. In the first step, a line is obtained – called rotated axis – that captures the convergence in 1987–96, ensuring that it crosses the reference year in normalizing the data. The next step is to draw a perpendicular line on the rotated axis at 1996 = 100 to form a modified plane. Thus an orthogonal of Chart 1 is obtained.

Chart 2 shows that the crisis-affected economies have remained below the rotated axis in the decade after the crisis. With the possible exception of South Korea, economic performance has been increasingly worse relative to the decade before the crisis, as if continuously plunging below the rotated axis. Indonesia and Thailand have moved the farthest and were still departing from the rotated axis in 2007. Malaysia and the Philippines have similar trends after 2005, but at a higher level compared to Indonesia and Thailand. For the Philippines, Chart 2 reveals that its trend has actually been on a constant decline since 1987. In fact this downward direction started much earlier if the data are extended back to 1980.

More importantly, Chart 2 shows the counterfactual economic performance of the crisis-affected economies between 1997 and 2007. The conjecture is that the socio-economic conditions in the period 1987–96 might have continued into the succeeding period had the deterioration in economic fundamentals been addressed; had captured bureaucracies and institutional rigidities been remedied; had the governments maintained effective management of their economies, even allowing for proper sequencing of deregulation and financial liberalization such that progressive industrialization and broad-based economic expansion could be sustained; and so on.[3] Of course, the counter-argument to this scenario is that the crisis-affected economies would nevertheless have experienced a deceleration in economic performance by the early 2000s if they had sustained the same level of economic expansion. Still, the deceleration would not be as dramatic as the one they experienced in 1997. Adjustments were done in the counterfactual that would avert the economic debacles. Nevertheless, Chart 2 highlights the observation that what occurred over 1987 to 1996 was desirable, notwithstanding other issues that came with robust economic expansion such as increasing inequalities and adverse environmental consequences. It is therefore clear that while it can be argued that the crisis-affected economies have already exceeded their 1996 GDP per capita, they unfortunately have not regained the robust economic expansion that distinguished the Asian miracle economies before the crisis.

Costing the Crisis

Chart 2 means that, for the crisis-affected economies, counterfactual economic expansion can be obtained as $y_{t,i} = \alpha + \beta\,year + \varphi\,y_{t-1,i} + e_{t,i}$ where $y_{t,,i}$ is GDP per capita (in 2000 prices) of an economy i. In other words, current GDP per capita can be obtained using the general direction of economic expansion proxied by a period indicator (that is, year), past information as embedded in past GDP per capita (that is, y_{t-1}), and other factors affecting y_t as represented by e_{ti}.[4] If there are transitory impacts on the economy, the difference between the estimated GDP per capita, y_t, and the actual value, y_t, is small. Subsequent amounts are smaller and decreasing to zero in period $t+j$. The reverse is the case if there are permanent impacts of a crisis or when no real economic recovery has occurred, so $(y_t - y_t)$ is large and the subsequent differences are larger over time. It is not discounted that growth acceleration can occur in some future period and that full recovery takes place then.

With y_t, the total accounting cost of a crisis is obtained as the annual foregone output per capita, $y_t - y_t$, multiplied by the population. Using the United States Treasury Bill rate, r, the total economic cost of a crisis, ec_t, is obtained as the opportunity cost per capita $[(1+r_t)\,(y_t - y_t)]$. Lastly, the total social cost of a crisis, sc_t, is the accumulated cost per capita, $[(1+r)sc_{t-1} + (ec_t - ec_{t-1})]$, multiplied by the population. Both ec_t and sc_t are assumed to be zero in period $t-1$. Note that using r is a rudimentary way of calculating the costs, but it is used to allow for easy comparison of the figures. More importantly, other items are not included in the calculations, such as the costs of unemployment, poverty, or the psychological impacts of the crisis, etc. Put simply, the economic and social costs are rough measures. Obviously, if other costs are included, ec_t and sc_t are much larger than those estimated here. The costs for each economy are discussed next.

Indonesia

As the crisis intensified in 1998, Indonesian GDP per capita fell to US$ 777 from US$ 906 in 1997. It further fell to US$ 773 in 1999. That is, GDP per capita contracted by 14.3 per cent in 1998 and another 0.5 per cent in 1999. The contraction meant that the foregone output per capita was US$ 175 in 1998 and US$ 223 in 1999. The opportunity costs per capita were US$ 184 and US$ 233, respectively. The accumulated cost per capita was US$ 241 for the two years, about 30 per cent of GDP per capita in 1999.

Five years after the crisis, Indonesian GDP per capita remained below its 1996 level, reaching US$ 844 in 2002. The foregone output per capita in 2002 then was US$ 280, while the per capita opportunity cost on the foregone output and accumulated cost reached US$ 284 and US$ 321, respectively. By that time, those amounts were 30 per cent and 40 per cent of GDP per capita, respectively. In fact, Chart 3 indicates that GDP per capita remained below the counterfactual scenario and thus the costs have risen over time. In other words, there was no economic recovery. As such, the foregone output per capita was larger than the previous amounts, reaching US$ 306 in 2004. The opportunity cost per capita reached US$ 310, while the accumulated cost per capita was US$ 355. These figures remained around 30 per cent of GDP per capita in 2004.

Provided that GDP per capita growth does not slow down in the coming years, the costs are expected to flatten out, suggesting that at least the foregone output per capita and opportunity cost per capita do not exceed US$ 350. What is a cause of concern, however, is the continuing rise in accumulated cost per capita, projected to reach US$ 418 in 2007. This is still growing in the medium

CHART 3   *Costs of the 1997 Crisis for Indonesia* (per capita in 2000 prices)

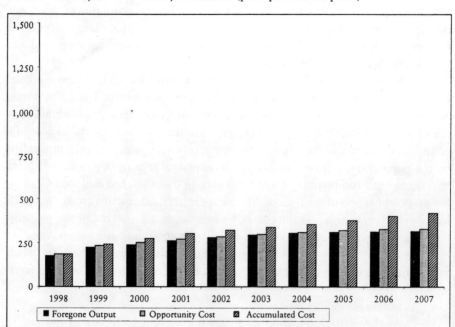

Source: Asian Development Outlook 2007 and World Development Indicators 2007.

term even with the current rate of economic expansion. Only with accelerated GDP per capita expansion – faster than the projected growth rates – are the trends reversed and the costs recovered. At present, however, it is disappointing that because of unaddressed constraints to economic growth, including weakened public investments, deteriorating public services and falling competitiveness, Indonesia cannot move to a higher gear of economic performance. Significant progress in addressing growth constraints is crucial in the coming years.

Malaysia

Malaysian GDP per capita fell from US$ 3,938 in 1997 to US$ 3,560 in 1998 as its economy contracted by 9.7 per cent. This reduction meant a foregone output per capita of US$ 571 and an opportunity cost per capita of US$ 598, about 16 per cent of GDP per capita in 1998. GDP per capita grew by 3.7 per cent in 1999, enabling Malaysia to regain its pre-crisis GDP per capita by 2000. But the expansion in these years was not enough to recoup the losses of 1998. Foregone output per capita was down to US$ 614 per capita in 2000 from US$ 646 in the previous year. The opportunity cost per capita was US$ 650, and the accumulated cost per capita was US$ 719. The gains in this period were reversed with an economic recession in 2001 as the economy sputtered to a –1.9 GDP per capita growth.

The effect of the recession on the costs was expected. The foregone output

CHART 4   *Costs of the 1997 Asian Crisis for Malaysia* (per capita in 2000 prices)

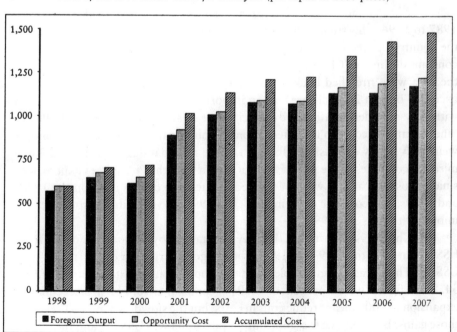

Source: *Asian Development Outlook 2007* and *World Development Indicators 2007.*

per capita rose to US$ 891, the opportunity cost per capita increased to US$ 922, and the accumulated cost per capita became US$ 1,015. It is clear that sustaining economic expansion in the recovery period is crucial to recouping the losses. As economic expansion slowed down in subsequent years, the costs continued to increase. In 2006, the foregone output per capita reached US$ 1,130, and the opportunity cost per capita was US$ 1,193. These figures were 25 per cent of GDP per capita in 2006. The accumulated cost per capita was US$ 1,434 or 30 per cent of GDP per capita.

The estimated figures for 2007 suggest even larger costs: a foregone output per capita of US$ 1,178, an opportunity cost per capita of US$ 1,225 and an accumulated cost per capita of US$ 1,487. It is unclear, however, if a flattening in the trends is taking shape in the medium term because of cyclical economic expansion. That is, costs increase as economic growth slows down, flatten during economic recovery and then increase as growth eases up. Because of this pattern of growth, the accumulated cost per capita is expected to continue to increase. Only robust economic expansion – again, faster than the projected rates – can arrest the rise in costs and reverse the trend. The economic performance of Malaysia appears to be constrained by global economic performance or, at least, that of its major trade partners, making robust economic growth contingent on external factors. While the exports sector remains crucial to buoy Malaysia in the short and medium term, in the long term it also needs to deal with the infrastructural and human capital constraints to keep the economy competitive.

The Philippines

Chart 1 showed that Philippine GDP per capita remained steady from 1987 to 1996. This trend reflects the boom-and-bust economic performance of the country between the 1980s and 1990s. In fact, the Philippines had been in constant decline, as Chart 2 illustrates, and this would be even more evident if the data were stretched back to 1970. The GDP per capita level of 1982 was exceeded only in 2002. There was an important economic turnaround in 1993 with large-scale deregulation and financial liberalization. In this period, the Philippines regained access to the international capital markets. In fact the economy went on a steady expansion, albeit not at the rate that distinguished the Asian miracle economies in the pre-crisis period. In a way, the Philippines experienced smaller costs because it was overlooked by the large capital flows in the 1980s and 1990s. An economic crisis in 1991 and 1992 also contributed to reduce the impact of the crisis in 1997.

Chart 5 shows that GDP per capita fell by a small amount, from US$ 970 in 1997 to US$ 945 in 1998. The foregone output per capita in 1998 was US$ 51. There was a comparable amount of opportunity cost per capita at US$ 54. These figures were 5 per cent of GDP per capita in 1998. The strong economic expansion in 2000 meant reductions in costs, but the slowdown in 2001 reversed those gains. By 2002, the foregone output per capita was US$ 89, and the opportunity cost per capita was US$ 90. The accumulated cost per capita stood at

CHART 5 *Costs of the 1997 Asian Crisis for the Philippines* (per capita in 2000 prices)

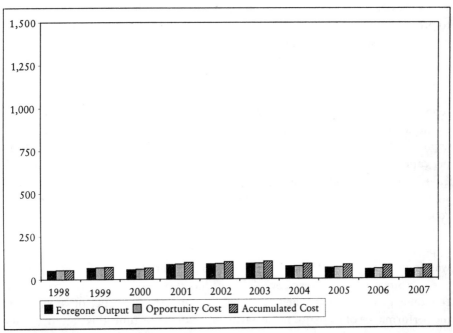

Source: Asian Development Outlook 2007 and World Development Indicators 2007.

US$ 100. These figures were about 10 per cent of GDP per capita in 2002. The costs were further reduced as economic growth was sustained into 2005. By 2006, the foregone output per capita and opportunity cost per capita were comparable to their 1998 levels. The accumulated cost per capita stood at US$ 77, down to 7 per cent of GDP per capita. It is clear that the Philippines has started to recoup the costs of the crisis. What must be pointed out is that because of the relatively mild economic expansion in the post-crisis period, the recouping has been slow.

The forecasts for 2007 suggest that there are steady reductions in the costs, though not large reductions. If the forecasts hold, the figures for 2007 are: foregone output per capita of US$ 53, opportunity cost per capita of US$ 55, accumulated cost per capita at US$ 78. These amounts are not significantly different to those for 1998 and 2006. As with the other crisis-affected economies, the Philippines has to sustain robust economic expansion in order to recoup the costs of 1997. But for the Philippines to recoup the lost opportunities from its earlier crises, there certainly needs to be exceptional economic expansion.

Even with positive developments in recent years, there are concerns that recent economic expansion has been weak. Notwithstanding the role of overseas workers' remittances in saving the economy from a balance of payments crisis in 2005, there is a budding Dutch disease as economic performance remains narrow (confined to electronics), shallow (with limited domestic linkages) and hollow (limited industrialization). It is vulnerable to global economic performance as well as to swings in domestic agricultural production. While reforms are expected to proceed at pace as in the earlier years, political instabilities haunt the present government, such that the economy may not reach higher growth trajectories.

South Korea

While South Korea faced an economic collapse in 1998, its economy rebounded quickly in 1999. Such a turnaround confirms the fundamental strength of the economy. The crisis produced large costs nonetheless. In 1998, GDP per capita fell to US$ 9,307 from the 1997 level of US$ 10,064. The foregone output per capita in 1998 was US$ 1,281, and the opportunity cost per capita was US$ 1,343. These amounts were 14 per cent of GDP per capita. These costs were significantly cut down with robust economic growth of 8.7 per cent in 1999. The economic expansion continued into 2002, cutting the costs to half even with a setback in 2001. Consequently, the foregone output per capita fell to US$ 666, opportunity cost per capita was at US$ 677 and the accumulated cost per capita was down to US$ 850. These amounts were 6 per cent of GDP per capita in 2002.

Since 2001, however, South Korea has experienced a cyclical pattern of economic growth, constrained by global economic performance or, at least, by the performance of its major trade partners. At the same time, this pattern points to some challenges for South Korea as its economy navigates through the reforms

CHART 6 *Costs of the 1997 Asian Crisis for South Korea* (per capita in 2000 prices)

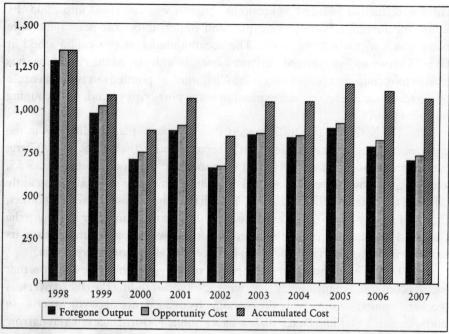

Source: *Asian Development Outlook 2007* and *World Development Indicators 2007.*

along with competing domestic interests. As such, there have been no significant reductions in costs in 2006, at least relative to the successes achieved by 2002. The figures were US$ 795 foregone output per capita, US$ 834 opportunity cost per capita and US$ 1,117 accumulated cost per capita. In fact, with the exception of 2005, the latter cost was higher than the levels of the preceding five years.

The forecast for 2007 is encouraging. Steady economic expansion is expected in the medium term, which will strengthen confidence in South Korea and support further economic growth. After the consumer credit problem in 2003 there was a re-examination of the reform programme, and there is steady progress on this, contributing to positive sentiments about the economy. It is to be expected that there will be further reductions in costs in the coming years. The figures for 2007 are: foregone output per capital, US$ 717; opportunity cost per capita, US$ 745; accumulated cost per capita, US$ 1,074. A steady pace of economic growth is crucial to cut the opportunity costs and accumulated costs per capita. But for South Korea to significantly reduce the accumulated cost per capita, it will be necessary to reignite robust economic growth of the type seen during the pre-crisis period.

Thailand

The crisis was thought to have inflicted a modest cost on Thailand. Its GDP per capita in 1997 shrank by 2.2 per cent, falling to US$ 2,101 from its 1996 level of US$ 2,154. As the crisis gained momentum and extended, serious costs became apparent. Economic growth further contracted by 12 per cent in 1998. Foregone output per capita became US$ 612 and opportunity cost per capita was US$ 641. The accumulated cost was US$ 652, which was 35 per cent of GDP per capita.

In 2000, the government of Thailand embarked on an expansionary fiscal policy to put the economy on track for a strong recovery. But economic growth tumbled to 1 per cent in 2001 as the global economic slowdown affected Thailand. By 2001, the foregone output per capita was US$ 892, the opportunity cost per capita US$ 922 and the accumulated cost per capita US$ 1,040. The amounts for 2002 were higher, as can be observed from Chart 7. Except between 2002 and 2004, when some momentum in economic expansion was seen leading to a flattening of the costs, economic growth since 2005 has decelerated. The costs rose quickly as a result, especially the accumulated cost. So, by 2006, the foregone output per capita was US$ 1,040, the opportunity cost per capita was US$ 1,089 and the accumulated cost per capita stood at US$ 1,345. What is alarming to note is that the accumulated cost in 2006 stood at 50 per cent of GDP per capita.

It is interesting to note that the pattern of cost recovery in Thailand since 2001 is similar to that of Malaysia. Thailand was unable to achieve an acceleration of growth and, consequently, the costs continued to increase. A flattening in the trends is expected as decent economic growth continues, but the social cost per capita is expected to increase steadily. To date, the prospects are

CHART 7   *Costs of the 1997 Asian Crisis for Thailand* (per capita in 2000 prices)

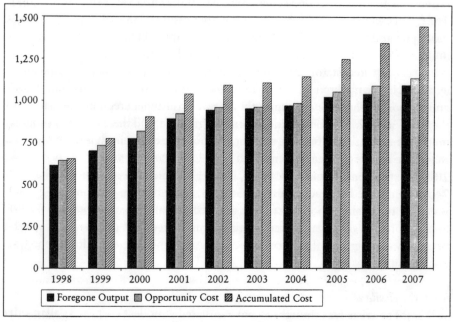

Source: *Asian Development Outlook 2007* and *World Development Indicators 2007*.

not good compared to the previous years, especially with economic growth at its lowest rate in six years. The estimated costs for 2007 are: foregone output per capita of US$ 1,093, opportunity cost per capita of US$ 1,136 and accumulated cost at US$ 1,444. In 2007, these costs relative to GDP per capita were not significantly different from the preceding years. The trends can be reversed if robust economic expansion is sustained in the medium term.

Nonetheless, problems hit the economy that limited economic expansion. The tsunami in December 2004 adversely affected the tourism industry that, in turn, affected economic growth. Tourism went into a lull for most of 2005, which was further hit by political unrest in the southern region. However it has now recovered. Export performance is expected to be unstable with high oil prices. Of course, large public infrastructure projects contributed to the economic expansion in the past, and this remains an option for the government.

Recent developments have raised concerns about the capacity of the economy to regain robust economic growth, particularly after the coup d'état in September 2006 sparked fears that political issues are once again being resolved through military intervention, as in earlier decades. This was compounded by the economic faux pas in December 2006, in which capital controls were introduced but quickly reversed when they did not work out as planned, indicating that the programme was not well thought out. Such uncertainties may weaken the prospects for robust economic expansion.

Summing Up

The above discussion emphasizes two points: the crisis-affected economies experienced inferior performance in the post-crisis decade, and their losses had not been recouped by 2007. While there was robust economic growth in the immediate years after the crisis that resulted in some reductions in costs, subsequent sluggish economic expansion meant that further cuts in the costs were not realized, and the costs increased as a result. The persistent gaps between the counterfactual and actual GDP per capita suggest that the crisis has had long-lasting effects.

Among the crisis-affected economies, the Philippines and South Korea illustrate success in recovering the losses. While the experience of the Philippines was to be expected as it did not face large costs, that of South Korea clearly demonstrates the crucial role of strong and sustained economic expansion in recouping the costs. Its strong economic rebound in 1999 meant that cost recovery started almost immediately after the crisis, although further progress was delayed when economic growth eased up. The patterns for Indonesia, Malaysia and Thailand clearly demonstrate what weakening economic expansion can do to increase the costs of crisis.

The aggregate figures on costs (see Appendix) substantiate the contention that the crisis-affected economies have endured the trauma of the crisis. For 2007, the projected total social cost of the crisis in Indonesia is US$ 95 billion (41 per cent of GDP); in Malaysia, US$ 39 billion (31 per cent of GDP); in the Philippines, US$ 7 billion (7 per cent of GDP); in South Korea, US$ 53 billion (8 per cent of GDP); in Thailand, US$ 95 billion (55 per cent of GDP). In the aggregate, Indonesia and Thailand have had the worst experience from the crisis. The conclusion is clear: robust economic expansion in the post-crisis period is crucial to recoup the costs of the crisis. Subsequent shocks that reduce economic performance need to be compensated as well with robust economic expansion, and appropriate policies are needed for growth acceleration. If economic growth has moderated or been deliberately adjusted to supposedly tolerable levels in the post-crisis period, it makes it difficult to recoup the lost opportunities.

Without doubt, how each of the crisis-affected economies responded to the crisis in 1997 is another dimension to consider. In part, the large costs in Indonesia and Thailand were a result of the way both economies handled the crisis, and the International Monetary Fund (IMF) had an important role in that process. The IMF is liable to the extent that it pressed for incorrect responses, albeit modified when belatedly found that the prescriptions were not working or worsening the situation. In Indonesia, for instance, contractionary policies mixed with sectoral reforms that were not directly related to the crisis were demanded by the IMF. While Indonesia tried to resist the IMF, the political crisis that compounded the situation complicated the policy responses and limited the options available to the country. In Thailand, the closure of banks following the standard stabilization prescriptions of the IMF, such as raising interest rates, fiscal austerity and so on, produced a panic that escalated the crisis. The backlash was contagion as confidence in the region dried up and insecurity prevailed. Malaysia, likewise, pursued IMF-style pro-cyclical policies in 1997 even though the IMF was not involved in the economy. Perhaps because Malaysia did not have the IMF impinging on its policy space, it was able to reverse its strategy and introduce countercyclical measures to insulate the economy from further damage. To some extent, the 1998 capital controls helped reduce the losses. Needless to say, the political events in Malaysia intensified the impact of the crisis. The Philippines had to go to the IMF because its economy was still recuperating from an earlier crisis and it clearly was not strong enough to withstand any attack. Ironically, the IMF intervention provided some shield. Nonetheless, the Philippines experienced some costs because, to an extent, it could not follow a Malaysia-style strategy. South Korea experienced a combination of the IMF-inspired strategies that were applied in Indonesia and Thailand, although there was a more systematic approach in terms of the amounts of loan extended and the attention to economic recovery. In a way, the IMF may have helped to ease the recovery process. Interestingly, South Korea was also able to act cautiously in going about policy adjustment: while vigorous but effective reforms were made, South Korea smartly ignored IMF advice to restructure its economy drastically. Instead, it salvaged the economy by focusing on institutional rigidities yet not resorting to Malaysian-type capital controls, thereby igniting economic growth and supporting the recovery process.

Another Declaration of Interdependence[5]

Ten years after the crisis, what are the policies required to realize robust economic expansion and prevent future crises in the crisis-affected economies? Five important elements are discussed below.

Economic Growth

More than before, robust economic expansion is needed. Domestic economic management must support economic growth, expand incomes and create jobs. Since GDP per capita can be enhanced either when nominal output increases or when population decreases, complementary social programmes for basic needs and social insurance are needed to stabilize population and improve labour productivity. This need not mean that governments should supply all that is required for economic growth and capabilities formation, but the essentials do need to be provided. While current investment in the crisis-affected economies has come down compared to the excessively high levels prior to the crisis, it must be stressed that the previous flows were mainly facilitated by ignoring the long-term implications of weak governance. Sound management of investment is needed to facilitate capital-deepening, enhance competitiveness, avoid unnecessary indebtedness and thereby support economic expansion.

It is clear from sections 3 and 4 that economic growth must be higher than the current levels and sustained for some time for full recovery to occur. Chart 1 shows that GDP per capita needs to expand at a rate of at least 6 per cent each year, which is the low-end average for the period 1987 to 1996. Downgrading economic growth in the economic plans so that they conform to projections of international institutions and rating agencies is unwarranted, considering that sufficient capacity is available for robust expansion. It is important, though, for past growth strategies not to be replicated. The potential destruction of natural resources and the environment brought about by mindless economic expansion must be considered in drawing up economic plans. It is also necessary to avoid the destabilization that comes with rapid economic transformation.

International Flows of Capital and Trade

There is a large literature on the causes of the crisis, and there is no need to repeat them here. One important dimension is that financial liberalization with loose regulation and weak or weakened management of international flows underpinned the crisis and produced large costs. Therefore the burden of proof is on those who argue that the purported benefits of unrestrained international capital flows not only materialize but, more importantly, accrue to domestic residents. If capital flows out of developing countries in the form of capital flight or even as legitimate capital outflows, while capital surges generate fragilities or reduced effectiveness of economic policies, there is a strong case for intervention. In any case, the management of capital flows is important. As long as the rules are clear and enforcement is fair, such intervention can contribute to increasing economic welfare in so far as capital flows support the expansion of production and increase economic growth. There may be concerns if the fear of regulation causes capital to stop flowing into the region.

A complementary intervention is trade management. Beyond issues associated with trade access and facilitation, trade coordination is important to avert domestic disintegration and social dislocation. The focus on export-oriented growth is difficult to sustain if there is no clear direction to push industries to higher levels of production and learn how to compete, beyond just being competitive. The crowding of global exports market must also be addressed. Obviously, intensive production can generate robust economic expansion despite structural inefficiencies, but it cannot go on forever. Trade management techniques are important to administer production, facilitate industrial deepening and propel the economy to higher levels of industrialization. As such, sound industrial policies and planning are crucial, though they need to be flexible to allow adjustment to changing circumstances. Similar to the case of capital flows, it must be demonstrated that the benefits of trade flows not only materialize and exceed the costs, but, more importantly, that the gains from trade accrue to the domestic residents. Again, as long as the modes of intervention are clear and fair, trade management techniques can contribute to increasing economic welfare. However, it would be unfortunate if uneasiness with strategic domestic intervention results in a situation in which economies shut their borders or introduce protectionist policies that constrain global economic performance.

Role of Governments

The role of the government in economic management and execution of reforms must be rethought. Governments that are unsuccessful face larger pressures to remove themselves from further participation in the economy. In turn, they become weaker or more ineffective. Weak governments cannot sustain stability in their economies or secure the basic needs of their people. And they experience increasing difficulties in regaining the level of effectiveness they once enjoyed. Governments that allow external forces to undermine their autonomy and capacity find that they degenerate quickly. As a result, years of economic progress can be reversed with the costs imposed on the people. Governments that wait for the market or events to unfold so as to produce the needed stability and security are bound to fail. Similarly, those afraid to take serious measures in the interest of the domestic economy also fail. When governments weaken or fail in this manner, they violate fundamental human liberties and the rights of their people to a decent, meaningful and substantive existence.

Strong governments therefore remain important, at least to ensure economic growth and progress. Strong governments mean effective governance, with governments at the centre of domestic management and policy-making. They effectively respond to domestic challenges while negotiating external demands. They facilitate cooperative relations with the private sector and civil society, rather than obstruct broad-based initiatives. They have long-term plans but pace reforms such that adequate regulatory institutions and supervisory mechanisms are in place, thus reducing vulnerability. Those that maintain autonomy and continuously improve capacity to respond to changing conditions are the ones that succeed in steering economies to higher growth trajectories and raising economic welfare. Thus it is important to challenge the governments of the crisis-affected economies to take decisive actions to stabilize their economies and ensure security for their people. It is important that they consider legitimate social concerns, such as a balanced and clean environment, a peaceful society and so on, rethink how reforms have been done in the past and the costs of misguided policies or wrong implementation, and the consequences of lost autonomy and capacity. This challenge is important for proactive engagement that leads to identification of legitimate alternatives for broad-based economic expansion.

On Opportunism and Hesitation

There is no doubt that misdiagnosis of the causes of the crisis and over-loading of rescue packages for the crisis-affected economies contributed to the escalation of the crisis. To an extent, the interventions by the IMF and others were opportunistic, driven by the desire to bring in reforms that were politically difficult to introduce earlier. The crisis provided an opportunity to strengthen that engagement. Recall that the crisis-affected economies were quickly branded as principals of crony capitalism, corruption, large-scale inefficiencies, etc. External intervention forced structural changes when economic environments went increasingly volatile and uncertain, thus undermining the reforms, which in turn became part of the crisis.

The initial hesitation of international institutions to provide support in a crisis situation was understandable, but their extended reluctance to help was not. While concerns about moral hazard were valid, the inaction or delayed action of the international institutions during the crisis produced outcomes that, in hindsight, were largely preventable. When these interventions did come, they targeted perceived structural problems rather than first ensuring economic stability. The crisis-affected economies could have avoided some of the large costs if measures had been introduced in a timely and appropriate manner. Concerns such as moral hazard could have been addressed if guidelines existed on lender–creditor duties and responsibilities.

On International Cooperation

At the global level, there is a need to foster international cooperation. Efforts that enhance the transparency of international flows, mechanisms to monitor the regional dimensions of vulnerabilities and so on, are in the right direction. The crisis illustrated how a shock in one place can snowball into a serious crisis in another. This underlines the need for democratic rules of operation that reduce uncertainty and create greater stability in the international economy. In the event of a crisis, the international community must take up the challenge to provide a quick response in order that it is not extended to other countries or transformed into a more virulent form. Ultimately, international coordination is needed so that global economic expansion raises incomes and reduces poverty.

Conclusion

This paper has presented a review of the economic performance of Indonesia, Malaysia, the Philippines, South Korea and Thailand in the decade following the 1997 Asian crisis. It shows that these crisis-affected economies have performed unsatisfactorily relative to previous performance. Full recovery requires sustained robust economic expansion to compensate for the losses of 1997. If economic growth moderates to supposedly 'pragmatic' levels, it will be difficult to recoup the costs.

As of 2007, the crisis-affected economies continue to endure the trauma of the crisis. They have exceeded their 1996 GDP per capita, albeit with years of significant lost opportunities. For 2007, the total social cost of the crisis in Indonesia is US$ 95 billion (41 per cent of GDP) or a per capita social burden of US$ 418. Malaysia is burdened with US$ 39 billion (31 per cent of GDP) or, in per capita terms, US$ 1,487. In the case of the Philippines, the total social cost is US$ 7 billion (7 per cent of GDP) or per capita social cost of US$ 78. South Korea needs to deal with US$ 53 billion (8 per cent of GDP) or a per capita social cost of US$ 1,074. Thailand is overloaded with US$ 95 billion (55 per cent of GDP) or a per capita social cost of US$ 1,444.

To realize robust economic expansion in the region, decisive policies are needed from the governments of the crisis-affected economies. These actions must ensure economic stability and preserve political security in the region. While reforms have been introduced after 1997, challenges remain – old and new ones – that must be addressed so that economic growth is raised to levels that characterized the Asian miracle economies before the crisis. Short of a positive direction in policies – taking up the useful components of past arrangements and putting in important missing elements like sustainable and equitable growth, sound domestic and external management, solid international cooperation – economic progress is limited and punctuated by crises.

Notes

[1] Versions of sections 3 and 4 of this paper have appeared in Beja (2007).

[2] Only the trend for Singapore is closest to the convergence of Indonesia, Malaysia, South Korea and Thailand. There was convergence among the five Asian miracle economies in 1986–96.

[3] Even in the mid-1990s, the International Monetary Fund (IMF) and the World Bank were optimistic that robust economic growth rates in the region would continue for another five years or till the early 2000s. In the early/mid-1980s, the governments of Indonesia, Malaysia, South Korea and Thailand embarked on economic reforms and adjustments to produce robust economic performance in the following decade. In the counterfactual, these economies could have done similar reforms and adjustments in the 1990s to sustain robust performance. While this scenario may be difficult to defend for the Philippines, considering its dismal economic performances in the 1980s and early 1990s, it must be pointed out that the policy mistakes and misguided economic agenda of the mid-1980s could have been avoided had the government maintained policy autonomy and capacities to institute sound economic reforms. The economic history of the Philippines also points to the fact that the deterioration of governance and capacities started much earlier, in the 1970s. It is also important to note that in the 1950s and 1960s, the Philippines had solid foundations, that the country provided capacity-building skills and training to the Southeast Asian countries for them to embark on sound structural transformation and economic expansion.

[4] In addition, $y_{t,i} = \alpha + \beta\ year + e_{t,i}$ was estimated and the geometric mean of the estimated values is used as y_t. Arguably, obtaining the geometric mean is an approximation to the Inada conditions in economic growth theory.

[5] Section 5 is another take on Chapter 14 of Rubin and Weisberg (2003).

References

Asian Development Bank (ADB) (2007), *Asian Development Outlook 2007*, Manila: Asian Development Bank.

Beja Jr., Edsel (2007), 'The Tenth Anniversary of the Asian Crisis: A Retrospective on East Asian Economic Performance', *Challenge*, 50 (5), September/October.

Burton, David and Alessandro Zanello (2007), 'Asia Ten Years After', *Finance & Development*, 44 (2), June.

Ito, Takatoshi, Akira Kojima, Colin McKenzie and Shujiro Urata (2007), 'Ten Years After the Asian Crisis: What Have We Learned or Not Learned', *Asian Economic Policy Review*, Special Issue, 2 (1): 1–168.

Rubin, Robert and Jacob Weisberg (2003), *In an Uncertain World: Tough Choices from Wall Street to Washington*, New York: Random House.

United Nations Economic and Social Council for Asia and the Pacific (UNESCAP) (2007), *Economic and Social Survey of Asia and the Pacific 2007*, Bangkok: United Nations Economic and Social Council for Asia and the Pacific.

World Bank (2007), *10 Years After the Crisis: Regional Update*, Washington, DC: World Bank.

Appendix

TABLE 1 *Total Accounting Costs of the 1997 Asian Crisis* (in US$ million and 2000 prices)

Year	Indonesia	Malaysia	Philippines	South Korea	Thailand
1998	35,159.4	12,528.2	3,717.7	59,288.1	37,231.2
	22.5	16.0	5.4	13.8	32.9
1999	45,289.3	14,529.4	4,906.6	45,489.7	42,904.1
	28.8	17.5	6.9	9.6	36.3
2000	49,095.4	14,125.1	4,253.1	33,469.8	47,872.3
	29.8	15.6	5.6	6.5	38.6
2001	54,596.8	20,928.6	6,625.9	41,650.6	55,792.8
	31.9	23.1	8.6	7.8	44.1
2002	59,212.8	24,192.9	6,967.8	31,705.8	59,566.9
	33.1	25.6	8.7	5.6	44.7
2003	63,193.0	26,408.3	7,182.5	41,094.3	60,631.6
	33.7	26.5	8.6	7.0	42.5
2004	66,463.8	26,767.1	5,993.3	40,588.2	62,302.8
	33.8	25.1	6.7	6.6	41.2
2005	68,504.3	28,800.8	5,350.9	43,421.5	66,155.7
	33.0	25.6	5.7	6.8	41.8
2006	69,894.1	29,409.8	4,653.3	38,569.2	67,958.4
	31.8	24.6	4.7	5.8	40.7
2007	71,658.8	30,958.6	4,560.2	34,937.5	72,003.1
	30.9	24.5	4.4	5.0	41.5

Note: Calculations of author. Numbers below aggregate figures represent shares of GDP.

TABLE 2 *Total Economic Costs of the 1997 Asian Crisis* (in US$ million and 2000 prices)

Year	Indonesia	Malaysia	Philippines	South Korea	Thailand
1998	36,853.8	13,131.9	3,896.8	62,145.3	39,025.5
	23.6	16.8	5.7	14.4	34.4
1999	47,398.6	15,206.1	5,135.2	47,608.3	44,902.3
	30.1	18.3	7.2	10.1	38.0
2000	51,962.2	14,949.9	4,501.4	35,424.2	50,667.7
	31.5	16.6	6.0	6.9	40.9
2001	56,481.3	21,651.0	6,854.6	43,088.2	57,718.6
	33.0	23.9	8.9	8.1	45.6
2002	60,167.6	24,583.0	7,080.2	32,217.0	60,527.4
	33.6	26.0	8.8	5.7	45.4
2003	63,833.4	26,675.9	7,255.3	41,510.7	61,246.0
	34.1	26.8	8.7	7.1	43.0
2004	67,376.5	27,134.7	6,075.6	41,145.6	63,158.5
	34.2	25.4	6.8	6.7	41.7
2005	70,663.3	29,708.5	5,519.6	44,790.0	68,240.7
	34.0	26.4	5.9	7.0	43.2
2006	73,194.3	30,798.4	4,873.1	40,390.3	71,167.2
	33.3	25.7	5.0	6.0	42.6
2007	74,479.8	32,177.3	4,739.8	36,312.9	74,837.6
	32.2	25.5	4.6	5.2	43.1

Note: Calculations of author. Numbers below aggregate figures represent shares of GDP.

TABLE 3   *Total Social Costs of the 1997 Asian Crisis* (in US$ million and 2000 prices)

Year	Indonesia	Malaysia	Philippines	South Korea	Thailand
1998	36,853.8	13,131.9	3,896.8	62,145.3	39,678.3
	23.6	16.8	5.7	14.4	35.0
1999	49,138.2	15,832.4	5,320.3	50,523.4	47,427.3
	31.2	19.1	7.5	10.7	40.1
2000	56,632.0	16,535.9	5,007.1	41,338.6	56,011.9
	34.3	18.3	6.6	8.1	45.2
2001	63,194.2	23,854.2	7,546.2	50,483.4	65,062.8
	36.9	26.3	9.8	9.5	51.4
2002	68,003.2	27,223.6	7,909.0	40,471.7	68,995.7
	38.0	28.8	9.9	7.1	51.8
2003	72,473.1	29,649.0	8,181.1	50,218.0	70,493.3
	38.7	29.7	9.8	8.6	49.4
2004	77,142.2	30,578.3	7,132.6	50,588.3	73,460.3
	39.2	28.6	8.0	8.2	48.5
2005	83,026.8	34,196.0	6,823.9	55,875.8	80,964.5
	40.0	30.4	7.3	8.8	51.2
2006	89,700.4	37,011.5	6,528.2	54,174.8	87,853.9
	40.8	30.9	6.7	8.1	52.6
2007	94,790.6	39,067.3	6,685.6	52,300.3	95,153.4
	40.9	31.0	6.5	7.5	54.8

Note: Calculations of author. Numbers below aggregate figures represent shares of GDP.

Thai Capital after the Asian Crisis

Pasuk Phongpaichit & Christopher Baker

What is the future for domestic capital in the economies of what we used to call 'developing countries'? The idea of development in the era after the Second World War imagined that any country could repeat the economic transition of the west by accumulating capital, reallocating labour and developing industry. Development policy and planning was about nurturing entrepreneurial capitalists by creating the institutions that would help them to flourish.

Over the last quarter-century, that model has been discarded. Most of the techniques for nurturing local capitalism in that development era are now outlawed under the rules of the world economy. The new orthodoxy is that capital should have the freedom to roam the world. In practice this means that big companies with the resources to develop technology and invest in marketing can generally out-compete their smaller, weaker and latecomer rivals. The production of all kinds of goods and services is being concentrated under the control of large transnational companies, most based in the advanced economies but with some new additions from the emerging giant economies of China and India.

For China and India, this issue is not so critical. They have huge internal markets that can incubate corporations of global scale. Their governments have the weight to bargain with the outside world to retain some protection of these markets in defiance of the new economic order. But for other developing countries, these special conditions do not apply.

Major economic crises serve as a kind of reality check. In the short term, economies may be able to resist or disguise the implications of changes in the global environment. For many countries in Asia, the 1997 crisis brought home the realities of the new global economic order.

This paper summarizes findings from a wide-ranging study on the impact of the 1997 crisis on domestic capital in Thailand.[1] It argues that the crisis marks a major shift in the role and prospects of private domestic capital, but that this is part of a major adjustment to globalization with far-reaching implications.

Background

At the end of the Second World War, Thailand was one of the most backward economies in Southeast Asia, trailing far behind Burma and the Philippines. Thailand had a colonial economy based on rice exports without the improvements in institutions and infrastructure that had tended to accompany colonial rule.

Over the next half century, the economy averaged growth of 7 per cent a year, multiplying real per capita incomes around eight times (Chart 1). By the early 1990s, Thailand was tipped as the most likely candidate among Southeast Asian countries to follow the East Asian route to newly industrializing country status. This half-century of spectacular growth can be attributed to a clutch of factors.

First, the US appointed itself as Thailand's international patron, and helped to provide the institutions, infrastructure, seed capital and planning expertise for industrial growth. The government concentrated on building infrastructure, maintaining a stable macroeconomic environment and refraining from any more drastic interference in the economy. A cadre of families of Chinese origin, stranded in Thailand by the 1949 Chinese revolution, supplied entrepreneurship, using the migrant's classic package of self-exploitation, high saving, heavy investment in the education of future generations and mutual cooperation. The new infrastructure (especially roads) gave the entrepreneurs access to massive untapped reserves of human and natural resources. The entrepreneurs responded flexibly to the rapid changes in competitive advantage brought about by changing domestic and international conditions. Beginning with agricultural exports, they transferred successively to agri-processing, starter industries such as textiles, joint ventures for export-

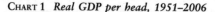

CHART 1 *Real GDP per head, 1951–2006*

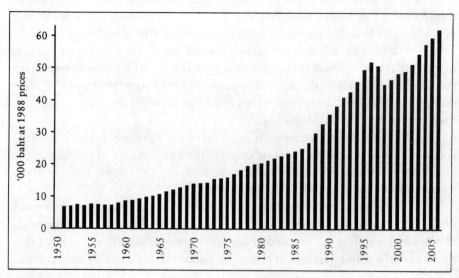

Source: NESDB.

oriented manufacturing and a range of service industries to meet rising domestic demand. Over this half-century, the political structure made a stuttering transition from military rule to a qualified parliamentary democracy. Rivalries among military factions in the early stages, and among political factions in the later ones, ensured there was no monopoly control on the distribution of political favours and rent-seeking opportunities.

Three features of this economy are worth noting. First, the rates of domestic savings and investment were very high (around 40 per cent of gross domestic product/GDP). The main mechanism of the capital market was a cartel of around fourteen commercial banks. A stockmarket was opened in 1975 and expanded after 1986, but remained a minor contributor to capital formation. Foreign direct investment also expanded from the late 1970s onwards, largely as a result of the outmigration of Japanese manufacturing, but remained a small percentage of overall capital formation. Second, virtually all domestic business was family business conducted by settled families of Chinese origin. At the end of this period, there was an estimated 150 entrepreneurial families of significance. A few families which had good access to the flow of capital through the banks, which had good political connections to access and defend business opportunities, and which were successful in expanding their internal management resources through demographic expansion and investment in education, developed into conglomerates spanning several economic sectors. In 1997, a hundred business groups had combined revenues equivalent to half of total GDP (Suehiro 2003). Third, the economy was highly geared to exporting, and relatively open compared to its immediate neighbours. Trade was substantially liberalized in the early 1980s, and the capital market was opened up around 1990.

Crisis Policy-making

At the onset of the 1997 crisis, those involved in making policy in Thailand had no strategy to rescue Thai domestic capital. The argument emanating from Washington tended to blame the crisis on Asia's bad capitalism and vaunt the benefits of the 'creative destruction' in the market mechanism. Local policy makers were nervous of being seen to show any favour to 'crony capitalists'. Hence, unlike in Korea or Malaysia, there was no attempt to bargain with the initial IMF (International Monetary Fund) strategy to manage the crisis.

The IMF proposals, as now widely recognized, were designed to manage a crisis brought on by government mismanagement and public indebtedness, and were totally inappropriate for a crisis brought on by failure to manage flows of commercial finance. The combination of the crisis and the IMF's initial package was calamitous for Thai capital in the one year following the crisis. As the currency dropped to half its value, foreign debts doubled in value, wrecking the balance sheets of the vast majority of major firms who had been tempted by the cheaper price of foreign borrowing over the prior five years. The IMF's deflationary package raised domestic interest rates above 20 per cent, adding to the costs of financing and blocking opportunities to convert foreign into domestic debt. The

CHART 2 *Per Capita Private Consumption, 1993–2006*

Source: Bank of Thailand.

IMF's deflationary package also succeeded in reducing per capita consumption by a fifth (Chart 2), with immediate effects on firms' profits and cash flows.

The first casualty was the bank-based capital market. In the past, loan default had been virtually unknown as it would deny a firm future access to funding. Almost overnight, default became conventional. With their balance sheets and cash flows wrecked, many firms were unable to service their debts and others joined the trend in order to minimize the damage. Bad loans soared to almost half the credit in the system.

Banks and other financial institutions were especially hit. Many had borrowed in dollars and lent on in local currency, and needed to increase capital to cover the damage to their balance sheets. The IMF's insistence on rapid compliance with Basle standards of capital adequacy increased the amounts required. Also on IMF insistence, government summarily closed down 56 finance firms on grounds that they had little hope of repairing their capital base. In August 1998, government proffered a scheme to help remaining banks and financial companies by providing counterpart funding for new capital raised. However, in the general atmosphere of blame and antagonism against domestic capital, most commercial financial firms feared the scheme would lead to government takeover, forced merger or other shotgun solutions. Only one bank and one finance firm entered the scheme. Over the following few years, four medium-sized commercial banks were sold into majority foreign ownership, four others effectively collapsed and were merged with other institutions, and all but a handful of the remaining finance firms disappeared. The larger banks survived by raising capital on their

CHART 3 *Distribution of Commercial Bank Lending, 1990–2006*

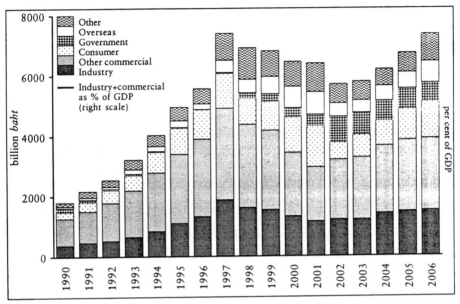

Source: Bank of Thailand.

own efforts, largely from the international capital market, and by gradually shrinking their loan portfolios by severely restricting any new lending. Over four years, the credit provided by the banks to the productive sectors of the economy steadily shrank to a little over half its pre-crisis level (Chart 3; banks lent their excess to consumers, government and overseas borrowers). The old bank-based capital market died.

Investment Inflows

Prior to the crisis, most multinationals were required to operate in Thailand through a 49:51 joint venture. US firms were exempt under a special arrangement, and the restriction had been slightly eased to encourage export-oriented manufacturing. In 1997–98, when Thailand's real sector was hit by widespread technical bankruptcy, government's solution was to remove these capital restrictions in the hope that an inflow of foreign funds would prevent a drastic drop of production and exports. The capital restriction was removed for most manufacturing, especially those sectors geared to export. For the service sector, government passed a revised Alien Business Law which appeared to continue the capital restrictions for most service sub-sectors. However, over the past two decades, as the economy became more liberalized, government turned a blind eye to growing use of a simple workaround for these capital restrictions using nominees and pyramid shareholdings. In the eye of the crisis, government winked at wholesale use of this workaround. These measures set up a fire sale of distressed Thai companies.

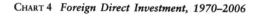

CHART 4 *Foreign Direct Investment, 1970–2006*

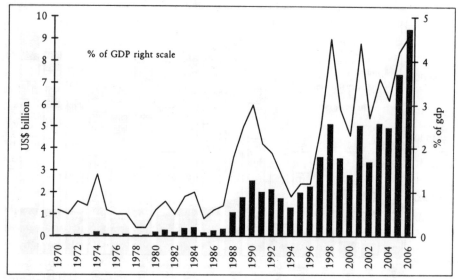

Source: Bank of Thailand.

Inflows of foreign direct investment (FDI) and foreign portfolio investment spurted from the second half of 1997 (Chart 4). In the ten years following the crisis, the average annual inflow of FDI was almost three times higher than in the boom decade in dollar terms, almost five times higher in *baht* terms, and over double as a proportion of GDP.[2] Flows of foreign portfolio investment, while more erratic, were on average almost double in the post-crisis decade compared to the boom decade. As a proportion of the total stock of direct investment in Thailand since 1970, the foreign share increased from around 10 per cent prior to the crisis to over double that ten years later (Pavida 2006).

By far the single largest source of FDI was Japan, its share rising from 29 per cent in the boom decade to 38 per cent in the post-crisis era. The US share dwindled slightly, while those of Taiwan and Hong Kong were reduced a lot. The share of FDI originating from Singapore increased from 9 per cent in the boom decade to 13 per cent in the post-crisis era. Singapore also dominated the flows of foreign portfolio investment, accounting for over two-thirds of the total in the post-crisis decade. To some extent this reflected the fact that many international financial firms maintained a regional headquarters in Singapore. But Singapore corporations also plunged into Thailand in the post-crisis era, taking special interest in banks and property.

These inflows were concentrated in certain sectors including export-oriented manufacturing, finance, large-scale retail, property, construction-related business and a range of service industries.

Manufacturing: Automotive

The post-crisis pattern in manufacturing industry is best exemplified by the automotive industry. Under the aegis of a long-term industrial policy, Thailand had developed an automotive industry with seven major Japanese joint venture assemblers geared to supply the domestic market, and some 1,200 parts suppliers, including domestic, foreign and joint venture firms, producing for both the domestic market and export. In the five years following the crisis, this structure dramatically changed. In all the major assemblers, the Japanese multinational corporation bought out the local partner completely or almost completely. Two US firms entered the market with full or almost full ownerships. To compensate for the fall in domestic consumption, all the assemblers reoriented towards export and raised the export volume to half of total production over the following decade. To achieve the higher quality demanded in the international market, the assemblers diverted more parts production to their worldwide suppliers, sometimes encouraging them to relocate to Thailand. Several of these parts makers in turn sourced components, sub-assemblies and services from their worldwide suppliers, prompting another wave of foreign investment in the sector from 2002 onwards. Some assemblers took greater control over distribution, displacing local dealers and specialist finance houses with their own subsidiaries or partners.

In a handful of years, multinational capital penetrated down several levels of Thailand's automotive industry. Only around a dozen domestic firms survived as first-tier suppliers of parts, often by selling off other business interests

CHART 5 *Automotive Exports, 1988–2006*

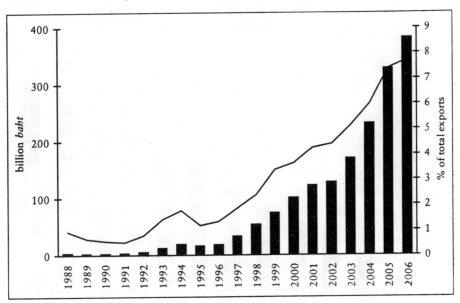

in order to invest in upgrading. Several hundred domestic firms were reduced to supplying the less lucrative spare-parts market, or withdrawing altogether. From this process, Thailand emerged as a minor but significant hub of the transnational automotive industry, and automotive exports made a major contribution to the recovery from the crisis (Chart 5). But Thailand now served as host, for multi-national automotive and domestic capital had very limited participation in the industry.

A similar process was seen in electrical, electronic and other manufacturing sub-sectors. Thai capital's involvement in manufacturing for export was reduced to some labour-intensive sectors such as garments and shoes, mainly producing on contract for brandname multinational corporations, and some resource-based industries, especially food processing.

Services: Retail

Three domestic business groups had ventured into large-scale retailing in the latter stages of the great boom which preceded the crisis. After 1997, the three were bought out by multinationals – Carrefour, Tesco and Casino.[3] All three used a nominee structure to evade the Alien Business Law. These firms took advantage of low land prices and the lack of regulation to expand from 11 to 148 stores over the following decade (Chart 6). In the four years 1998–2002, Tesco invested over a billion US dollars in Thailand, and within six years, Thailand had become the second largest operation for Tesco outside its UK base (as measured by floor space).

CHART 6 *Number of Hypermarket Outlets, 1995–2006*

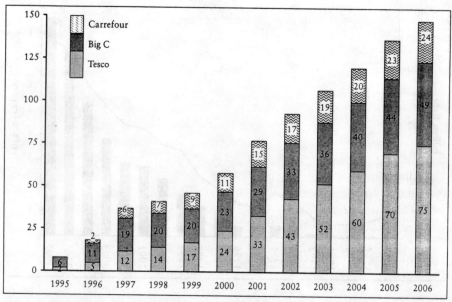

Source: Nipon *et al.* (2002) and corporate websites..

Until 2001, this expansion was confined to the capital Bangkok, but subsequently overflowed into the major provincial towns. Because of the lack of any regulation, the multinational firms were able to locate megastores in prime city-centre locations without having to bear the social and environmental costs. In a provincial town, these megastores typically engrossed over half the retail volume, driving large numbers of local retailers out of business. The turnover of the three multinational chains expanded to 92 billion *baht* (*c*. US$ 2.2 billon) in 2001, and 173 billion *baht* (*c*. US$ 5 billion) in 2006.

From 1998 onwards, there were scattered protests by retail groups against the unregulated invasion by the multinational megastores, but government was reluctant to make any move that might be seen as antagonistic towards foreign investment. In the campaign that elevated him to prime minister in 2001, Thaksin Shinawatra promised to regulate the retail sector and protect the interests of domestic capital. On achieving power, he initiated the drafting of a law. But in late 2002, Thaksin announced that the idea of legislating any protection for local retail had been abandoned. A minister explained that this decision had been taken 'simply because we don't want to send a wrong signal to the foreign community'. Thaksin added: 'External trade is important to the Thai economy since it generates new investment and increases our productivity' (*The Nation*, 17, 18 and 20 November 2002).

In most localities, domestic capital cooperated with the megastore chains, particularly by selling them the land for prime locations. However, in a handful of local towns, business groups were successful in excluding the megastores, sometimes by resort to local planning laws and sometimes through openly threatening campaigns ('You build, we burn'). In 2004, when Tesco proposed to penetrate another segment of the retail trade by building another 400 smaller-sized stores, domestic retail protesters forced government to impose a delay on Tesco's expansion while government drafted a regulatory law (still in process).

Many other service firms entered Thailand in the aftermath of the crisis. Some of these were simply taking advantage of low office rentals and the ease of evading the capital restrictions. Some came in order to service multinational manufacturers who were their worldwide clients. Some were attracted by the demand for special expertise generated by the crisis. The arrivals included firms in property, law, specialized finance, accountancy, consultancy, repair and maintenance. In 2007, when government threatened to close the conventional loophole in the Alien Business Law, estimates of the number of companies which had exploited this loophole ranged up to 40,000 (*Prachachat Thurakit*, 11 January 2007). This number included a vast number of restaurants and other petty businesses, but also some major ventures in property, retailing and other services.

Some parts of the service sector were protected through political influence, but even this became uncertain after the crisis.

Mobile phone services were provided by an oligopoly of three domestic firms, headed by a firm in the Shin business group owned by the prime minister's family. This oligopoly repelled four prospective local competitors through political influence, and kept foreign firms at bay through a Telecommunications Law prescribing a maximum foreign shareholding of 25 per cent. For twenty years, this oligopoly delivered the highest volumes of profit gleaned by Thai domestic capital. But as the mobile phone business matured on a global scale, these local firms were affected by a global trend towards concentration. They needed to make further investments to keep up with the pace of technological development, but could only justify those investments if the business achieved a scale larger than that possible within the Thai domestic market. In 2005–06, two of the Thai firms sold out to multinational firms which were intent on expanding to achieve that scale. (The sector's political influence was now used to remove the capital restriction to make the sale possible.)

In finance, manufacturing and services, the inflow of foreign capital in the aftermath of the crisis was a sudden and marked change from past practice. Overall, the involvement of foreign capital in the economy increased substantially. In 1988, 122 of the world's top 450 multinational companies had an operation in Thailand. By 2000, the number had doubled to 248 of the top 500, and the number of their subsidiaries had tripled from 214 to 630, of which 305 were in manufacturing (Suehiro 2003). The amount of tax paid by multinational companies increased by 80 per cent over the four years 2000–04 (Deunden *et al.* 2007).

Impact on Domestic Capital

It is difficult to give an accurate picture of the impact on Thai domestic capital as a whole, but a rough conclusion is that one quarter of all business groups of any significance suffered serious damage.

Among the top 50 business groups on the eve of the crisis, one quarter either disappeared or sank to the lower reaches of the ranking table. Among a larger list of 200 top business groups, a quarter disappeared completely. Among the roughly 400 domestic firms listed on the stock exchange, around 100 or almost a quarter were delisted over 1997–2004 (compared to only eleven delistings over the prior decade). Of these 100, 53 were mandatorily delisted, usually because of bankruptcy proceedings. Among the other 47, many were Thai or joint-venture firms which had been bought out by a foreign parent company and removed from the exchange. Examples are Prudential Assurance and American Standard (Suehiro and Natenapha 2004).

Two factors seem to have determined the Thai business groups' chances of survival – sector and structure. Several of those which were badly affected had their core business in sectors overwhelmed by multinational capital. These included groups which had specialized in manufacturing joint ventures with foreign firms, groups involved in the more speculative parts of the finance industry, and groups with a heavy commitment to property development.

Most Thai business groups had started out in the family-based structure of Chinese origin known as *kongsi*, which roughly translates as 'partnership'. Under this system, all members and branches of the family are considered part of a single enterprise. The patriarch (or, more rarely, matriarch) has absolute control over both the direction of the enterprise and the distribution of the profits. All adult males, and many females too, are expected to work in the family concern. On the occasion of a son's marriage, the patriarch allocates the son a segment of the business for his family upkeep, though still within the patriarch's overall control. On the patriarch's death, control usually passes to the eldest son, but this may vary if another family member is clearly better qualified.

Some family firms had grown into sprawling conglomerates over time. They not only accumulated financial capital but also acquired intangible assets through their relations with banks, politicians and foreign partners which gave them advantages in exploiting new areas of profitable opportunity. Families often branched into new areas by indulging the ambitions of sons, especially those who had been educated overseas and returned with new skills and a different view of the future. In the crisis, some of the most vulnerable firms were those which had developed into such conglomerates without modifying the internal structure. A patriarch remained in authoritarian control. Other family members monopolized management positions. Such firms were reluctant to hire outside professionals who would be difficult to integrate with the family structure. They also failed to attract the best middle management because there was no upward career path. Such groups may have floated some of their units on the stockmarket to raise additional funds, but retained family control through a pyramid structure topped by a non-listed family company.

Such firms had often accumulated large amounts of debt behind a screen of non-transparency. The prime example was the TPI group of the Leophairatana family. When the crisis struck, it emerged that TPI owed US$ 3.2 billion in external debt to some 400 creditors. Such firms also did not have enough depth and expertise of management resources. The Leophairatana family was soon embroiled in acrimonious negotiations with its creditors and eventually was ejected from the management by court process in 2005. Several other firms which collapsed in the crisis had a similar structure under a powerful patriarch with little or no professional management. These included the Tejapaibul financial conglomerate, taken over by government in January 1998, and the Srifuengfung's Cathay Trust group. Several groups which maintained a similar structure but a much narrower range of business interests also suffered badly. These included the Chansrichawla family's Siam Vidhya group in finance, Sukree Phothiratanakun's TBI group in textiles, Akorn Huntrakun's New Imperial Hotel group and Charn Uswachoke's Alphatech Electronics group. Others entered bankruptcy proceedings, underwent restructuring and ultimately survived, but in much reduced form. Such firms include the Horrungruang family's NTS steel group, the SSP (Siam Steel Pipe) group led by the Leeswadtrakul family and the Modernform furniture group led by the Usanachitt family.

Business groups which had modernized their operations while retaining the family structure had a much better chance to survive. Such groups organized their interests on a divisional basis, listed most of their operational firms in the stockmarket and complied with its rules of disclosure, recruited professional management and allowed them to rise to executive and board positions, while at the same time retaining family control through non-listed family investment companies. The prime example was the Charoen Pokphand (CP) group which, by the 1990s, had around 100 companies spread across twenty countries with a work force of more than 120,000. It had employed professionals in finance and technology from the 1950s, introduced an American-style multi-division organizational system in 1985, listed affiliate companies from 1987 to raise funds, established a holding company and headquarters to centralize decision-making in 1990, and launched an intensive human resource development programme from 1995. While many family members were employed within the group, they were not exempt from the training and appraisal imposed on other executives, and could only hope to rise on merit.

In the crisis, the CP group hired management consultants for advice and underwent a drastic restructuring, shedding many companies to concentrate on two core areas of agri-business and telecommunications, streamlining its divisional structure, recruiting more outside directors, and pulling out of the crisis through its ability to raise extra finance from the stockmarket (Suehiro 2001). On a smaller scale, the Saha Union and Sahapat manufacturing groups, the Kasikorn bank group and the Shin group, all emerged strongly from the crisis through a similar strategy.

CHART 7   *Top 150 Business Groups by Assets, 2000*

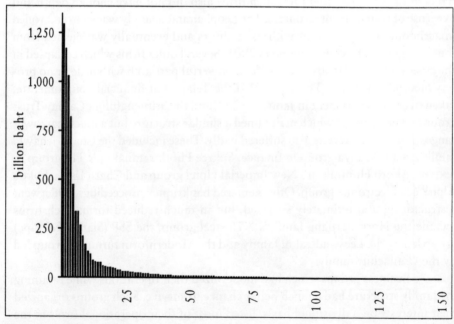

Source: Suehiro database.

Capital Concentration

As a general rule, concentration of control over capital significantly increased in the aftermath of the crisis as a result of two processes.

First, among local business groups the crisis tended to create a large number of losers and a much smaller number of winners who expanded into the space created by the collapse of their rivals. In finance, for example, the five leading commercial banks held on to their two-thirds share of all banking credit, while the banking sector as a whole expanded into the space created by the collapse of finance companies. In the alcohol beverage market, the TCC group of Charoen Sirivadhanabhakdi strengthened its monopoly control over locally produced spirits while simultaneously grabbing a 60 per cent share of the beer market. On the exit from the crisis, an informed observer reckoned that only 150 significant business families remained. Among these 150, the top dozen accounted for four-fifths of total assets (Chart 7).

The second process of concentration resulted from the intrusion of multinationals. In the retail market, three multinational chains displaced tens of thousands of smaller stores. In the automotive industry, some 200 mostly multinational parts firms replaced several hundred local and multinational firms operating before the crisis. In the downstream steel industry, three Thai firms were first merged into a single conglomerate which was subsequently bought by an Indian multinational. In the mobile phone market, two multinationals acquired a dominant position.

CHART 8 *Trade as per cent of GDP, 1995–2006*

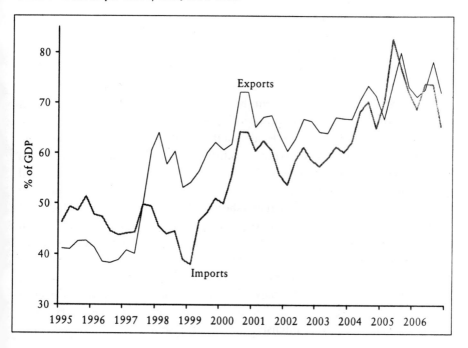

CHART 9 *Export Shares by Sector, 1985–2006*

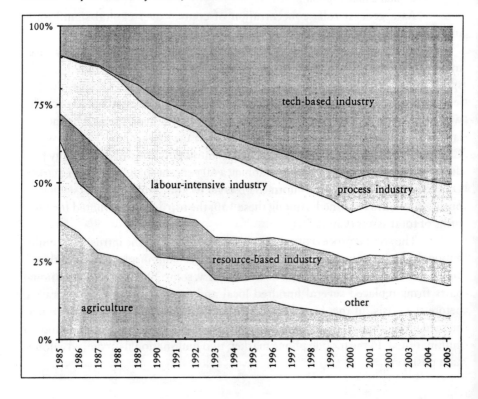

Export Dependence

Over the crisis and recovery, the economy became significantly more open, more integrated into global markets and more dependent on foreign investment and foreign demand.

The fall in the value of the currency in 1997–98 repriced Thai exports whose growth had begun to falter in the mid-1990s as a result of rising costs of labour and other local inputs. Many companies, including multinationals such as the automotive assemblers and local manufacturers such as Sahapat, transferred portions of their capacity to export production, to compensate for the fall in domestic demand. Large increases in export volume and value were the principal mechanism that pulled the economy out of the crisis. In most years from 1999 onwards, growth-accounting exercises showed that exports accounted for all or almost all of GDP growth.[4] The ratio of foreign trade to GDP rose steadily from around 90 per cent on the eve of the crisis to around 150 per cent in the mid-2000s – an exceptionally high level for an economy of Thailand's size (Chart 8). Moreover, the major contributors to this growth in export were manufacturing sectors dominated by multinationals. The three sub-sectors of automotive, electronic and electrical goods expanded to over 50 per cent of total exports, while the export shares of labour-intensive industries, resource-based industries and agriculture, in which domestic capital still had a significant stake, showed a marked trend of decline (Chart 9; automotive, electrical and electronic goods comprise most of the 'tech-based industry' category).

Collapse of Domestic Investment

Despite the strong export performance, the growth rate of the Thai economy appeared to move down a notch as a result of the crisis. The average rate had been around 7 per cent over the prior four decades. Now it moved down to 4 to 5 per cent (Chart 10).

While the multinational-dominated export-oriented segment of the economy boomed in the decade following the crisis, domestic investment stubbornly failed to recover. From 1998, the government ran a fiscal deficit to stimulate consumption, and from 2001 sustained the stimulus by stimulating consumer credit. As a result, real private consumption rebounded from its precipitate 20 per cent fall, recovered its pre-crisis level by late 2002, and continued a similar trend of growth through to 2006 (Chart 2). Yet investment failed to respond to this growing demand. At first this could be explained by the high levels of excess capacity created by overinvestment in the later stages of the boom. Yet by 2004, capacity usage had also returned to pre-bubble levels, while domestic investment remained sluggish.

The pattern of high domestic savings and high domestic investment which had characterized the long period of growth in the late twentieth century had been broken. In the pre-crisis era, domestic savings had already begun to decline from its 40 per cent plateau as per capita GDP grew and more of the population was transferred to the urban sector. Yet, over the crisis and recovery, gross domestic savings dropped further from around 35 to 30 per cent of GDP. The major contribution to this fall came from households whose savings fell from around 10 to 6 per cent of GDP (Chart 11). Partly this might be explained by changes in the distribution of income, but this has not been thoroughly analysed. Partly it could be explained by the government policy to stimulate private consumption through greater use of credit including credit cards, housing loans, rural micro-finance and several other schemes. Household debt significantly increased.[5]

Gross domestic investment fell from a 40 per cent level prior to the crisis to a trough of 20 per cent in the immediate aftermath, before recovering slowly and incompletely to 31 per cent in 2005 (Chart 12). Part of the drop can be attributed to a fall in public investment. In the immediate aftermath of the crisis, government funds were diverted to recovery programmes, leaving little surplus for the capital budget. But thereafter the Thaksin government simply failed to prioritize public investment until 2005, when the government was already crumbling.

Several reasons can be adduced to explain the fall in private domestic investment. First, the bank-based capital market which had prevailed in the pre-crisis era had been deliberately destroyed in the belief that weak banking was a major cause of the crisis and that an Anglo-Saxon stockmarket model was inherently superior. Banks had learnt risk management and replaced their personalized

CHART 10   *Quarterly Real GDP Growth, 1994–2007*

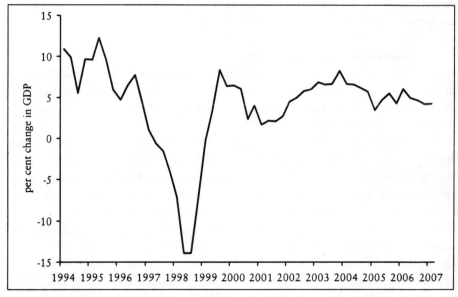

Source: Bank of Thailand.

CHART 11   *Gross National Savings, 1994–2005*

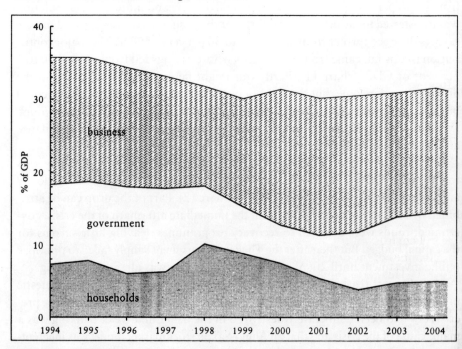

Source: NESDB.

CHART 12   *Gross Domestic Investment, 1994–2005*

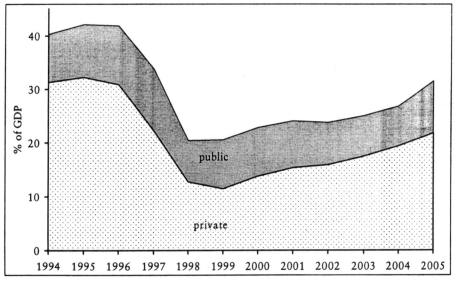

Source: NESDB.

methods for assessing customers with technical credit analysis. Banks had also diverted their attention to consumer banking, or developed specialisms in such areas as housing or automotive loans. The absolute volume of credit made available by banks to the productive sectors of the economy shrank steadily from 1997 to 2002, before recovering slightly in absolute terms but continuing to decline as a proportion of GDP to less than half the level before the crisis (Chart 3).

Newer forms of financing were limited. Only a handful of the largest firms were able to borrow abroad or to issue bonds. Government tried to promote the stockmarket by offering tax incentives for listed firms and opening a secondary board (the MAI), but failed to significantly increase the number of listed firms. Some family firms were simply unwilling to subject themselves to the disciplines required by listing. But the stockmarket was also unattractive in other ways. The movement in the overall level of the stockmarket bore little or no relation to the profits of listed firms, or even to the overall performance of the economy. The principal factors moving the market were flows of international finance. Given the relative thinness of the Thai stockmarket, relatively small flows in international terms could significantly move the local index. The decisions of international finance to invest in such a peripheral market were based on changes in trends, currency values and sentiments in markets on the other side of the world. Analysts attempting to predict the Thai bourse paid almost no attention to local GDP rates or corporate profits, but tracked the value of the dollar, the price of gold and oil, and the trends in major markets in the financial centres of the world.

A second source of movement in the market was domestic manipulation. Scandals over manipulation of individual companies were a regular occurrence.

Several of the largest domestic investors in the Thai stockmarket were directly or indirectly connected to the Thaksin government installed in 2001. A proposal to install a real-time stockmarket indicator in the parliament building was indicative of the close relationship between politics and the market. One minister had to resign after his listed family company was embroiled in flagrant accounting fraud. Partial privatization of some state enterprises through the stockmarket suspiciously created windfall gains for some prominent political figures.

For domestic entrepreneurs, the stockmarket could not be relied upon to reflect the value of their investment.

In the aftermath of the crisis, surviving Thai domestic capital was heavily concentrated in service sectors (including property and finance). Only four major domestic business groups retained significant interests in manufacturing. Several families still had interests in agri-processing, but conspicuously channelled most of their new investment into ventures such as hotels, property and retail development. Although a large slab of the finance sector had passed into foreign ownership, four families still retained minority shareholdings but management control in leading commercial banks. Some of the most successful business families on the exit from the crisis were clustered in service sub-sectors where there was still some protection under the Alien Business Law, concession arrangements or other regulations. These sub-sectors included media, entertainment and telecom. Despite the devastation in the property market in 1997–98, entrepreneurial families flocked back to this sector once it stabilized in the early 2000s. Two of the most successful business groups in the crisis aftermath specialized in developing industrial estates to host multinational manufacturing. Several others found they could draw profits from renewed urban expansion underpinned largely by the multinational-dominated export economy.

Over the second half of the twentieth century, Thai domestic capital had played a key role in the expanding the productive potential of the economy. After the 1997 crisis, it was confined mostly to a rentier and service role in an economy dominated by multinational firms.

Conclusion

Does it matter if multinational capital becomes dominant while domestic capital is confined to minor corners of the economy and a rentier-like role? Is this not inevitable in the context of globalization?

Multinationals bring several built-in advantages. They import technology. They train people. They have a tendency to be highly efficient because of international competition. They contribute to growth. For a country highly dependent on exporting, tapping into global production chains through multinational companies appears to be a highly successful strategy. Of course, there are problems over profit drain and risks that the multinationals will be footloose, but the very rapid spread of multinationals in recent years has happened in part because host governments perceive that the advantages outweigh the disadvantages.

Here we are not so much concerned with the pros and cons of multinationals *per se*, but with the consequences of becoming so dependent on multi-national capital that domestic capital is fatally weakened. An export-oriented, multinational-owned manufacturing sector tends to be capital-intensive, to have low labour absorption and to have relatively few linkages with the rest of the economy. In several Latin American countries, a series of economic crises has progressively debilitated domestic capital to the point that its role in the local economy is insignificant. Is Thailand (and possibly other non-giant Asian economies) on the same path? If so, the government needs to concentrate on two key policy areas. First, it needs policies to develop support industries, human capital, infrastructure and logistics which encourage the multinational exporters to deepen their production base in the local economy. Second, it needs to promote and facilitate domestic firms venturing overseas since that is the only route of survival for domestic capital.

Notes

[1] This article is based on our book, provisionally entitled *Thai Capital After the Crisis*, which will be published by Silkworm Books, Chiang Mai in early 2008. That book in turn is based on a research project supported by the Thailand Research Fund, to which the following researchers contributed: Chaiyon Praditsil, Natenapha Wailerdsak, Nophanun Wannathepsakun, Nualnoi Treerat, Olarn Thinbangtieo, Pavida Pananond, Porphant Ouyyanont, Rattaphong Sonsuphap, Sakkarin Niyomsilpa, Thanee Chaiwat, Ukrist Pathmanand, Veerayooth Kanchoochat, Viengrat Nethipo. We have limited the referencing in this article to sources other than the researches under this project.

[2] The Bank of Thailand figures used for this calculation underestimate the contrast as they exclude investments in the banking sector, which increased after the crisis with the sell-off of controlling holdings in four banks.

[3] The local firms retained minority stakes. Delhaize also entered but failed, and withdrew in 2003.

[4] The contribution of exports to GDP was 113 per cent in 1999, 210 per cent in 2000, 135 per cent in 2002 and 63 per cent in 2004 (Warr 2005: 30). 2001 was an exception because of a slump in the US.

[5] Debt per household rose from 68,405 *baht* in 2000 to 132,263 in 2007 (*Bangkok Post*, 24 August 2007).

References

Deunden, Nikomborirak *et al.* (2007), 'Khrongkan botbat khong borisat kham chat nai prathet thai: raingan khwam kaona khrang thi 2' ('Project on the role of multinational companies in Thailand: second progress report'), Bangkok: Thailand Research Fund.

Pavida, Pananond (2006), 'Foreign Direct Investment and the Development of Thai Firms: A Case Study of Electronics Industry', Proceedings of the Annual Seminar of the Faculty of Economics, Thammasat University, entitled *Thai Economy in the Changing Global Economy and Society*, Bangkok.

Suehiro, Akira (2001), 'Family Business Gone Wrong? Ownership Patterns and Corporate Performance in Thailand', ADB Institute Working Paper, 19, Tokyo: ADB Institute.

———— (2003), 'Big Business Groups, Family Business and Multinational Corporations in Thailand 1979, 1997 and 2000 Surveys', paper presented at Medhi Wichai Awuso Project, 8 January 2003, Faculty of Economics, Chulalongkorn University.

Suehiro, Akira and Natenapha Wailerdsak (2004), 'Family Business in Thailand: Its Management, Governance, and Future Challenges', *ASEAN Economic Bulletin*, 21, 1, April.

Warr, Peter, ed. (2005) *Thailand Beyond the Crisis*, London/New York: Routledge/Curzon.

Ten Years after the Crisis

A Bright Future for Capitalism in Thailand?

Bruno Jetin

This paper studies twenty-five years of growth and development in Thailand (1980–2005) to show that the 1997 financial crisis had deep-rooted productive origins. It further argues that despite a near eradication of absolute poverty, Thai capitalism is unable to combine long-term growth and social progress, and is indeed dependent on the permanent repression of labour incomes.[1] In section 1, we start with an analysis of structural changes in employment, the distribution of income and the evolution of real income versus labour productivity, to show the continuous imbalance of power between labour and capital. In section 2, we analyse the impact of the distribution of income on the competitiveness of Thailand. Our analysis relates to the Thai economy as a whole and not only to manufacturing. One reason for this is that, while manufacturing may be the driving force of economic development, in terms of employment it represented only 15 per cent of the labour force in Thailand in 2005 and therefore cannot be representative of the distribution of income at the national level. A second reason is that manufacturing, a component of the 'formal' economy, cannot be competitive without the support of the 'informal' economy, which not only provides food but also supplies industrial products and services, and mitigates the adverse effects of the absence of a welfare system.

The Distribution of Income in Thailand: Who Benefited from Growth?

Thailand has witnessed a tremendous change in the composition of its employment (Chart 1). Family helpers, who work mainly in agriculture, accounted for 53 per cent of employment in 1969. They now represent merely 19 per cent. The proportion of self-account workers remains stable at around 30 per cent. Together, they form what is usually called informal employment,[2] which fell dramatically in Thailand from 86 per cent in 1969 to about 50 per cent in 2006. The other half of employment is essentially constituted of wage earners (in state and private companies) and employers who together make up formal employment. Wage labour, which is the backbone of capitalism, is bound to be the major part of employment in the near future in Thailand, while it represented only 14 per cent almost forty years before. Because the labour force is now roughly divided into two equal parts, any attempt to calculate the share of labour income in GDP

CHART 1 *Share of Formal and Informal Employment in Thailand, 1969–2006*

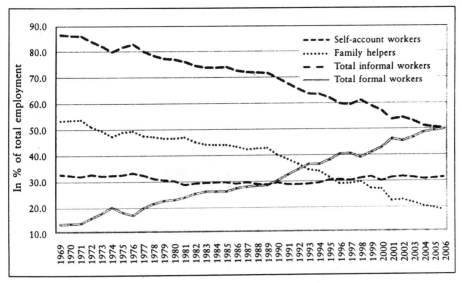

Source: Computed by the author from Labour Force Survey, NSO, various issues.

(gross domestic product) must take into account the income share of 'informal workers' and not only the share of 'formal workers'. One possibility is to use the National Income and Product Accounts (NIPA). Wage earners' income is registered as 'compensation of employees' while informal workers' income is registered as the 'operating surplus of private unincorporated enterprises' (OSPUE). It represents, in fact, a mix of wages and profits of the self-employed and their employees, which gives an estimate of the informal sector.[3]

In order to reduce the bias introduced by the presence of profit in OSPUE, the methodology proposed by D. Gollin (2002) is applied.[4] The result is the adjusted labour share presented in Chart 2. One can see that there is a historical downward trend in the share of labour. The labour share fell from about 83 per cent in 1980 to a trough of 62 per cent in 1996, then recovered during the crisis years because of the fall of profit, but declined again to 70 per cent during the period of recovery (Chart 2). These movements are explained by the sharp decline in the income share of all categories of informal workers until 1996, while the income share of wage earners was increasing but at a slower pace. Since the crisis, these trends have been reversed. The share of wage earners declined from its peak of 42 per cent in 1999 to 38 per cent in 2005, while informal workers' share recovered and then stabilized at around 38 per cent.[5]

The share of capital mirrors the evolution of the labour share because it is calculated as 1 minus the labour share. The capital share increased from 17 per cent in 1980 to a maximum of 38 per cent in 1996 at the end of the boom period (1986–96), fell to 25 per cent in 1999 and then increased again to 30 per cent during the recovery period, benefiting from the decline in the wage earners'

CHART 2 *Labour and Capital Shares of GDP in Thailand, 1980–2005*

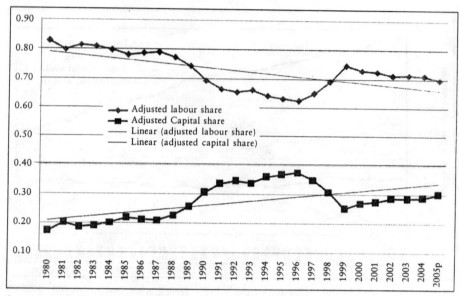

Source: Calculated by the author based on NESDB and NSO data.

CHART 3 *Determinants of the Profit Rate*

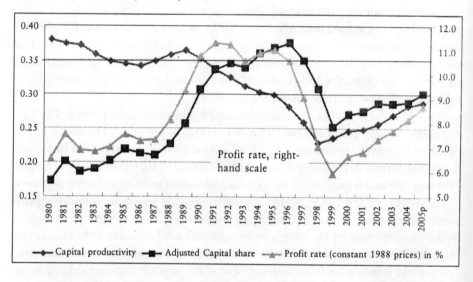

income share. The increase in the income share of capital until 1996 was crucial for the observed creditable profit rates, because the productivity of capital has performed poorly from 1980 to 1996 (Chart 3). The profit rate can be written as:

$$\frac{P}{K} = \frac{P}{Y} \times \frac{Y}{K}$$

where P is the volume of profit, K the stock of capital and Y the GDP (gross domestic product) at factor cost. The profit rate is the product of the capital share $\frac{P}{Y}$ times the productivity of capital $\frac{Y}{K}$. One can see from Chart 3 that the strong increase in the share of capital enabled the profit rate to increase sharply, from an average of 7 per cent in 1980–86 to an average of 11 per cent during 1990–96. The drop in the share of capital during the crisis added to the decline of capital productivity that started in the 1980s but deepened in the 1990s. In 1995, the deceleration in capital productivity was not compensated for by the increase in the capital share, so the profit rate started to decrease before the financial crisis and then dropped sharply in 1997 when the crisis started. The overaccumulation of capital laid the ground for the crisis, which was not purely financial but was rooted in the productive sphere. The recovery of the profit rate to around 9 per cent in 2005 was due to the combined increase of capital's share of income and the productivity of capital (which, thanks to the elimination of excess capital, is on the rise for the first time in the whole period).

Because the increase in the capital share has played such a determining role in maintaining the profit rate at a high level, it is necessary to understand the evolution of its counterpart, the labour share of income. Table 1 presents the determinants of the evolution of the labour income share. If the real average compensation[6] per worker increases less than labour productivity, then the labour income share decreases and vice versa. One can see that before (1981–85) and during (1986–96) the boom years, labour productivity increased nearly two times more than the real average compensation per worker. Clearly, the growth did not benefit workers, with the surplus created by productivity increases being channelized in favour of profit.

This was not the result of any economic law but rather of an unfavourable balance of power between workers – who were subject to a long series of dictatorial governments – and companies which increased their share of income. After the episode of the crisis, when both productivity and real compensation registered negative growth, it is worth noting that real compensation resumed its previous pattern. Its growth rate (2.7 per cent) is not negligible but still lower than the rate of increase of labour productivity (3.8 per cent), although the gap has narrowed. As a consequence, the labour income share declined at a rate of –1.1 per cent per year, from 75 per cent in 1999 to 70 per cent in 2005. Chart 4 shows that the coefficient of restitution of productivity gains to workers was 46 per cent for the whole period. During the boom years, it was much higher (Chart 5), with 60 per cent of labour productivity growth being distributed to workers through

TABLE 1   *Determinants of the Decline in the Labour Income Share*

	1981–85	*1986–96*	*1997–98*	*1999–2005*
Real average compensation	0.6	3.4	−1.3	2.7
Labour productivity	1.7	6.7	-6.5	3.8
Labour income share	−1.1	−3.3	5.2	−1.1

Source: Calculated by the author based on NESDB and NSO data.

CHART 4 *Real Compensation and Productivity in Thailand, 1981–2005*

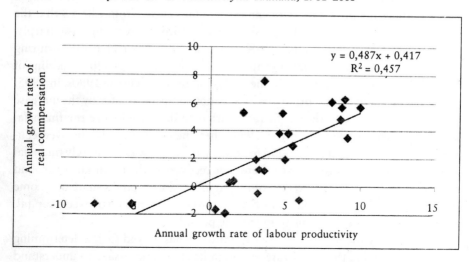

CHART 5 *The Boom, 1986–96*

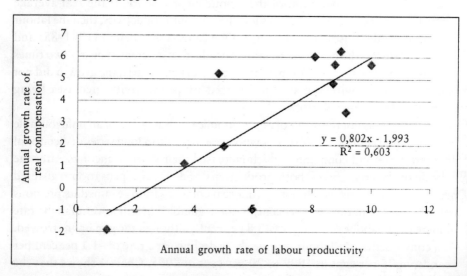

compensation increases. But since the crisis, the figure has fallen to 44 per cent which is closer to the long-term average. Since the working hours in Thailand are among the highest in the world (Lee, McCann and Messenger 2007), we can be sure that productivity gains have not been used to reduce the working time.[7] This means that 54 per cent of productivity gains are on average transformed into profit. If we compare the Thai case with the historical experience of Europe taken as a benchmark, we can draw the following lessons. During the 'golden age' of post-war growth (1960–73), labour productivity gains in Europe reached 4.5 per cent on average, and real wages followed very closely at 4.4 per cent (Husson 2000). In comparison, we can see that labour productivity gains in

CHART 6 *The Crisis and its Aftermath, 1997–2005*

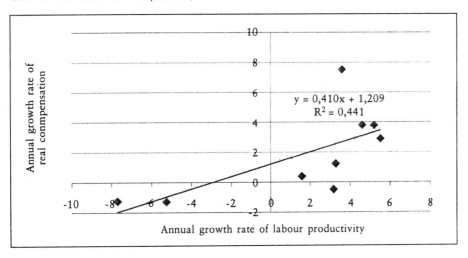

Annual growth rate of labour productivity

$$y = 0{,}410x + 1{,}209$$
$$R^2 = 0{,}441$$

Thailand (6.7 per cent, see Table 1) were quite high during the boom. The difference lies in real compensation that lagged behind. Real compensation increases never followed productivity gains closely.

The Distribution of Income and its Impact on Competitiveness

The accumulation process depends on the rate of profit: $r = \dfrac{\pi}{K}$ where π is the volume of profit and K the stock of capital. If the country is not in the middle of a crisis and if the future is not too uncertain, a high rate of profit raises the degree of entrepreneurs' optimism and induces them to invest more. The 'Cambridge equation' (Pasinetti 1962) formalizes this idea (also at the core of Marxian economics, see Shaikh 1999) by stating that the propensity to save out of profit multiplied by the profit rate determines the growth rate of capital stock, i.e. the pace of accumulation.

$$\frac{I}{K} = g_k = s_p \frac{\pi}{K} = s_p r$$

where s_p is the propensity to save out of profits and g_k is the growth rate of the capital stock. It follows that when all profits are saved ($s_p = 1$) and turned into investment (I_{max}), the maximum rate of accumulation (g_{kmax}) is achieved:

$$I_{max} = \pi, \text{ so that } \left(\frac{I}{K}\right)max = \left(\frac{\Delta K}{K}\right)max = (g_k) = \frac{\pi}{K} = r$$

When this is the case, the ratio of the actual growth rate to the maximum growth rate of capital $\left(\frac{gK}{R}\right)$ can be interpreted as an indicator of the degree to which the growth potential of the economy is being exploited (Shaikh 1999). If the ratio is close to 1, the growth potential is fully utilized. If it is superior to 1, then there is excess demand, leading to inflation rather than higher growth. If it is inferior to 1, there are idle capacities and slow growth. This has been the case

CHART 7   *Profit Rate, GDP Growth, Capital Stock Growth*

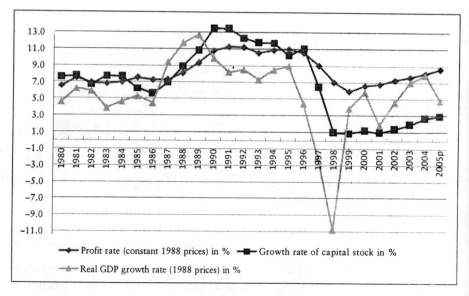

in the Philippines since the mid-1980s until at least 2002: the capital stock growth (around 3 per cent on average) has been well under the rate of profit (around 11 per cent on average) (Felipe, Sipin 2004). In Thailand, it was quite the contrary until the 1997 crisis. The growth of the capital stock (6.8 per cent) has been close to the profit rate (7.2 per cent during 1981–85, but far exceeding the profit rate during most of the boom period, 1986–96), leading to over-accumulation (Chart 7). Inflation has been in fact moderate[8] because the GDP growth rate declined from 13 per cent in 1989 to 4 per cent in 1996, and because of wage repression. The sharp drop in the accumulation rate from 11 per cent in 1996 to 1 per cent in 1997 (until 2001) testifies to the intensity of the crisis. The accumulation of capital resumed only in 2002 at a slow pace and reached 3 per cent in 2005, well below the profit rate (9 per cent). This explains why the present GDP growth rate is well under its potential rate, because investment remains low (see Chart 8).

Gross fixed capital formation has remained at around 21 per cent of GDP since 1999, around half of the record level of the 1990–96 period (41 per cent) and well below the pre-boom years (29 per cent over 1980–85). Chart 8 shows that part of the decline is due to contraction by the state, which used to invest more than 8 per cent of GDP in the pre-boom period; this reached 10 per cent in 1996 and was down to 5 per cent in 2007. The Thai state did not play a counter-cyclical role after the crisis although it had paid its debt to the IMF (International Monetary Fund). Private investment increased from its minimum of 11 per cent in 1999 to 17 per cent in the first half of 2007, close to its pre-boom level of 20 per cent, and was therefore almost solely responsible for the modest recovery of investment. Had the state maintained its investment expenditure at 10 per cent of GDP, the aggregate investment rate would have been 27 per cent, close to the pre-boom years.

CHART 8 *Private and Public Investment Rate in Thailand*

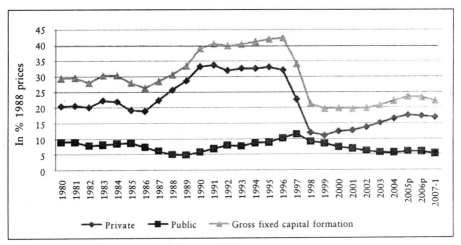

Source: Computed by the author from NESDB data.

CHART 9 *Private Investment as a Share of GDP, 1988 prices*

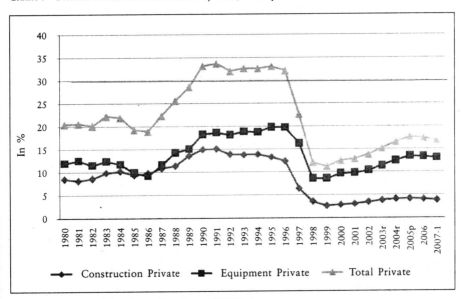

Source: Computed by the author from NESDB data.

When we look at the structure of private investment (Chart 9), we note that the recent increase of investment was due to expenditure on equipment (13 per cent in 2007), while investment in construction remained depressed at around 4 per cent against 13 per cent on average in the boom years and 9 per cent in the pre-boom years.

One limiting feature of this positive trend in productive investment is that most of it came from multinational companies. In 2006, 'private investment growth was supported almost entirely by the 18 per cent real growth in FDI. This reflected low, if not negative, investments by domestic investors amidst political uncertainties' (World Bank 2007: 28). This was probably not the case in 2007 as there was no return of domestic investors' confidence, which represents around three-fourths of total private investment. At best, there was a return to the investment pattern of the pre-boom years at 11 per cent. If this were indeed the case, Thailand would enter a new period of slow growth.

In the short term, this situation is due to several factors. First, there are still excess capacities in the economy that have not been eliminated by the crisis. Second, there is also a fundamental uncertainty regarding the future, due to the political instability and the absence of a long-term growth strategy on the part of the state. If excess capacity can be eliminated, the capacity of the state to define a new strategy for development remains an open question.

Another source of concern is the evolution of unit labour costs, which is one measure of cost competitiveness. The unit labour cost is defined as the ratio of the nominal compensation rate (*baht* per worker) to labour productivity, where the latter is defined as the volume of GDP per worker.[9] Therefore:

$$ULC = \frac{Wn}{\dfrac{VAn_{/p}}{L}} = \left(\frac{Wn}{VAn}\right) P = Sl \times P$$

where W_n denotes the nominal compensation rate, VA_n is the nominal value added or GDP at the aggregate level, P is the output deflator, L is the employment, Sl the labour income share. The equation shows that the unit labour cost can also be expressed as the labour income share multiplied by the GDP deflator. When one wants to assess competitiveness, the GDP deflator can be divided by a foreign exchange index. There is therefore a direct link between the distribution of income and competitiveness, as expressed by ULC (Felipe, Sipin 2004: 6–8). Neoclassical economists would say that the lower the labour income share, the better competitiveness is. As it is easier to repress compensation than to increase labour productivity and growth, the temptation is to engage in a race to the bottom. The counter-argument is that in the long run, repression of workers' compensation depresses domestic demand, leading to a reduction of investment that affects productivity negatively. Chart 10[10] presents three indicators of Thailand's cost competitiveness, namely, the unit labour cost expressed in *baht* (*ULC baht*), the unit labour cost expressed in US$, and the unit labour cost expressed in a basket of currencies of Thailand's main trading partners (*ULC* real effective exchange rate). One can see that despite the decline of the labour income share from 83 per cent in 1980 to 70 per cent in 2005, the unit labour cost expressed in *baht* has increased steadily all through the period. The reason is the continuous increase in inflation (the GDP deflator), which more than compensated the decrease of the labour share. In terms of international competitiveness, it is worth observing that due to the dollar peg that prevailed in the 1980s until 1996, the unit labour cost expressed

CHART 10   *Three Indicators of Thailand's Competitiveness*

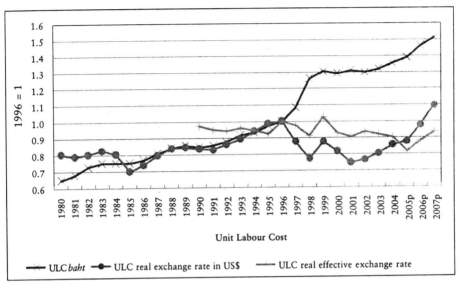

Unit Labour Cost

—— ULC *baht*   —●— ULC real exchange rate in US$ ⸺ ULC real effective exchange rate

Source: Computed by the author from NESDB, Bank of Thailand and NSO data.

in US$ followed closely the unit labour cost expressed in *baht*. As a consequence, competitiveness shrunk by 43 per cent from 1985 to 1996. This contributed strongly to the current account deficits that eventually led to the massive outflows during the crisis.

The adoption of the 'dirty float' regime after the crisis changed the situation dramatically. Following the sharp devaluation of the *baht* in 1997–98, the dollar remained at a low level in the following years, reaching a post-crisis low in 2001. This 'cheap *baht*' period turned the rising 'domestic' unit labour cost into a decreasing unit labour cost in dollar terms. The evolution of the real effective exchange rate was less favourable, but still helped to decrease the unit labour cost of Thailand compared to its main trading partners. This favourable period is now finished. Since 2001, the *baht* is appreciating against the US$, with an acceleration since 2005. In real effective terms the appreciation of the *baht* started only in 2005, but is following the same path. This means that the rising 'domestic' labour cost is no more compensated by depreciation of the *baht*; quite to the contrary, the two factors combine to erode Thailand's competitiveness. This is putting Thai exporters under stress because the investment failure makes it difficult to increase productivity as a way to improve unit labour cost. As a consequence, the downward pressure on workers' compensation will probably be stronger.

Conclusion

The evidence presented in this assessment of Thailand ten years after the crisis leads us to the following conclusions. The first is that the origin of the crisis has to be traced back to the overaccumulation of capital inherited from the boom. The pace of accumulation was slowing down since 1990 and the productivity of capital was also declining all through the period. The financial crisis triggered the economic crisis, but was not the deep cause. Second, the profit rate showed a surprising capacity to remain at a high level even during the crisis and to recover rather quickly, due to the capacity of employers to capture the major part of labour productivity at the expense of workers' compensation. Third, the rate of accumulation which had moved in line with the profit rate in the past seems now to be disconnected from profit, a feature that is also found in the developed countries since the beginning of the 1980s (Husson 1999). This disconnection has given birth to the financialization of capitalism, with the excess of profit being invested in financial markets instead of in the productive sphere. This financialization was not observed as such in developing countries up to now, at least in Asia, because the rate of growth was high for decades. The deceleration of growth in the Southeast Asian countries since the crisis, unlike in China and now India, raises the question of the prospect of financialization in these countries. Is the difference observed in Thailand between the rate of profit and the rate of accumulation (5.6 per cent on average in the period 1999–2005) a transitory phenomenon or a new permanent feature? If it proves permanent, financial crises, unfortunately, have a bright future.

Notes

[1] To make our point, we use the National Income and Product Accounts (NIPA) provided by the National Economic and Social Development Board (NESDB), www.nesdb.go.th. Data for capital stock also comes from NESDB. Data for employment comes from the Labour Force Survey of the National Statistical Office (NSO), http://web.nso.go.th/eng/stat/stat.htm. Data for exchange rate come from the Bank of Thailand, http://www.bot.or.th/bothomepage/index/index_e.asp.

[2] Defining the informal economy and its workers is controversial and goes beyond the scope of this paper. We will refer to a simple definition: the informal economy encompasses 'all economic activities that contribute to the officially calculated (or observed) gross national product but are currently unregistered' (quoted in Felipe, Sipin 2004).

[3] The share of OSPUE in Thailand has sharply declined from 58 per cent of national income in 1980 to less than 38 per cent in 2005, while the share of formal workers has increased from 32 to about 38 per cent. Together, they represent 76 per cent of national income, which is a bit of an overestimate because of the presence of profits in OSPUE. The decline in OSPUE is explained by the decrease in the number of family helpers noted above.

[4] This consists of two adjustments. Adjustment 1 calculates the labour share using the ratio of the sum of the shares in GDP of employees and OSPUE to 1 minus the share in GDP of indirect taxes and subsidies and provision for consumption of fixed capital. This adjustment treats all OPSUE as labour income, so it gives an overestimated labour income share. In the case of Thailand, it leads to a labour share that declines from 0.90 in 1980 to 0.77 in 2005. Adjustment 2 calculates the labour share using the ratio of the share of compensation of employees in GDP to 1 minus the share of OPSUE and minus the share of indirect taxes and subsidies and provision for consumption of fixed capital. The labour share is then underestimated. It declines from 0.75 in 1980 to 0.63 in 2005. The 'adjusted labour income' is the average of adjustments 1 and 2. See Gollin (2002) for further details.

[5] This reflects probably long-lasting employment movements from salary employment to self-employment. A section of wage earners who lost their jobs during the crisis and became self-employed have not returned to salary jobs after the crisis. So the income

share of self-employed has increased from 22 per cent to 29 per cent of GDP. On the contrary, farmers' income share has continued to decline steadily from 20 per cent in 1980 to 10 per cent of GDP in 2005. There was no sustained return to the countryside.

[6] For the sake of simplicity, we use the term compensation both for 'formal' and 'informal' workers, although it is not appropriate for the last category which is composed of workers of varying status.

[7] According to the ILO report, 46.7 per cent of Thai workers work more than 48 hours a week, defined as the threshold of excessive hours; 57 per cent of self-employed work more than 50 hours. Thailand is the only country in the sample of 50 countries where the average working hours in manufacturing are over 59 per week, exceeding working hours in the service sector. Most recent data for Thailand are for 2000.

[8] The inflation rate (GDP deflator), although positive, has been moderate for a developing country: 4.1 per cent per annum during 1981–85, 4.8 per cent during the boom period 1986–96, and 1.3 per cent when the accumulation of capital resumed in the years 1999–2006.

[9] 'A specific characteristic of unit labour cost measure is that the numerator, which reflects the labour cost component of the equation, is typically expressed in nominal terms, whereas the denominator, which is productivity, is measured in real or volume terms' (Ark, Monnikhof 2000). This apparent contrast can be understood when interpreting the unit labour cost measure as an indicator of cost competitiveness. It then adequately represents the current cost of labour (the numerator) per 'quantity unit' of output produced (the denominator) which can only be proxied at the aggregate level by deflated value added.

[10] Chart 10 is based on the following hypothesis: because the data was not yet published, the income labour share for 2005, 70 per cent, was supposed to be constant for 2006 and 2007, which is reasonable because incomes do not fluctuate a lot from year to year. For 2007, the foreign exchange rates used cover the first semester only.

References

Ark, Van B., E.J. Monnikhof (2000), 'Productivity and unit labour cost comparisons: a data base', Employment Paper, No. 5, Geneva: ILO.

Felipe, J., G.C. Sipin (2004), 'Competitiveness, Income Distribution, and Growth in the Philippines: What does the Long-run Evidence Show?', ERD Working Papers Series, No. 53, Manila: Asian Development Bank, June.

Gollin, D. (2002), 'Getting Income Shares Right', *Journal of Political Economy*, 110 (2): 458–74.

Husson, M. (2000), 'Les racines de l'euro-chômage', in *Les marchés du travail en Europe*, Collections Repères, Paris: La Découverte; http://hussonet.free.fr/textes.htm.

——— (1999), 'Surfing on the Long Wave', *Historical Materialism*, No. 5, Winter; http://hussonet.free.fr/surfing.pdf.

Lee, S., D. McCann, J.C. Messenger (2007), *Working Time around the World: Trends in Working Hours, Laws, and Policies in a Global Comparative Perspective*, Geneva: ILO.

Mallikamas, P.R., D. Rodpengsangkaha, Y. Thaicharoen (2003), 'Investment Cycles, Economic Recovery and Monetary Policy', Discussion Paper, Monetary Policy Group, Bank of Thailand.

Pasinetti, L.L. (1962), 'Rate of Profit and Income Distribution in Relation to the Rate of Economic Growth', *Review of Economic Studies*, 29: 267–79.

Pholphirul, P. (2005), 'Competitiveness, Income Distribution and Growth in Thailand: What Does the Long-Run Evidence Show?', Bangkok: International Economic Relations Program, Thailand Development Research Institute, May.

Shaikh, A. (1999), 'Explaining Inflation and Unemployment: An Alternative to Neoliberal Econo-mic Theory', in *Contemporary Economic Theory*, A. Vachlou, ed., London: Macmillan.

World Bank (2007), *Thailand Economic Monitor*, April, World Bank.

Monetarist and Neoliberal Solutions in Indonesia

Old Wine in New Bottles?

Rizal Ramli & P. Nuryadin

The epithet 'East Asian economic miracle' bestowed upon some Asian countries by the World Bank was in the event not strong enough to protect them from the crisis that befell the region ten years ago. The exchange rate crisis that emerged first in Thailand had a devastating impact on the economies of Malaysia, Korea and Indonesia as well as Thailand. Unfortunately, the economic contraction suffered by Indonesia was much worse than in the other affected countries. Indonesia experienced the entire cycle of economic crises from exchange rate collapse to a liquidity crisis to a banking crisis and, finally, generalized bankruptcy in the corporate sector. In 1998, the Indonesian economy contracted by 12.8 per cent, the worst economic reversal in the world outside of the former Soviet Union and Eastern bloc.

At the time, government bureaucrats blamed the crisis on external factors. But this was more a reflection of their refusal to take responsibility for their role in the crisis and their eagerness to find a scapegoat. Events in Thailand did give rise to the initial shock, but the subsequent developments were a consequence of structural weaknesses in the Indonesian economy. Moreover, the impact of the crisis was made much worse by the failure of policy makers to anticipate it, and a series of misjudgements and policy errors as it unfolded.

The social and economic costs of these policy errors were massive. Tens of millions of people lost their jobs and half the population fell below the poverty line. The riots and looting of May 1998 were a direct result of the breakdown of the economy. The cost of recapitalizing the banks reached Rp 650 trillion (including Bank Indonesia Liquidity Credits) in addition to new public sector foreign borrowing. The domestic and foreign debt of this period remains a burden on the national economy till today.

These are bitter memories, but there is much we can learn from this tragic experience, especially in the context of Indonesia's continuing economic vulnerability.

The Pre-Crisis Economy: Moderate Growth and Repeated Crises

Indonesia enjoyed moderate rates of economic growth prior to the crisis.[1] During 1970–96, the real growth of gross domestic product (GDP) averaged 6.7

per cent per annum.[2] But this moderate economic growth concealed some structural weaknesses that carried the risk of destabilizing the national economy. These weaknesses, among others, were as follows.

Cross-Ownership and Cross-Management in the Financial Sector

A specific policy change that had a huge impact on the financial sector in the early 1990s was the October 1988 deregulation package, better known as 'Pakto 88'. An important provision of Pakto 88 was the relaxation of restrictions on establishing new banks, in particular the low minimum capital requirement of Rp 10 billion. The new rules certainly contributed to the rapid increase in the number of banks in Indonesia, from 111 in 1988 to 240 in 1995 – more than double in just seven years. More banks meant more credit supplied to the real sector, which supported moderate growth in the 1990s. But this policy also had a negative impact that greatly endangered national economic stability. The ease with which banks could be opened triggered an increase in the number of aggressive banks, as well as cross-ownership and cross-management in the financial sector.

Data from 1996 indicate that most of the large banks in Indonesia were affiliated to other banks and financial institutions. In other words, the concentration of ownership in the banking sector before the crisis was very high. Cross-ownership and cross-management in the banking sector was a major cause of increased systemic risk and economic instability in the Indonesian economy. A study conducted by ECONIT and the Indonesian Institute of Bankers (IBI) in 1997 found that concentration of ownership and management was especially dangerous because of the associated tendency to exceed intra-group legal lending limits.[3]

In this context, external supervision by Bank Indonesia was completely ineffective because of the many loopholes designed to enable groups to avoid the legal lending limits. Loan swaps among group banks and the use of finance companies, vertical corporate structures, and management and ownership nominees were some of the mechanisms deployed to help groups avoid legal lending limits.

Overvaluation of the Rupiah

Another risk to the Indonesian economy that emerged before the crisis was the current account deficit, which increased throughout the 1980s. Two years before the crisis the current account deficit ballooned. For example, in 1994 the deficit was just US$ 3.1 billion, but by 1995 it had more than doubled to US$ 7.2 billion. The increase in the current account deficit added to economic vulnerability and was a signal that clouds were gathering over the Indonesian economy.[4] Countries with large current account deficits are more likely to be targeted by domestic and international speculators ready to make large bets against the national currency.

Moreover, the monetary authorities attempted to defend a fixed exchange rate of around Rp 2,200 to 2,300 per US dollar. Yet the continued rise of the current account deficit demanded a more flexible exchange rate. In other words, the policy of the monetary authorities to defend a fixed exchange rate resulted in an overvalued *rupiah*. In November 1995 ECONIT estimated that the exchange rate against the US dollar was overvalued by at least 16 per cent.[5]

Over-leveraging with International Debt in the Private Sector

A major component of the current account deficit was debt service payments on international loans to both the public and private sectors. Indonesia's private international debt in 1997 was conservatively estimated at US$ 60 billion, or about 50 per cent of total foreign debt. When we add short-term borrowing such as dollar and *rupiah*-denominated promissory notes, commercial paper and other short-term debt instruments held by foreigners, total private foreign debt was as high as US$ 75 billion. Thus Indonesia's total foreign debt, including that of the public sector, was of the order of US$ 135 billion in 1997.

This is an exceptionally high and risky level of debt, implying a debt service ratio in excess of 40 per cent. The accumulation of private foreign debt in the absence of a government monitoring and information system gave rise to sudden increases in the demand for foreign exchange and resulting fluctuations in the exchange rate that endangered national economic stability. Moreover, much of this foreign debt was used to finance consumption and investment in the non-traded sectors such as speculation in the property market. The situation would have been different if foreign loans had been invested in productive, foreign exchange-earning businesses.

CHART 1 *Indonesia's Estimated Foreign Debt, 1992–98* (US$ billion)

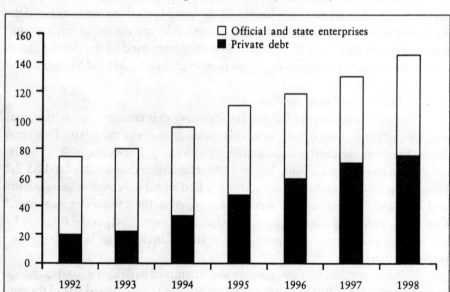

Source: ECONIT.

Disregarded Warning Signals

In November 1996, well before the onset of the economic crisis, ECONIT was alone in calling attention to the warning signs on the horizon.[6] Other institutions such as the World Bank, the International Monetary Fund (IMF) and international investment banks repeated time and again that Indonesia's economic fundamentals were very strong. Bank Indonesia in fact issued a fierce rebuttal of ECONIT's analysis at the time.

In the *Economic Outlook 1996* published in November 1995, ECONIT noted that the current account deficit had doubled in size from US$ 3.1 billion in 1994 to US$ 7.2 billion in 1995, and that the resulting potential for volatility represented 'gathering clouds' over the Indonesian economy. The main reason for this conclusion was the threat of a speculative attack on the currency, which had occurred repeatedly over the previous years in countries with weak economic fundamentals, in particular large current account deficits.

ECONIT warned at the time that the three main characteristics of countries likely to be subjected to speculative attacks were: (1) an overvalued exchange rate in the presence of a large current account deficit; (2) a weak banking system; (3) a large differential between domestic and foreign interest rates. Four ASEAN countries, namely, Thailand, Indonesia, the Philippines and Malaysia, met these three criteria and therefore needed to take preemptive action. To reduce the current account deficit and overvaluation of the *rupiah*, the ECONIT Advisory Group, at the end of November 1995, recommended that Bank Indonesia should allow the *rupiah* to depreciate by at least 16 per cent in 1996 to forestall a speculative attack on the currency. Of course the depreciation would have to be carried out gradually and in stages so as not to trigger speculation against the *rupiah*. Yet this recommendation was ignored and in fact the opposite policy implemented, namely, a deceleration of depreciation (3.6 per cent), by end-1996. In other words, the extent of overvaluation of the *rupiah* actually increased, and with it the vulnerability of the Indonesian economy.

ECONIT also recommended that the private sector should consolidate and strengthen corporate financial structures to reduce over-leverage. These precautions were necessary to reduce exposure to economic and political risks in 1997. Managers who reduced leverage and reinforced their corporate financial structures were much better able to protect their businesses from monetary shocks. Unfortunately, these warnings were ignored. In 1998, the gathering clouds released a hailstorm of a full-blown monetary crisis, the impact of which fell upon all of the Indonesian people.

The Policy Response Intensifies the Crisis

The exchange rate crisis was impossible to avoid in the end. Through August 1997, the value of the *rupiah* fell about 18 per cent against the US dollar. Unfortunately, the response of the monetary authorities to the depreciation was panic. Bank Indonesia applied a 'Super Tight Monetary Policy', which effectively gave rise to a liquidity crisis that was more dangerous than the currency crisis itself. The panicky response of the monetary authorities undermined market faith in the *rupiah*. In the midst of a crisis, psychological factors are more important than market fundamentals when it comes to determining the exchange rate. The impact of the 1997 tight money policy was even harsher than that of the 'Sumarlin Shock II' in 1991. The latter only targeted the money supply while allowing the market to set interest rates. The 1997 tight money policy attempted to control three things at the same time: the money supply, the price of money and the allocation of money. The impact of this attempted 'triple fix' was nothing short of disastrous.

It is not a coincidence that the *rupiah* fell to a new low on the morning of 6 October 1997 (Rp 4.000 per US$), reflecting the market's negative perception of the policy intervention of the monetary authorities. This overshooting of the appropriate level of the *rupiah* against the dollar was a vote of no-confidence in the monetary policies that had just been adopted.

The World Bank and even the government itself stated publicly that the country was experiencing a 'crisis of confidence'. These pronouncements were self-destructive in that they undermined the very confidence that the authorities were trying to re-establish. The comments also revealed the extent of the policy confusion that had paralysed the government and the international organizations. A financial or cash-flow crisis is a much simpler problem, and one that can be resolved through the extension of new borrowing to restore liquidity to the system. But a crisis of confidence suggests that the markets have lost faith in the monetary authorities and economic policy in general. Under these conditions, new lending simply provides additional ammunition for the speculative attack on the currency. Confidence can only be restored by putting in place credible policy makers and credible policies to convince the markets that the tide has changed, and that speculation against the currency has become more risky.

It is interesting that ten years after the event, J. Soedradjad Djiwandono (who was Governor of Bank Indonesia in 1993–98) admitted that monetary policy at the onset of the crisis was excessively tight. In an interview published in *Info-Bank* magazine in 2007, Djiwandono said that 'monetary tightening in the third and fourth week of August 1997 was indeed excessive'.[7]

Enter the IMF: The Beginning of a New Disaster
Reflecting the feelings of inadequacy and self-doubt that emerged among policy makers during the crisis, some officials began to talk openly about the need to ask for the assistance of the International Monetary Fund (IMF). Newspapers in Indonesia and abroad advised Indonesia to immediately request a loan from the IMF. According to these official and mass media pundits, only an IMF loan could help Indonesia recover from the monetary crisis.

However, ECONIT's Public Policy Review of 8 October 1997 warned that inviting the IMF would only push Indonesia into a deeper crisis. ECONIT compared Indonesia to a patient in need of hospitalization because of some economic risks and because of the accumulation of financial and monetary misjudgements

CHART 2 *Stages of the Crisis*

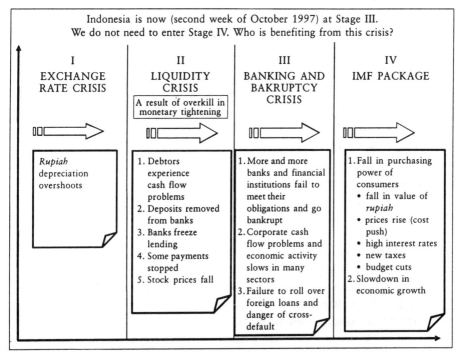

Indonesia is now (second week of October 1997) at Stage III.
We do not need to enter Stage IV. Who is benefiting from this crisis?

I	II	III	IV
EXCHANGE RATE CRISIS	LIQUIDITY CRISIS	BANKING AND BAKRUPTCY CRISIS	IMF PACKAGE
	A result of overkill in monetary tightening		
Rupiah depreciation overshoots	1. Debtors experience cash flow problems 2. Deposits removed from banks 3. Banks freeze lending 4. Some payments stopped 5. Stock prices fall	1. More and more banks and financial institutions fail to meet their obligations and go bankrupt 2. Corporate cash flow problems and economic activity slows in many sectors 3. Failure to roll over foreign loans and danger of cross-default	1. Fall in purchasing power of consumers • fall in value of *rupiah* • prices rise (cost push) • high interest rates • new taxes • budget cuts 2. Slowdown in economic growth

Source: *Public Policy Review*, ECONIT, 8 October 1997.

and policy errors. But Indonesia's economic fundamentals were much better than those of Mexico and Thailand, and therefore Indonesia did not need to be treated in the intensive care unit. ECONIT divided Indonesia's crisis into four stages. At the time, Indonesia was still in the early phases of Stage III (See Chart 2). Many options were still available short of IMF intervention.

There were two possible explanations for why Indonesia was being told to invite the IMF even though the situation did not warrant a trip to the intensive care unit. The first possibility was that the groups that were urging Indonesia to seek IMF assistance (Widjoyo and his colleagues) in fact wanted Indonesia to enter into a more dangerous stage of the crisis, to experience a sharper economic decline with wider social and political implications. The recommendation to allow cross-defaults to occur to teach the borrowers a lesson suggests pettiness and a disregard for the fate of the nation, since cross-defaults would certainly leave Indonesia no option but to go to the IMF. It was well understood at the time that cross-defaults would result in sudden and massive capital outflows, leaving Indonesia dependent on the IMF for access to foreign exchange.

The second possibility was that the people recommending IMF involvement did not understand the consequences of doing so or the historical experience of countries that had borrowed from the IMF. Clearly, they were not sufficiently aware of the impact of IMF loans in the countries affected, or that IMF programmes had resulted in a dramatic slowdown in economic growth, a sharp reduction in purchasing power among consumers, and an increase in poverty. The IMF was not a 'saviour' but rather a 'surgeon' that would carry out an unnecessary emergency room amputation and then put the patient on a strict diet, with long-term consequences.[8]

Indonesia's economic turbulence had resulted in serious losses for international creditors, since the fall in value of the *rupiah* had made it impossible for domestic borrowers to meet their obligations. The use of IMF loans only to enable Indonesian debtors to make principal and interest payments would only benefit international lenders. But in the long run the Indonesian people would have to pay back the IMF in the form of an excessive contraction in aggregate demand. Only with reduced consumption could the economy produce the financial surplus needed to repay the country's debt to the IMF.[9]

In this connection, the following question arises: 'Who benefited from the advice to call in the IMF – international creditors or the Indonesian people?' Monetary contraction would certainly save some creditors from losses but would also result in the loss of purchasing power, a shift in the structure of asset ownership and the acceleration of 'economic condemnation' of small and medium-sized enterprises. Small and medium-scale businesses are not able to withstand the liquidity problems stemming from an extended monetary contraction, causing bankruptcy rates among these firms to increase.

In fact the government had begun to take some positive steps to bring the country out of the monetary crisis. Minister of the State Secretariat Moerdiono, on the orders of President Soeharto, had requested corporate borrowers that had not hedged exchange rate risk to queue for access to foreign exchange (24 September 1997). But, unfortunately, the Berkeley mafia intentionally ignored this order to coordinate repayments of unhedged corporate borrowers. It is no surprise that unhedged private debtors rushed into the market to buy foreign exchange to repay their loans, with the result that in early October the exchange rate plummeted.[10]

When some corporate borrowers were finding it difficult to roll over their loans, the government could have helped them by forming a private sector negotiating committee to attempt to convert the debt into equity (debt to equity conversion/swap). Debt to equity swaps achieve three things: (i) over-leverage in the corporate sector is reduced; (ii) corporate financing is strengthened; (iii) in many cases the quality of management improves with the involvement of international managers.

Still other options were available, which suggests that the IMF was called in too quickly. Lack of self-confidence and indecision paralysed the government precisely at the time when decisive action was needed. In economics, as in politics and war, the quality of leadership is tested during times of crisis.

The experience of other countries has shown that many of the IMF's patients recover briefly only to experience a relapse and revert to being a patient. There are many examples in Africa and Latin America of how the IMF applies ineffective, generic prescriptions.

Yet these concerns were ignored. The government, then represented by Minister of Finance Marie Muhammad and BI Governor Sudradjad Djiwandono, insisted on signing the first Letter of Intent (LoI) with the IMF on 31 October 1997. At the request of the Berkeley mafia led by Widjojo Nitisastro, President Soeharto signed the second Letter of Intent in January 1998, witnessed by IMF Managing Director Michel Camdessus. In fact, the head of state rarely signs IMF agreements, which are typically signed by the minister of finance or head of the central bank. But the Berkeley mafia deliberately talked President Soeharto into signing so that later they could dissociate themselves from the deal.

The involvement of the IMF broadened and deepened the crisis. As a consequence of its misdiagnosis and incorrect prescription, the Indonesian economy contracted in 1998 by 12.8 per cent. Of course, even without the IMF Indonesia would have suffered an economic crisis in 1998, but most likely on a smaller scale – economic growth of –2 to 0 per cent. The policy recommendations of the IMF pushed Indonesia into a more serious crisis. For example, the liquidation of sixteen banks in November 1997 triggered a run on tens of banks including Bank BCA and Bank Danamon, precipitating the collapse of the national banking system and the sinking of the *rupiah*.

In many cases in Latin America and Africa, IMF recommendations have triggered mass demonstrations, riots, loss of life and the fall of governments. In addition, in the Indonesian case, the involvement of the IMF forced tens of millions of people out of work, bankrupted the private and public sectors, and imposed long-term costs on the economy such as the more than Rp 600 trillion given over to recapitalize the banks and tens of billions of dollars in new international debt.

The IMF also triggered social unrest through its recommendations. The economic and social costs of the crisis led to the IMF-provoked riots of May 1998. At the behest of the IMF, the government raised the price of kerosene by 25 per cent and gasoline by 71 per cent on 4 May 1998 to reduce fuel subsidies. One day later, thousands of students protested the price hikes in Makasar, and buildings and cars were set on fire. Over the next several days, the protests spread to Medan, Surabaya, Solo, Yogyakarta and finally to Jakarta on 12 May 1998. As a result of this IMF advice, hundreds of people died across Indonesia, thousands were wounded, and hundreds of buildings and thousands of vehicles destroyed. This is an example of what has occurred time and again in the developing world: social unrest as a result of the IMF.

The irony is that Marie Muhammad, one of the key officials who invited the IMF to Indonesia – and who at the time applied IMF policies enthusiastically – acted in later years as if he had no responsibility for what had transpired. In an interview with *Tempo* magazine in July 2007, Marie Muhammad said that 'the IMF's prescription was based on analysis that was indeed off the mark. The reason is that the IMF acts as if all countries have identical problems.' This is an astonishing statement from an official who, when in office ten years ago, had implemented with great enthusiasm the IMF policies that thrust Indonesia into the depths of economic crisis.

The Slow Recovery

As mentioned above, Indonesia suffered the worst economic contraction among the crisis-hit Asian countries. Compared to Malaysia, Thailand and South Korea, Indonesia's post-crisis recovery was also the slowest. One year after the crisis, South Korea recorded economic growth of about 9.5 per cent. Meanwhile, Thailand and Malaysia grew by 4.4 and 6.6 per cent respectively in 1999. In the same year, the Indonesian economy grew by less than 1 per cent.

South Korea's rapid recovery cannot be considered in isolation from steps taken by its government to roll over the foreign loans of South Korean banks with the help of US Treasury Secretary Robert E. Rubin and Federal Reserve Chairman Alan Greenspan. These efforts reduced pressure on South Korean borrowers and restored public and investor confidence in policy makers. Malaysia and Thailand introduced monetary and fiscal stimuli immediately after the crisis, including the development of infrastructure to raise domestic demand in a classic Keynesian manner.

The Indonesian government pursued policies of a very different sort. In accordance with IMF recommendations, Indonesia in fact transformed private debt into public debt, which imposed a massive burden on the government budget. The government also tightened monetary and fiscal policy to ensure that the government could service its debts, including its IMF loans. Yet when economic conditions are deteriorating, it is the responsibility of the government to use whatever means are at its disposal to bring it back to life, not to slow down the

CHART 3 *Economic Recovery: Indonesia is the Slowest*

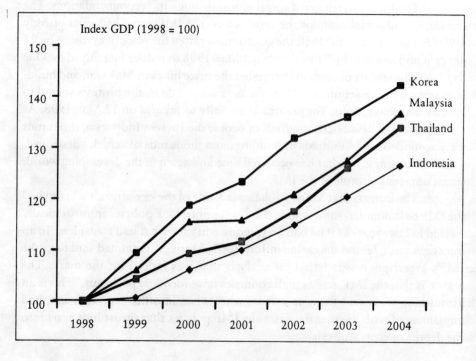

recovery with tight fiscal and monetary policies. Therefore it is not surprising that Indonesia's recovery was the slowest in Asia.

It must be recognized that political instability and the deterioration of the security situation in 1998 were partly to blame for Indonesia's slow recovery. But the incorrect prescription of the IMF supported by the New Order Economic Mafia[11] was the main reason. The IMF's errors can be seen from the perspective of the three policy stages beginning in October 1997.

In the first stage, IMF recommendations created financial instability and mass bankruptcies. Instability was triggered by the super-tight monetary policy, when the inter-bank rate rocketed from 20 per cent to 300 per cent after the third quarter of 1997. Super-tight monetary policy resulted in a liquidity crunch in the Indonesian banking system because many banks relied for some of their liquidity on the inter-bank market. The IMF recommendation to close sixteen banks without adequate preparation in November 1997 destroyed public confidence in the domestic banking system. This step immediately triggered US$ 5 billion in capital outflows, undermining the value of the *rupiah*. The depreciation of the *rupiah* could not be controlled because it had been allowed to float on 14 August 1997. Under conditions of financial instability, allowing the *rupiah* to float without controls triggered capital outflows that pushed the *rupiah* down even further. As a result, the business world suffered the twin blows of *rupiah* depreciation and super-high interest rates. In the end, businesses suffered a liquidity crisis followed by mass bankruptcies and lay-offs affecting millions of workers.

In the case of banking, the IMF was invited in to stabilize the sector, but in the end destabilized it. The IMF misdiagnosed the problem and prescribed the wrong treatment, with the result that the Indonesian economy experienced the hardest of hard landings. In 1998 the economy contracted by 12.8 per cent, the worst performance in the country's history.

The second stage was the transformation of private debt into public debt. IMF recommendations had already raised public debt to extremely high levels, especially domestic public debt, of which there was very little prior to the crisis. Before the 1997 crisis, Indonesia's total debt burden was US$ 136 billion, consisting of $ 54 billion in public sector debt and $ 82 billion in private foreign debt. But by 2001, the government's international debt had risen to $ 74 billion, plus debt to the domestic private sector of Rp 647 trillion (about US$ 65 billion). Meanwhile, private foreign debt had fallen to $ 67 billion owing to accelerated repayments and debt restructuring. Indonesia's total debt at that time was greater than its gross domestic product (GDP), which was only about $ 150 billion. As a consequence of the financial crisis and the incorrect prescription put forward by the IMF, Indonesia's debt doubled over the four years following the onset of the crisis in 1997.

In the third stage, the consequences of the IMF's errors began to exert a broader impact on the government budget. In the 2002 fiscal year, for example, debt payments on domestic and foreign debt reached US$ 13 billion (Rp 130 trillion). Debt service payments in this year were more than three times as large as salaries for the entire civil service and military, and more than eight times the size of the education budget. The size of the domestic debt has been closely connected to Bank Indonesia's monetary policy. With the encouragement of the IMF, Bank Indonesia was certain that control over inflation could only be achieved through tight monetary policy and high interest rates on Bank Indonesia Certificates (SBIs). But this disregarded the obvious fact that much of the inflation recorded during this period was a direct result of price hikes implemented by the government. Inflation was not in this instance simply a monetary phenomenon. Moreover, an unintended consequence of Bank Indonesia's tight money policy was a mounting burden on the government budget, as debt service payments were linked to domestic interest rates. At that time, every 1 per cent increase in the SBI rate resulted in an increase in the government deficit of Rp 2.3 trillion.

With such a large burden on the state budget, the government was confronted with a difficult dilemma. Unpopular measures were needed to reduce the deficit, many of which would make life difficult for millions of Indonesians. In addition to raising taxes, electricity and fuel prices, the government was under intense pressure to sell state assets as quickly as possible and at bargain basement prices. The case of Bank Central Asia (BCA) in 2002 is an interesting example. With a target price of Rp 5 trillion, the government would still have to carry the burden of interest payments on BCA recapitalization debt of between Rp 7 and 8 trillion per year, assuming no change in the government's position on recapitalization debt.

The policies of the New Order Economic Mafia, supported by the IMF, relied on debt rather than investment for development, and thus drove the economy into a deeper debt trap. The IMF's misdiagnosis, forced on Indonesia, led to the government assuming responsibility for an additional debt burden that should have been shouldered by the private sector – that is, the debt incurred by the private sector from Bank Indonesia Liquidity Credits (BLBI) of Rp. 144 trillion and bank recapitalization. Indeed the misuse of BLBI is the largest financial scandal in the nation's history.

Policy Change Blocked by Myths

In 2002, economists grouped together as Tim Indonesia Bangkit (TIB) recommended that the government immediately cancel the IMF programme, and suggested alternative policies to accelerate economic growth after its discontinuation. Unfortunately, these efforts to bring an end to the IMF programme were blocked by the Berkeley mafia, which put forward several myths about the IMF and Indonesia's policy choices, and effectively deepened Indonesia's dependence on international debt.

The first myth was that IMF programmes strengthen investor confidence in Indonesia. After so many Letters of Intent and seven years under IMF supervision, investor confidence in Indonesia is still not restored. The main problem is not the presence or absence of the IMF but, rather, political stability, physical security and the rule of law. If these three factors are present, investor confidence will increase with or without the IMF.

The second myth is that IMF loans lead to inflows of private capital. In fact, the opposite has occurred. Under Indonesia's various IMF programmes, the country has experienced a decoupling of multilateral and private capital inflows: indeed private capital has left Indonesia (see Chart 4). Once again, the main reasons are political stability, security and rule of law.

The third myth is that the IMF can stabilize the value of the *rupiah*. This has become something of a joke among Indonesians, who know the opposite to be true. Since October 1997, every time an IMF team has come to Jakarta the value of the *rupiah* has fallen. And on each occasion, Bank Indonesia has been forced to intervene to strengthen the *rupiah* at a cost of millions of dollars. In general, as noted by Dr Didik Rachbini, the relationship between the IMF and the value of the *rupiah* is asymmetrical. When the IMF makes positive statements about Indonesia the *rupiah* does not strengthen, but when the IMF criticizes Indonesia the *rupiah* falls. The strengthening of the *rupiah* in the first half of 2002 was not a result of the IMF's performance but of the weakening of the US dollar against major world currencies. Another factor was political stability, as President Megawati avoided controversy and political parties agreed to stabilize the political situation in the lead-up to 2004.

The fourth myth is that the IMF can collude with other creditors to deny credit to countries that do not take on IMF programmes, and extend credit to

CHART 4 **Misleading Myths** *(Private capital flows remain negative under Indonesia's IMF programme)*

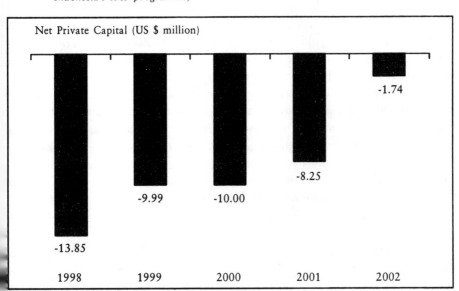

Source: Statistik Ekonomi Keuangan Indonesia, October 2003, Bank Indonesia.

countries that do. This ignores that fact that each creditor has its own strategic and economic interests in Indonesia. At the time that I was Coordinating Minister of the Economy, we signed loan agreements with the World Bank, Japan and the Asian Development Bank even though the IMF Letter of Agreement had not been finalized. Indeed many official creditors also view the IMF as too obstinate, and object to the rolling conditionalities in IMF programmes. Creditors are aware that collusion among themselves could result in cash flow problems in borrowing countries and even default, which would not be in their interest.

These myths were spread continuously by the New Order Economic Mafia, to the point that the public was persuaded that without the IMF the country would become bankrupt and break to pieces. But Malaysia overcame the crisis without an IMF programme. The Thaksin government in Thailand did not renew its IMF programme and Thailand did not fall to pieces. We should also remember that terminating the IMF programme would not mean withdrawing Indonesia's membership from the IMF.

Indeed since 2002, Indonesia has not needed IMF credit. IMF loans are a second-tier defence, meaning that the US$ 400 million pledged by the IMF is only used if Indonesia experiences a balance of payments crisis and runs out of international reserves (which at that time totalled some US$ 28 billion). This is unlikely to occur, particularly in the presence of a flexible exchange rate regime under which the value of the currency adjusts to the balance of payments situation. In other words, Indonesia cannot actually use its IMF loans but must still pay interest on them. The statement of the Coordinating Minister of the Economy that IMF loans carry the lowest interest rate is therefore not accurate, since the loans are not used but they must still be serviced. For the year 2001, for example, Indonesia received IMF loans worth US$ 400 million and paid US$ 2.3 billion to the IMF, consisting of $ 1.8 billion in principal and interest payments of $ 500 million. These are fees paid to a doctor who has consistently been guilty of malpractice, but demands payment plus interest for unnecessary emergency room amputations. Too bad if the patient is still in a coma.

Increasing foreign borrowing through the IMF to 'inflate' the balance of payments is an artificial solution because it does not come about through private capital flows or net exports. Borrowing to inflate the balance of payments also reduces Indonesia's capacity to finance projects such as infrastructure rehabilitation, irrigation development and labour-intensive public works. In other words, borrowing from the IMF carries an opportunity cost for the Indonesian economy in the form of investments not undertaken. Meanwhile, Indonesia cannot make use of IMF credit.

In an interview in *Business Week* (19 November 2001), Nobel prize-winning economist Joseph Stiglitz of Columbia University said that 'IMF programmes longer than two years in duration are evidence of IMF failure'. Indonesia is from this perspective an example of massive failure on the part of the IMF because the IMF programme lasted for six years (1997–2003). According to Stiglitz, 'The IMF demands too many conditionalities, some of which are political in nature, and often enter into the domain of microeconomics, which are outside of the mandate and competence of the IMF [which is limited to the macroeconomy].'

Ten Years Later

The crisis of 1997/98 taught us many policy lessons. But in the event, Indonesian policy makers have not learned much. Economic policy-making is still conservative and geared towards stabilizing financial and monetary indicators. Even though the IMF has left Indonesia, conservative monetary and fiscal policies are still practised, if only to smarten up indicators such as the inflation and exchange rates. Yet the main economic target should be to reduce poverty and unemployment. This can only be achieved through investment and increasing productivity in the real economy, particularly in labour-intensive manufactures. Financial indicators are only an intermediate target on the way to the ultimate goals of prosperity and employment.

Financial stability is of course important for the economy. Yet efforts to stabilize financial indicators in Indonesia have too often sacrificed the performance of the real sector, resulting in increases in poverty and unemployment. Efforts to control inflation have prevented the economy from growing to its full potential. The monetary authorities have even tried to control inflation caused by rises in government-administered prices with tight money, as in the case of the fuel cost increases in October 2005.

On the fiscal side, rather than use the budget as an economic stimulus, the government has attempted to reduce deficits as far as possible. For the period 2002–06, the budget deficit as a per cent of GDP fluctuated between 0.5 and 1.7 per cent, much lower than the legal limit of 3 per cent.

As a result of the obsession with fiscal and monetary targets, the real sector has recorded exceptionally slow growth rates over the past four years. Over the period 2002 to 2006, the industrial production index for medium and large-scale firms rose by only 2.1 per cent per year. In 2006, the production index of manufacturing actually fell compared to the previous year (see Chart 5). Other developments also point to the beginning of a process of deindustrialization in the form of low investment rates, low rates of capacity utilization, relocation of manufacturing to other countries, and the substitution of trade and distribution of imported products in the place of domestic production. The quality of growth is also very low. The number of additional workers for every one percentage point of GDP growth has fallen from 500 to only 240 thousand. It is therefore hardly surprising that open unemployment has jumped from 9.1 million workers in 2002 to 10.5 million by February 2007 (see Chart 6).

The irony is that the stagnation in the real economy is not reflected at all in the financial sector. Some financial and monetary indicators point in the opposite direction. The Jakarta Stock Exchange (JSX) Index is up three to five-fold, from 700 in 2004 to 2.380 on 23 July 2007. Foreign exchange reserves have also increased sharply, from US$ 35 billion in 2006 to $ 51 billion in July 2007, which has helped to stabilize the value of the *rupiah*.

CHART 5 *GDP Index vs Production Index (Economic growth over the past three years not supported by manufacturing)*

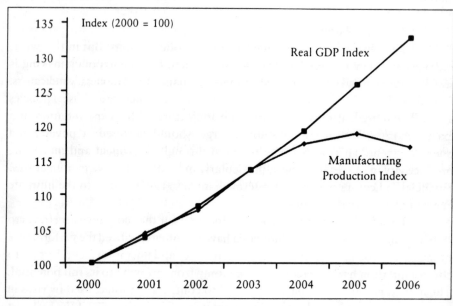

Source: BPS.

CHART 6 *Rising Unemployment (The unemployment rate has increased dramatically over the past six years)*

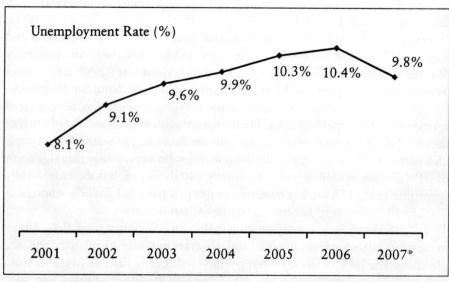

Note: * Modified method of calculating employment. See TIB paper, 'Challenging the Credibility and Independence of BPS', 28 May 2007.
Source: BPS.

Asset Bubbles

In January and May of 2006, economists grouped together as the Tim Indonesia Bangkit (TIB) stated that the contradiction between financial and real indicators represented a warning sign for the Indonesian economy.[12] The improvements in the financial indicators would prove temporary if not supported by a recovery of the economic fundamentals. The danger is that asset bubbles would form that appear solid and safe from the outside, but are in fact empty and liable to burst.

The main cause of the disjuncture between the real economy and financial indicators in Indonesia was hot money from abroad flowing into the Asian region, including Indonesia. By June 2007, foreign ownership of financial instruments in Indonesia was Rp 797 trillion, with about Rp 670 trillion (84 per cent) in the form of shares purchased on the Jakarta Stock Exchange (see Table 1). Inflows of hot money drove up the JSX Index and strengthened the *rupiah*. From early 2006 to mid-July 2007 the JSX Index rose from 1,600 to 2,400. The *rupiah* also strengthened, rising to Rp 8.600 per US dollar by the middle of May 2007.

TABLE 1   *Foreign Control (Foreign ownership of financial instruments has increased over the past five years)*

	Stock	Government Bond	SBI
Foreign Ownership on Indonesia's Financial Instruments, June 2007			
Foreign ownership (Rp trillion)	669.7	81.8	45.0
Foreign shares (%)	43.5	18.0	17.3
Changes of foreign ownership from the beginning of 2007 (%)	28.2	48.9	149.0

Source: BI, KSEI, BEJ.

Asset bubbles created by hot money are dangerous because capital inflows are a double-edged sword. As domestic assets are bought up by foreign money they rise in value, taking with them the value of the *rupiah* which is also in demand to acquire these assets. But if financial flows reverse direction they can be a disaster for the financial markets and the *rupiah*. Right now, about 65–70 per cent of share transactions on the JSX involve foreign investors. The direction of the JSX is under the control of international investors, mostly global hedge funds. Even a small economic shock, either domestic or external, could result in reverse flows and a massive correction in asset prices.

The conditions for the Indonesian Economic Crisis, Book 2, are now falling into place. Consider the following.

The Increase in Export Values and Reserves are the Result of Hot Money and High Commodity Prices

Over the last two years Indonesia's foreign exchange reserves have increased dramatically, from US$ 35 billion in 2005 to $ 51 billion. This reserve position is supported not by export competitiveness or an increase in foreign direct investment, but rather by windfalls such as high international commodity prices and inflows of hot money.

Since 2004, the international prices of a number of commodities have increased sharply (see Chart 7). These price rises have increased the value of Indonesian exports, while also strengthening the reserves position and the *rupiah*. In 2006, Indonesian exports exceeded the US$ 100 billion mark. But from the perspective of the composition of exports following SITC codes, it is clear that export growth was driven by commodities such as rubber, metals, vegetable oils and spices, among others.

Another factor that has strengthened the country's reserves position and the value of the *rupiah* is the flow of hot money to Indonesia triggered by the gap between domestic and foreign interest rates. Since the middle of 2005, the volume of hot money that has entered Indonesia is thought to be in excess of $ 20 billion.

The rise in reserves and export values and the strengthening of the *rupiah* have led some observers, particularly within the government, to conclude that all is well on the economic front. But this overconfidence could prove fatal if the government fails to realize that the factors responsible for these improvements are temporary and not sustainable. If domestic industries are not helped to become more competitive, exports and foreign exchange reserves will fall in time as international commodity prices follow their normal, cyclical trends.

CHART 7 *Price-driven Export Growth: Rising Commodity Prices as the Source of Export Growth*

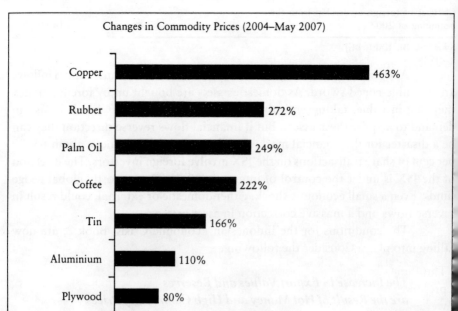

Source: Bank Indonesia.

Illusory Growth in the Banking Sector

In 2006, the banking industry recorded rising profits. Net Interest Margins (NIM) in January 2007 were 6.6 per cent and among the highest in the world. In the wake of rising profits resulting from these high margins, Indonesian banking sector shares soared, driving the JSX Index to new heights. But the favourable situation in the banking sector was not supported by improvements in the economic fundamentals, as reflected in trends in credit growth. In fact credit growth slowed down over 2005–07. In 2006 bank credit grew by only 4 per cent, while in May 2007 credit growth was only 17 per cent, much lower than the historical trend of 25–30 per cent per year.

In other words, rising profits in the banking sector are not a reliable indicator of financial stability because these profits are not derived from sustainable sources of revenue such as corporate lending. When the SBI rate comes down, the banks' profits will suffer.

Oversupply in the Property Sector

Another phenomenon observed over the past five years is the boom in the property sector, including residential, commercial and office properties. From 2002 to 2006, capitalization of office space increased at a rate of 45 per cent per year.

Yet the rapid growth of supply in the property sector has not been met by an increase in demand. The supply of office space has risen sharply, but the slow growth of investment suggests that demand will not be increasing any time soon. In 2006 gross investment increased by only 3 per cent. The supply of residential and commercial properties has also increased rapidly, but the purchasing power of the public has not recovered since the high inflation rate of 17 per cent in October 2005.

Not surprisingly, occupancy rates have fallen sharply across all sectors. According to Bank Indonesia data, occupancy rates of leased offices in Jakarta fell nine percentage points, from 89 per cent in 2005 to 80 per cent in the first quarter of 2007. The situation is the same for commercial space in the Jakarta–Bogor–Tanggerang–Bekasi region. Normally occupancy rates for shopping centres are around 94 to 95 per cent, but in the first quarter of 2007 they had fallen by six to seven percentage points, to 88 per cent. Lately, developers have attempted to raise rents and maintenance costs to meet their operational expenses.

Of greater concern is the fact that financing for property developments comes from the banking sector, especially mortgages and business loans used to purchase residential and commercial properties. In the absence of an improvement in the real economy, the level of non-performing loans is certain to rise sharply. This is the situation in the United States, which is experiencing a crisis due to the proliferation of sub-prime loans – mostly mortgages extended to households that were not in a position to continue to service their loans if interest rates rose or incomes fell. As in the United States, Indonesian borrowers are ill-prepared for a slowdown in the real sector. In other words, the property bubble has increased the risk of a liquidity crisis that is not yet apparent in non-performing loan data.

Overvalued Shares

The JSX Index rose dramatically over the period 2005 to mid-2007. It rose 55 per cent in 2006, and another 32 per cent over the period January to June 2007. The rise in the index is in part a reaction to high international commodity prices, which raises profits in the plantation and mining sectors. But the main cause is the flow of hot money into the Asian region, including Indonesia. Based on Ministry of Finance data, from January to June 2007 US$ 1.6 billion in hot money flowed into the Jakarta Stock Exchange. Such is the torrent of capital inflows that investors no longer appear to care about market fundamentals. Price-earning ratios (PER) have risen to extraordinary levels. In July 2007, forty-nine issues had PERs above 50, twenty-five stocks had PERs over 100, and the prices of eight stocks had risen to more than 400 times earnings.

High share prices in the absence of strong market fundamentals signal the formation of a dangerous asset bubble. Any sudden shift in capital flows could result in a sharp fall in equity prices. We should remember that such a reversal of capital flows was one of the causes of the 1997 economic crisis.

Poor Government Track Record in Reducing Economic Fluctuations

The government's track record in reducing economic fluctuations, especially the prices of basic commodities, is very poor. Its efforts to address price rises of basic commodities such as rice, cooking oil and sugar over the past year have been unsuccessful, largely due to the inability of cabinet members holding economic portfolios to solve practical problems. The poor performance of the government's economic team risks triggering social unrest because the living standards of the people are closely tied to the prices of basic commodities. The situation could become even more dangerous if the bursting of the financial sector bubble leads to more price fluctuations for basic needs.

Politics Heats Up Earlier than Expected

Many observers predicted that the political situation leading up to the 2009 general elections would not heat up until 2008. But given continued stagnation in the real economy and persistently high poverty and unemployment rates, the political situation has already become very dynamic. The main consequence of this acceleration of the political calendar is that the government is distracted from the country's economic problems. In addition, if the country were to be subjected to an external financial shock, political factors could cause the situation to deteriorate further as it did ten years ago.

As was the case prior to the 1997/98 crisis, a combination of risks have come together to form the 'gathering clouds' over the Indonesian economy. Any domestic or external shock could release a dangerous hailstorm as it did ten years ago.

The sub-prime lending crisis in the United States is one such external shock. Sub-prime mortgages are loans to house buyers with low credit ratings who must borrow at high interest rates to cover the extra risks associated with these loans. Global hedge funds, seeking high returns on their capital, bought up these sub-prime mortgages in the form of mortgage-backed securities. But as home owners began to default on their sub-prime loans, hedge funds came under pressure. At the end of July, Bear Stearns, the fifth largest investment bank in the United States, closed two hedge funds linked to sub-prime mortgages. This announcement immediately caused a correction on the world's stockmarkets, including Indonesia's.

The failure of two Bear Stearns hedge funds was only the beginning of the sub-prime loan crisis. Since then another hedge fund, this time one owned by BNP Paribas, has gone bankrupt. Some observers predict that the sub-prime loan crisis will result in losses of US$ 100 to 150 billion, and extend over a period of at least three years. Analysis by the TCW Group concludes that there is a 60 per cent probability that the United States will experience a recession in 2007 as a result of the sub-prime mortgage problem.

When corrections like this occur, the first thing that hedge funds do is to unwind their existing positions to acquire sufficient liquidity to cover their obligations. Indonesia's inflated stockmarket is a likely candidate for a sell-off by global funds. If this were to occur, the likely result would be a sharp fall in the JSX Index and a weakening of the *rupiah*.

Events in the first two weeks of August 2007 confirmed these suspicions. The effects of the sub-prime loan crisis were felt beyond Bear Stearns and BNP Paribas as bankruptcies and losses mounted around the world. Some of the biggest names in global finance were not spared. The US equity markets took a big hit followed by exchanges across the globe. But the effects in Indonesia were the worst. Over the period 1 to 16 August 2007, the JSX Index fell by 18.7 per cent, a much larger correction than that experienced in the US and other Asian markets (see Chart 8). This is a reflection of the deeper structural weaknesses of the Indonesian economy.

Fortunately, central banks in North America, Europe and Japan immediately intervened to inject billions of dollars of liquidity into the markets and lower key interest rates. Some hedge funds on the brink of collapse were bailed out. Global markets appear to be recovering as a result of this timely intervention. But since the injection of liquidity has not resolved the origins of the problem – that is, the systemic risk associated with sub-prime loans – it is likely that the effects of intervention will be felt in the short term, and global markets will remain volatile for the rest of the year.

This volatility carries serious risks for Indonesia because of the country's relatively weak economic situation. The large correction on the Indonesian market is an indicator of things to come. Although the JSX Index recovered in the third week of August, the cumulative fall of about 8 per cent for the period 1 to 28 August 2007 was still steep relative to the US and other Asian markets. For example, over the same period the Hang Seng rose 0.8 per cent, the Dow Jones

Chart 8 *Cumulative Correction on International Markets (1–16 August 2007)*
        (JSX experiences largest correction)

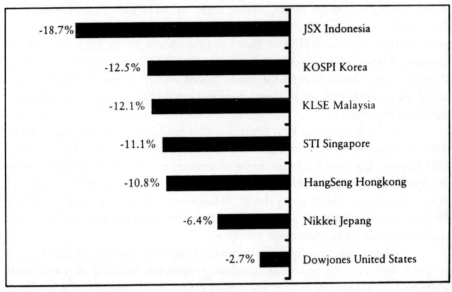

Source: Yahoo Finance.

fell 1.3 per cent, Korea's KOSPI fell 5.4 per cent, the Nikkei dropped 5.6 per cent, Singapore fell 5.8 per cent and Malaysia's KLSE was down 6.9 per cent.

Lessons Not Learned by the Government's Economic Team

The government has not learned anything from its botched response to the 1997/98 crisis and from the intervention of the IMF at that time, which deepened the crisis even further. Ten years on, the government's economic team considers the financial bubble as a source of pride, and they continue to do whatever they can – directly and indirectly – to attract hot money to Indonesia (see Iman Sugema, *Bisnis Indonesia*, 3 August 2007, p. 2).

Yet, as discussed above, hot money is a double-edged sword. One moment capital inflows are driving up stock and other asset prices, and the next moment they are sending them crashing down. Consciously or unconsciously, in chasing after hot money the government's economic team has increased the vulnerability of the Indonesian economy to a financial and economic crisis. The more hot money that flows into Indonesia, the more vulnerable the Indonesian economy becomes.

Moreover, the sharp rise in asset prices represents another obstacle to the growth of the real economy. As profits in the financial sector continue to outpace those available in other sectors, investors forego ventures in industry, agriculture and services in favour of speculation. This creates even higher asset prices, attracting even more capital. As the bubble develops, the other sectors are starved of capital until the point that the financial bubble bursts under the weight of a stagnant economy.

Other countries in Asia have already woken up to the dangers of hot money. They have taken preemptive action to prevent financial bubbles. For example, the government of China increased taxes on stock transactions at the end of May 2007 and has imposed heavy sanctions on international banks to prevent large capital inflows. Thailand has taken numerous actions to devalue the *baht*, fearing that exchange rate appreciation would threaten the export industries that account for two-thirds of the country's GDP.

These concerns of other countries should stand as a warning to the government of Indonesia that it should not be overconfident in the face of asset inflation caused by hot money inflows. Ten years ago the overconfidence of Indonesia's policy makers plunged the country into the worst economic crisis in the country's history. Let us hope that it is not too late to learn something from that bitter experience.

Notes and References

[1] Moderate relative to higher growth of Asian economies (8 to 10 per cent per annum.)
[2] Indonesia's historical GDP growth has been revised upward by back-casting techniques
[3] ECONIT Advisory Group and the Indonesian Institute of Bankers, 'Study of Structure and Strategic Policy in the Indonesian Banking Industry Post-2000', 1997.
[4] As noted in 'ECONIT's Economic Outlook 1996: A Year of Consolidation,' Part 2, p. 28, November 1995.
[5] See 'ECONITS's Economic Outlook 1996: A Year of Consolidation,' Part 3, p. 17, November 1995.
[6] 'ECONIT's Economic Outlook 1997: A Year of Uncertainty', 5 November 1996.
[7] 'Ten Years since the Monetary Crisis: Preparing to Face the Second Crisis', InfoBank, July 2007.
[8] Econit Public Policy Review (EPPR), 'Calling in the IMF: Treachery or Ignorance?', 8 October 1997, p. 3.
[9] Ibid., p. 4.
[10] Ibid.
[11] See the paper prepared by the Anti-Debt Coaliation (Koalisi Anti Utang), 'The Berkeley Mafia: The Failure of Indonesia to Become a Leading Country in Asia', 6 June 2006.
[12] See two papers produced by Tim Indonesia Bangkit: 'The Indonesian Economy in 2006: The Delayed Renewal', 26 January 2006, p. 3; 'Slow Economic Recovery and Widening Inequality', 18 May 2006.

The Role of Foreign Capital in the South Korean Financial Crisis and Recovery

Doowon Lee

Introduction

It has been ten years since the outbreak of the South Korean financial crisis in 1997. To many observers inside and outside the Republic of South Korea, it was a surprise to see South Korea become the victim of the contagion effect of financial crisis in other Southeast Asian economies. However, what was even more surprising was the subsequent rapid pace of recovery out of the crisis. In the process of this recovery, the South Korean economy has undergone painful structural reforms in four major areas: the corporate sector, the financial sector, the government sector and the labour sector. As a result of these reforms, the South Korean economy has transformed into a very different economy as of 2007. Much of this transformation has produced positive results, although there are some adverse effects as well.

The main focus of this paper is on the role played by foreign capital in the outbreak and in the aftermath of the crisis. During the crisis, many observers blamed foreign capital for the sudden outflow from the South Korean capital market, and criticized the capital account liberalization that was associated with the government's decision to join the OECD (Organization for Economic Cooperation and Development) in 1996. This paper examines this criticism based on the existing literature and available data. There are also contrasting views with regard to the role of foreign capital in the aftermath of the crisis. Some argue that inflow of foreign capital has produced positive effects such as improved transparency and profitability, while others feel that the inflow of foreign capital has had negative effects such as increased volatility in the capital market. This paper also examines these hypotheses. By examining the outbreak of and recovery from the financial crisis in South Korea, the paper aims to draw lessons and policy implications that may be useful to economic policy makers not only in South Korea, but also in other developing countries.

The Nature of the Financial Crisis and Recovery in South Korea
Outbreak of the Crisis

When Southeast Asian countries such as Thailand and Indonesia were hit by the financial crisis in mid-1997, not many people believed that South

Korea would be the next victim. The South Korean government had repeatedly pacified the market by claiming that the fundamentals of the country's economy were strong, and that the central bank had enough foreign exchange reserves to defend its exchange rate. However, the economy had shown several signs of internal problems since the early 1990s. After the economic boom of the late 1980s, the South Korean economy neglected much-needed structural adjustment. As a result, by the mid-1990s it was clear that South Korean firms were losing international competitiveness due to the so-called 'low-efficiency and high-cost' economic structure.[1] Despite these problems, South Korean firms, in particular the large conglomerates, continued to make large and ambitious investments by borrowing money from banks. This pattern of growth inevitably produced a mounting debt problem in the corporate sector, which resulted in a growing problem of non-performing loans (NPL) in the financial sector. Table 1 compares the debt–equity ratio of South Korean firms with those of other leading economies, and shows that the debt–equity ratio of the former was three to four times higher. It was clear that this high ratio of debt could not be sustained. Table 2 shows the share of non-performing loans in total loans made by commercial banks. Compared to its own past standards, it seemed that South Korea's bad loan problem in 1999 was not so serious as to be classified as a crisis. However, the international comparison shows that South Korean banks were heavily burdened with non-performing loans as compared to banks of the other leading economies.

What made the situation even worse was the external economic policy of the South Korean government. In 1996 the South Korean government had joined the OECD and partially liberalized the capital account. The inflow of foreign capital through this partially opened capital account had been rapidly absorbed by South Korean firms, which had an almost insatiable demand for

TABLE 1   *International Comparison of Debt–Equity Ratios of Manufacturing Industry*

South Korea 1997 -> 2004 -> 2006	Germany 1996	Japan 1999 -> 2003	Taiwan 1995	US 1999 -> 2004
3.96 -> 1.04 -> 0.99	0.98	1.74 -> 1.45	0.86	1.64 -> 1.41

Source: Krueger and Yoo (2001); *Bank of South Korea Information*, Bank of South Korea (June 2001, September 2005); *Principal Economic Indicators*, Bank of South Korea (May 2007).

TABLE 2   *International Comparison of NPL out of Total Loans* (per cent)

South Korea 1999	South Korea 2001	South Korea 2006	US* 2000	Japan* 2000	Germany** 1999	U.K.** 1999
12.90	3.41	0.84	1.21	5.44	1.3	2.17

Notes: * Average of ten biggest commercial banks' NPL.
    ** Average of five biggest commercial banks' NPL.
Source: Lee (2001, Table 11); South Korean data for 2001 and 2006 from Financial Supervisory Service (www.fss.or.kr).

CHART 1   *Causes of the Crisis*

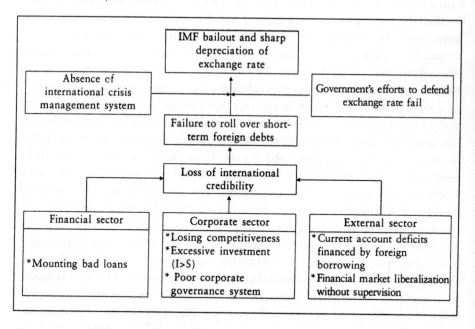

capital. Therefore, by the mid-1990s the South Korean economy was running chronic current account deficits, financed by the equivalent capital account surpluses.[2] Furthermore, the South Korean government maintained a *de facto* fixed exchange rate until the crisis broke. In order to maintain the existing exchange rate in the face of a large current account deficit, the South Korean government had to pour a substantial amount of its foreign exchange reserves into bolstering the value of its domestic currency in the first half of 1997. When the government realized that it did not have enough foreign exchange reserves to defend the exchange rate, there was no option but to ask for a rescue package from the IMF (International Monetary Fund). A more detailed analysis of the causes of the crisis can be found in Lee (2000, 2001), and is summarized in Chart 1.

Recovery from the Crisis

After the South Korean government received the emergency rescue package of $57 billion from the IMF and other leading economies,[3] it initiated major reforms in four areas under the guidance of the IMF: in the corporate sector, the financial sector, the labour sector and the government sector. Notwithstanding some debate, the general direction of the reforms was agreed upon by both the IMF and the South Korean government.

The first area of reform was the financial sector, which was heavily burdened with large non-performing loans. One of the first things the South Korean government did was to set up a fairly large public fund, and inject some of its resources into troubled banks in order to keep them solvent and prevent a bank run. Thanks to the sound fiscal position of the government, approximately

64 trillion *won* of public funds were hastily raised. In order to carry out the financial sector reforms more effectively, two powerful institutions – the Financial Supervisory Service (FSS) and the Financial Supervisory Commission (FSC) – were established by combining the existing three supervisory bodies of banks, insurance companies and security companies. At the same time, a painful restructuring job had to be carried out. Several troubled banks had to be either closed down or merged, and numerous non-bank financial institutions had to be closed, as shown in Table 3. In particular, virtually all the merchant banks, which had triggered the financial crisis, had to be closed. In the process of this painful restructuring effort, about one-third of the employees in the commercial banking sector were laid-off.

The second area of reform was the corporate sector. The corporate sector was responsible for the massive amount of NPLs, as it kept on borrowing from the financial sector to finance its excessive investment. In particular, many large conglomerates of South Korea continued with excessive and overlapping investment projects, in the belief that they were simply too big to die. As a result of this heavy borrowing, the average debt–equity ratio of South Korean listed firms in the manufacturing sector was approximately 400 per cent while the equivalent numbers for the leading economies were less than 150 per cent, as shown in Table 1. Therefore, one of the immediate concerns was to reduce this high debt–equity ratio to around 200 per cent. Even though there was a controversy over whether it would be appropriate to apply a uniform criterion of 200 per cent debt–equity ratio to every industry, the South Korean government insisted on applying it to every industry and virtually every firm. For many financially stressed South Korean firms, achieving a debt–equity ratio of 200 per cent in the middle of a severe credit crunch was a gruelling job. In the end, only eighteen conglomerates out of the thirty listed in 1997 could remain listed in the stockmarket

TABLE 3 *Number of Financial Institutions*

Financial Sector	End of 1997	March 2007	Change
Commercial Banks	26	13	−13
Specialized and Development Banks	7	5	−2
Merchant Banks	30	2	−28
Securities Firms*	36	54	+18
Insurance Companies	50	51	+1
Investment Companies	31	51	+20
Leasing Companies	25	35	+10
Mutual Savings & Finance Companies	231	110	−121
Credit Unions (Credit Cooperatives)	1,666	1,020	−646
Total	2,102	1,341	−761

Note: * The number of security firms increased due to the establishment of foreign-owned security firms. Also, some merchant banks were transformed into security firms.

Source: Lee (2001, Table 3); data for 2007 is from the Financial Supervisory Service of South Korea (www.fss.or.kr).

by 2001. Eventually, by 2000 the South Korean companies' average debt–equity ratio went down to the target rate of 200 per cent, and it was further lowered to less than 100 per cent in 2006. As the debt–equity ratio went down along with lower interest rates, the financial costs of South Korean firms declined rapidly, as indicated in Chart 2.

Not only did the debt–equity ratio change substantially, but so did the way firms financed their investment. Traditionally, South Korean firms used to rely heavily on external sources such as bank loans rather than internal sources such as retained earnings. However, after the crisis, they became more reliant on

CHART 2 *Financial Costs of Manufacturing Companies*

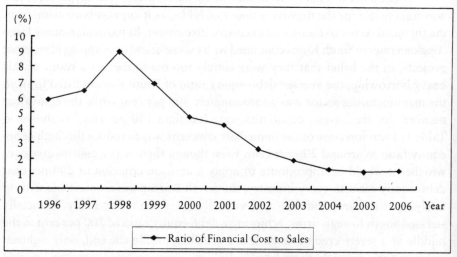

Source: Economic Statistics System, Bank of South Korea (http://ecos.bok.or.kr).

CHART 3 *Proportion of Direct Finance out of External Sources*

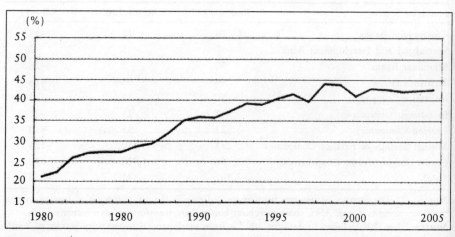

Source: Hahm, Joon-Ho (2007, Figure 2).

direct sources such as the issue of equities, bonds or corporate papers, as is evident from Chart 3.

Another important focus of reform in the corporate sector was to make the corporate governance system healthier and improve the accounting system to be more transparent. In order to achieve this, the protection of small shareholders' rights was enforced along with the introduction of external directors. Also, inter-national accounting standards were introduced in 1998, reinforcing the duties and liabilities of boards of directors.

The third area of reform was the labour market. The South Korean labour market enjoyed *de facto* full employment before the crisis, with a rate of unemployment lower than 3 per cent. However, the restructuring of the corporate and financial sectors made massive layoffs inevitable. To carry out such restruc-turing, one of the first actions of the government was to establish a 'tripartite commission' composed of representatives of labour, management and government. This commission was then encouraged to reach an agreement among these three players regarding the expediency of layoff. In the circumstances, the labour unions had no choice but to accept the agreement reached by the commission. As a result, the unemployment rate soared rapidly to reach 7 per cent in the first half of 1998 (Chart 4).

With the unemployment rate at 7 per cent, the government had to establish a social safety net system in a hurry. Unemployment benefits and the employment insurance system were expanded. Also, the government poured a large amount

CHART 4 *Unemployment Rate* (quarterly data, per cent)

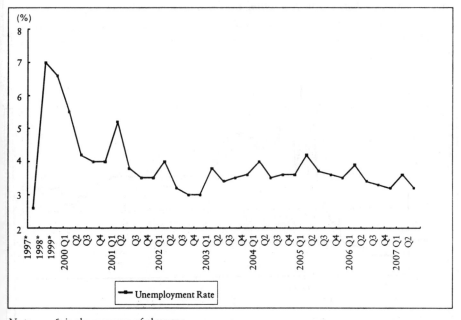

Note: * is the average of the year.
Source: Economic Statistics System, Bank of South Korea (http://ecos.bok.or.kr).

of money into a public works programme through which temporary jobs were created immediately after the crisis. Thanks to these efforts, the South Korean labour market became more flexible and the social safety net system improved. However, as has been analysed in Lee (2006), the labour market has become tight again after the recovery from the crisis.

The final area of reform was the government and the public sector. The goal of this reform was to achieve a small and efficient government sector through deregulation and privatization. In terms of deregulation, the South Korean government under President Dae-Jung Kim achieved noticeable results, as shown in Table 4. However, as with the reform effort in the labour market, there has been a slowdown after 2003. Similarly with regard to privatization: while several large state-owned enterprises such as POSCO, South Korea Telecom and South Korea Heavy Industries and Construction Company were privatized under President Dae-Jung Kim, no noticeable privatization has occurred since 2003.

The inflow of foreign exchange and the achievement of these four major reforms made the South Korean economy regain its international competitiveness

TABLE 4 *Number of Administrative Regulations*

Year	1998	1999	2000	2001	2002	2003	2004	2005	2006
Number	10,190	7,127	7,156	7,460	7,723	7,836	7,846	8,017	8,083

Source: Regulatory Reform Committee (http://www.rrc.go.kr/rrc/situation).

CHART 5 *Exchange Rate Fluctuation during the Crisis* (*won* per $)

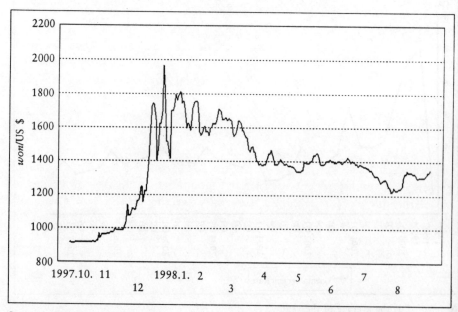

Source: Economic Statistics System, Bank of South Korea (http://ecos.bok.or.kr).

CHART 6 *Recovery from the Crisis*

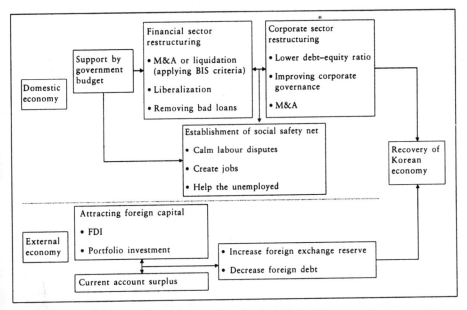

in a short period of time. As export earnings began to accumulate along with the inflow of foreign capital into the South Korean stockmarket, the exchange rate of the *won*, which peaked to almost 2,000 *won* per US $, was rapidly stabilized. (Chart 5).

Summarizing the reform efforts of the South Korean economy to overcome the crisis, it can be said that both internal and external factors played positive roles. Domestically, painful reforms removed excessive debt and NPLs from the corporate and financial sectors, which helped South Korean firms to regain their international competitiveness. Externally, the devalued exchange rate helped South Korean firms to increase their exports. Subsequently, the inflow of foreign capital into the South Korean capital market helped to stabilize the exchange rate. Chart 6 is a graphical summary of these reform and recovery processes.[4]

Role of Foreign Capital in the Outbreak of the Crisis

As is now well known, the South Korean economy was suffering from a substantial current account deficit in the mid-1990s. In order to maintain a stable exchange rate under this chronic current account deficit, the country needed to rely on the inflow of foreign capital. Generally speaking, there are three channels for foreign capital inflow: FDI (foreign direct investment), portfolio investment into the securities market, and commercial loans by financial institutions. Before the crisis, South Korea had relied mostly on the last channel. Little effort was made to attract FDI before the crisis. As a result, FDI inflow was only a couple of billion US dollars annually (Table 5), which was not sufficient to finance the current account deficit.

Therefore, South Korea had to rely on two alternative ways to finance

TABLE 5   *Inward FDI and Current Account Balance* ($ million)

	1994	1995	1996	1997
Invested FDI[1]	809.0	1,775.8	2,325.4	2,844.2
Reported FDI[2]	1,317	1,947	3,203	6,971
Current Account Balance[1]	−4,024.2	−8,665.1	−23,120.2	−8,287.4

Source: [1] Economic Statistics system, Bank of South Korea (http://ecos.bok.or.kr).
[2] Ministry of Commerce, Industry and Energy (http://www.mocie.go.kr).

its current account deficit: it had to either rely on inflow of foreign capital into the South Korean stockmarket or commercial loans. When these two channels dried up, it was clear that South Korea could not sustain its current account deficit and service its international debt. Therefore, we need to examine which of these two sources of foreign capital caused problems in 1997.

The first culprit could have been the foreign capital inflow into the stockmarket. Based on the experience of the Mexican crisis of 1994 and the Southeast Asian crisis of 1997, many people initially suspected that the sudden outflow of foreign capital from the South Korean stockmarket caused the problem. For example, in the case of Mexico, net financial inflows into Mexico amounted to about 8 per cent of Mexican GDP during 1992 and 1993, which was almost equivalent to Mexico's current account deficit during the same period. When this inflow of foreign capital dried up, the Mexican government had no other choice but to devalue its currency and ask for an IMF-led bail-out in 1994.[5] However, a closer look at the South Korean stockmarket tells a different story. Even though there was a certain degree of capital outflow from the South Korean securities market, it was not sufficiently large to cause the crisis. As shown in Chart 7, only $2 billion worth of foreign capital was withdrawn between August and November 1997. Furthermore, this trend of capital drain was soon reversed to a net inflow of capital after December 1997. This implies that the main factor that triggered the financial crisis was not the sudden outflow of short-term speculative money invested in the South Korean stockmarket.

Not only was the net outflow of foreign capital from the stockmarket negligible, but the relative weight of foreign shareholders in the stockmarket was not significant enough to cause major fluctuations. When the South Korean stockmarket was partially opened to foreign investors in 1992, the government had imposed many restrictions on the share ownership of foreign investors. For example, their total share could not exceed 10 per cent of a listed company in 1992. Even though this upper limit of foreign share ownership increased gradually, it was still limited to 20 per cent in 1996.[6] As a result of these restrictive measures, the relative importance of foreign shareholders in the South Korean stockmarket before the crisis remained small, if not negligible, as shown in Table 6.

This means that it must have been the withdrawal of commercial loans that triggered the crisis in 1997. In particular, the sudden withdrawal of loans by Japanese banks was the main reason. By the mid-1990s, many Japanese banks

CHART 7 *Flow of Foreign Portfolio Investment into the South Korean Stockmarket*

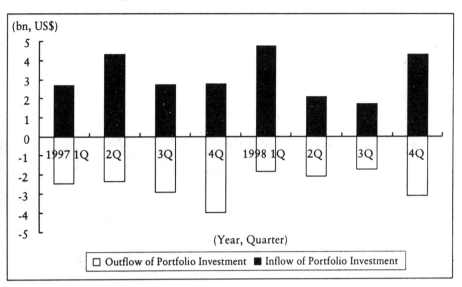

Source: Economic Statistics System, Bank of South Korea (http://ecos.bok.or.kr).

TABLE 6 *Stock Shareholding of Foreigners* (number of shares)

Unit/year	1992	1993	1994	1995	1996	1997	1998
thousand shares	220,634	500,083	634,855	762,311	989,201	816,107	1,181,311
%		4.13	8.74	9.11	10.12	11.58	9.11	10.39

Source: Securities Statistics Yearbook 2002, South Korea Exchange (http://krx.co.kr).

were suffering from insolvency problems because of Japan's long domestic recession. When the Thai and Indonesian currencies collapsed, in particular, a large number of loans made by Japanese banks to these regions became non-performing loans (NPLs). Therefore, when the loans made to South Korean financial institutions matured, the Japanese banks refused to roll them over and began to collect the matured loans from South Korean firms in order to meet the capital adequacy norm of 8 per cent. As emerged during the hearings of the South Korean National Assembly, Japanese banks had collected $12 billion from South Korea in 1997.[7] Chart 8 shows this graphically. There was a sudden decrease in commercial banks' liabilities from the second half of 1997, which implies that South Korean banks had to repay their loans in massive volume to foreign creditors in this period.

From this analysis, we can say that it was the mismanagement of foreign loans that triggered the South Korean financial crisis in 1997. As argued in Lee (2000), there were two kinds of mismanagement. First, there was a mismatch of maturity, as South Korean financial institutions borrowed short-term foreign loans and lent long-term to South Korean firms. Second, there was a miscalculation of

CHART 8 *Composition of Foreign Liabilities*

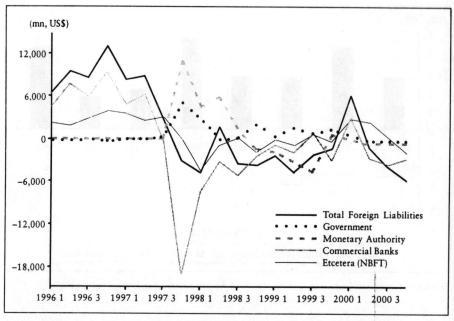

Source: *Economic Statistics System,* Bank of South Korea (http://ecos.bok.or.kr).

the amount of usable foreign exchange reserves. Even though the official foreign exchange reserves of the Bank of Korea exceeded $30 billion, the usable foreign exchange reserves were far short of this official amount. In this respect, the immediate cause of the South Korean financial crisis was different from that of the Mexican and Southeast Asian crises.

So the mismanagement of foreign loans by South Korean financial institutions, the lack of proper supervision by the government and the contagion effect of financial crisis were the main culprits behind the South Korean crisis. In particular, the massive losses of Japanese banks in the other Southeast Asian financial markets had a fatal negative contagion effect on South Korea. This kind of contagion effect has been analysed by Calvo and Mendoza (2000), and Nilsen and Rovelli (2001), who have shown that in the globally integrated financial market, it is possible to cause a bank run-style financial crisis in one country through the contagion effect from other countries. However, not every country in East Asia was inflicted by such contagion. Although most economies in East Asia suffered from economic fluctuations in the late 1990s, not all of them fell into a crisis.

Many analysts have also claimed that the hasty and unprepared entry into the OECD in 1996 was responsible for the sudden inflow of foreign capital into South Korea, which eventually resulted in the crisis. However, when we examine the situation of South Korea's capital account in the mid-1990s, this claim is hard to accept. In fact, it was the five-year blueprint for the reform of the foreign exchange system issued by the South Korean government in 1994 that had allowed the inflow of short-term foreign capital; so the capital account was already open to foreign capital to a large degree even before 1996. Furthermore, even when South Korea joined the OECD in 1996, the government did not fully open its capital account to foreigners. In the negotiation process before joining, South Korea had secured a substantial number of capital controls. Out of the 91 counts of capital liberalization measures, South Korea had liberalized only 50 counts in 1996. This implies that joining the OECD in 1996 was in fact not as hasty or unprepared as many suspected.

Furthermore, it is not quite true that international institutions such as the IMF had pressed the South Korean government to fully liberalize its capital account in 1996. The attitude and approach of the IMF with regard to capital account liberalization is well summarized in Chapter 5 of IMF (2005). In principle, the IMF advocated capital account liberalization as it could benefit the developing countries by providing greater access to the international capital market. Since the mid-1990s, however, the IMF has paid more attention to the potential risks of capital flow volatility, and some economists had apparently begun to appreciate the effectiveness of capital control policies in Chile. However, this concern was not formally addressed in the IMF's policy advice to individual countries with regard to capital account liberalization. The IMF now agrees that it was only after the East Asian crisis that its approach changed to a more cautious approach to capital account liberalization, emphasizing the pace and sequence of liberalization policies. It now admits that until the late 1990s it had encouraged premature capital account liberalization in some countries without fully emphasizing the potential risks of capital flow volatility. Based on this analysis, it is difficult to claim that South Korea joining the OECD in 1996 and the subsequent measures of capital account liberalization were responsible for the 1997 crisis. Rather, as argued above, it was essentially the mismanagement of foreign liabilities by South Korean financial institutions in the mid-1990s that was responsible for the outbreak of the crisis.[8]

Role of Foreign Capital in Post-Crisis Recovery

The South Korean economy recovered from the trough of the crisis much faster than expected. With just three quarters' experience of negative growth rate, from the fourth quarter of 1997 to the second quarter of 1998, the South Korean economy rebounded strongly from the fourth quarter of 1998. As has already been mentioned, there are many internal and external factors behind this strong recovery. We now focus on the role of foreign capital in the recovery process.

Positive Effects

The first and most important role foreign capital played in the early stage of recovery was the injection of much-needed foreign exchange liquidity into South Korea. Immediately after the crisis, there were two major sources from which South Korea built up its depleted foreign exchange reserves: the current account surplus and the capital account surplus. With the substantial depreciation of the *won*, South Korean export industries regained international price competitiveness, while the sharp recession in 1998 slashed South Korea's demand for foreign imports. As a result, South Korea's current account surplus soared from 1998 and this continues into the present. However, our main focus here is on the inflow of foreign capital into South Korea's capital account. As noted above, foreign capital inflows can be in the form of FDI, portfolio investment into the stockmarket and foreign loans. With regard to the flow of foreign loans, South Korea reversed the pattern from inflow to outflow as it began to repay loans from 1998. Also, there was some success in attracting FDI until the early 2000s. However, as is shown in Chart 9, the major inflow of foreign capital was through the stockmarket. Immediately after the crisis, the upper limit of foreign share ownership was removed and foreigners were allowed to own up to 100 per cent of any listed company. In every year since 1999, the inflow of foreign capital into the South Korean stockmarket exceeded $ 50 billion, and it reached approximately $ 240 billion in 2006. Even though there was a substantial outflow of portfolio investment, the net inflow into the stockmarket remained positive for most of the years after 1998, as is evident from Chart 9. The inflow of foreign currency through current and capital accounts helped the South Korean central bank to rebuild its foreign exchange reserves rapidly, and by July 2007 South Korea had the fifth largest foreign exchange reserves in the world, at $ 254.8 billion.[9]

The massive inflow of foreign capital played a positive role in stabilizing

CHART 9   *Net Inflow of Foreign Capital*

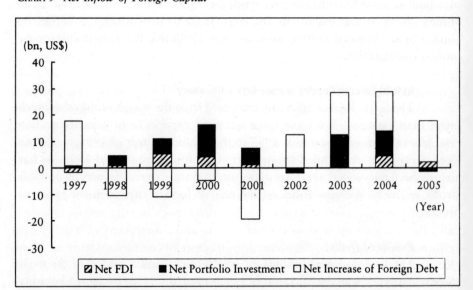

Source: Economic Statistics System, Bank of South Korea (http://ecos.bok.or.kr).

CHART 10   *Exchange Rate Movement after the Crisis (won/$)*

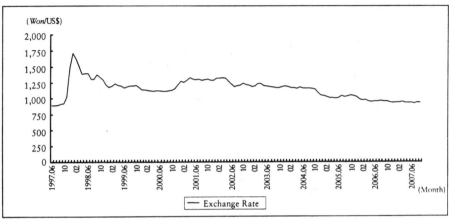

Source: Bank of South Korea (http://ecos.bok.or.kr).

the exchange rate. As is shown in Chart 10, South Korea succeeded in stabilizing the exchange rate within two to three years after the crisis. In fact, the continuous inflow of foreign currencies because of surpluses on capital and current accounts since the crisis caused the exchange rate to appreciate to pre-crisis levels by 2007.[10] With abundant accumulation of foreign exchange reserves, the government was able to pay back the IMF loan ahead of schedule and officially declare the end of the crisis.

Second, the inflow of foreign capital greatly altered the structure of the corporate governance system in South Korea. Foreign shareholders pressed the existing managers of South Korean companies to improve their transparency and accounting structures, and to strengthen the rights of small shareholders (as has been stressed in Suh 2006 and Wang 2007). These measures improved the external image of South Korean companies and helped to remove the so-called 'South Korea discount' phenomenon in the stockmarket.[11] As shown in Chart 11, the presence of foreign shareholders peaked in 2004 when shares held by them exceeded 40 per cent of the total market capital. The inflow of foreign capital also contributed substantially to the increasing market capitalization of the South Korean stockmarket, as is indicated in Chart 12. Although there was concern initially that the presence of foreign shareholders would overwhelm the South Korean stockmarket, this concern has faded since 2005 as local investors have started to invest more in the stockmarket.

Third, the presence of foreign capital in the South Korean financial system, especially in the banking system, has improved not only the transparency but also the profitability of banks. After painful and comprehensive restructuring efforts in banking sector, the ownership structure of commercial banks in South Korea has greatly changed. Some banks such as South Korea First Bank and South Korea Exchange Bank were sold to foreign capital, while other banks such as Hana Bank[12] and Kookmin Bank were owned both by domestic and foreign

CHART 11   *Ownership Proportions in the South Korean Stockmarket* (per cent)

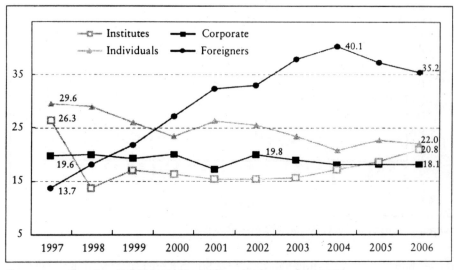

Source: *Securities and Futures,* South Korea Exchange, May 2007.

CHART 12   *The Size of the South Korean Stockmarket after the Crisis*

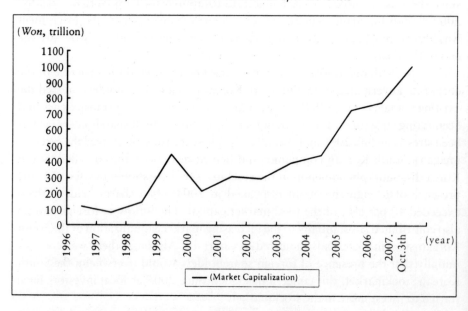

capital. The former banks are classified as foreign banks and the latter as compounded banks. The rest of the commercial banks are classified as domestic
banks where there are no major foreign shareholders. Even though there are
some differences in terms of their performance, the financial performance of all
three kinds of banks improved greatly after the crisis. The figures in Chart 13
summarize the performance of commercial banks in South Korea in terms of BIS

CHART 13a   *Performance of Commercial Banks after the Crisis: BIS Ratio*

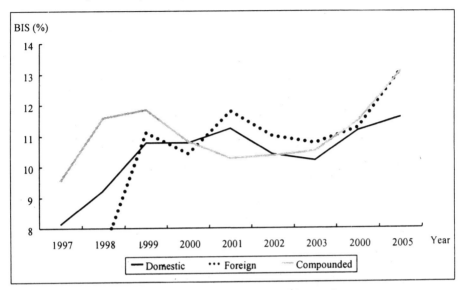

Notes: Foreign bank is a bank whose largest shareholder is a foreigner.
Compounded bank is a bank whose largest shareholder is not a foreigner, but there exists a foreign shareholder who owns more than 5 per cent of the total share.

Source: Bank Management Statistics of Financial Supervisory Service, South Korea (www.fss. or.kr).

CHART 13b   *Performance of Commercial Banks after the Crisis: ROE Ratio*

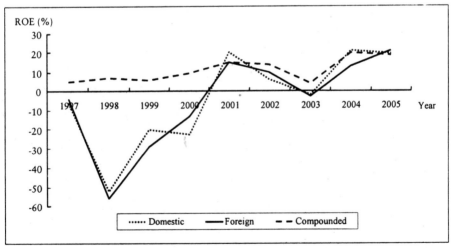

Source: Bank Management Statistics of Financial Supervisory Service, South Korea (www.fss. or.kr).

CHART 13c   *Performance of Commercial Banks after the Crisis: ROA Ratio*

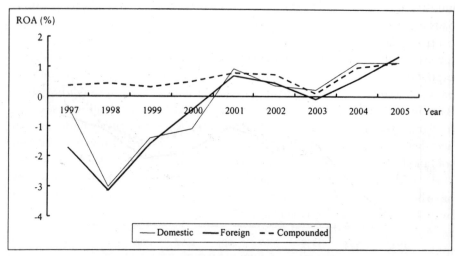

Source: Bank Management Statistics of Financial Supervisory Service, South Korea
             (www.fss. or.kr).

ratio, ROE (return on equity) and ROA (return on assets). The performance of
these three kinds of commercial banks has been synchronized since 2001.

Not only did the profitability of the financial sector improve after the
crisis, but also the size of South Korean financial institutions increased rapidly.
This was mostly due to an aggressive process of mergers and acquisitions, which
was inevitable in the wake of the massive restructuring of the financial sector.
The number of financial institutions reduced by 35 per cent, as shown in Table 3.
Although it is difficult to measure numerically, it is likely that the inflow of
foreign capital with advanced know-how played a major role in this.

Adverse Effects

One of the most frequently criticized and controversial negative effects
of foreign capital is the short-term speculative nature of investment. In South
Korea, there are several such cases that have drawn public attention. Most notably,
several foreign PEFs (private equity funds) took over South Korean financial and
real estate assets at discounted prices after the crisis, and sold them at higher
prices with windfall profits.[13] In each case, the foreign PEF purchased a troubled
South Korean bank from the South Korean government and sold it with hefty
capital gains within four or five years. The possibility of acquiring such a large
profit within a short period of time without paying any capital gains tax has led
several observers to criticize the transactions of these PEFs as speculative.

Even though these transactions seem legal on the surface, they have
created some controversy. First, there is concern about whether they used any
inside information when they purchased South Korean banks in the first place.
Also, there is concern as to whether the transfer of ownership from the South

Korean government to PEFs has impaired the public good nature of the banking industry and its ability to meet broader social functions. Whether the transactions of foreign PEFs were in the nature of speculation or investment is still very controversial and hard to verify, since the large capital gain can be justified as a reward for the risky investment made by a PEF. It is also true that not all foreign capital made such a huge gain in the financial market. For example, Commerzbank, a German commercial bank, purchased shares of South Korea Exchange Bank in 1998 immediately after the crisis. In fact Commerzbank was the first foreign financial institution to invest in the South Korean financial market, which was then perceived as too risky by other foreign investors. However, in 2003 it sold its shares to Lone Star at a lowered price and suffered considerable losses.

The second major criticism levelled against foreign banks is that they have been responsible for depressing the investment spirit of South Korean firms by demanding very high dividend payments and posing threats of hostile takeover. Several instances of this can be cited. For example, after Soros' Quantum Fund took over the then-troubled Seoul Security Company in 1999, it surprised many people by paying a very high dividend, equivalent to 60 per cent of the book value of a share in 2002. In the extreme case, some companies had to pay dividends that were even higher than the net profit. In 2003, when SK Co. Ltd. was under the threat of a hostile M&A from Sovereign Fund, it had to pay a dividend as much as six times higher than its net profit to appease its shareholders. Also in 2003, when Hermes Fund, a UK PEF, became the third largest shareholder of Samsung Co. Ltd., it spread rumours of a hostile M&A against Samsung, which

CHART 14   *Falling Potential Growth Rate*

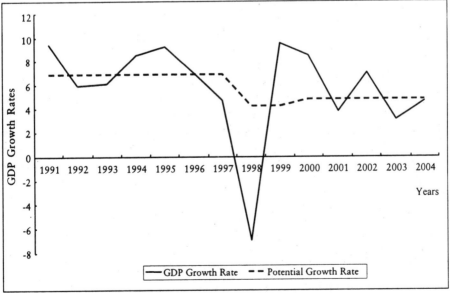

Source: Economic Statistics System, Bank of South Korea (http://ecos.bok.or.kr).

forced the company to purchase its own stocks to defend its corporate governance. Eventually, Hermes Fund sold its shares at higher prices and exited the market with a huge capital gain. It has been argued that a series of such incidents caused by foreign capital depressed the investment spirit of South Korean firms as they (especially the large firms) had to pay more attention and money to defend their corporate control than to set up a long-term investment plan. As a result of this negative impact, foreign capital has been blamed for being responsible for depressing the growth potential of the South Korean economy. Chart 14 shows how the growth potential of the South Korean economy deteriorated after the crisis, mainly because of the falling investment ratio.

However, all this has also had a positive effect. In order to defend their corporate control against the threat of hostile takeovers, South Korean firms have improved their governance structure and taken better care of small shareholders. As a result, SK Co. Ltd., which was the victim of a hostile takeover, won 'The Excellent Company Prize' in the 2007 Corporate Governance Service South Korea awards. Also, there is a possibility that the negative implications of hostile M&A for investment have been exaggerated. Youn and Choi (2007, in South Korean), for instance, conclude that the negative impact is exaggerated. They suggest that there is little evidence to show that foreign capital has increased stockmarket disturbance, as foreign investors seldom follow 'herd behaviour'. Also, to the surprise of many, they conclude that the existence of foreign capital has not increased the propensity to pay dividends. Rather, foreign capital has increased both profit and dividends, thereby leaving the propensity to pay dividends largely unchanged, and that the increase of foreign capital in the South Korean stockmarket has had little influence on the investment ratio. In general, Youn and Choi reject many of the hypotheses related to foreign investors after rigorous empirical tests, mainly because of the fact that foreign investors are not homogeneous and it is therefore meaningless to distinguish them from domestic investors.

Lastly, foreign banks have been criticized for focusing too much on household loans without providing sufficient amounts of corporate loans, thereby making them responsible for the deteriorating investment potential of South Korean firms. However, domestically owned banks have shown similar behaviour after the crisis. As shown in Chart 15, the proportion of household loans out of total loans made by commercial banks increased rapidly after the crisis. The rapid rise of household loans was also fuelled by the government policy of easy credit in 1999 and 2000.

This combination of commercial banks' attempts to increase household loans and the government policy of easy credit increased the ratio of household debt to GDP. Chart 16 shows that the household debt ratio increased rapidly until 2002, when the easy credit policy was finally reined in. The increased debt ratio of households in turn was the major reason for depressed domestic consumption in recent years, which hampered the full recovery of the business cycle.

CHART 15   *Proportion of Corporate Loans and Household Loans in Commercial Bank Credit*

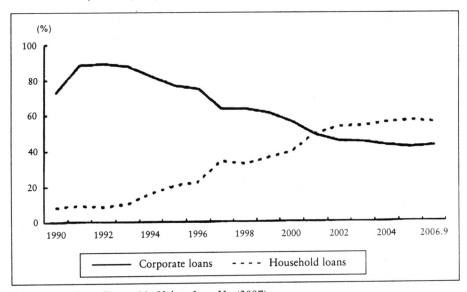

Source: From Figure 6 in Hahm, Joon-Ho (2007).

CHART 16   *Household Debt and Credit* (per cent of GDP)

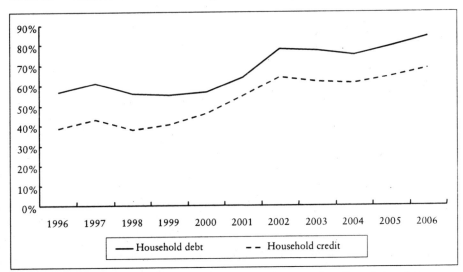

Source: Economic Statistics System, Bank of South Korea (http://ecos.bok.or.kr).

Policy Implications and Concluding Remarks

There are several policy implications we can draw from the experiences of the South Korean financial crisis. One of the most critical lessons it teaches is that it is difficult to adhere to a fixed exchange rate system without proper measures to stabilize the exchange rate. Even though South Korea did not employ such a system before the crisis, its exchange rate mechanism was *de facto* a fixed exchange rate system. That is why the government tried to defend its exchange rate by pouring tens of billions of dollars into the foreign exchange market until the very last minute. This lesson can be applied to almost any country in East Asia and Latin America that has gone through a currency crisis. Another important lesson is that the fundamental elements of a national economy, such as sound fiscal policy and qualified human capital, matter greatly in the process of recovery from crisis. As has been outlined in this paper, it was the fiscal muscle of the South Korean government that enabled it to establish approximately 168 trillion *won* worth of public funds to carry out the financial and corporate sector restructuring effort. Also, the highly qualified human capital of South Korean firms enabled rapid improvement of exports once the exchange rate depreciated.

It has been pointed out by many observers that sequential liberalization of the capital market is necessary. In this respect, however, South Korea did not commit any serious mistake. In the case of South Korea, it was not the sequence of capital market liberalization but the lack of proper supervision after the liberalization that induced the crisis. This point is emphasized by Shin and Wang (2000). They mention several lessons that can be drawn from the South Korean financial crisis, such as proper supervision of banks, improved corporate governance and the importance of foreign direct investment. They argue that the sequencing problem of capital account liberalization in South Korea prior to the crisis was not the major reason for the crisis, as South Korea had liberalized mainly trade-related capital flows. Rather, structural deficiencies in the South Korean corporate and financial sectors were the major reason for the outbreak of the crisis.

With regard to the role of foreign capital, which is the main concern of this paper, the conclusion is not straightforward. There have been many misconceptions and exaggerations, but to sum up we may say that foreign capital can be a 'double-edged sword'. In some respects, it can help the development of a country by providing the necessary capital. However, it can also affect the possibility of stable growth when foreign capital withdraws suddenly from developing countries. Foreign capital can produce positive effects such as improving the corporate governance structure and enhancing transparency. However, it can also disturb the market by posing threats of hostile M&A. Therefore, it is necessary to sequence capital liberalization policies as well as to distinguish short-term speculative investors from long-term strategic investors.

Notes and References

[1] There were three areas where the South Korean economy was seen to suffer from high costs: high logistic costs, high labour costs and high interest payment costs.

[2] For example, the current account deficit in 1996 was $ 23 billion, which was 4.15 per cent of GDP. Cf. Economic Statistics System, Bank of South Korea (http://ecos.bok.or.kr).

[3] South Korea borrowed $ 35 billion from the IMF. Foreign financial institutions also rolled over their matured loans of $ 23 billion. Further, the South Korean government issued $ 4 billion worth of Foreign Exchange Stabilization Bonds. See 'Achievement and Tasks of 5 Years of IMF Program' (in Korean), Ministry of Finance and Economy (2002: 11); http://www.mofe.go.kr/.

[4] A more detailed description of crisis recovery can be found in Chopra, Kang, Karasulu, Liang, Ma and Richards (2001).

[5] Andrew B. Abel and Ben S. Bernanke, *Macroeconomics*, Addison Wesley Longman, Inc. (2001: 190).

[6] According to 'Chapter 2. Securities Trading by Foreigners' of Regulation on Supervision of Securities Business, the upper limit of foreign share ownership increased to 50 per cent in December 1997, and it was abolished in 1998. Cf. Financial Supervisory Service (http://fss.or.kr).

[7] In early 1999, the National Assembly of South Korea had a hearing in order to verify the causes of the economic crisis. For further details, see *Sisa Journal* (18–25 February 1999).

[8] This is similar to the analysis of Kwon (1996, in Korean) and Wang (2007, in Korean), both of whom acknowledge the South Korean government's effort to liberalize its capital market in a cautious manner in the mid-1990s, but conclude that both the South Korean government and the South Korean financial institutions failed to impose proper supervision once the capital market was liberalized.

[9] As of July 2007, China has the largest foreign exchange reserve with $ 1,034 billion, followed by Japan ($ 923.7 billion), Russia ($ 416.2 billion) and Taiwan ($ 280.6 billion). See Data Template on International Reserves and Foreign Currency Liquidity, Data and Statistics, IMF, at http://www.imf.org, and Rank Order Reserves of Foreign Exchange and Gold, CIA World Factbook, at http://www.cia.gov.

[10] The South Korean *won* per US dollar exchange rate was 913.5 on 2 October 1997, before the crisis. During the crisis, it plummeted to 1,964.80, on 24 December 1997. However, after continuous appreciation from early 1998, it stood at 913.7 on 1 October 2007.

[11] Share prices of South Korean companies suffered from low evaluation, which was reflected in the PER (price earnings ratio), due to geopolitical factors such as the North–South Korean nuclear issue and lack of transparency.

[12] Hana Bank was classified as a compounded bank until the third quarter of 2005 when Allianz held more than 5 per cent of its shares. However, since the establishment of Hana Financial Group in the fourth quarter of 2005, it has been classified as a domestic bank.

[13] They were New Bridge Capital, Lone Star and the Carlyle Group; and their victims were South Korea First Bank, South Korea Exchange Bank and Hanmi Bank, respectively.

References

Calvo, Guillermo A. and Enrique G. Mendoza (2000), 'Rational Contagion and the Globalization of Securities Markets', *Journal of International Economics*, 51.

Chopra, Ajai, Kenneth Kang, Meral Karasulu, Hong Liang, Henry Ma and Anthony Richards (2001), 'From Crisis to Recovery in South Korea: Strategy, Achievements, and Lessons', IMF Working Paper No. 01/154.

Hahm, Joon-Ho (2007), 'Changes and Evaluation of the Financial System' (in South Korean), paper presented at the seminar on 'A Decade after Financial Crisis: Process and Problems', South Korea Economic Association.

IMF (International Monetary Fund) (2005), *The IMF's Approach to Capital Account Liberalization* (Washington: IMF).

Kwon, Jae Joong (1996), 'Capital Mobility and Non-Current Account Transaction' (in South Korean)', in *Sectoral Evaluation and Expectations for South Korea's Entry to the OECD*, KIEP (South Korea Institute for International Economic Policy).

Krueger, Anne O. and Jungho Yoo (2001), 'Falling Profitability, Higher Borrowing Costs, and Chaebol Finances during the South South Korean Crisis', paper presented at the IMF–KIEP conference on 'The South Korean Crisis and Recovery', Seoul, South Korea.

Lee, Doowon (2000), 'South Korea's Financial Crisis and Economic Restructuring', in *South Korea Briefing 1997–1999: Challenges and Change at the Turn of the Century*, edited by Kongdan Oh (New York: M.E. Sharpe in cooperation with Asia Society).

—— (2001), 'The Economic Reform and Its Aftermath in South Korea', *Global Economic Review*, Vol. 30, No. 4.

—— (2006), 'The South Korean Economy in Transition: In Search of a New Model', *Global Economic Review*, Vol. 35, No. 2.

Nilsen, Jeffrey H. and Riccardo Rovelli (2001), 'Investor Risk Aversion and Financial Fragility in Emerging Economies', *Journal of International Financial Markets, Institutions and Money*, Vol. 11, Nos. 3/4.

Shin, Inseok and Yunjong Wang (2000), 'How to Sequence Capital Market Liberalization: Lessons from the South Korean Experience' (KDI).

Suh, Sangwon (2006), 'The Influence of Foreigners' Stock Investment on South Korean Stock Prices and Its Implications' (in South Korean), *Economic Papers*, Vol. 12, No. 1, (Institute for Monetary and Economic Research, Bank of South Korea).

Wang, Yunjong (2007), 'Structural Transformation of the South Korean Economy: Focused on External Sector' (in South Korean), paper presented at seminar on 'A Decade after Financial Crisis: Process and Problems', South Korea Economic Association.

Youn, Taehoon and Yong-Seok Choi (2007), 'Hostile M&As in South Korea after the Financial Crisis', in *Institutional and Policy Reforms to Enhance Corporate Efficiency in South Korea* (South Korea Development Institute).

The End of Developmental Citizenship?

Economic Restructuring and Social Displacement in Post-Crisis South Korea

Chang Kyung-Sup

Introduction

A decade after it occurred, what South Koreans call 'the IMF crisis' has transformed the South Korean economy and society in an irreversible direction. Although the economy has been seemingly resuscitated in a way that is as impressive as the earlier industrial build-up, most South Koreans express increasing fatigue and hopelessness about their socio-economic status.

During the three pre-crisis decades, South Koreans at the grassroots had been enfranchised by successive developmentalist governments to attain what I propose to call *developmental citizenship*. In that period, the South Korean developmental state managed to industrialize and expand the national economy at a pace that could incorporate almost all economically motivated individuals through increasing jobs and better incomes – but not through the comprehensive social security benefits that, in European welfare states, constitute 'social citizenship' in T.H. Marshall's (1964) explanation. South Koreans responded to this dynamic economic process by fully mobilizing private material and human resources as economic investment.

The economic crisis of 1997 and its emergency rescue measures – in large part coerced by the International Monetary Fund (IMF) – dealt a fatal blow to this state–grassroots interactive developmentalism. As clearly shown in formal statistics, labour-shedding was the most crucial measure adopted for rescuing South Korean firms, many of which were on the verge of bankruptcy. Even after the worst was over, most major firms continued to undertake organizational and technological restructuring in an employment-minimizing manner, and thereby got reborn as globally competitive leading exporters.

The sustained economic growth in the new century, buttressed by phenomenal increases of exports by a handful of major *chaebol*[1] firms, has not been accompanied by meaningful improvements in grassroots employment and livelihood. Instead, temporary and underpaid jobs have become normal, and on-the-job poverty has increased sharply. Income inequality has expanded continuously, and even those under the conservatively set official poverty line have drastically increased in numbers and proportions.

Such social polarization may now worry major South Korean firms far less than before because they are not as dependent now upon domestic labour supplies and because their ownership, if not their management, has been internationalized at appalling speed. Foreign corporate shareholders could not wish for more at a time when South Korea's economic growth is accounted for mostly by rapidly rising corporate income (as opposed to stagnant labour income).

The two arguably progressive governments under Kim Dae-Jung and Roh Moo-Hyun, respectively, have tried to come to the rescue of grassroots South Koreans by implementing and strengthening various elements of the so-called social safety net. However, even after increasing social expenditure for several years, South Korea's public budget for social security, not to mention its social services, is far behind that of serious social policy states in the west. Income transfers through public welfare programmes seem to have only marginal effects on reducing inequality and poverty.

South Korea's organized labour, despite its international reputation for militant activism, has been surprisingly incompetent in resisting and redressing this proletarian crisis. Their expressed willingness to cooperate with the government and business on the eve of the impending national economic crisis was only abused by the latter as a convenient pretext for unrestrained neoliberalization of labour markets involving unrestrained layoffs and proliferating severely underpaid transitory employment. By contrast, corporate and governmental pledges for workers' stable employment and livelihood, as well as for their own structural reforms, have remained as permanent rain-checks. Paradoxically, the rapid segmentation of labour markets between surviving regular employees in large *chaebol* and public corporations (who constitute the core of union membership) and underpaid temporary workers (who constitute an overwhelming majority of new employment) now fatally threatens the social sustainability of organized labour causes.

Developmental Citizenship vs. Social Citizenship

The economic and social calamities accompanying the national financial collapse of 1997 paradoxically made South Koreans realize what kinds of social entitlements had been ensured for them during the previous few decades under successive developmentalist governments. Apparently, such entitlements were not social security measures that could have been used to stabilize living conditions in a volatile situation like the 1997 crisis. Whatever the social programmes of the state, they failed to alleviate in any meaningful way the material difficulties of grassroots South Koreans caused by sudden and massive unemployment under widespread corporate bankruptcies. What came as a totally alien experience to most South Koreans was their sudden and irreparable exclusion from work. For almost three decades, almost all willing adults not only had been employed, but also used to work more hours each week than most other working populations in the world. All of a sudden, their willingness to work was no longer respected by the economy or the state.

South Koreans' entitlement to work had been a core element of the develop-

TABLE 1   *Size and Sectoral Composition of Employment, and Unemployment Rate, 1963–97*

	Total no. of employed persons (1000)	By sector (%)			Unemployment rate (%)
		Agriculture/ fishery	Manufacture/ mining	Service	
1963	7563	63.0	8.7	28.3	8.1
1970	9617	50.4	14.3	35.3	4.4
1980	13683	34.0	22.5	43.5	5.2
1990	18085	17.9	27.6	54.4	2.4
1997	21048	11.0	21.4	67.6	2.6

Source: NSO, *Fifth Year's Economic and Social Change seen through Statistics*, 1988, p. 97.

mentalist rule of Park Chung-Hee and his political successors (Chang 2002), but it had not been legally codified as a political responsibility of the state. This reflected a fundamental difference of the capitalist developmental state from the socialist state, whose political constituencies (that is, the proletarian population) have a citizenship right to work. Nevertheless, the constant provision of abundant jobs and business opportunities through sustained economic growth was an undeclared responsibility of the South Korean developmental state, which had only a flimsy legitimacy in historical origin and recurrently turned to authoritarian measures for political control.

As shown in Table 1, the authoritarian developmental state may well have taken pride in guaranteeing its political constituencies a *de facto* entitlement to work ever since the onset of industrialization – a sort of 'developmental citizenship', as opposed to what T.H. Marshall (1964) dubs 'social citizenship' in European welfare states. The unemployment rate in South Korea drastically fell from 8.1 per cent to 2.6 per cent during the 1963–97 period, whereas the total size of employment nearly tripled simultaneously. Most of the new jobs were of course created in the manufacturing and service industries, so that the proportion of the rural population precipitously declined. At least on the economic front, one of the most rapid urbanizations in human history coupled with an explosive population growth ensuing from the post-Korean War baby boom was successfully managed by a political regime of single-minded developmentalism.

Although South Koreans – middle-class citizens in particular – never stopped politically challenging the historical illegitimacy and undemocratic governance of the military-led state, they nonetheless positively responded to the developmental initiative of the regime. They did not criticize the developmentalist bias (that is, the social policy conservatism) of the state. They even allocated most of their own private material resources to 'individually developmental' causes, including savings, education, etc.[2] The undisputed dependence of the South Korean economic success on rich human capital and abundant savings, among various other factors, was crucially conditioned by ordinary citizens' active response to the developmentalist initiative of the state.

In almost every opinion poll on politics, South Koreans used to choose economic performance as the foremost responsibility of the government. They believed in the possibility that the government could determine the state of their economic life. In this context, the protracted governmental negligence over social welfare did not worry grassroots South Koreans. Ruled by a political regime *satisficing* with occasional political reminders of the necessity to preserve Confucian virtues of family support, South Korean citizens were equally conservative or audacious in their entrepreneurially biased lives. This kind of developmental politics and attitude turned out to be untenable by late 1997 as too many grassroots South Koreans found themselves without any meaningful public or private mechanisms for weathering the sudden economic crisis. Developmental citizenship could not replace social citizenship permanently.

Financial Crisis Resolved through Proletarian Crisis: Neoliberal Developmental Statism as Remedy

As the Asian financial crisis enveloped South Korea against all predictions to the contrary, the developmental nature of the South Korean state became unevenly distributed between the grassroots and business (*chaebol*). Saving the economy was considered tantamount to saving industrial and financial enterprises. And, as shown in Table 2, many industrial and financial enterprises were rescued by dumping their employees under the IMF-demanded consent of the newly sworn-in government of Kim Dae-Jung. Even South Korea's powerfully organized unions had to compromise on this asymmetrical arrangement (see Appendix). The vague hope for re-enfranchising masses of discharged workers after the recovery failed to materialize even after the national economy returned to a stable growth path.

I have elsewhere documented the economic miseries and desperate social responses of grassroots South Koreans in the immediate wake of the economic crisis (Chang 2002). Unfortunately, as shown later in this paper, such miseries and desperation have not disappeared, but have become very much normal aspects of life in the new century. From middle-aged South Koreans who have unsuccessfully struggled to recover their pre-crisis employment status to young South Koreans who have been denied regular (that is, non-temporary) employment opportunities from the beginning of their career, the South Korean state is clearly an anti-proletarian, neoliberal defector.

TABLE 2 *Corporate Management Performance in the First Half of 1997 and 1998* (n=2,328)

Performance item	1997	1998
Total sales increase rate	9.1	5.0
Sales profit ratio	7.5	8.8
Total profit ratio	1.4	−0.4
Per worker sales increase rate	13.9	20.0
Per worker value-added increase rate	11.4	9.3
Per worker expense increase rate	8.3	−4.7
Worker expenses to sales ratio	12.0	9.4

Ironically, such neoliberal defection of the state in labour policy is very much an integral element of its reinstated developmentalism towards the export industry and finance. The Kim Dae-Jung government wanted to ensure the survival of most of South Korea's major export firms, which in turn required the survival of financial institutions whose near-defunct loans to these firms threatened such survival. Furthermore, the government realized that the un(der)developed industry of finance was a crucial pitfall of the South Korean economy and decided to aggressively promote its international competitiveness (mainly against would-be foreign rivals in the domestic financial market). Thereby a new developmental statist project was initiated in an industry whose underdevelopment was a paradoxical outcome of decades of developmental statism (Kong 2000). The so-called 'structural adjustments' of export firms and banks involved radical changes in labour relations (including, of course, massive layoffs), as well as organizational transitions in ownership and management.

As an ultimate public guarantee for this simultaneously neoliberal and developmental project, the government devised a scheme called *gongjeokjageum* (public funds).[3] Under this scheme, state funds would be poured into designated banks, firms and projects in pace with pre-targeted processes of structural adjustment, in most cases entailing massive layoffs under the rubric of 'flexible labour relations'. (Many will be reminded of South Korea in the 1970s when Park Chung-Hee's developmental state dealt with business and labour quite similarly.) In addition, the public funds helped to finance aggressive technological restructuring that enabled industries to radically streamline the current work force and minimize new demands for labour. Post-crisis industrial restructuring above all implied 'jobless economic development'.

Interestingly, but not surprisingly, the IMF and other major parties of global finance soon agreed to this ostensibly developmental initiative of the South Korean government. It was not surprising because large shares of major South Korean corporations and banks had already been sold off to foreign investors at IMF-set bargain sale terms (of plummeting nominal prices of stocks, skyrocketing exchange rates and shock-therapy interest rates). As major stakeholders of numerous South Korean manufacturers and banks, global financial institutions and investors began to develop an interestingly congenial perspective on the reinstated proactive industrial policy of the South Korean state which is financially buttressed by South Korean citizens' tax payments. For the same reason, they did not reserve praise for the neoliberal side of the government's policy that would ensure sustained increases in corporate profits vis-à-vis suppressed labour incomes.

Table 4 reveals how successful the developmental-cum-neoliberal policy in South Korea has been. It is nothing but startling that the spectacular growth of corporate incomes in the first few years of the new millennium had no positive impact whatsoever on workers' incomes. The post-crisis South Korean economy seems to have fundamentally disenfranchised the worker population, whether or not they actually work. If the rapidly increasing income gap between different classes of wage workers is taken into account, the figures in Table 4 indicate that

TABLE 3 Foreigners' Shareholding in Major South Korean Companies (2006 end)

Company	Share by the biggest holder (A)	Restriction on foreign ownership	Share by foreigners (B)	Difference (B–A)
Samsung Electronics	15.84		47.24	31.4
POSCO	4.74		59.34	54.6
KB	5.46		84.32	78.86
KE	53.89	40	75.48 (30.2)	–23.69
Shinhian Financial	9.06		60.96	51.9
Woori Financial	77.97		9.95	–68.02
SK Telecom	23.1	49	100.00 (49)	25.9
Hyundai Motors	26.11		41.86	15.75
Hynix	9.16		20.19	11.03
Hyundai Heavy Machinery	23.27		22.32	–0.95
LG Phillips	70.78		50.53	N/A
KT	7.99	49	97.40 (47.7)	39.71
SK	15.65		45.27	29.62
Hana Financial Holdings	9.62		80.64	71.02
Shinseqve	29.61		42.85	13.24
Lotte Shopping	68.88		21.83	–47.05
Korea Exchange Bank	64.62		80.37	N/A
LG Electronics	34.82		35.53	0.71
KT&G	10.33		54.08	43.75
Samsung Fire Insurance	18.44		53.77	35.33
Industrial Bank of Korea	57.69		21.04	–36.65
LG Card	22.93		1.39	–21.54
S-Oil	35.23		48.66	N/A
SK Networks	40.59	49	2.09 (0.01)	–40.58
Hyundai Mobis	33.49		45.35	11.86
Daewoo Ship Building	31.26		34.07	2.81
Daewoo Construction	32.54		11.78	–20.76
NHN	10.47		56.82	46.35
Doosan Heavy Machinery	41.39		20.22	–21.17
LG	49.61		30.14	–19.47

Note: Share by foreigners is as of 30 March 2007.
Source: Herald Business, 23 April 2007, www.heraldbiz.com.

TABLE 4 Individual versus Corporate Disposable Income Growth (%)

	1980–89	1990–96	2000–03
Economic Growth	8.7	7.9	5.6
Individuals	9.9	6.6	0.3
Corporations	6.1	4.3	62.6

Source: Yoon Jin Ho (2005).

a majority of the grassroots population has actually experienced income reductions.

The End of Growth-with-Equity: Bipolarization of South Korea

More specifically, the neoliberal policy has fundamentally altered the qualitative nature of labour relations. Alongside South Korea's rapid economic recovery, the magnitude of unemployment did decrease substantially (excepting among young people). However, most of the newly offered jobs are temporary, contractual ones and thus do not assure employees' stable living conditions. The so-called *bijeonggyujik* (non-regular position) has become a norm in most of the private sector. As shown in Chart 1, non-regular workers are offered only half of the regular workers' wages and an almost negligible portion of regular workers' non-wage benefits. An entirely different group of working class has emerged to be abused in the process of South Korea's rapid economic recovery.

Under the mounting pressure and criticism of workers and would-be workers as its political constituency, the state stepped in to enact a law prohibiting discrimination based upon different employment statuses and requiring regular employment after three years of contractual work. Its actual effect has been to generalize under-three-year contractual employment. In 2007, the first year under this law, a majority of the non-regular workers who have suffered from discriminatory treatment and wages for three years are required to leave their jobs (and, if they wish, to enter another three years of exploitation elsewhere).

As temporary and underpaid jobs have become normal, poverty – even at absolute levels – is no more an exclusive outcome of joblessness. That is, rapidly increasing numbers of people have suffered from on-the-job poverty. According to a study by a government-affiliated research organization (Lee *et*

CHART 1 *Gap between Regular and Non-Regular Workers, 2003*

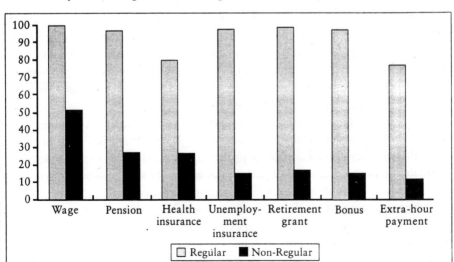

Source: Yoon Jin Ho (2005: 120).

TABLE 5   *GINI Index, Poverty Rate, Poverty Gap Ratio, 1996–2006*

	GINI	Poverty rate		Poverty gap ratio	
		Policy poverty line (minimum livelihood income)	Relative poverty line (50% of median income)	Policy poverty line (minimum livelihood income)	Relative poverty line (50% of median income)
1996	0.2782	3.1	9.0	27.3	27.1
2000	0.3307	8.2	13.4	30.4	32.0
2003	0.3449	10.4	16.0	35.4	36.8
2006	0.3364	11.6	16.7	45.0	43.3

Note: 2006 covers the first and second quarters only.
Source: Combined figures from Lee, Hyun-Ju *et al.* (2006: 61–67).

al., 2006: 132), the proportion of employed people under the official poverty line (in terms of minimum livelihood income) increased from 5.7 per cent in 1996 to 9.2 per cent in 2000, slightly declined to 7.4 per cent in 2003, but rose again to 8.8 per cent in (the first two quarters of) 2006. The poverty rate was of course much higher among unemployed people (34.3 per cent in 2000 and 31.9 per cent in 2003) and slightly higher among economically inactive (that is, dependent) people (19.8 per cent in 2000 and 13.7 per cent in 2003).

The same study documents that the poverty rate (in terms of the official poverty line) for the entire population rose from 3.1 per cent in 1996 to 8.2 per cent in 2000, and further to 10.3 per cent in 2003 and 11.6 per cent in (the first two quarters of) 2006 (see Table 5). One out of ten Koreans has to struggle below a very conservatively estimated level of minimum livelihood. In a related process, the GINI index jumped from only 0.2782 in 1996 to 0.3307 in 2000, and remained at similar levels of 0.3449 in 2003 and 0.3364 in 2006. A return to the 'growth-with-equity' model seems well beyond sight. Even more disturbing are the poverty gap ratios which indicate how much of the poverty line on average has to be additionally earned to escape poverty. The sharply accelerated increases of the ratio in recent years cannot but be disheartening to any caring observer of the country. As of 2006, those who were officially poor earned only 55 per cent of the minimum livelihood income on average. This means not only that the proportion of people under the poverty line has risen sharply, but also that such officially poor people are much poorer now than before.

Whereas poor people see their poverty continuously worsening, rich people see their income and wealth increasing. Rich households have become richer through heightened corporate profits, soaring prices of corporate stocks, skyrocketing prices and rents of real estate, gradually rising interest rates, etc. (The same process implies unbearable inflation in grassroots living costs such as room rents.) Consequently, the gap between the rich and the poor as measured by the inter-class ratio of household incomes has kept widening. According to official government data, the household income ratio between the richest 20 per cent and the poorest 20 per cent was 8.22 in 2005, 8.36 in 2006 and 8.40 in the first quarter of 2007 (*Yonhapnews*, 15 May 2007).

Social Safety Net: Neoliberal or Social Democratic?

The 'successful failure' of the post-crisis economic policy with regard to grassroots livelihood obviously necessitated a much more active stance on the part of the South Korean state in favour of social policy. In fact, even neoliberal financial predators led by the IMF concurred on the need to urgently establish a so-called 'social safety net' in this crisis-hit society. For a citizenry whose social citizenship remained hollow except in terms of virtual full employment, the layoff-centred economic structural adjustment could mean nothing but a total breakdown of livelihood. Hence the social safety net, as a buffer against potential life-and-death insurrections of stressed workers and the jobless, was as much a neoliberal as a social democratic prescription.

Without a serious ideological conversion to social democracy, the developmental-cum-neoliberal state in post-crisis South Korea embarked upon various schemes for providing emergency relief to unemployed or underemployed workers and their families. The two relatively less conservative (not progressive!) governments under Kim Dae-Jung and Roh Moo-Hyun have respectively focused on unemployment protection and socio-economic bipolarization, but without proud results. To begin with, even after increasing social expenditure for many years, South Korea's public budget for social security, not to mention its social services, is nowhere near that of serious social policy states in the west (see Chart 2).

Likewise, income transfers through public welfare programmes seem to have only marginal effects upon reducing inequality and poverty. According to a Korean scholar's estimation (see Table 6), all social security programmes involving income transfers reduced the household poverty rate by less than 2 per cent (that is, from 10.6 per cent to 8.8 per cent) in 2001. At the individual level, their

CHART 2 *Social Expenditure as Proportion of GDP in 2004*

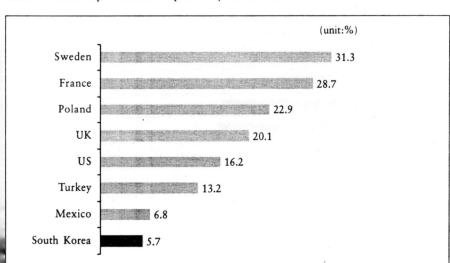

Source: *Kyunghyang Daily*, 4 March 2007; www.khan.co.kr.

TABLE 6   *Absolute Poverty Rate (below Official Minimum Livelihood)*
before and after Public Income Transfers in 2001

		Household poverty rate (%)	Individual poverty rate (%)
Pre-transfer		10.6	8.4
After all transfers		8.8	6.9
Social Insurance	Public pensions	9.9	7.8
	Industrial accident payments	10.6	8.3
	Unemployment payments	10.6	8.3
Other subsidies		10.4	8.2
Poverty assistance		9.9	7.8

Source: Ku Inhoe (2006: 112).

CHART 3   *Relative Poverty Rate (% Earning Less than 50% of the Median Income)*
before and after Public Income Transfers

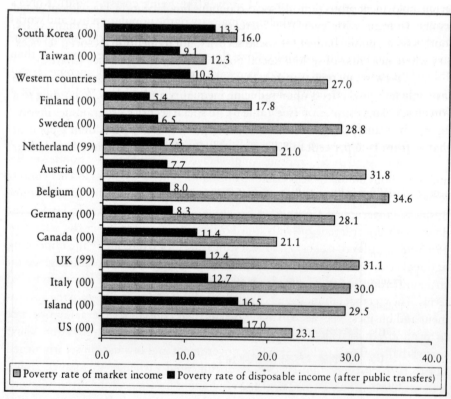

Source: Ku Inhoe (2006: 113).

combined effect was just 1.5 per cent. Only pensions and poverty assistance measures had slightly noticeable effects. Unemployment payments and industrial accident payments, which had been ambitiously prepared as counter-crisis measures, had almost no effect. These programme-specific effects did not significantly differ between households and individuals.

In an international comparison for 2004 by the same scholar (see Chart 3), South Koreans' relative poverty rate (below 50 per cent of the median income) decreased by only 2.7 per cent (that is, from 16.0 per cent to 13.3 per cent) after all public transfers of income. Western countries as a whole were able to reduce the same rate by 16.7 per cent (that is, from 27.0 per cent to 10.3 per cent). Even the UK, the origin country of neoliberalism, reduced it by 18.7 per cent (that is, from 31.1 per cent to 12.4 per cent). All European continental welfare states managed to keep the after-transfer-rate of relative poverty under 10 per cent.

It is true that pre-transfer income is much more equally distributed in South Korea than in the western countries. But such market income equality has to be weighed against the absolute level of South Korean income, which is far below that of western countries. Moreover, the living costs in South Korea's leading cities (where an overwhelming majority of the population live and work) have been estimated by various agencies as belonging to the world's most expensive group. In particular, Seoul is sometimes surveyed as more expensive than Tokyo.[4] Material survival in South Korea without generous public income protection requires extraordinary individual efforts, including the world's longest working hours.[5]

Divided-and-Ruled: Dilemma of Organized Labour

Amidst all these symptoms of proletarian crisis, how could South Korea's militant labour unions have become so dormant? Where has their globally famous social and political activism gone? As shown in the Appendix (the Labour–Business–Government Committee Co-Declaration), national union leaders sat down with government officials and business representatives in the winter of 1997–98 in order to discuss emergency measures for overcoming the impending national economic crisis. After a stormy debate, two national unions agreed on structural adjustments of corporate management and labour relations in broad terms. The fact that labour leaders publicly spoke of 'cooperation' with the government and business was soon exaggerated as their consent to liberal lay-offs, not to mention 'adjustment of wage and working hours' in the Co-Declaration. What was verbally offered to labour by the government and business in return turned out to be permanent rain-checks, as documented earlier in this paper. Union leaders quite naturally refused further consultations for cooperation in the following years, but the critical moments were already over. Their half-voluntary loss of socio-political momentum in organized activism soon became a fatal source of social indifference to organized labour causes. The election of a handful of labour leaders into the national parliament, for the first time in South Korean political

TABLE 7   *Union Participation Rate of Regular and Non-Regular Workers, 2006*

	Total number (10,000)	Unionized number (10,000)	Unionization rate (%)	Change from 2005 (% point)
Regular employees	693	150	21.6	−1.1
Non-regular employees	841	23.4	2.8	−0.4

Source: Korea Non-Regular Labour Center (2007).

history, could not change the stalemate because the voters regarded it more as a symbolic political development than a qualitative political transition.

The economic (and demographic) consequence of the labour unions' compromise has been even more devastating to organized labour causes. In a very recent instance of labour dispute, (regular) workers of Hyundai Motors tried to appeal to public sympathy by explaining the details of their working and living conditions on the web. The overwhelming majority of responses, however, were extremely hostile. Hyundai Motors workers' complaints about working and living conditions became an object of jealousy among young netizens, most of whom were perhaps frustrated by underpaid and unstable jobs offered in flexible labour markets.[6] These unsympathetic sentiments of supposed class allies may not have been unrelated to the immediate compromise of Hyundai Motors workers with their employer. Ordinary members of organized labour, most of them regular employees of large *chaebol* companies or public corporations (see Table 7), have suddenly joined the ranks of a 'labour aristocracy' in the eyes of young netizens (and, in fact, the general public).[7]

The neoliberal labour regime has successfully incapacitated organized labour's public legitimacy. In a national economy with structurally segmented labour markets, labour activism is too easily portrayed as egoism. A decade after the economic crisis, and a decade after organized labour's ineffective reaction to it, South Korean labour unions find themselves surrounded by paradoxical critics within the proletarian population. The latter's sentimental defection and/ or economic disarticulation imply unions' lack of reproducible social constituencies. That is, the pervasiveness of 'non-regular' employment in most industries (as well as the relocation of industrial jobs overseas) has made labour activism even a demographically abortive project. It is not coincidental that national and industrial labour unions are now investing their entire energy and resources into assisting non-regular workers' struggles against opportunistic employers and the ambivalent state.

Appendix

'Nosajeongwiweonhoe (Labour–Business–Government Committee) Co-Declaration' of 20 January 1998 (translated by the author)

(1) The Government shall prepare the basis for sound economic development by sincerely accepting the responsibility for the current economic crisis and inspecting its causes thoroughly. In order to cope with the expected rapid increase of unemployment, the Government shall prepare a landmark unemployment measure and a stabilization measure for workers' living including price stabilization by the end of January, and seek measures for cutting the 1998 budget and reshuffling and reducing government organizations by mid-February. Also, the Government shall prepare a master plan for increasing corporate managerial transparency by the end of February, which will include prohibiting the mutual payment guarantee between corporations, the writing of integrated financial statements, etc. In addition, the Government shall make efforts to ensure the creativity and autonomy of corporate management and the basic labour rights of workers, and to protect the livelihoods of the low-income strata by expanding social security measures.

(2) Corporations shall pursue active structural adjustments and do their best to prevent indiscreet lay-offs and unfair labour practices in this process. Also, corporations shall take the lead in improving corporate managerial transparency, for instance, through the sincere disclosing of managerial information, and for the normalization of corporate management, for instance, through the improvement of corporate financial structures.

(3) Labour unions shall do their best to improve productivity and quality for the resuscitation and competitiveness and strengthening of corporations and, under urgent managerial causes, make strong efforts for the adjustment of wages and working hours in order to minimize unemployment.

(4) Workers and employers shall try to maintain industrial peace by solving every problem through dialogue and compromise. Also, the Government shall strictly counter unlawful activities at industrial sites which take advantage of the economic crisis.

(5) We, *Nosajeongwiweonhoe* (Labour–Business–Government Committee), shall do our best to prepare an environment for inviting overseas capital and, in consideration of the schedule of the provisional session of the National Parliament in February, reach a package settlement on the agendas agreed on and adopted by this Committee as soon as possible through labour–business–government grand compromises.

Notes

[1] *Chaebol* is a special term (in Korean) for a South Korean business conglomerate that operates multiple corporations in diverse industries with tight ownership and management control by a family (Kang 1996). *Chaebols'* indiscreet borrowings from international lenders in the 1990s were mainly held responsible for the national financial crisis of 1997 (Kong 2000).

[2] I have elsewhere conceptualized such a developmental attitude of private families in education as *the social investment family* (Chang 2007).

[3] The first issue of the *White Book of Public Fund Administration* in 2002 revealed that 156.7 trillion *won* had been mobilized and used under this scheme by June 2002. Interest payments in this fund amounted to 24.3 trillion *won* (Ministry of Finance and Economy, 12 September 2002).

[4] There are controversies over the price levels of Seoul (*Hankook Ilbo*, 12 June 2007). The United Nations allocates 366 US dollars to its officials for a day's stay in Seoul as compared to 347 dollars in New York and 280 dollars in Tokyo. *Business Travel News* recently reported that 396 US dollars are needed for an American business traveller for a day in Seoul, the eighth most expensive among 100 top cities outside the US. The South Korean government, quoting the price figures of various international agencies, insists that the costs of ordinary people's livelihood in South Korea are less expensive than in the major western countries.

[5] According to the 2007 edition of the International Labour Organization's *Key Indicators of the Labour Market* (KILM), South Korea topped 54 countries surveyed in the annual hours of work in 2006. South Koreans, who on average worked 2,305 hours in 2006, were closely followed by peoples of other Asian countries such as Bangladesh, Sri Lanka, Hong Kong, Malaysia and Thailand, all working more than 2,200 hours annually.

[6] The conservative media love to make a critical issue of such cold responses of netizens to organized labour actions. See 'Hyundai Motors Union Violence . . . Hot Internet: Netizens, Anti-Union On-Line Protest' (*Korea Economic Daily*, 5 January 2007).

[7] See Kim Won (2007), 'The Social Isolation of South Korea's Big Factory Unions: With a Focus on Hyundai Motors in Ulsan' (in Korean), unpublished paper.

References

Bank of Korea (1998), 'The Analysis of Corporate Management in the First Half of 1998' (in Korean), unpublished survey report.

Chang Kyung-Sup (2002), 'South Korean Society in the IMF Era: Compressed Capitalist Development and Social Sustainability Crisis', in Pietro P. Masina, ed., *Rethinking Development in East Asia: From Illusory Miracle to Economic Crisis* (London: Curzon Press), pp. 189–222.

—— (2007), 'Politics of *The Social Investment Family*: Education and State–Family Relations in South Korea', paper presented at the conference on 'The Changing Asian Family as a Site of (State) Politics', Asia Research Institute, National University of Singapore, 26–27 April 2007.

Hankook Ilbo (www. hankooki.com).

Herald Business (www.heraldbiz.com).

International Labour Organization (ILO) (2007), *Key Indicators of the Labour Market* (KILM), fifth edition, Geneva: ILO.

Kang, Myung Hun (1996), *The Korean Business Conglomerate: Chaebol Then and Now* (Berkeley: University of California Press).

Kim Won (2007), 'The Social Isolation of South Korea's Big Factory Unions: With a Focus on Hyundai Motors in Ulsan' (in Korean), unpublished paper.

Kong, Tat Yan (2000), *The Politics of Economic Reform in South Korea: A Fragile Miracle* (London: Routledge).

Korea Economic Daily (www.hankyung.com).

Korea Non-Regular Labour Center (2007), 'Union Participation Rate of Regular and Non-Regular Workers' (in Korean), unpublished report.

Ku Inhoe (2006), *Income Inequality and Poverty in Korea: Worsening Income Distribution and* the *Need for Social Policy Reform* (in Korean), Seoul: Seoul National University Press.

Kyunghyang Daily (www.khan.co.kr).

Lee Hyun-Ju *et al.* (2006), *The Structure of Poverty in Korea* (in Korean) (Seoul: Korea Institute for Social Development and Policy Research).

Marshall, T.H. (1964), *Class, Citizenship, and Social Development* (Garden City: Doubleday).

Ministry of Finance and Economy, Republic of Korea (2002), *White Book of Public Fund Administration, 2002* (in Korean).

National Statistical Office (NSO), Republic of Korea (1998), *Fifty Years' Economic and Social Change Seen through Statistics* (in Korean).

Nosajeongwiweonhoe (Labour–Business–Government Committee) (1998), 'Labour–Business–Government Committee Co-Declaration' (in Korean), 20 January 1998.

Yonhapnews (www.Yonhapnews.co.kr).

Yoon Jin-Ho (2005), 'The Causes for Income Bipolarization and the Direction for Policy Responses' (in Korean), in Seoul Social and Economic Research Center, ed., *The South Korean Economy: Beyond Globalization, Structural Adjustment, Bipolarization* (Seoul: Hanul), pp. 110–48.

Financial Liberalization, Crises and the Role of Capital Controls

The Malaysian Case

Jomo K.S.

Analysts have increasingly acknowledged the role of easily reversible capital flows in precipitating the 1997–98 crises in East Asia. They now generally accept that the national financial systems in the region did not adapt well to international financial liberalization (Jomo 1998). Financial liberalization undoubtedly succeeded in temporarily generating massive net capital inflows into East Asia, unlike into many other developing and transition economies, some of which experienced net outflows. However, it also exacerbated systemic instability and reduced the scope for the government interventions responsible for the region's economic miracle. Foreign capital inflows adversely affected factor payment outflows, export and import propensities and the terms of trade, and thus the balance of payments. In particular, increased foreign capital inflows reduced foreign exchange constraints, allowing the financing of additional imports, but thereby also resulted in current account deficits. This created the conditions for the loss of investor confidence that resulted in the capital reversals of 1997.

The bank-based financial systems of most of the East Asian economies affected by the crises were especially vulnerable in the face of a sudden drop in the availability of short-term loans as international confidence in the region dropped suddenly during 1997. Available foreign exchange reserves were exposed as inadequate to meet financial obligations abroad, requiring governments to seek temporary credit facilities to meet obligations that had been incurred mainly by their private sectors. Data from the Bank of International Settlements (BIS) showed that the banks were responsible for much of this short-term debt, though some of it did consist of trade credit and other short-term debt deemed essential for ensuring liquidity in an economy. However, the rapid growth of short-term bank debt during stockmarket and property boom periods suggests that much of the short-term debt was due to factors other than trade credit expansion.

In Malaysia, the temporary capital controls the central bank introduced in early 1994 momentarily dampened the growth of such debt, but by 1996 and early 1997, a new short-term borrowing frenzy was evident that involved not only the banks, but also other large, private companies with enough political influence to circumvent the central bank's guidelines. However, the sequence of policy events that led up to the crisis was very different in Malaysia from the scenario elsewhere. This was due to a tightening of regulatory control with the Banking and Financial Institutions Act of 1989 that was adopted in the wake of a serious recession and banking crisis in the mid-1980s. In the beginning of the 1990s, there was an attempt to increase capital market activity in Malaysia, with a split between the stock exchanges of Singapore and Kuala Lumpur. The Malaysian authorities at that time staged what were essentially 'road shows' in order to try and lure foreign investors to invest in the Malaysian stockmarket. The efforts were successful, and during 1992 and 1993 a major influx of capital into Malaysia from international investors occurred. However, towards the end of 1993, there was a sharp reversal of capital flows out of the country, resulting in a collapse of the stockmarket. In 1994, the Malaysian Finance Minister at that time, Anwar Ibrahim, introduced capital controls on financial inflows. These controls were subsequently lifted in the second half of 1994 due to effective lobbying by those with a strong interest in seeing a dynamic stockmarket.

As a result of these capital market-oriented policies, Malaysia' situation at the time of the crisis was different. Whereas the other three crisis-affected East Asian economies succeeded in attracting considerable, mainly short-term, US dollar bank loans into their more bank-based financed systems, Malaysia's vulnerability was mainly due to the volatility of international portfolio capital flows into its stockmarket. As a consequence, the nature of Malaysia's external liabilities at the beginning of the crisis was quite different from that of the other crisis-stricken East Asian economies. A greater proportion of Malaysia's external liabilities consisted of equity rather than debt. Compared with Malaysia's exposure in the mid-1980s, many of the liabilities, including the debt, were private rather than public. In addition, much of Malaysia's debt in the late 1990s was long-term rather than short-term in nature, again in contrast to the other crisis-affected economies. Further, monetary policy and banking supervision had generally been much more prudent in Malaysia than in the other crisis countries. For example, Malaysian banks had not been allowed to borrow heavily from abroad to lend on the domestic market. Such practices involved currency and term mismatches, which increased the vulnerability of countries' financial systems to foreign bankers' confidence and exerted pressure on the exchange rate pegs.

These differences have lent support to the claim that Malaysia was an innocent bystander that fell victim to regional contagion by being in the wrong part of the world at the wrong time. Such a view takes a benign perspective of portfolio investment inflows, and does not recognize that such inflows are even more easily reversible and volatile than bank loan inflows (Jomo 2001). Contrary to the innocent bystander hypothesis, Malaysia's experience actually suggests greater vulnerability because of its greater reliance on the capital market. In mid-1994, as the rising stockmarket renewed foreign portfolio investors' interest in Malaysia, those who stood to gain from a stockmarket bubble successfully lobbied for abandoning the early 1994 controls on portfolio capital inflows.

As a consequence, the Malaysian economy became hostage to international portfolio investors' confidence. Hence, when government leaders engaged in rhetoric and policy initiatives that upset such investors' confidence, Malaysia paid a heavy price as portfolio divestment accelerated. This rendered Malaysia vulnerable to the 1997–98 portfolio capital flight, resulting in a stockmarket collapse by about four-fifths of its market capitalization in February 1997.

After the crisis broke in Thailand in July 1997, the regional economies responded in ways that were predominantly influenced by the prevailing market sentiment and by the IMF (International Monetary Fund). The exception was Malaysia, which tried to stem the consequences of the crisis through a number of initiatives. Initially, the Malaysian government spent about 9 billion Malaysian *ringgit*, at that time worth about US$ 4 billion, in a period of three weeks, in an urgent attempt to defend the *ringgit*. This endeavour was unsuccessful, and the Malaysian authorities consequently gave up. Other countries in the region did not try to defend their currencies and therefore did not lose as much money in the process. However, by late 1997, after disagreements between Malaysian political leaders and lobbies, there was a brief period when IMF-type policies became more influential.

Thailand, Indonesia and South Korea had received IMF emergency credit and were subject to its deflationary conditionalities, which had aggravated the regional recession and crises. Although the Fund continued its emphasis on strict monetary policy, it seemed more willing to abandon its earlier insistence on 'fiscal discipline'. By late 1998, it lifted curbs on counter-cyclical (reflationary) fiscal policies by allowing debtor nations to run budget deficits – perhaps belatedly, recognizing that most East Asian crisis economies (not including Indonesia) had run budget surpluses for years.

In the last quarter of 1998, the regional turmoil came to an end as East Asian currencies strengthened and stabilized, partly as a result of the US Federal Reserve Bank's decision to lower interest rates. This effectively halted capital flight from Asia to the US. Given that respite, Asian currencies strengthened and stabilized. In the first quarter of 1999, Thailand, Indonesia and South Korea posted positive growth rates. Malaysia, on the other hand, slipped into its fifth quarter of recession. However, matters changed soon. By the end of 1999 and into 2000, Malaysia's recovery was second only to South Korea's.

In Malaysia, fourteen months after the crises were sparked off by the floating of the Thai *baht* in July 1997, Prime Minister Mahathir Mohamad introduced several controversial currency and capital control measures. Malaysia's bold introduction of capital controls on 1–2 September 1998 in response to the crisis elicited mixed reactions. Amidst the debate, both critics and advocates tended to exaggerate their case with little regard for accuracy. Proponents of capital account liberalization generally opposed capital controls because they were viewed as a setback to the gradual capital account liberalization that had taken place over the previous two decades. They claimed that the measures undermined freer capital movement and capital market efficiency – reducing net flows from the capital-rich to the capital-poor, limiting access to cheaper funds, increasing financial volatility, aggravating inflation and lowering growth – besides encouraging reversal of the larger trends towards greater economic liberalization and globalization. Market fundamentalists loudly prophesied Malaysia's doom, little anticipating that Malaysia's recovery would be stronger than Thailand's or Indonesia's and second only to South Korea. Since then, the critics have reversed their opinion.

Neoliberal critics referred to the fact that despite the administration's efforts to attract capital, foreign direct investment (FDI) flows had decreased after 1996. They claimed that this was due to the Malaysian authorities' reduced credibility after the imposition of the September 1998 controls. However, this was not a purely Malaysian phenomenon. There is considerable evidence of a decline in FDI throughout Southeast Asia, including in the countries that maintained open capital accounts. Considering this, a more plausible explanation for reduced FDI flows to Southeast Asia would be that the 1997–98 crises dramatically highlighted the region's declining competitiveness and attractiveness compared to, say, China.

Some of the more doctrinaire neoliberals also disagreed with the IMF's interventionism, albeit minimalist, on the grounds that the Fund represents a super-state of sorts and such intervention undermined market forces. Meanwhile, counter-cyclical interventionists condemned the IMF's early pro-cyclicality. The Fund's own policy stance has also changed over time, and has often been shown to be doctrinaire, poorly informed and heavily politically influenced, especially by western interests led by the US.

As compared to these views, most – though not all – heterodox economists endorsed the Malaysian challenge to contemporary orthodoxy for the opposite reasons. They emphasized that financial and capital account liberalization had exacerbated financial system vulnerability and macroeconomic volatility. More importantly, they pointed out that such measures created conditions for restoring the monetary policy autonomy considered necessary for fostering economic recovery.[1] The Malaysian experience does suggest that the orthodoxy's predictions of disaster (as, for example, by the late Nobel Laureate Merton Miller) were inaccurate, as plainly proven by later events. However, it is much more difficult to prove that the Malaysian controls were the resounding success portrayed by its advocates and supporters.

The actual efficacy of Malaysia's measures is difficult to assess. Malaysia's recovery (6.1 per cent in 1999 and 8.3 per cent in 2000) was more modest than South Korea's (10.9 per cent in 1999 and 9.3 per cent in 2000). Since South Korea was also subject to an IMF bail-out programme, one cannot attribute the different rates of recovery in 1999 to different monetary policy measures or IMF conditionalities. It seems likely that the relatively stronger recovery in Malaysia and South Korea, when compared to the other crisis countries, was due to stronger fiscal reflationary efforts as well as increased electronics demand.

Besides, after September 1998, Thai interest rates fell below Malaysian rates after being well above Malaysian rates for years (Jomo 2001: 206, Figure 7.1). This suggests that the US Fed's interest rate reduction did more to reduce interest rates in the East Asian region than did the September 1998 Malaysian initiatives. But it also points to an element of truth in the general observation that monetary policy is far less effective than fiscal measures in reflating the economy.

It also needs to be noted that the capital control measures were significantly revised in February 1999. The modifications represented attempts to mitigate some problematic consequences of the capital controls regime. As of 1 September 1999, the September 1998 regime was fundamentally transformed, ending the original curbs on capital outflows. There have since been no new curbs on inflows; rather, strenuous efforts to encourage the return of capital inflows (including short-term capital) have been undertaken.

Did Mahathir's September 1998 Controls Succeed?

Did Malaysia's September 1998 selective capital control measures realize their objectives? The merits and drawbacks of the Malaysian government's capital controls regime in dealing with the regional currency and financial crisis will be debated for a long time to come as the data does not lend itself to clearly support any particular position. The diverse interpretations of the data enable proponents to claim that the economic decline and stockmarket slide halted soon after the onset of the controls, while opponents can counter that such reversals have been more pronounced in the rest of the region.

Industrial output, especially in manufacturing, declined even faster after the introduction of capital controls in Malaysia until November 1998, and continued downward till January 1999 before turning around. Even after that, with the exception of a few sectors (notably electronics), industrial output recovery was not spectacular, except in comparison with the preceding deep recession. Meanwhile unemployment rose, especially affecting those employed in construction and in financial services. Domestic investment proposals almost halved, while 'greenfield' FDI seems to have declined by much less, though cynics noted that actual trends had been obscured by quicker application processing, approval of previously rejected applications and some redefinitions of the FDI measures (see Jomo 2001: Figure 7.2).

Further, as is now generally recognized, the one-year lock-in of foreign funds in the country came too late to avert the crisis or help retain the bulk of foreign funds that had earlier fled. Instead, the funds 'trapped' were those that had not already left in the preceding fourteen months, inadvertently 'punishing' those investors who had not already withdrawn funds from Malaysia.

It appears that the actual contribution of capital controls to the strong economic recovery in Malaysia in 1999–2000 is ambiguous at best. It may even have slowed down the recovery led by fiscal counter-cyclical measures and the extraordinary demand for electronics, thus explaining the weaker recovery in Malaysia compared to South Korea. In the longer term, many critics claim that it diminished the recovery of foreign direct investment – which has compelled the authorities to seek more domestic sources of economic growth, though the evidence to support this argument is inadequate.

More importantly, the regime remains untested in terms of its contribution to checking international currency volatility, as such instability abated throughout the region at around the same time following the US Fed's interest rate reduction. Although recovery of the Malaysian share market – which had declined more than other stockmarkets during the crisis – lagged behind the other (relatively smaller) markets in the region, it is not clear what should be made of this.

If, indeed, Malaysia's capital controls stemmed from near-desperation, as Mahathir said at a symposium on the first anniversary of the controls, then its timing was most fortunate. When it was introduced the external environment was about to change significantly while the economy had seen the outflow of the bulk of short-term capital, so that, in a sense, the regime was never tested. If the turmoil of the preceding months had continued until the end of 1998 or longer, continued shifts and re-pegging would have been necessary, with deleterious effects.

Malaysian authorities set the peg at RM 3.8 to the US dollar on 2 September 1998, after it had been trading in the range of RM 4–4.2 per US dollar, in a bid to raise the value of the *ringgit*. Since mid-September 1998, however, other regional currencies stabilized – after the US Federal Reserve Bank lowered interest rates in the aftermath of the Russian and LTCM crises, strengthening the *yen* and other regional currencies. Thus the *ringgit* became undervalued for about a year thereafter, which – by chance rather than by design – boosted Malaysian foreign exchange reserves from the trade surplus, largely due to import compression, as well as some exchange rate-sensitive exports. Malaysia's foreign exchange reserves depleted rapidly from July until November 1997 before improving in December, and especially after the imposition of capital controls in September 1998 (Jomo 2001: Figure 5.10). Thus the *ringgit* undervaluation may have helped Malaysian economic recovery, but certainly not in the way the authorities intended when initially pegging the *ringgit*.

While the undervalued *ringgit* backed an export-led recovery strategy, this was not the intent, as government efforts were focused on a domestic-led recovery strategy. The undervalued *ringgit* is said to have had a (unintentional) 'beggar-thy-neighbour' effect. Due to trade competition, the undervalued *ringgit* is said to have discouraged other regional currencies from strengthening earlier for fear of becoming uncompetitive relative to Malaysian production costs and exports. There were also fears that the weak Southeast Asian currencies might cause China's authorities to devalue the *renminbi*, which could have had the undesirable effect of triggering another round of 'competitive devaluations', signalling danger for all.

Clearly, the *ringgit* peg brought a welcome respite to businessmen after more than a year of currency volatility. But, as noted earlier, exchange rate volatility across the region abated shortly thereafter. Moreover, it is ironic that a presumably nationalistic attempt to defend monetary independence against currency traders should, in effect, hand over determination of the *ringgit*'s value to the US Federal Reserve through partial or quasi-dollarization. If the US dollar had strengthened significantly against other currencies, then Malaysia may have had to re-peg against the US dollar to retain export competitiveness. However, the greenback initially weakened due to lowered US interest rates. After strengthening from 1999, it again weakened after 2001, which created much less pressure for re-pegging or de-pegging.

While interest rates were undoubtedly brought down by government decree in Malaysia, the desired effects were limited. Interest rates have been reduced dramatically across the region, in some cases even more than in Malaysia, without others having to resort to capital controls. As noted earlier, while interest rates in Thailand were much higher than in Malaysia for over a year after the crisis began, they declined below Malaysian levels during September 1998. Perhaps more importantly, loan and money supply growth rates actually declined in the first few months after the new measures were introduced despite central bank threats to sack bank managers who failed to achieve the 8 per cent loan growth target rate for 1998. It has become clear that credit expansion is a consequence of factors other than capital controls or even low interest rates. Across the region, especially in South Korea and Thailand, counter-cyclical spending also grew, without resorting to capital controls.

The Malaysian authorities' mid-February 1999 measures effectively abandoned the main capital control measure introduced in September 1998, that is, the one-year lock-in. While foreign investors were prohibited from withdrawing funds from Malaysia before September 1999, they were allowed to do so from mid-February 1999 after paying a scaled exit tax (lower taxes for longer-term investment in Malaysia), in the hope that this would reduce the rush for the gates come September 1999.

The very low volume of actual capital outflows after the lock-in ended on 1 September 1999 has been interpreted in different ways. One view was that since the stockmarket had recovered and could be expected to continue rising, there was little reason to flee. A second view emphasized the role of the nominal exchange rate, which had been fixed against the US dollar at RM 3.8. With the greenback perceived to be still strengthening, there was little exchange rate risk to discourage investors from holding *ringgit*. A third perspective held that the low rate of exit indicated that capital controls were probably unnecessary, having been introduced fourteen months after the crisis began, that is, after most of the capital flight had already taken place.

Meanwhile, in an attempt to attract new capital inflows, new investors were granted a less onerous capital gains tax. However, it is unlikely that the capital gains tax will deter exit in the event of a panic as investors rush to cut their losses. At best, it could discourage some kind of short-selling from abroad owing to the higher capital gains tax rate of 30 per cent as opposed to 10 per cent on withdrawals performed within less than a year. The differential may have discouraged some short-selling from abroad, but would not have deterred capital flight in the event of financial panic. In September 1999, the capital gains exit tax rate was set at a uniform rate of 10 per cent, thus eliminating the only feature of the February 1999 revised controls that might have deterred short-selling from abroad.

The desirability of some measures associated with the capital controls is also in doubt as evidence of favouritism or cronyism mounts, while the contribution of 'rescued' interests to national economic recovery efforts is dubious (Wong 2002). Simon Johnson and Todd Mitton (2003) have shown that the market prices of stocks associated with Mahathir cronies rose disproportionately more after the introduction of the September 1998 capital controls. However, the evidence does not really allow one to conclude that the capital controls *per se* were solely or principally responsible for this outcome. As the Malaysian authorities had also undertaken several other important measures from mid-1998, more careful analysis is required before one can conclusively attribute this favourable effect on Mahathir crony stock prices to the capital control measures.

After all, counter-cyclical fiscal spending had been reintroduced by the then Finance Minister Anwar Ibrahim from around May–June 1998, possibly with an eye to the ruling party's annual general assembly at the end of that month. Around this time, the IMF had begun to reconsider its earlier policy conditionality and advice for the crisis-affected East Asian economies to avoid budgetary deficits. During this time too, the Malaysian authorities set up three important institutions to facilitate restoration of bank liquidity by taking over many large non-performing loans (Danaharta), bank recapitalization (Danamodal) and corporate restructuring (Corporate Debt Restructuring Committee, or CDRC). Furthermore, the popularity of crony stocks before the crisis – contrary to the neoliberal presumption that minority investors have an aversion to such shares – suggests that portfolio investors understandably preferred such stocks, especially after intense political conflict preceding the capital controls suggested that Anwar-connected stocks were doomed, while those linked to Mahathir would be the principal beneficiaries of government policy interventions.

Some Policy Lessons

Malaysian Prime Minister Mahathir's September 1998 capital controls were correctly seen as a bold rejection of both market orthodoxy as well as of IMF market-friendly neoliberalism. Where Thailand, South Korea and Indonesia had gone cap in hand – humiliatingly accepting IMF-imposed conditions to secure desperately needed credit – the Malaysian initiative reminded the world that there were alternatives to capital account liberalization. For many, enthusiastic support for the Malaysian controls and claims of its success are crucial in opposing market fundamentalism and IMF neoliberalism. But many opponents of capital account liberalization have gone to the other extreme, with some exaggeration about the actual implications of the measures undertaken by Malaysia and their achievements. For example, one supporter has extolled the virtuous consequences for labour resulting from capital control measures, with scant regard for the

Malaysian authorities' self-confessed motive of protecting big business interests, professedly to protect jobs.

The coincidental timing of an article by Paul Krugman in *Fortune* magazine advocating capital controls reinforced the impression that the measures were primarily intended to provide monetary policy independence to reflate the economy. However, as noted earlier, foreign developments from August 1998 also created new international monetary conditions that facilitated the adoption of reflationary policies in the rest of the region. Though Malaysia missed out on most of the renewed capital flows to the region from the last quarter of 1998, it is not clear that such easily reversible capital inflows are all that desirable. The more serious problem was the credibility of government policies, which appeared to adversely affect the inflow of FDI (despite official protests to the contrary) as well as risk premiums for Malaysian bonds.

The subsequently undervalued pegged *ringgit* also had negative implications for a broad recovery, which depended upon imported inputs. It is not clear that the peg gave a major boost to exports, as the official export figures suggest. The post-September 1998 regime has also not produced other desired effects as the export base remains narrow, with the most significant growth coming from electronics due to external demand increases and with the increase in foreign reserves largely resulting from massive import compression.

There are costs to maintaining an undervalued *ringgit*, especially in the context of an economic upturn of what is still a very open economy. Undervaluation may help some exports in the short term, but it also makes imports of capital and intermediate goods more expensive, thus impeding recovery and capacity expansion in the medium term. (Before the crisis, imports were almost equivalent to GDP.) The trade surplus subsequently declined as import compression due to the undervalued *ringgit* declined. Coupled with an apparently stubborn negative services balance, a reduced current account surplus accompanied the economic upturn.

Contrary to official claims, the controls may also have had some negative effects on desired long-term FDI, for example, among potential foreign investors who might mistrust a government for apparently reneging on an implicit commitment to not impose capital controls on outflows. However, there is no conclusive evidence to this effect. In fact, surveys by Japanese government agencies – notably the Japan External Trade Organization (JETRO) and Japan Bank for International Cooperation (JBIC) – suggest that such investors have been indifferent to or even approving of the controls. In any case, FDI throughout the world had declined significantly since the late 1990s, with China receiving a much greater share of such investments.

The subsequent reduction of FDI cannot be conclusively attributed to the September 1998 measures. The authorities attributed the FDI decline to misperceptions, and had to spend inordinate energy and resources trying to rectify the situation. But confidence in the consistency and credibility of the Malaysian government's policy was seriously eroded, as were years of successful investment promotion. This was not helped by unnecessarily hostile and ill-informed official rhetoric.

The capital controls regime was thus counter-productive in terms of the overall consistency of government policy, and probably had some adverse long-term consequences. The problem was exacerbated by the prime minister's declared intention to retain the regime until the international financial system was reformed. Since the desired reforms to the international financial architecture are unlikely to materialize in the foreseeable future, the Malaysian government should institute a permanent but flexible, market-based regime of prudential controls to moderate capital inflows and deter speculative surges, both domestic and foreign, in order to avert future crises. This would include a managed float of the currency with convertibility but no internationalization, minimally meaning no offshore *ringgit* accounts and limits on offshore foreign exchange accounts and foreign borrowings.

There is also an urgent need for some degree of monetary cooperation in the region. It is now clear that currency and financial crises have primarily regional effects. Hence regional cooperation is a necessary first step towards establishing an East Asian monetary facility. Only responsible Malaysian relations with its neighbours will contribute to realizing such regional cooperation.

In conclusion, it is relevant to point out that our critical evaluation of Malaysia's unorthodox crisis management measures should not obscure their potential and desirability, especially when such problems cannot be avoided or overcome by other means. The window of opportunity offered by the capital controls regime was abused by certain powerfully connected business interests, not only to secure publicly funded bail-outs at public expense, but also to consolidate and extend their corporate domination, especially in the crucial financial sector. Capital controls have been part of a package focused on saving friends of the regime, usually at public expense. For example, while indirectly not involving public funds, the government-sponsored restructuring of the ruling party-linked Renong conglomerate was estimated to cost the government, and hence the public, billions of *ringgit* in toll and tax revenue. Also, the non-performing loans (NPLs) of the thrice-bankrupted Bank Bumiputra – taken over by politically well-connected banking interests – have not been heavily discounted like NPLs of other banks, although it has long abandoned its 'social agenda' of helping the politically dominant Bumiputera community.

Other elements in the Malaysian government's economic strategy after the imposition of controls reinforce the impression that the capital control measures were probably motivated by political considerations as well as the desire to protect politically well-connected businesses. In sum, the Malaysian experiment with capital controls has been compromised by political bias, vested interests and inappropriate policy instruments. Hence it would be a serious mistake to reject the desirability of capital controls on account of the flawed Malaysian experience.

Note

[1] Many intermediate positions also emerged, for example, the IMF's then Deputy Managing Director Stanley Fischer endorsed Chilean-style controls on capital inflows, implying that the September 1998 Malaysian controls on outflows were far less acceptable, presumably because they involved controls on outflows rather than inflows, besides undermining government credibility, and thus were likely to generate more adverse consequences.

References

Johnson, Simon and Todd Mitton (2003), 'Cronyism and Capital Controls: Evidence from Malaysia', *Journal of Financial Economics*, 67, pp. 351–82.

Jomo K.S., ed. (1998), *Tigers in Trouble: Financial Governance, Liberalization and Crises in East Asia* (London: Zed Books).

——— (2001), *Malaysian Eclipse: Economic Crisis and Recovery* (London: Zed Books).

Wong Sook Ching (2002), 'The Role of Government in Managing Corporate Distress after the 1997 Crisis: Theories and Case Studies of Selected Malaysian Corporations', M. Ec. Research Paper, Faculty of Economics and Administration, University of Malaya, Kuala Lumpur.

The Philippines
Ten Years after the Asian Crisis

Joseph Anthony Lim

Low-Quality Growth before and after the Crisis

The impact of the Asian crisis in the Philippines amounted to one of the busts in a set of boom–bust cycles that affected the country over a span of three decades. The downturns occurred in 1984–85, 1991–93, 1998–99, 2001 (see Chart 1). These busts made Philippines a laggard among the East Asian economies.

The growth rates after the Asian crisis from 2002 to the first quarter of 2007 appear to mark a return to pre-1998 growth rates. This process of growth has also been accompanied by a continuing rise in overseas workers' remittances, which makes GNP (gross national product) growth even higher than GDP (gross domestic product) growth.

But there are reasons to believe that these growth rates may be overestimated. The high growth rates during 2002–06 occurred in a statistical context

CHART 1 *GDP and GNP Per Capita*

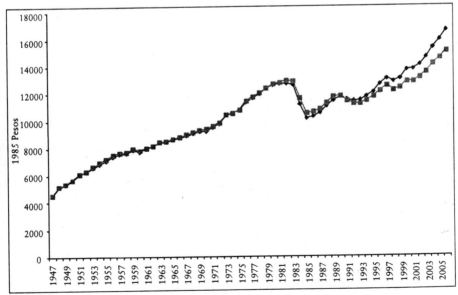

Source: National Statistics Coordination Board (NSCB).

TABLE 1   *GDP and GNP Growth Rates* (per cent)

	1995	1996	1997	1998	1999	2000	2001	2002	2003	2004	2005	2006	2007 1Q	2007 2Q
GDP growth	4.68	5.85	5.19	–0.58	3.40	5.97	1.76	4.45	4.93	6.18	4.97	5.37	6.91	7.5
GNP growth	4.88	7.24	5.25	0.41	3.73	7.07	2.26	4.18	5.95	6.72	5.64	6.21	6.64	8.3
NFIA, % of GDP	2.78	4.13	4.20	5.23	5.57	6.67	7.20	6.92	7.96	8.51	9.19	10.07	9.27	

Source: National Statistics Coordination Board (NSCB).

CHART 2   *Statistical Discrepancy, % of Nominal GDP*

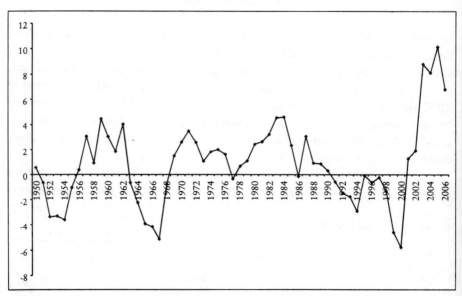

Source: Calculated from National Income Accounts, NSCB.

marked by exceedingly high and positive statistical discrepancies, which makes one suspect that the supply-side data are overestimated (see Chart 2). The base year for the national income accounts is 1985, relative prices based on which are still being used despite being obsolete and bearing no semblance to relative prices today. Most economists suspect that the growth rates for 2004–06 and the first two quarters of 2007 are significantly overestimated.

Furthermore, the quality of the growth is marred by a number of factors, explained below.

Falling Investment Rates

To start with, high rates of growth have been registered at a time when both savings and investment rates (as a percentage of GDP) were falling, as

CHART 3 *Demand Components of GDP, % of Nominal GDP*

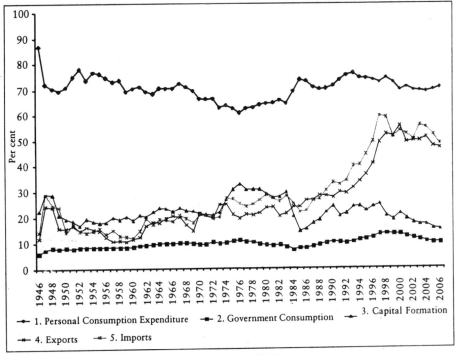

Source: National Statistics Coordination Board (NSCB).

CHART 4 *Gross Domestic Savings and Gross Investments, % of GDP*

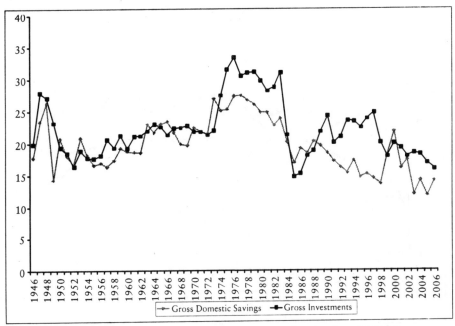

Source: Calculated from data of National Statistics Coordination Board (NSCB).

shown in Chart 3. Savings and investment rates have been declining in the years after the crisis since 2000. Chart 4 shows a clear continuing decline in the share of investment in GDP after the Asian crisis. The share of consumption increases with each recession and remains high (around 70 per cent). There were large investment–savings gaps (representing trade deficits) before the crisis. This gap was reduced after the crisis as the investment share fell, even as gross domestic savings as share of GDP also fell. Thus growth during 2005–07 was spurred by consumption and declining trade deficits.

Stagnant Industrial and Manufacturing Base

A second disconcerting feature of recent growth is that, as earlier, it is spurred by services, and does little to correct for the low manufacturing and industrial base in the country.[1] Chart 5 shows that the economic collapse in the mid-1980s brought down the shares of industry and manufacturing in GDP, and these have remained stagnant ever since. As the share of agriculture falls, the main spur to growth comes from services. This is continuing now, as business process outsourcing and call centres are the fastest growing activities in the economy. This sector is being touted as a saviour that will help improve the economic performance of the country. But its linkages with other sectors of the economy

CHART 5   *Shares of Economic Sectors, % of Nominal GDP*

Source: National Statistics Coordination Board (NSCB).

are weak and it does not carry positive externalities in terms of human capital development (since the main skill is to speak English with an appropriate accent, usually American).

Jobless Growth

A third feature of growth in recent times is its limited contribution by way of employment growth. As Chart 6 shows, after the Asian crisis, as GDP growth rates improved, unemployment rates continued to increase. This persistence of high unemployment, especially from 2000 to the present, is due to the high rates of entry into the labour force and the low employment absorption in agriculture and industry.

Chart 7 shows the employment rates (as percentages of the labour force) in agriculture going down steeply in the 1990s and 2000s. Employment rates in manufacturing and industry are stagnant. Only the services sector is currently absorbing workers and therefore the unemployment rate is inching upwards. This picture mirrors the value-added picture shown earlier of a declining agricultural share, stagnant industrial and manufacturing shares, and a rising share of services.

This is further corroborated by Chart 8, which shows labour productivity (output per employed person) going up faster than GDP per capita. There is increasing labour productivity in agriculture and industry as these sectors resort

CHART 6 *Unemployment Rate vs. GDP Growth*

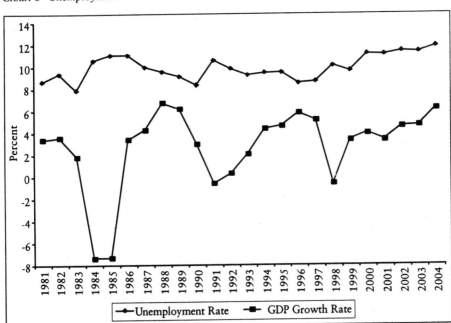

Source: Labour Force Survey, NSCB.

CHART 7 *Employment by Sector and Unemployed, as % of Labour Force*

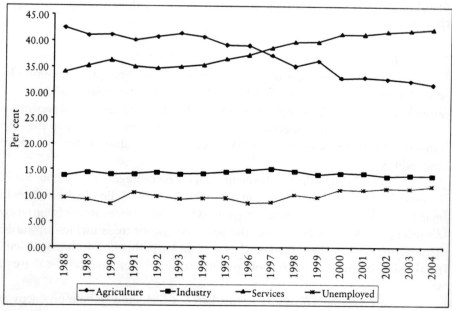

Source: Labour Force Survey, NSCB.

CHART 8 *Labour Productivity and GDP Per Capita* (in 1985 prices)

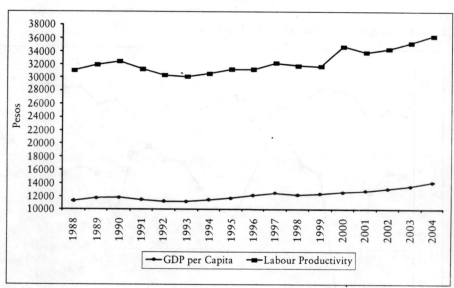

Source: Labour Force Survey, NSCB.

to reducing labour cost, as a means of coping with the increased import competition resulting from trade liberalization in an adverse production environment characterized by high electricity costs and poor infrastructure.

The unemployment rate was supposed to have declined in the first quarter of 2007 when GDP growth zoomed to 6.9 per cent. But this may not be sustainable because fiscal weakness and missed revenue targets (to be discussed later) are jeopardizing the pump-priming and infrastructure building required to sustain economic growth.

The External Sector and Economic Crisis in the Philippines

The Philippines has usually entered a crisis whenever international reserves have fallen below two months of imports (see Chart 9).

The Philippines experienced balance of payments crises in 1958, 1960–62, 1970, 1983–85, 1991 and 1998. As can be seen from Chart 9, these were periods when international reserves fell below two months of imports. Until the Asian crisis, high growth inevitably led to large current account deficits, which precipitated balance of payments crises. Thus recessions were preceded by high current account deficits. As recessions were accompanied by sharp devaluations due to the capital flight triggered by the crisis, the devaluations and recessions ensured a reduction in the current account deficit through a sharp fall in imports. (see Chart 10).

CHART 9 *International Reserves in Number of Months of Imports of Goods and Services*

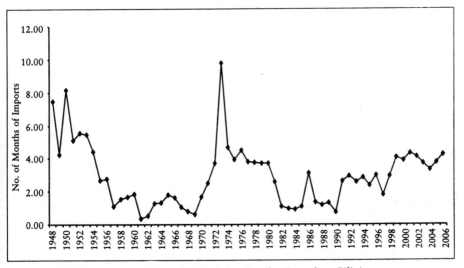

Source: IMF, *International Financial Statistics*; Bangko Sentral ng Pilipinas.

CHART 10   *Current Account Balance as % of GDP vs. Growth Rate of GDP Per Capita*

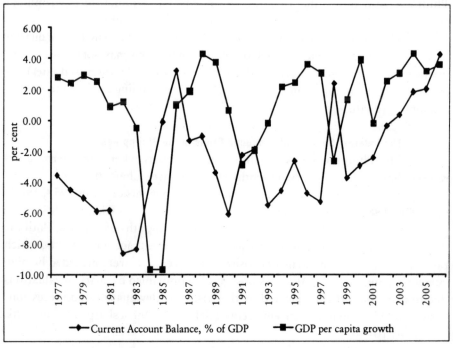

Source: IMF, *International Financial Statistics*; NSCB.

A Replay of the Asian Crisis?
Continuing Capital Account Volatility due to
Capital Account Liberalization

There appears to be a change in aggregate growth patterns since 2002, with positive and relatively high growth rates being accompanied by an improvement in the current account, leading to a significant surplus in 2006. This is largely due to the high remittances from overseas Filipino workers. While this should have brought some stability to the external account, the capital account liberalization appears to have aggravated external volatilities (see Table 2).

The external capital account was marked by high portfolio and 'other' investments in 1996 (pre-crisis), which fell in 1997 and 1998 due to the Asian crisis. There was a fleeting and partial resumption of flows in 1999 and 2000, and then a return to net outflows during 2001–04 because of political instabilities and a fiscal crisis under Presidents Estrada and Arroyo. There was a return to positive direct and portfolio investments in 2005 and 2006, but increased outflows from residents under 'other investments' in the same years. Between July 2007 and late 2007, there were massive outflows from the stocks and sovereign bonds of the Philippines due to the sub-prime crisis in the western countries. The risk premium for sovereign debt, which had improved in recent years due to the waning of the fiscal crisis and political instabilities, was increasing again as foreign investors frantically abandoned low-tiered emerging markets like the Philippines and Indonesia.

Overall, starting from the 1980s, capital account liberalization has resulted in greater volatility in exchange rates because of massive inflows and outflow of capital due to internal and external shocks (see Chart 11). The spectre of the Asian crisis is still very much present.

TABLE 2   *Balance of Payments, % of GDP*

	1996	1997	1998	1999	2000	2001	2002	2003	2004	2005	2006
Current Account	−4.8	−5.3	2.4	−3.8	−2.9	−2.4	−0.4	0.4	1.9	2.0	4.3
Goods and Services	−9.4	−12.3	−4.1	−10.0	−10.3	−12.0	−9.8	−9.8	−8.6	−9.3	−6.5
Goods 1/	−13.7	−13.5	0.0	−7.8	−7.9	−8.8	−7.2	−7.3	−6.6	−7.9	−5.9
Net Services	4.2	1.2	−4.0	−2.1	−2.5	−3.2	−2.6	−2.5	−2.0	−1.4	−0.6
Net Income and Current Transfers	4.7	7.0	6.5	6.2	7.4	9.6	9.5	10.2	10.5	11.3	10.8
Capital and Financial Account	10.0	1.5	−0.4	8.7	2.3	1.5	0.6	−0.5	−2.2	0.4	−1.8
Net Financial Account	13.6	7.9	0.7	5.5	4.3	0.5	0.5	0.6	−1.9	2.2	−1.6
Net Direct Investment	1.6	1.3	3.3	1.5	2.8	0.5	1.9	0.2	0.1	1.7	1.9
Net Portfolio Investment	6.4	0.7	−1.4	4.8	−0.7	0.1	1.0	0.7	−0.7	3.5	2.3
Net Financial Derivatives	0.0	0.0	0.0	0.0	0.1	0.0	0.0	−0.1	0.0	0.0	−0.1
Net Other Investments	5.6	5.9	−1.1	−0.8	2.1	0.0	−2.3	−0.3	−1.4	−3.0	−5.7
Net Errors and Omissions	−3.6	−6.4	−1.2	3.0	−2.1	0.9	0.0	−1.1	−0.3	−1.8	−0.3
Overall BOP Position	5.2	−3.8	2.0	4.9	−0.6	−1.0	0.2	−0.1	−0.3	2.4	2.5

Source: IMF, *International Financial Statistics*; Bangko Sentral ng Pilipinas.

CHART 11   *Growth Rate of Nominal Exchange Rate*

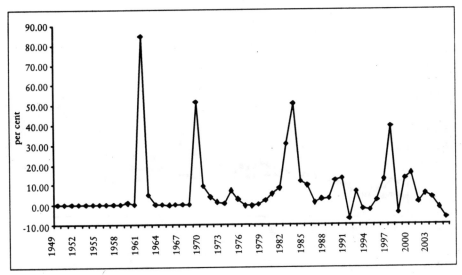

Source: IMF, *International Financial Statistics*.

The strong appreciation of the Philippine *peso* from 2005 up to August 2007 was due to the global weakness of the dollar, strong remittances from Filipino workers, and portfolio inflows into the stock and sovereign bond markets. This led to complaints from exporters and import-competing domestic sectors that their prices may no longer be competitive. Overseas Filipino workers also were alarmed at how the strong appreciation had dissipated the purchasing power of their remitted earnings.

But in August 2007, the *peso* started to weaken again as speculative foreign capital flowed out of the country due to the sub-prime crisis, because it viewed the country's near-junk rating from the rating agencies as similar to the hedge funds related to the sub-prime loans. The resulting flight to safety to US Treasury Bills hit the low-tiered emerging markets (Indonesia and the Philippines) the hardest. Sovereign bond risk premiums increased again and it will once again be more costly for the Philippines to borrow from the international market. One can see clearly that the Asian crisis is actually continuing due to the lack of corrective measures to prevent it from happening again.

Continuing Low Confidence in the Financial Sector

This is even more true in the Philippines as the loss of confidence in the financial system continues. The low financial confidence can be seen in the declining M2 and domestic credit as percentage of GDP after the Asian crisis (see Chart 12).

It is also manifested in banks not wanting to lend to the private sector because of several factors, such as strict capital adequacy ratios and high loan-loss provisions, the need to quickly dispose of non-performing assets, low interest rates and declining gaps between lending and deposit rates, political instabilities, fiscal crisis and other economic instabilities, including high oil prices.

CHART 12   *M2 and Domestic Credit, % of GDP*

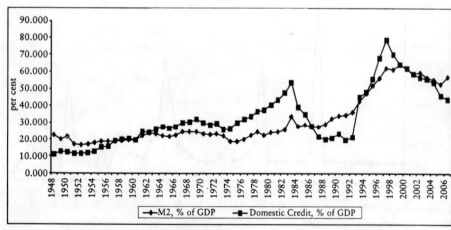

Source: IMF, *International Financial Statistics.*

The weak financial confidence mirrors the almost decade-long financial decline from the mid-1980s to early 1990s as the Philippines joined the Latin American countries afflicted by the infamous debt crisis of the 1980s (see Chart 12). As a result, financial institutions prefer to hold government securities rather than lend to the private sector due to the perceived safety of the former. This has kept interest rates low despite the fiscal crisis of the government.

The Fiscal Crisis

The similarities of the current situation with the period of the Asian crisis are further enhanced by the fiscal crisis the Philippines is facing. This crisis was caused by high national government deficits and initial losses of the state-owned National Power Corporation. One can see from Chart 13 that the Philippines achieved a fiscal surplus before the crisis. This deteriorated into deficits during the crisis, and deteriorated even more after the crisis, reaching a deficit of more than 5 per cent of GDP in 2002.

The main problem is that even with the economic recovery after the crisis, the tax effort continued to deteriorate, as Chart 14 shows. The tax revenue improved in 2006 due to the R-VAT law, which expanded value-added taxation to services, oil products and other previously exempted products. The law further increased the VAT tax rate from 10 to 12 per cent.

Although there were improvements in the tax effort in 2005 and 2006, the decline in the fiscal deficit from 2003 to 2006 was primarily a result of expenditure cutbacks at a time when the interest burden was increasing. This is shown in Chart 15. Thus the fiscal crisis, though widely publicized as possibly leading to an Argentina-like debt default and economic collapse, actually led to cutbacks

CHART 13   *National Government Deficit, % of GDP*

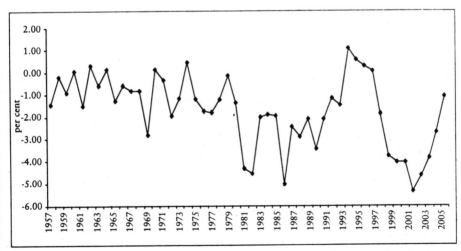

Source: IMF, *International Financial Statistics*; Department of Finance, Bangko Sentral ng Pilipinas.

CHART 14   *Tax Effort: Tax Revenue to GDP Ratio* (%)

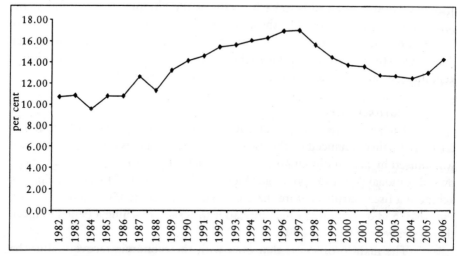

Source: *ADB Key Indicators,* various years; Department of Finance, Bangko Sentral ng Pilipinas.

CHART 15   *Share to Government Revenue of Various Government Services*

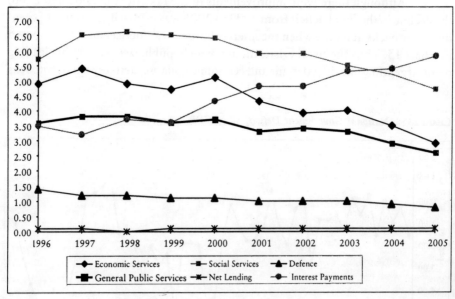

Source: Bangko Sentral ng Pilipinas.

in social and economic services that increased the difficulties of the population. It also meant cutbacks in infrastructure spending that adversely affected the domestic economy, exports and the majority of the population.

The extreme burden of public debt service and high public debt burden is shown in Table 3. More than 80 per cent of government revenues was going towards meeting principal and interest payments on public debt. This necessitated further cuts in expenditures and the accumulation of more debt. And so the fiscal crisis returned in 2007 despite the improvements in 2006. The tax effort fell to 11.6 per cent in the first quarter of 2007 despite the economy growing at 6.9 per cent. Revenue collection and budget deficit targets from January to May 2007 were missed, causing renewed concerns of a fiscal crisis all over again.

By late 2007 this situation resulted in:

- S & P, Moody's and Fitch refusing to upgrade Philippine sovereign credit rating in 2007.
- The IMF, the credit rating agencies and international financial capital demanding new tax measures. The government is officially resisting because of its defeat in the senatorial elections of 2007.
- The government admitting the need to improve tax administration and concentrate on collections from big corporations and rich individuals, though many doubt if it has enough political will.[2]
- Government plans to sell and privatize government assets and companies, to make up for the missed targets.
- Promises to invest heavily in infrastructure building to pump-prime the economy, though low revenue collections make this unlikely.

TABLE 3   *Indicators of Burden of Public Debt and Public Debt Service*

	1998	1999	2000	2001	2002	2003	2004	2005	2006
As % of NG Revenues:									
NG Debt Service Payments	35.6	42.9	44.3	48.4	61.9	73.5	85.1	83.2	87.2
Interest	21.6	22.2	27.4	30.8	32.1	35.4	36.9	36.7	31.7
Principal	14.0	20.7	16.9	17.6	29.8	38.1	48.2	46.5	55.6
As % of GDP									As of July 2006
Total National Govt Debt	56.1	59.6	64.6	65.7	71.0	78.2	79.0	72.3	69.6
Domestic	31.9	32.9	31.8	34.4	37.1	39.7	41.5	40.2	38.2
Foreign	24.2	26.8	32.7	31.3	33.9	38.5	37.5	32.0	31.4
As % of GDP									
Total Public Sector Debt	94.6	101.5	108.0	106.0	110.2	118.2	109.8	93.4	n.a.
Domestic	35.2	32.8	32.1	32.7	34.4	35.7	35.4	33.0	n.a.
Foreign	59.5	68.7	75.9	73.3	75.9	82.5	74.4	60.4	n.a.

Source: Department of Finance, Bangko Sentral ng Pilipinas.

The government's fiscal targets – inspired by the IMF (International Monetary Fund), sovereign credit agencies and international finance – are indeed very strict. The target year for achieving fiscal balance has been advanced from 2010 to 2008. It now looks like the government has shot itself in the foot. The inability to achieve its own fiscal target has caused a loss in confidence. (This sounds familiar as the very tight fiscal targets set by the IMF during the Asian crisis caused losses of confidence not only in the Philippines, but in Indonesia and the other IMF-assisted countries.)

Recipe for Another Crisis?

The ingredients of another Philippine-style Asian crisis is in the making, with a mixture of external shocks – massive outflows due to external shocks such as the sub-prime crisis – and a potentially explosive political situation following the guilty decision on ex-President Estrada, the re-opening of President Arroyo's election rigging case in the last presidential election, and a new scandal concerning an allegedly corrupt deal with a Chinese firm to bring broadband services to the government system.

Thus the signs that a 1997-type crisis is being replayed are many. To start with, there is evidence of external sector volatility, with an initial strong appreciation of the *peso* and then a weakening as speculative investors left within weeks of the sub-prime crisis. Second, banks have not been lending to the private commodity-producing sectors, but there has been a rise in bank lending in early 2007 to the property sector with indications of a property bubble. What is more, just when bank lending recovered in 2007, the central bank decided to mop up liquidity because it feared that high inflows of remittances would spur inflation in excess of its targets. Third, the stockmarket has also been volatile, with the benchmark index rising by almost 100 per cent between 2004 and September 2007 (pointing to a speculative bubble), and falling by as much as 25 per cent in the wake of the sub-prime crisis. Fourth, this has occurred in a context of growing portfolio flows, especially into and out of the stockmarket and sovereign bonds. The only missing ingredient is a current account deficit, but the danger is there because even though the Philippines' international reserves have increased significantly, they are much smaller than in other countries.

An Alternative Economic Programme

All this emphasizes the vulnerability of the current economic regime to the vagaries of international financial markets. It is therefore high time that serious thought be put to alternative economic policies that protect the country from the capriciousness of international speculative capital. I detail some possible alternatives in what follows.

Undervalued Currency with Market-Based Capital Controls

The first proposal involves establishing a *peso* narrow band at an undervalued level. To be successful, this has to be supported by a Chilean-style tax on short-term capital inflows, or an exit tax (Malaysian style) for capital outflows on funds staying less than one year in the country. The purposes of this would be to reduce exaggerated short-term capital inflows and outflows; to ensure more exchange rate and price stability; to protect export and import-competing sectors; to protect the purchasing power of overseas workers; and to bias monetary policy towards a more accommodating rather than a contractionary stance.

Reduce Fiscal Tightness and Focus Tax Collection on Big Corporations and Rich Families

The second policy consists of relaxing overly strict fiscal targets, and implementing progressive taxation and policies to reduce the debt burden. Instead of imposing indirect taxes and targeting taxation of fixed income earners, the government should improve tax administration, and remove the high exemptions for corporations and rich individuals. In the implementation of tax collection there should be strong pursuit of big tax evaders, and severe, visible and widely publicized punishment of these corporations and individuals. The fiscal deficit targets should be revised to around 1 to 2.5 per cent of GDP in the next few years. This will allow more time and room to improve the tax structure and institutions, as well as ensure financing for already constricted social and economic services, and infrastructure building.

The current high public debt service burden should be reduced by strong negotiations for debt and interest reduction, and, if this is not possible, at least long-run rescheduling at lower interest rates to reflect current international lending rates.

A More Progressive Industrial Policy

The third set of policies consists of improving the industrial policy to tackle both market failures and government failures. It should be noted that despite espousing free trade, the government still does have some sort of industrial policy, which consists of: promotion of business process outsourcing and call centres, with little multiplier effects and sectoral linkages; export of semiconductors and electronics, with little value-added due to high import content; and reliance on injections of remittances from overseas workers as the driver for growth.

Instead, it is recommended that industrial promotion be more focused on viable sectors with greater multiplier effects, higher technological spillovers, more employment generation and greater economies of scale, via providing complementary infrastructure, direct or credit subsidies and tax incentives for such sectors. Promotion of a strong industrial and manufacturing base requires promoting vibrant and competitive steel, cement, petrochemical, electronics and metal productive sectors. Employment-generating programmes and measures to facilitate upward mobility from unskilled to skilled labour for the majority of workers should be planned and implemented. All this requires an efficient and honest government that implements these policies with transparency and fairness, which can only be ensured through political struggle.

Rethinking Restrictive Inflation Targeting and Financial Liberalization Policies

Monetary and credit policies should be supportive of the integrated industrial policy, so that liquidity in the system will not be wasted in speculative activities (too much investments in high-end real property and the stockmarket). Instead of mopping up liquidity for fear of inflation or overspeculation, the low lending to the private sector should be corrected by redirecting liquidity to the priority sectors through proper economic and credit incentives. The rediscount windows of the central bank should be made more active in credit allocation to banks with loan portfolios that are more productivity- and employment-sensitive with healthy repayment rates. Financial instruments and bonds can be created with the cooperation of the business sector to target savers from the domestic economy and overseas workers to invest in priority sectors.

Social Policies for the Poor and Vulnerable

The market and the capitalist system are not kind to the poor, the un-educated, the unskilled, and victims of natural and human disasters. It is imperative that poverty reduction not be dependent on economic growth alone, especially in the current jobless growth situation. That is why fiscal policies must be designed to accommodate social programmes and skill development programmes which ensure that the poor and the vulnerable will not only have access to basic needs and services, but will also be able to experience upward mobility – not only in their employment but in their total human development.

If programmes and policies such as these are adopted, the low-quality growth as well as the extreme vulnerabilities to external shocks and contagion can be addressed. And ten years from now, hopefully, the Asian crisis will be an event in the past.

I would like to thank Mr Alvin Firmeza for his research help.

Notes

[1] In a country of more than 80 million people, there is hardly any operating steel or petrochemical industry.
[2] The head of the Bureau of Internal Revenue was sacked on 21 June 2007, but the structure of tax collection – which reeks of corruption – remains intact.

References

Lim, Joseph, 'Philippine Monetary Policy: A Critical Assessment and Search for Alternatives', to be published by Policy and Economic Research Institute (PERI), University of Massachusetts, Amherst, and International Review of Applied Economics.
Stiglitz, Joseph (2007), 'The Asian Crisis Ten Years After', Project Syndicate.

Economic Performance after
Financial Crisis in Other Emerging Markets

Latin American Financial Crises and Recovery

Jan Kregel

Although the financial crises that struck emerging market developing countries in the 1990s were all characterized by large and abrupt capital reversals, the causes of the conditions that first generated the capital inflows and then triggered the capital reversals were very different in Latin America as compared to Asia. In Asia, savings and investment rates were extremely high, stable growth at double digit rates had become commonplace in conditions of stable prices, and exchange rates were stable with contained fiscal and external balances. Although it was questionable whether these countries actually needed additional financial resources from external capital inflows, an increasing number of foreign investors were attracted by what appeared to be a successful long-term growth process with high and stable returns to investment.

In Latin America, on the other hand, savings and investment rates had been persistently low, with chronic fiscal and external disequilibrium associated with hyperinflation and high exchange rate volatility. There was little in the actual performance of the Latin American economies emerging from the 1980s debt crisis to attract foreign investors. Instead, the inflow of external finance was induced by the policies that were introduced to deal with the aftermath of the 1980s debt crisis – the Brady Plan and the structural adjustment policies that accompanied it. It was the expectation of quick profits from the liberalization of what had been highly regulated economies, as they privatized state-owned companies and replaced import substitution with market-led liberalization and deregulation, that brought capital inflows. But, in distinction to Asia, the inflows were primarily directed to financial assets, rather than to real assets such as export facilities or real estate.

The fact that these capital inflows were soon reversed in the 1994–95 Tequila crisis in Mexico, the Brazilian exchange rate crisis of 1999 and the Argentine crisis of 1998–2001 can be seen as confirmation of the failure of the adjustment policies to provide sustainable recovery from the 1980s debt crisis. To date, all three countries have avoided a third round of financial crisis, but with widely differing real economic performance. While Brazil and Mexico have persisted with modified versions of their previous policies and have maintained price stability, this has come at the cost of a lower trend growth rate than they had experienced in the 1960s and 1970s. Argentina, on the other hand, has made a sharp break with its previous policies, defaulting on its foreign debt and concentrating on domestic demand. It has seen a sharp increase in its trend growth rate and a recovery in employment, although with some evidence of emerging inflationary pressures and supply bottlenecks, especially in energy.

The lessons from a comparison of Latin American and Asian recovery from crisis must be drawn against the background of the very different causes that attracted the inflows and their subsequent reversal, in particular the failure of post-crisis adjustment policies.

Policy-Induced Capital Inflows

After the declines in income growth that occurred after 1982 as Latin American debtor countries attempted to produce current account surpluses large enough to meet outstanding debt service proved to be politically unacceptable, the Brady Plan shifted the focus of the resolution of the outstanding debt: from policies to create large current account surpluses by reducing activity levels, to policies that would allow Latin American countries to access the international capital markets. This was intended to allow them to return to growth by refinancing the majority of their outstanding debt to commercial bank syndicates in the US and Europe by shifting it to the private sector institutional lenders in those countries.

Thus Latin American countries were encouraged to introduce changes in their domestic policy framework to make them more attractive as destinations for international portfolio and direct investment flows. The primary objective of domestic stabilization policies, in addition to the elimination of extremely high inflation and, in some cases, hyperinflation, was thus the creation of conditions that would allow the countries to return to international capital markets to refinance their outstanding indebtedness and their existing levels of external deficits. The preferred avenue was via the stabilization of exchange rates and rapid return to full convertibility of currencies at a targeted exchange rate or fluctuation band. Thus Mexico and Brazil introduced exchange rate regimes based on tight fluctuation bands, and Argentina opted for a fixed rate of exchange for the *peso* to the US dollar through the Convertibility Law. Not only were they initially successful in reducing nominal exchange rate volatility, they all experienced substantial real exchange rate appreciation.

These stable exchange rate regimes were supported by policies to introduce market-based resource allocation through a reduction in the role of government in the economy, through privatization of state-owned enterprises, deregulation of financial and goods markets, and the creation of primary government budget surpluses. Tight restrictions on expansion of the domestic money supply were put in place, and all these countries eventually introduced legislation to increase the autonomy of the central bank. Domestic goods markets were opened to competition from foreign imports to reinforce the price stabilization policy.

The privatization of state-owned enterprises through direct sale or by flotation in domestic equity markets served to draw the attention of foreign portfolio investors to what were to become known as 'emerging equity markets'. Further financial market deregulation, capital account liberalization and active policies to support the growth of domestic equity markets were introduced to encourage capital inflows to purchase domestic financial assets and provide foreign exchange to repay, as well as the opportunity to refinance, the accumulated debt burden from the 1980s.

The basic difference from the multitude of previous failed attempts to fight hyperinflation, and the major reason for the success of these policies in eliminating inflation so rapidly, was the increased liberalization of foreign capital inflows. Previous attempts at stabilization had seen the rise in domestic incomes and consumption and imports, along with the decline in domestic export competitiveness that was caused by real or nominal exchange rate appreciation resulting from the use of an exchange rate anchor, produce balance of payments crises, devaluation and a return of inflation. This also occurred in the 1990s, but because capital inflows were more than sufficient to cover the external deficits and caused reserves to increase and reinforce market perceptions of strength, instead of devaluation, there was currency appreciation.

Thus it was the Brady Plan and the success of the structural adjustment policies to open investment opportunities in conditions of low inflation that brought the capital inflows which would then produce the reversal and the crisis of the 1990s, as the policies failed to deliver long-term increases in growth and profitability. A number of factors that were crucial to the success in fighting inflation were also important in preventing a return to sustained growth.

As mentioned, in most countries successful inflation reduction was accompanied by real appreciation of exchange rates. Tight monetary policies in the presence of falling inflation rates led to extremely high real interest rates that caused a deterioration in external accounts and dampened incentives to invest to increase domestic productivity. The capital inflows had little impact in increasing domestic savings and investment, and were primarily in portfolio assets rather than real assets.

Thus, although most Latin American countries introduced market-based stabilization policies that achieved success in eliminating inflation, and have been praised for introducing policies that produce good 'macroeconomic fundamentals', they were not able to harness free trade and capital flows as engines of stable growth in per capita incomes. The success of the policies adopted to produce stability in macroeconomic fundamentals – low inflation, primary budget surpluses and control of money supply – overlooked more traditional macroeconomic fundamentals such as high levels of aggregate demand, low real interest rates and competitive real exchange rates. As a result, they created an overall macroeconomic environment that impeded the required structural changes at the micro level to meet the challenge of the substitution of state controls by market forces through external competition. This failure recreated difficulties at the macro level that appear to have undermined the sought-after return to growth and financial stability. In addition, these changes at the macro level have reduced the possibility to use traditional stabilization policies, and thus have tended to aggravate the response to crisis when it occurred.

Thus, five areas can be identified in which structural adjustment policies undermined the stability of the macroeconomic fundamentals and the adjustment of the production structure. The first is the overvaluation of the exchange rate; the second is the high level of real interest rates; the third is the composition of the fiscal budget; the fourth, the composition of the external account; and the fifth, the failure of adjustment of the industrial production structure to reduce the dependence of increased investment and increased export capacity on imported inputs.

Exchange Rates

Success in fighting inflation in the presence of a stable nominal exchange rate produces real exchange rate appreciation. In the presence of unilateral trade liberalization, this makes it more difficult for domestic industry to respond to the new price and productivity structure after opening the domestic economy to global competition through trade. While overvaluation of the exchange rate is beneficial in reducing the price level of imported goods and creating competition for domestic producers, it also allows foreign importers to gain competitive advantage relative to domestic producers. This is especially so if domestic producers cannot adjust their cost and production structures rapidly while foreign producers are simply faced with increasing output, which can be done rapidly and with declining costs in conditions of excess capacity.

Interest Rates

Tight monetary policies that were considered necessary to bring inflation under control, as well as the perceived need to provide attractive returns to external investors in order to ensure the capital inflows required to refinance outstanding debt and to provide finance for the modernization of domestic industry, produced high nominal interest rates. In conditions of rapidly falling inflation rates, these translated into extremely high real interest rates. Thus, on the one hand, domestic industry faced excessively high interest rates to finance restructuring, while banks (who, during hyperinflation, had ceased to provide credit to the private sector) found it more attractive to increase holdings of high-yielding government securities, often financed by borrowing in international markets at cheaper external interest rates, or to take advantage of the deregulation of financial markets to offer credit to consumers. Business firms, facing a lack of domestic credit and extremely high domestic interest rates, also were attracted to borrowing abroad at much lower rates of interest, creating increased foreign exchange exposure that was usually not hedged because of the confidence in exchange rate stability created by the elimination of inflation and the return of foreign capital inflows. The result was that domestic banks concentrated on financing government debt and provided virtually no lending to the private business sector, although consumer lending expanded as a result of deregulation. Private sector business financed production either from own funds or by borrowing at lower rates in foreign currency from abroad, creating implicit asset–liability mismatches and increased financial fragility.

On the other hand, governments found themselves in a position of having to refinance and issue new debt at real interest rates that were far higher than real domestic growth rates, creating conditions in which reduction in the debt burden became impossible, irrespective of the restrictiveness of the government's financial policy. Indeed, the restrictive fiscal policy often only served to depress domestic activity and tax yields, thus increasing the size of the deficits to be financed, while it did little to reduce government borrowing costs that were set by international risk premia.

One of the basic reasons for implementing anti-inflation policies linked to exchange rate stability was that these policies would bring about a decline in interest rates and thus a decrease in financing costs that would provide support for investment. High interest rates were believed to be caused by a large inflation premium and the risks of exchange rate depreciation. Lower inflation would reduce the inflation premium and exchange rate stability would reduce exchange rate risk, bringing about a reduction in nominal interest rates that would provide a boost to domestic investment without any negative impact on external capital inflows. Indeed one of the main justifications for pegging the *peso* to the dollar under the Convertibility Law was the expectation that domestic interest rates would converge towards those prevailing in the US. However, the need to attract international capital and induce residents to maintain local currency deposits along with differential credit risks of Latin American financial institutions offset many of the benefits of lower inflation and exchange rate stability.

Further, the deregulation of financial markets increased the costs of financial transactions in domestic credit markets disproportionately for small and intermediate businesses that did not benefit from the preferential access accorded to large businesses in international capital markets. The differential in interest rates and disparate financial costs contributed to the consolidation and concentration of private national economic groups in many countries in the region. The persistence of large interest rate differentials also generated inflows based on interest rate arbitrage similar to those that had been prevalent in Asia.

Government Expenditure

The reliance on external capital inflows for the success of the inflation policies that was inherent in the Brady Plan produced a resumption of external debt accumulation. This caused a structural shift in the composition of government expenditures on current account. First, rapid and unforeseen declines in inflation tended to increase labour costs as a share of government expenditure, as wages adjusted less rapidly than other elements of government expenditure. At the same time, the increasing debt burden, and the failure of interest rates to fall, increased the interest component of current government expenditure. With fiscal austerity measures aimed at balancing the budget, declining expenditure on goods and labour services was in many cases offset by the fall in income and thus tax yields, and the increased interest service on outstanding debt due to increased indebtedness and higher real interest rates. This negative impact on government finances was reinforced by the negative carry on the increased reserves due to the difference between the domestic interest rate paid on the bonds issued to sterilize the capital inflows, and the developed country short-term rate earned on the deposit of the reserves in dollars in New York.

External Account Balances

A similar shift occurred in the composition of the current account, as the share of factor services increased relative to goods and services trade as a result of the increasing size of debt service payments. This shift was further reinforced by the fact that with global financial integration, an increasing share of domestic government debt was being held either directly or indirectly by non-residents. In addition, the sharp increase in direct investment flows also increased non-resident claims on current account in the form of non-repatriated profits. Thus, just as the interest cost of government debt became an increasingly important component of government budgets, factor services became an increasingly important component of the current account balance for countries engaged in successful structural adjustment to conditions of hyperinflation.

Changed Response to Economic Policies

The return of substantial capital inflows, and the shifts in the structure of internal and external account balances that resulted, brought about an important change in the way these economies responded to traditional stabilization policy measures. For example, in Argentina the rapid increase in the external deficit after stabilization was not a cause for policy concern, since, under its currency board system, it was considered impossible for the central bank to provide financing for a fiscal or an external deficit. Instead, an autonomous adjustment mechanism similar to that which was presumed to have existed under the gold standard was expected to operate. Any deficit on the external account that was not financed by the private sector would produce an outflow of foreign exchange reserves and thus a decline in the domestic money supply that would cause domestic wages and prices to fall, restoring external competitiveness, increasing exports and reducing imports until external balance was achieved. However, this automatic adjustment process can be severely disrupted if other factors determine the quantity of reserves, and other components of the external account dominate trade in goods and services. As a result of the liberalization and deregulation of domestic goods and financial markets after the introduction of the Convertibility Law in Argentina, private capital inflows more than offset the current account deficit. Indeed, up to the period of the Tequila crisis, non-financial private sector inflows alone more than covered the current account deficit. Although the central bank did not finance the current account deficit, external creditors did, and, as a consequence, the constraint on domestic money supply growth was inoperative. Indeed, the flows were so large as to create impetus in the opposite direction. There was thus no automatic adjustment to ensure external equilibrium.

There is an equivalent argument for the automatic adjustment of the fiscal balance, since under the currency board system the central bank cannot monetize government debt unless it also acquires foreign exchange. Thus, when government fiscal receipts fail to cover its expenditures, it must either increase taxation or reduce expenditures, unless it can borrow from the private sector. Any of these responses should have the same general effect of reducing domestic demand and exercising downward pressure on wages and prices. This should cause imports to fall, exports to rise and external demand to expand sufficiently to offset the fall in internal demand. However, this adjustment mechanism can also become inoperative because of external capital flows. For the first half of the decade, the government could count on revenues from the sale of state-owned property, and in the second, on a captive market for government debt created by reform of the pension system and of banking laws.

Thus, as long as private sector lenders are willing to finance imbalances, the automatic adjustment mechanisms may not function as expected. It is often argued that no action should be taken to offset such flows since they are the expression of the private market – known as the Lawson Doctrine; nonetheless, they offset the possibility of the market providing the automatic adjustment to external and internal imbalance that eventually produces financial crisis.

The build-up of external and internal indebtedness that large private sector capital inflows create also means that there is a change in the way economies respond to Keynesian policy measures. By cutting government expenditure, traditional Keynesian balance of payments adjustment policies aim to create a fiscal surplus that is reflected in a balance of payments surplus, as declining incomes reduce imports and the resulting excess productive capacity is directed to increasing exports. But when fiscal expenditure and external claims are dominated by debt service payments, policies that influence income levels may have little impact on net internal and external balances. If the restrictive demand policies increase international risk premia because international investors view falling growth and profit rates as increasing the likelihood of exchange rate adjustment or of a reversal of stabilization policy, the resulting increase in interest costs may more than offset any improvement in spending, leading to a deterioration in the accounts. The basic difficulty is that while government expenditure policy may influence imports and exports of goods and services, the debt service component of internal and external expenditure is determined by other factors such as international interest rates, the maturity structure of the debt and repayment patterns over which governments have little direct control.

Thus, while Mexico, Brazil and Argentina all managed to tame high or hyperinflation and enjoyed exchange rate stability, booming financial markets and rising foreign investment, by the middle of the 1990s they were also experiencing rising external and fiscal deficits, increasing external indebtedness and faltering growth performance. The underlying logic of the Washington Consensus that import substitution growth strategies could be replaced by eliminating inflation distortion and restoring the profitability of investment so that resources were more efficiently allocated, and by foreign direct investment creating a competitive export platform to eliminate the external constraint, proved to be mistaken.

The Post-Crisis Recovery Experience in Brazil, Mexico and Argentina

There is one common characteristic of the recovery in all three countries: the crisis forced them to abandon their exchange rate policies. Since these policies had been under threat due to the rising levels of internal and external deficits, they required increasingly tight monetary and fiscal policies to attract the external inflows needed to keep exchange rates stable. The possibility to relax policy provided an opening for recovery and higher growth that was experienced in all countries. However, after crisis, both Brazil and Mexico took measures to restore their prior policy stance, although with nominally flexible exchange rates. Their expansions were thus shortlived, and they were soon experiencing a return of capital inflows and exchange rate overvaluation in conditions of low trend growth. Argentina, on the other hand, explicitly rejected a return to externally financed growth, and introduced policies to keep interest rates low and a policy of stabilization of the real exchange rate. It has experienced higher than trend growth on a sustained basis since the recovery began in mid-2002.

Brazil's 1999 Exchange Rate Crisis and Recovery

In Brazil the recovery was very shortlived, as restrictive policies were quickly reintroduced. President Cardoso campaigned on maintaining control of inflation through stability of the exchange rate. Thus, despite the deterioration of the external and fiscal balances, tight monetary and fiscal policy was maintained in order to generate the external capital inflows required to defend the *real* in the face of rising unemployment and falling growth. Real interest rates that had averaged around 20 per cent in the period of the Real Plan shot up above 40 per cent in the last half of 1998. Unemployment rose from just under 5 per cent in 1995 to over 8 per cent in 1998, while the growth rate fell from a Real Plan average of over 3 per cent to near-zero in 1998. This policy was reinforced by a $35 billion IMF support loan,[1] which required maintaining current policies. Despite this 'bullet-proofing' attempt to convince financial markets to sustain their investments in Brazil, net capital movements fell from $26 billion in 1997 to less than $16 billion at the end of 1998, and foreign exchange reserves fell from nearly $75 billion in April of 1998 to around $36 billion in January 1999.

Against a current account deficit running in excess of $30 billion in 1997 and 1998 and without signs of improvement in either the fiscal or external balance, and with the successful re-election campaign over, the exchange rate band was abandoned in January 1999. The result was extreme exchange rate uncertainty in which the *real* surpassed 2 *reis* to the US dollar and then stabilized. Against conventional expectations, the inflation pass-through was moderate and produced a permanent devaluation of the currency. When Arminio Fraga was appointed to

CHART 1 *Brazil: Real Annual GDP Growth, 1994–2006*

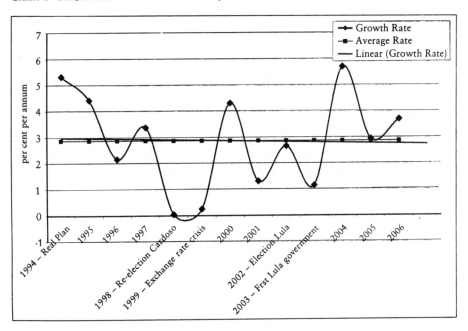

head the central bank, he introduced a policy of guiding interest rates downward, while the government persisted in its policy of running primary surpluses. The result was a short-term spurt in growth in 2000 that was quickly reversed by contractionary policies at the end of the Cardoso administration and the speculation and exchange rate volatility surrounding the incoming Lula administration, even though it largely adopted the policy stance of the outgoing government.

The Recovery from the Mexican Crisis of 1994–95

Mexico, like Brazil, had followed a policy of currency stability through an exchange rate band, and experienced capital inflows more than sufficient to cover its rising external and internal imbalances. At the end of 1994, just as the NAFTA treaty was being implemented, and following a period of modest economic growth but with increasing political turmoil surrounding the change in government and the announcement of a revolutionary movement in the south, foreign investors lost confidence in the ability of the government to maintain its exchange rate policy. Short-term government liabilities sold to foreigners could not be rolled over and the *peso* collapsed. The IMF, with the aid of the US and other governments, produced one of the largest aid packages ever granted.[2] In exchange for the funding programme, Mexico was required to implement a drastic adjustment package, similar to those seen in Asia after the 1997 crisis. Restrictive fiscal and monetary policy and wage controls formed the traditional structural adjustment policy. The result was a deep decline in output and employment, of over 6 per cent and over 5 per cent in 1994 and 1995, respectively, with inflation shooting up to around 51 per cent in 1995. However, much like in Brazil, the crisis was quickly reversed. The economy started to recover in the third quarter of 1995, and GDP grew over 5 per cent in 1996 and by over 6 per cent in 1997.

The immediate and most significant trigger was the fall in private expenditure, i.e. private fixed investment and private consumption. The drop of the latter was due to a 13 per cent (seasonally adjusted) decline of real wages. The reduction in government expenditure was also a contributing factor to the decrease of demand and output, but of lesser importance. On the other hand, non-oil exports responded quickly and robustly to the large depreciation of the *peso*, and the domestic receipts from oil exports also rose. The large improvement of the trade balance from the downward adjustment of imports and the growth of exports supported the level of demand and economic activity.

While the collapse in demand and output was partially offset by the growth of net exports, the growth of exports proved to be the single most important factor contributing to the recovery, with both oil and non-oil exports growing at a high rate. Eventually imports recovered, and the import coefficient also rose. The decline in government expenditure also reversed and offset its decline during the downswing – the growth rate from the quarter prior to the crisis until the upper point of the recovery exceeded the rate of growth of GDP. Private expenditure, however, did not recover from its decline during the downswing, and both consumption and fixed investment were lower at the upper point of the recovery than they had been prior to the crisis (8 per cent and 22 per cent below, respectively). Although employment was restored to its pre-crisis level, average real wages in manufacturing did not recover. In fact they were 23 per cent lower at the upper point of the recovery than in the quarter prior to the crisis.

The net additional demand generated by the government on the domestic market, deducting foreign interest payments, gives total government domestic expenditure (which is equal to government expenditure on goods and services, plus government transfers and wages, plus domestic interest payments). The deficit should refer to government expenditures over and above those financed with taxes levied on the population, which in Mexico includes government revenues from ownership of the oil industry. Thus, when a rise in the price of oil allows the government to increase domestic expenditure without changing the deficit, it will nonetheless create a net additional demand.

Therefore, in order to see the impact of fiscal policy, the government domestic deficit should be defined as the difference between government domestic expenditure and government domestic revenue. According to estimates made by Julio Lopez,[3] during both the 1980s and 1990s, Mexico always maintained a positive, and relatively high, domestic deficit: around 17 per cent of GDP in the first decade and 6 per cent in the second. That is, thanks to the ownership of the oil industry, the government has been able to exert an important positive influence on effective demand, thus stimulating employment and private profits. Also, revenues accruing from the oil industry have permitted Mexico to have a very low rate of taxation, which, obviously, has minimized social conflict.

CHART 2   *Mexico: Current Account and Fiscal Balance, 1989–98*

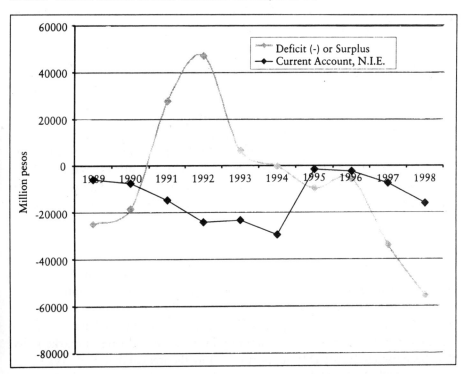

Government expenditure and the domestic deficit fell until the third quarter of 1995 and from then onwards they both recovered, remaining at a relatively high level during 1996. Finally, there was a tandem movement in the domestic deficit and total government expenditure. Indeed, the reductions in the former from a peak in the first quarter of 1996 did not provoke a fall in government expenditure, which further grew for two additional quarters – but now financed with the expansion of domestic government revenue ensuing from the recovery.

Both the domestic deficit and total government expenditure played important roles in triggering the recovery, by sustaining domestic demand and private profits when other components of domestic demand were collapsing. Once the recovery started, other factors such as private domestic expenditure revived to ensure its continuance.

Thus, while the government officially followed the orthodox structural adjustment policy, the rise in oil prices and the devaluation reduced the pressure to continue to cut expenditure because the total budget was balanced. The rise of the price of oil along with the devaluation of the currency was therefore an important factor which explains the fiscal policy stance.

Argentina's Recovery from the 2001 Default

The political stalemate that followed the resignation of the Argentine government in 2001 and the Christmas eve default of Argentina's sovereign debt meant that there was little time for a formal change in economic policy. However, the elimination of the need to meet external and internal debt service automatically created a less restrictive policy that was reinforced by the market-led devaluation of the exchange rate following the revocation of the Convertibility Law and the sharp increase in the terms of trade of Argentina's main agricultural exports. Thus the initial response was a sharp increase in exports and a collapse in imports due to the deepening recession.

After a period of political uncertainty and economic experimentation, a stable government was elected, and policy concentrated on domestic recovery as a prelude to reaching conciliation with creditors. Rapid reconciliation with creditors had been supported by the IMF in order to allow Argentina to return to international capital markets to borrow, so as to meet arrears in debt service. This had been the policy in the Brady Plan and all subsequent crisis resolution policy. But, as argued above, this approach does not provide a real solution to the crisis, but simply uses additional borrowing to replace prior borrowing.

Argentina faced special conditions because the IMF declined to continue to support the government programme, following suggestions by the US Treasury Secretary Paul O'Neill that the past history of IMF-supported bail-outs of debtor countries had created moral hazard amongst creditors who had come to believe in an IMF guarantee on emerging market debt. He also argued that the threat of contagion producing systemic instability in international capital markets that had been used to justify IMF support was more theoretical than real. As a result, not only did the IMF withdraw support, it failed to provide support for the Argentine recovery programme as it had done in the case of Brazil and Mexico.

Instead, the government argued that only by returning to sustained growth

CHART 3 *Argentina: Aggregate Demand Shares of GDP* (seasonally adjusted)

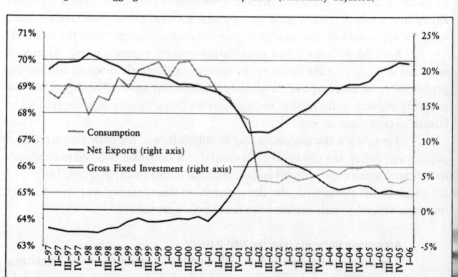

could Argentina make a credible commitment to sustainable debt repayment. The question at issue between the government and the IMF was whether the new government's surplus target would be one that maximized the probability of sustained growth (and thus implicitly also maximized the amounts received by creditors), or whether the surplus target would be one that maximized the amounts received by creditors (and thus implicitly jeopardized domestic growth and maximized the risk of another default and rescheduling in the short period). In response to the IMF's insistence on the latter stance, Argentina noted that while the Fund's new strategy of market resolution was supposed to remove the moral hazard guarantee created by an IMF bail-out, by supporting a policy that favoured the interests of the creditors, the Fund was still creating moral hazard, only now at the expense of Argentine citizens who are being asked to forego growth in order to repay debt at 100 per cent of its face value.

Indeed, a senior IMF official has confirmed that because of the Fund's position as a preferred creditor to Argentina, it was required to give priority to the interests of the private creditors. He argued that if the IMF did not participate in the debt restructuring process, then its position as a privileged creditor could be questioned and this would cause irreparable damage to the ability of the IMF to lend. As a result, he argued that the Fund must be involved in determining the fiscal policy of the debtor. This was because it makes no sense to follow a policy that leaves the determination of fiscal stance (above and beyond what is necessary to meet the debt service to the multinational lenders) to the debtor and the private creditors independent of the IMF, since it is the IMF that judges the sustainability of the debt restructuring that is reached with the private creditors.

The government argued that a surplus of 3 per cent of GDP along with a restructuring package repaying approximately 25 per cent of the debt would satisfy the requirement of producing sustained growth. Argentina eventually repaid

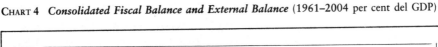

CHART 4 *Consolidated Fiscal Balance and External Balance* (1961–2004 per cent del GDP)

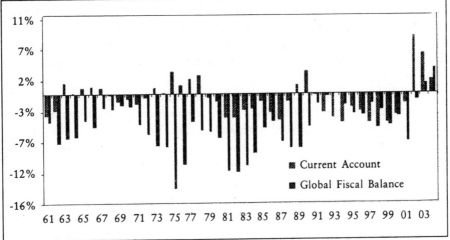

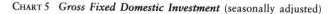

CHART 5 *Gross Fixed Domestic Investment* (seasonally adjusted)

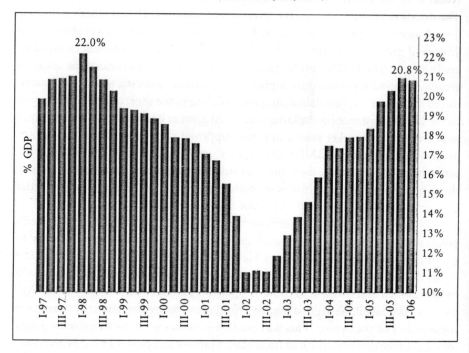

all of its outstanding borrowings to the IMF in order to maintain its policy auto-nomy. At the same time, the government refused to use tight monetary policy to return to foreign markets, instead using a policy of negative real interest rates to support the restructuring of the financial system and investment.

While net exports provided the initial impetus to the recovery of demand and the creation of internal liquidity and the increase in tax yields due to a tax on exports, internal demand soon became the driving force behind the recovery.

In particular, investment recovered sharply, and the decline in national income of nearly 11 per cent in 2002 was followed by an expansion of over 8 per cent in 2003 (peaking at an annual quarter on quarter rate of over 16 per cent in the second quarter of 2003). In a response similar to that of the Brazilian economy in 1999, removing the fixed exchange rate target allowed highly restrictive policies to be relaxed.

The recovery in economic activity dates from the last quarter of 2002 when output increased by a modest 1.2 per cent over the third quarter. However the recovery has not been as smooth and sustained as indicated by the annual growth rates, either when calculated on a year on year basis, or by annual rates calculated on the basis of comparison with the same quarter a year earlier. These annualized rates have been positive since 2003.

A particular characteristic of the recovery has been the stability of nomi-nal salaries in the private sector (around 50 per cent of total employment) that remained negative in real terms until around 2004, when real increases were

CHART 6 GDP: *Annual Rate of Change*

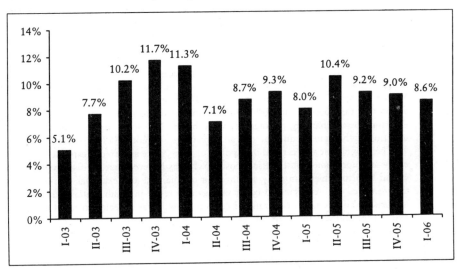

enjoyed. However, the public sector is still showing negative performance with relation to the pre-crisis period. This does much to explain the stagnant behaviour of consumption expenditure. Despite the rising levels of employment, the reduction in the poverty ratio and the Gini coefficient, the recovery has largely been to increase profits in agribusiness and manufacturing sectors at the expense of wages. As inflation is starting to resurface, this represents a potential hazard to the continuation of recovery.

Thus the positive Argentine recovery can be traced to the decision to forego a return to policies of external savings-financed investment and flexible exchange rates without capital controls. Indeed, although it was warned that it would never be able to borrow in international capital markets after the restructuring agreement, Argentina has found it necessary to introduce Chilean-style controls on capital inflows.

Notes

[1] Mr Camdessus described the programme as combining 'large up-front fiscal adjustment of over 3 per cent of GDP with reforms of social security, public administration, public expenditure management, tax policy and revenue sharing that confront head-on the structural weaknesses that lie at the root of the public sector's financial difficulties. Within this framework of structural reforms, Brazil's three-year fiscal program targets primary surpluses of 2.6 per cent of GDP in 1999, 2.8 per cent in 2000, and 3 per cent in 2001. The Brazilian authorities are also committed to further opening up the economy, ensuring firm monetary discipline and macroeconomic stability, and maintaining the current exchange rate regime, while reinforcing the exchange reserves and improving the competitiveness of the economy. The way is now open for the international community to provide financial support to Brazil that will enhance market confidence in the government's economic policies and help the success of the country's program.

Official creditors, multilateral and bilateral, will provide support totalling more than \$41 billion over the next three years, roughly \$37 billion of which is available, if needed, in the next 12 months. I say "if needed" because this is a program which has an important precautionary character, and Brazil, of course, feels free to draw on the resources for their entirety or only in part. I believe that the soundness of Brazil's program and the authorities' commitment to it together with the strong support demonstrated by the official international community provide the conditions for Brazil's private creditors now to act to help ensure its success.'

[2] The International Monetary Fund approved an eighteen-month stand-by credit for Mexico of up to the equivalent of SDR 12,070.2 million (about US\$17.8 billion) in support of the government's 1995–96 economic and financial programme. This was the largest-ever financing package approved by the IMF for a member country, both in terms of the amount and the overall percentage of quota, 688.4 per cent.

The programme was centred on a policy of wage, price and credit restraint supported by an improvement in the fiscal position. It was believed that the fiscal tightening would help to achieve an early stabilization of financial and exchange markets, and the measures were expected to boost savings and result in a substantial reduction in imports. In addition, an acceleration in export growth was expected to result from the real depreciation of the currency.

The policy on wages and prices that was formulated in the context of the Agreement of Unity to Overcome the Economic Emergency, signed between the government, the Bank of Mexico, and the labour and business sectors, implied a significant reduction in real wages on average, and represented a major contribution on the part of labour to set the basis for a resumption of growth. The pact also limited the increase in public sector tariffs, resulting in a revenue loss for the public sector to be compensated by other fiscal measures. A tight credit policy was seen as playing a critical role in achieving the objectives of the programme.

[3] 'Mexico's Economy: The Crisis, the Recovery, the Policy Options,' *Economia*, Niteroi, Vol. 1, No. 2, July–December 2000.

Patterns of Adjustment under the Age of Finance

The Case of Turkey as a Peripheral Agent of Neoliberal Globalization

Erinc Yeldan

Turkey experienced a severe economic and political crisis in November 2000 and again in February 2001. The crisis erupted when Turkey was following an exchange rate-based disinflation programme, engineered and led by the IMF (International Monetary Fund).[1] Over 2001, the GDP (gross domestic product) contracted by 7.4 per cent in real terms, wholesale price inflation (WPI) soared to 62 per cent, and the currency lost 51 per cent of its value against the major foreign currencies. The burden of adjustment fell disproportionately on the labouring classes, as the rate of unemployment rose steadily by 2 percentage points in 2001 and then another 3 percentage points in 2002. Real wages fell abruptly by 20 per cent in 2001 and have not recovered to pre-crisis levels even at the time of writing.

The IMF has been involved with the macro management of the Turkish economy both prior to and after the crisis, and provided net financial assistance of $20.4 billion between 1999 and 2003. Following the crisis, Turkey has implemented an orthodox strategy of raising interest rates and maintaining an overvalued exchange rate. The government was forced to follow a contractionary fiscal policy, and promised to satisfy the customary IMF demands: reduce subsidies to agriculture, privatize and reduce the role of the public sector in economic activity.

The post-crisis economic and political adjustments were overseen by the newly founded Justice and Development Party (AKP) which came to power enjoying an absolute majority in the parliament, in the November 2002 elections. Though maintaining a pro-Islamic political agenda, the AKP nevertheless distanced itself from the previous 'National View' orthodoxy of the traditional Turkish Islamic movement. The AKP refurbished itself with a more friendly view towards the west, ready to do business with global finance capital and willing to auction off strategic public assets to transnational companies. In the political arena, the AKP gave unequivocal support to US interests in the Middle East, including to the then approaching war in Iraq.[2]

With a new Stand-by Agreement on which the existing AKP government reached a consensus with the IMF in 2004, the international financial institutions (IFIs) and Turkish business were assured that the 'reform' process would continue up to 2008 along the course set by the IMF's structural adjustment programme since 1998. The programme was officially declared as a package of policies aimed at checking increases in both domestic and external debt, and channelling the country again to a path of 'stable' growth. However, it is widely known that beyond what has been declared officially, the programme envisages much more radical arrangements in restructuring political and social life as a whole. It is also common knowledge that the primary and the most important target of these arrangements is to eradicate public services and related achievements in the fields of social security, education and health, and to commodify the provision of these services through privatization. A critical point to be underlined is that all of the governments of the recent period, including the AKP, have displayed their 'most determined' political stand with respect to such policies (and in turn have been hailed as 'credible' and 'reputable') while neglecting reactions coming from the working classes and the people in general. On this basis, it can be asserted that Turkey constitutes one of the best examples of those societies where the formal aspects of political democracy are observed and nothing more (ISSA 2006).

In fact, shortly after it took office, the AKP abandoned the discourse that had manipulated the anti-IMF and anti-liberal reactions in the country, and showed no hesitation in fully adopting neoliberal policies, entrusting national resources and the economic future of the country directly to foreign capital and the unfettered workings of the market. The distinguishing feature of the AKP government in this respect has been that it has undertaken the mission of executing the neoliberal project using the discourse of a 'strong government', without confronting any strong popular opposition (ISSA 2006; Cizre and Yeldan 2005). The AKP has acted faster and more boldly than any preceding government in implementing the neoliberal economic agenda in an attempt to respond to the requests of international capital, on the one hand, and to settle its problem of adaptation to the state and administrative traditions of the country, on the other.

It is the purpose of this paper to portray the post-2001 crisis adjustment and transformations in the Turkish political and economic arena under the auspices of the Bretton Woods institutions. The focus is on the macroeconomics of the AKP period, rather than the evolution of the 2001 crisis *per se*. The paper is organized into four sections. The first provides an overview of macroeconomic adjustment in Turkey since the crisis, focusing on the speculative nature of growth with a detailed assessment of the modes of balance of payments financing during the AKP era. The second section examines the pattern of jobless growth and changes in labour markets. The deterioration of the position of wage labour, along with its role in generating the necessary economic surplus in the post-crisis adjustment, is documented in the third section. The fourth section concludes with a discussion on the political inferences of the neoliberal reforms of the post-crisis era.

Post-Crisis Characteristics of Growth
The current IMF programme in Turkey relies mainly on two pillars: (1) fiscal austerity that targets a 6.5 per cent of GDP surplus for the public sector

in its primary budget;[3] (2) a contractionary monetary policy operated by an independent central bank, that exclusively aims at price stability via inflation targeting.[4] Thus, the Turkish government is charged to maintain dual targets, a primary surplus target in fiscal balances and an inflation target, and is effectively divorced from all other concerns with respect to macroeconomic aggregates.

According to the logic of the programme, successful achievement of these fiscal and monetary targets would enhance the 'credibility' of the Turkish government, thereby ensuring a reduction in the country's risk perception. This in turn would enable reductions in the rates of interest that would then stimulate private consumption and fixed investment, paving the way to sustained growth. Thus, it is alleged that what is being implemented is actually an expansionary programme of fiscal contraction.

Post-2001 growth has indeed been high. Annual rates of growth of real GNP (gross national product) averaged 7.8 per cent over 2002 to 2006Q2. Growth, while rapid, had very unique characteristics. Firstly, it was mainly driven by a massive inflow of foreign finance capital, which in turn was lured by significantly high rates of return offered domestically; hence, it was speculative-led in nature (Grabel 1995). The main mechanism has been that the high rates of interest prevailing in the Turkish asset markets attracted short-term finance capital, and, in return, the relative abundance of foreign exchange led to overvaluation of the Turkish *lira*. Lower foreign exchange costs led to an import boom both in consumption and investment goods. Clearly, fiscal contraction involving severe retrenchment of public non-interest expenditure boosted the expectations of the financial arbitrageurs (see Table 1). The second characteristic of the post-2001 era was its pattern of jobless growth. Rapid rates of growth were accompanied by high rates of unemployment and low work participation rates. The rate of unemployment rose to more than 10 per cent after the 2001 crisis, and despite rapid growth, has not come down to its pre-crisis level of 6.5 per cent in 2000. Furthermore, together with persistent open unemployment, disguised unemployment has also risen. According to Turkstat data, 'persons not looking for a job, but ready for employment if offered a job' increased from 1,060,000 workers in 2001 to 1,936,000 by 2006, bringing the total (open plus disguised) unemployment ratio to 15.5 per cent (see Table 6).

Together with rapid growth, disinflation has been hailed as another area of 'success' for the AKP government. The central bank started to follow an open inflation-targeting framework in January 2006. The bank's current mandate is to set a 'point' target of 5 per cent inflation in consumer prices. The inflation rate, both in consumer and producer prices, was in fact brought under control by 2004. Producer price inflation receded to less than 3 per cent in late 2005. After a brief turbulence in asset markets in May–July 2006, inflation again accelerated to more than 10 per cent and could only be brought under control gradually to 9.6 per cent towards the end of 2006.

Despite the positive achievements on the disinflation front, rates of interest remained slow to adjust. For instance, the real rate of interest on the government

TABLE 1 *Key Macroeconomic Indicators, Turkey*

	IMF-Led Disinflation Programme	Crisis	Under 3-Party Coalition Government	IMF-Led Post-Crisis Adjustments Under Pragmatic and Western-friendly Islamism of the AKP			
	2000	2001	2002	2003	2004	2005	2006.Q3
GNP Growth Rate	6.3	−9.5	7.9	5.9	9.9	7.6	7.8
Inflation (CPI, 12 months averages)	54.9	54.4	44.9	25.3	10.6	8.2	9.6[1]
Real Wage Growth (%)	2.1	−20.1	1.1	5.1	3.9	−0.1	1.3
Unemployment Rate (%)	6.5	8.4	10.3	10.5	10.2	10.2	8.8
Budget Balance / GNP (%)	−10.9	−16.2	−14.3	−11.2	−7.1	−2.0	−0.6[2]
Non-Interest Primary Budget Balance / GNP (%)	5.7	6.8	4.3	5.2	6.1	7.4	6.3
Central Adm. Domestic Debt (billion $)	58.0	84.9	91.7	139.3	167.3	182.4	173.1
Central Adm. Domestic Debt / GNP (%)	29.0	69.2	54.5	54.5	52.3	50.3	45.7[2]
Total External Debt Stock (billion $)	118.5	113.6	130.1	144.9	162.2	171.1	198.3
External Debt / GNP (%)	59.3	78.0	71.9	60.6	54.2	47.4	52.4[2]
Foreign Trade Balance (billion $)	−23.8	−7.1	−11.4	−18.2	−30.6	−39.8	−32.0
Exports (fob, billion $)	30.7	34.3	40.1	51.1	66.9	76.7	63.9
Imports (cif, billion $)	54.5	41.4	51.5	69.3	97.5	116.5	95.9
Current Account Balance (billion $)	−9.8	3.4	−1.5	−8.1	−15.6	−23.1	−25.3
Current Account Balance / GNP (%)	−4.9	2.3	−0.8	−2.8	−5.3	−6.4	−6.7[2]

Notes: [1] As of end of 2006.
[2] As a ratio of last four quarters.

Source: TR Central Bank (www.tcmb.gov.tr); Undersecretariat of Treasury (www.treasury.gov.tr).

CHART 1 *Inflation* (WPI 1994 = 100) *and Real Interest Rate on GDIs*

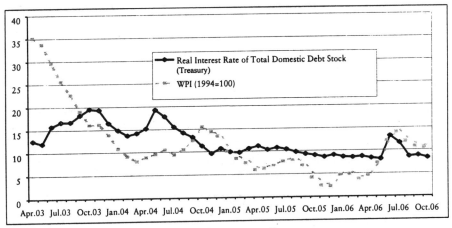

Source: Turkish Statistical Institute (Turkstat), www.die.gov.tr.

debt instruments (GDIs) remained above 10 per cent over most of the post-crisis period, and generated heavy pressure on the fiscal authority with respect to meeting its debt obligations (see Chart 1). The persistence of high real interest rates, on the other hand, was also conducive to attracting heavy flows of short-term speculative finance capital over 2003 and 2005. This pattern continued into 2006 at an even stronger rate.

The inertia of the real rate of interest is an enigma given the successful macroeconomic performance thus far on the fiscal front. Despite some decline in the general plateau of real interest rates, Turkish interest rates have remained significantly higher than those prevailing in most emerging market economies. The credit interest rate, in particular, has been stagnant at 16 per cent despite the deceleration of price inflation until the May–July turbulence. Thereafter, credit interest rates accelerated to 23.5 per cent (Turkstat 2006).

The high rates of interest were conducive to generating a high inflow of hot money finance into the Turkish financial markets. The most direct effect of the surge in foreign finance capital over this period was felt in the foreign exchange market. The overabundance of foreign exchange supplied by foreign financial arbitrageurs seeking positive yields led to significant pressures for appreciation of the Turkish *lira* (TL). As the Turkish central bank has restricted its monetary policies only to control of price inflation and left the value of the domestic currency to the speculative decisions of market forces, the TL appreciated by as much as 40 per cent in real terms against the US $ and by 25 per cent against the Euro (in producer price parity terms).

Chart 2 portrays the paths of the bilateral (vis-à-vis the US $) and the trade-weighted real exchange rates (in PPP terms, with producer prices as the deflator) over 2000–06. The currency crises of November 2000 through February 2001 are clearly visible in the chart. The recent blip in May–July 2006, on the other hand, had a minimal effect on the real value of the real exchange rate and

CHART 2   *Indexes of the Bilateral and Trade-Weighted Real Exchange Rate*

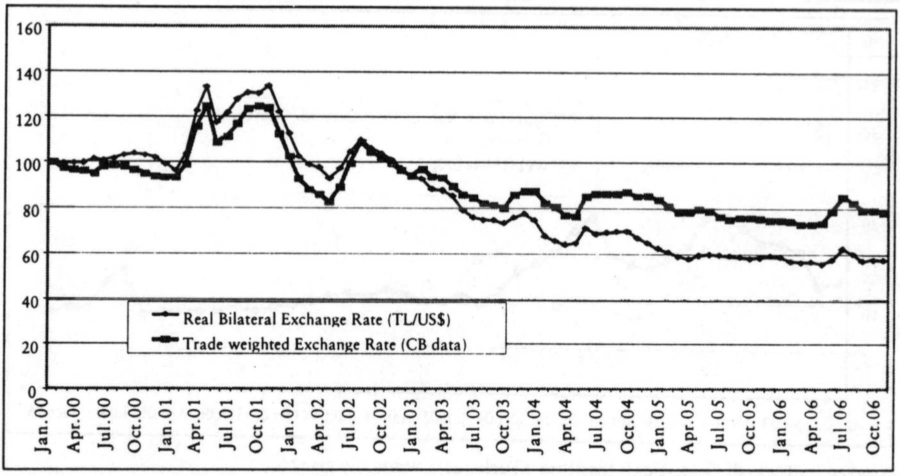

Source: TR Central Bank and Turkish Statistical Institute (Turkstat).

did not suffice to change the direction of the course of ongoing real appreciation.

Components of Balance of Payments and External Debt

The structural overvaluation of the TL, not surprisingly, manifested itself in ever-expanding deficits on the commodity trade and current account balances. As traditional Turkish exports lost their competitiveness, new export lines emerged. Yet, these have proved to be mostly import-dependent, assembly-line industries such as automotive parts and consumer durables. They use the advantage of cheap import materials, get assembled in Turkey at low value added and then are re-directed for export. Thus, being mostly import-dependent, they have a low capacity to generate value added and employment. As traditional exports dwindle, the newly emerging export industries were not vigorous enough to close the trade gap.

Consequently, starting 2003, Turkey has witnessed expanding current account deficits, with the figure in the third quarter of 2006 reaching a record-breaking magnitude of $25.3 billion, or 6.7 per cent of GNP. In this context, it has to be noted that Turkey traditionally has never been a current account deficit-prone economy. Over the last two decades (1980s and 90s), the average current account balance hovered around plus and minus 1.5–2.0 per cent of GNP with deficits exceeding 3 per cent, signalling the need for significant currency adjustments, as occurred in 1994 and 2001. In fact, the mechanics of the cumulative current account deficit of the post-2001 period can only be understood in the context of the speculative transactions embedded in the finance account of the balance of payments (BoP). Table 2 summarizes the relevant data.

The data in Table 2 indicate that the finance account has experienced a net surplus of $103.3 billion over the 'AKP period', 2003 through 2006 (September). About half of this sum ($51.2 billion) was due to credit financing of the banking

TABLE 2   *Selected Indicators on Balance of Payments and Foreign Debt* (million US$)

	2001	2002	2003	2004	2005	2006Q3	2006Q3–2003
Exports (fob)	34,373	40,124	51,206	67,047	76,595	63,916	258,764
Imports (fob)	–38,106	–47,407	–65,216	–90,925	–109,171	–95,922	–361,234
Trade Balance	–3,733	–7,283	–14,010	–23,878	–32,576	–32,006	–102,470
Current Account Balance	3,392	–1,524	–8,037	–15,604	–22,852	–25,334	–71,827
Finance Account Balance	–14,643	1,161	7,098	17,679	44,069	34,462	103,308
Foreign Direct Investment by Residents Abroad	–497	–175	–499	–859	–1,047	–361	–2,766
Foreign Direct Investment by Non-Residents	3,352	1,137	1,752	2,847	9,650	12,804	27,053
Non-Residents' Portfolio Investments in Turkey	–3,727	1,503	3,851	9,411	14,670	4,849	32,781
Residents' Portfolio Investments Abroad	–788	–2,096	–1,386	–1,388	–961	–1,284	–5,019
Other Investment, Net	–12,983	792	3,380	7,668	21,757	18,454	51,259
Net Errors and Emissions	–1,759	118	4,941	2,267	1,983	–659	8,532
Change in Reserves (–: Increase)	12,924	212	–4,097	–4,342	–23,200	–8,469	–40,108
Foreign Debt Stock	113,592	130,093	144,915	162,202	171,078	198,261	68,168
Short-term Foreign Debt Stock	16,403	16,424	23,013	32,569	38,247	43,322	26,898
Ratio of Short-term Foreign Debt Stock to Central Bank Reserves	0.87	0.61	0.68	0.90	0.76	0.74	

Source: TR Central Bank (www.tcmb.gov.tr).

sector and non-bank enterprises, while a third ($32.8 billion) originated from non-residents' portfolio investments in Turkey. Residents have exported financial capital of the magnitude of $5.4 billion, and if one interprets the net errors and omissions term of the BoP accounts as an indicator of domestic hot money flows (see Akyuz 2004; Boratav and Yeldan 2005), the total sum of net speculative finance capital inflows is calculated to reach $36.2 billion over the three years of the post-crisis adjustment.

Foreign direct investment (FDI) has been seen as an important source of financing the current account deficit, especially after 2005. It is true that the BoP data reveal a sudden increase in the flow of FDI, totalling $22.4 billion in the last two years. However, looking at FDI more closely, it is evident that the bulk of this flow has been due to privatization receipts plus real estate and land purchases by foreign residents. Neither of these items are sustainable sources of foreign exchange, and they were driven by speculative arbitrage opportunities rather than for enhancing the real physical capital stock of the domestic economy. In fact, as reported by the ANKA researchers, the stock of 'hot money' reached $52.3 billion by August 2006. This stock is fed by three sources: (i) foreigners' holdings of government debt instruments (£17.9 billion); (ii) foreigners' holdings of securities at the Istanbul Stock Exchange Market ($30.6 billion); (iii) foreign exchange deposits with the banking sector ($3.7 billion). The aggregate stock of hot money reached two-thirds of the cumulative current account deficit over the post-2001 crisis period.

A significant detrimental feature of hot money-led balance of payments financing is its foreign debt intensity. As evident from Table 2, the stock of external debt increased by a total of $63.5 billion from the end of 2002 to the second quarter of 2006. This indicates an increase of 48.8 per cent in US dollar terms over a period of three-and-a-half years. Despite this rapid increase, the burden of external debt as a ratio of GNP fell from 72 per cent (2002) to 47 per cent (2005). This fall was due to both the rapid expansion of the GNP and the unprecedented appreciation of the *lira* over the period. The appreciation of the TL disguises much of the fragility associated with both the level and the external debt-induced financing of the current account deficits. A simple purchasing power parity 'correction' of the real exchange rate, for instance, would increase the burden of external debt to 77 per cent of GNP in 2005.[5] This would bring the debt burden ratio to the 2001 pre-crisis level. Under the floating exchange rate regime, this observation reveals the persistent fragility of the Turkish external markets, as a possible depreciation of the *lira* in the days to come may severely worsen the current account financing possibilities. This persistent external fragility is actually one of the main reasons why Turkey was hit the hardest among the emerging market economies in the global turbulence of May–June 2006 (IMF 2006).

Another facet of the external fragility of Turkey's balance of payments regards the composition of debt. As far as the post-2001 era is concerned, two critical features of external debt-driven current account financing have been that (i) the foreign debt accumulation was mostly of short-term duration, and (ii) it was mostly driven by the non-financial private sector rather than the public sector. The relevant data are shown in Table 3.

As Table 3 attests, of the accumulated foreign debt of $68.2 billion over the AKP era, 43 per cent was short-term in maturity. Turkey's external short-term

TABLE 3   *Composition of External Debt Stock* (millions US$)

	2000Q4	2001Q4	2002Q4	2003Q4	2004Q4	2005Q4	2006Q3	2006Q3–2002Q4 Increase
External Debt Stock (1+2)	118,504	113,592	130,093	144,915	162,202	171,078	198,261	68,168
(1) Short-term Foreign Debt	28,301	16,403	16,424	23,013	32,569	38,247	43,322	26,898
Banks	16,900	7,997	6,344	9,692	14,529	17,740	19,828	13,484
Other Sectors	9,748	7,654	8,425	10,461	14,753	17,744	20,897	12,472
TR Central Bank	653	752	1,655	2,860	3,287	2,763	2,774	1,119
(2) Medium–Long-term Debt	90,203	97,189	113,669	121,902	129,633	132,831	154,939	41,270
(2.1) Public Sector	47,621	46,110	63,618	69,503	73,825	68,114	68,660	5,042
(2.2) TR Central Bank	13,429	23,591	20,340	21,504	18,114	12,654	12,921	-7,419
(2.3) Private Sector	29,153	27,488	29,711	30,895	37,694	52,063	73,358	43,647
(2.3.1) Financial Enterprises	7,581	4,789	4,637	5,060	8,284	15,316	21,264	16,627
Banks	4,550	3,211	3,026	3,140	5,750	12,231	17,310	14,284
Non-Bank Financial	3,032	1,578	1,611	1,920	2,534	3,085	3,954	2,343
(2.3.2) Non-Financial Enterprises	21,571	22,699	25,074	25,835	29,410	36,747	52,094	27,020

Source: Undersecreteriat of Treasury (www.hazine.gov.tr).

debt stock, which had reached $28.3 billion just before the eruption of the February 2001 crisis, was reduced to as low as $13.7 billion in the first quarter of 2002. The stock of short-term debt has increased rapidly, especially after 2003, to reach $43.3 billion as of the third quarter of 2006. A critical aspect is the ratio of short-term debt to the central bank's international reserves, which is regarded as one of the crucial leading indicators of external fragility (see, for example, Kaminsky *et al.* 1999), and has been interpreted as the 'most robust predictor of a currency crisis' (Rodrik and Velasco 1999). The path of this indicator over the post-2001 period is summarized in the last row of Table 3.

As the ratio of short-term external debt to central bank international reserves rises, it signals a decline in the capability of the central bank to meet the external liabilities of the domestic economy, and can be interpreted as a worsening of external fragility. This ratio stood at 0.87 by the end of 2001,[6] and after receding to 0.61 in early 2002, rose to 0.92 by the third quarter of 2005. It was brought back to 0.74 by the third quarter of 2006, thanks mainly to the very rapid build-up of foreign exchange reserves by the Turkish central bank over the previous year. By way of comparison, the aforementioned 'fragility ratio' was 0.60 in Malaysia, 0.91 in the Philippines and 1.50 in Thailand just before the 1997 Asian crisis broke. Thus it can be argued that 0.60 is regarded as a critical threshold from an international speculation point of view (see, for example, Kaminsky *et al.* 1999).[7]

The preceding discussion indicates that despite the brief deceleration of the turbulence of May–June, the Turkish economy continued to increase the intensity of its accumulation of external debt in 2006. Data of the first nine months of 2006 are summarized in Table 4.

In Table 4 we distinguish the BoP data of January–September 2006 over two axes. The first is the decomposition of the in/out-flows of foreign capital into two sources: foreign non-residents and domestic residents. Capital inflows originating from foreign sources increased by 48 per cent over the comparable period of 2005, and reached $38.1 billion. The domestic sources, on the other hand, displayed an tendency to flow out, and net flows therefore amounted to $ –7.2 billion.

TABLE 4   *Main Components of the Balance of Payments in 2006* (million US$)

	Jan–Sept 2005	Jan–Sept 2006	Difference
Current Account Balance	−15,870	−25,334	−9,464
Capital Originating from Foreign Sources	25,821	38,108	12,287
Capital Originating from Domestic Sources	−4,052	−7,188	−3,136
Change in Reserves ('−' indicates increase)	−8,561	−4,927	n.a.
Net Errors and Omissions	2,662	-659	−3,321
Net Capital Inflow	24,431	30,261	5,830
Foreign Debt-Inducing Capital Inflows	17,291	23,705	6,414
Net Hot Money Flows	11,959	−1,869	−13,828

Source: Boratav (2006); TR Central Bank.

CHART 3   *External Debt by Sectors*

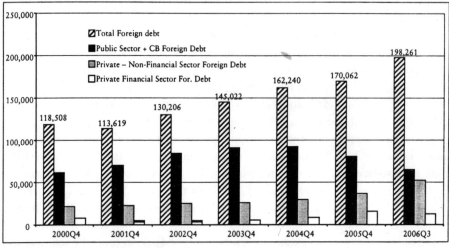

Source: TR Central Bank, www.tcmb.gov.tr.

This figure comprises outflows due to operations of the banking sector and enterprises, as well as domestic rentiers' decisions. Taking account of the net errors and omissions figure of $–0.7 billion, the overall net foreign capital inflow into Turkey reached $30.3 billion, a 24 per cent increase over the same period in 2005.

The data reveal significant deceleration of the hot money component of this transfer ($–1.9 billion), as the domestic outflows of hot money outpaced the speculative inflows of non-residents. Consequently, the role of hot money financing of the balance of payments was reduced in the first nine months of 2006. The period further reveals, however, a 38 per cent increase in net foreign indebtedness, to reach $23.7 billion. Given that the public sector is currently following a strict austerity programme and has generated a sizeable primary surplus, this increase in foreign debt has originated mainly from the private sector – and from the non-banking, private enterprise sector (see Table 3). The external debt obligations of the private sector ($73.4 billion) exceed aggregate public foreign debt ($68.6 billion) as of the third quarter of 2006.

Within the private sector, non-financial enterprises explain 60 per cent of the aggregate increase of private external debt over the post-2002 AKP period and account for 71 per cent of the total stock of private debt by 2006Q3 (see Chart 3).

The 'IMF Programme'

The rapid increase of private sector debt – of both financial and non-financial sectors alike, reveals the true essence of the IMF-engineered adjustment mechanisms following the currency and banking crises of February 2001. The Turkish post-crisis adjustment ultimately relied on maintaining high real rates of interest in anticipation of increased foreign capital inflow into the domestic economy. Coupled with an overall contractionary fiscal policy, the programme found the main source of expansion in speculative inflows of foreign finance. Persistently high rates of interest against the backdrop of lower inflation and fiscal primary surplus targets were the main attributes of the IMF programme as implemented both by the three-party coalition government under Mr Bulent Ecevit (until November 2002) and by the AKP government (post-November 2002).

The aforementioned elements of this adjustment path were clearly stated, in fact, in the *Turkey Country Report* prepared by the IMF staff in late 2001. Table 5 makes a reference to that report, which laid out the macroeconomic targets of the post-crisis adjustment path as envisaged by the IMF. It is illuminating to note that the targets of the IMF encompassing 2002 through 2006 have eventually become the official targets of both governments over that period. The targeted rate of real GNP growth, for instance, was persistently set at 5 per cent for each coming year, despite the observed rapid expansion of the economy by rates often exceeding 7 per cent in the preceding year! This choice was clearly no coincidence. Likewise, the inflation targets of the 'independent' central bank each year followed the path envisaged in the 2001 IMF report, beginning with 20 per cent for 2003 to 5 per cent for 2006. (Note that the Turkish central bank declared the onset of its official inflation targeting monetary regime on 1 January 2006.) Finally, the very sanctimonious primary surplus target for the public sector at 6.5 per cent of GNP clearly finds its origins in the IMF report.

That having been said, what remains noteworthy is the IMF's choice of a very high and persistent real interest rate, targeted at 18 per cent, throughout the programme horizon, despite the falling trajectory of the inflation rate. The actual rates of inflation and real interest that are shown in Chart 1 seem to find resonance in the adjustment path assumed by the IMF staff immediately after the 2001 crisis. It is clear that the main adjustment mechanism of the post-crisis IMF programme was embedded in maintaining significantly high real interest rates. These attracted short-term finance capital and the relative abundance of foreign exchange led to overvaluation of the *lira*. As noted above, lower foreign exchange costs led to an import boom both in consumption and investment goods, while fiscal contraction boosted expectations of finance.

In sum, contrary to the traditional stabilization packages that aimed at

TABLE 5   *Macroeconomic Targets of the Current IMF Programme*

	2002	2003	2004	2005	2006
GNP Real Growth Rate	3.0	5.0	5.0	5.0	5.0
Non-Interest Budget balance / GNP (%)	6.5	6.5	6.5	6.5	6.3
Inflation Rate	35.0	20.0	12.0	8.0	5.0
Nominal Rate of Interest on Domestic Debt	69.6	46.0	32.4	27.4	23.9
REAL Rate of Interest on Domestic Debt	25.6	21.7	18.2	18.0	18.0

Source: IMF, *Turkey Country Report*, 2001; www.imf.org.

increasing interest rates to restrict domestic demand, the new orthodoxy aimed
at maintaining high interest rates for the purpose of attracting speculative foreign
capital from the international financial markets. The end results in the Turkish
context were shrinkage of the public sector in a speculative-led growth environment; deteriorating education and health infrastructure which require increased
public funds urgently; and the consequent failure to provide basic social services
to the middle classes and the poor. Further, as domestic industry intensified its
import dependence, it was pushed towards adapting increasingly capital-intensive
foreign technologies, with adverse consequences on domestic employment.

Persistent Unemployment and Jobless Growth

Another key characteristic of the post-2001 Turkish growth path has
been its 'jobless' nature. The rate of open unemployment was 6.5 per cent in
2000; it increased to 10.3 per cent in 2002, and remained at that plateau despite
the rapid surges in GDP and exports. Open unemployment is a severe problem,
in particular, among the young urban labour force, reaching 26 per cent. Table 6
provides information on the Turkish labour market.

The civilian labour force (ages 15+) amounted to 51.8 million people in
the third quarter of 2006. The participation rate fluctuated between 48 and 50
per cent, due mostly to seasonal effects. In general, the participation rate is less
than the EU average. This low rate is principally due to women choosing to remain outside the labour force, a common feature of Islamic societies. However, the
recent decline may also reflect the increase in the number of discouraged workers
who have lost hopes of finding jobs. If we add the Turkstat data on underemployed
people, the excess labour supply (unemployed + underemployed) is observed to
reach 15.5 per cent of the labour force as of the third quarter of 2006.

TABLE 6   *Developments in the Turkish Labour Market* (1,000 persons)

	2000	2001	2002	2003	2004	2005	2006Q3
15+ Age Population	46,209	47,158	48,041	48,912	49,906	50,991	51,770
Civilian Labour Force	23,078	23,491	23,818	23,640	24,289	24,989	25,622
Civilian Employment	21,581	21,524	21,354	21,147	21,791	22,566	23,279
Unemployed (Open)	1,497	1,958	2,473	2,497	2,479	2,509	2,343
Open Unemployment Ratio (%)	6.5	8.4	10.4	10.5	10.3	10.2	9.1
Disguised Unemployment[a]	1,139	1,060	1,020	945	1,223	1,714	1,936
Total Unemployment Ratio[b] (%)	10.9	12.3	14.1	14.0	14.5	15.8	15.5
Civilian Employment by Sectors							
Agriculture	7,103	8,089	7,458	7,385	7,400	6,661	6,809
Industry	3,738	3,774	3,954	3,821	3,988	4,360	4,429
Services	9,738	9,661	9,942	10,080	10,403	11,545	12,041

Notes: [a] Persons not looking for a job yet ready to work if offered one: (i) seeking employment and
              ready to work within fifteen days, and yet did not use any of the job search channels in the
              last three months, plus (ii) discouraged workers.
              [b] Total (open + disguised) unemployment accounting for persons 'not in labour force'.
Source: Turkish Statistical Institute (Turkstat), Household Labour Force Surveys.

CHART 4 *Annual Rate of Change in GDP and Aggregate Employment*

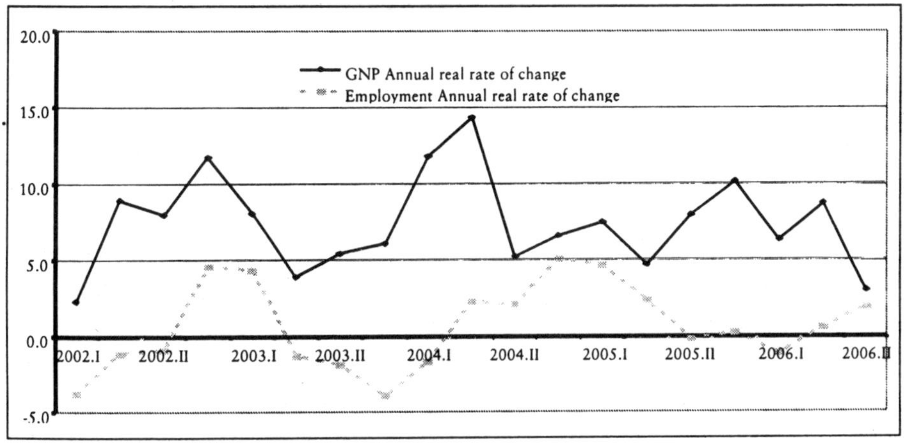

Source: Turkish Statistical Institute (Turkstat), Household Labour Force Surveys.

Yet, the most striking observation on the Turkish labour market over the post-2001 crisis era is the sluggish rate of employment generation. Despite the very rapid growth in industry and services, employment growth has been meagre, especially after 2002. Such jobless growth has been observed in many other developing economies as well.[8] The Turkish experience in this regard is evident from the quarterly growth rates of GDP contrasted with annual rates of change in employment, as plotted in Chart 4. In order to make the comparisons meaningful, the changes in employment are calculated relative to the same quarter of the previous year.

The chart discloses that between 2002.Q1 and 2006.Q3, the average rate of growth in real GDP was 7.5 per cent. In contrast, the rate of change of employment averaged only 0.8 per cent over the same period. Over the nineteen quarters portrayed in the chart, GDP growth was positive in all periods. Yet employment growth was *negative* in nine of those nineteen quarters.

A sectoral breakdown of the post-crisis employment patterns reveals a massive depopulation of the rural economy. Agricultural employment has fallen by 1,289,000 workers since 2001. Against this fall, there had been a total increase of employment in the services sectors by 2,380,000 and by 655,000 in industry. Simultaneous to this was the expansion of the aggregate labour supply from 47.158 million in 2001 to 51.770 million in 2006, adding to the acuteness of the problem of joblessness.

Thus, in conclusion, two important characteristics of the post-crisis adjustment path stand out. First, the post-2001 expansion was concomitant with a deteriorating external imbalance, which in turn was the end result of excessive inflows of speculative finance capital. This was characterized as 'speculation-led' expansion in the preceding section. Second, the rate of output growth contrasted with the persistent unemployment, warranting the term 'jobless growth'.

A further detrimental effect of the speculative-led, jobless growth era has

CHART 5   *Labour Participation Rates and Total Unemployment Rates*

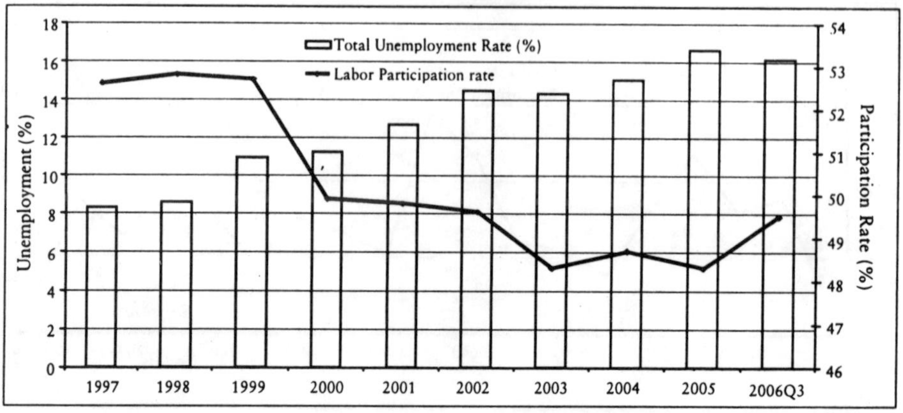

Source: Turkish Statistical Institute (Turkstat), Household Labour Force Surveys.

been the overall decline in labour participation rates. Though lower than in the comparable member countries of the European Union, labour participation rates were above 50 per cent through most of the 1990s. The participation rate first declined to less than 50 per cent during the implementation of the 2000 exchange rate-based disinflation programme. It continued its secular decline over the rest of the decade, as depicted in Chart 5.

Wage Labour as the Absorber of the Burden of Adjustment

A transfer of the financial surplus through very high real interest rates offered to the financial system would, no doubt, have repercussions on the primary categories of income distribution. It is clear that creation of such a financial surplus would directly necessitate a squeeze of the wage fund and a transfer of the surplus away from wage labour towards capital incomes, in general. It is possible to find some evidence of this from the path of the manufacturing real wages. Chart 6 portrays the dynamics of manufacturing real wages and offers contrasts with the productivity of labour.

The index of labour productivity, measured in real output per hours, showed a rapid increase with its level reaching 158 index points (1997=100) by 2006.Q3. Over the same period, however, average wage remuneration declined by 23.8 per cent in real terms. This exercise shows very clearly how in the Turkish economy, speculative financial gains were financed by squeezing real wages. Each rapid rise in financial returns has been closely associated with a downward movement of real wages, and has involved a direct transfer from labour incomes towards capital, both domestic and foreign.[9] Real wages contracted severely after the 2001 February crisis and this downward trend was maintained throughout 2002 and 2003.

A case can further be made here that the ongoing process of surplus transfer from wage labour to the financial–industrial conglomerates is nothing new,

CHART 6 *Real Wages and Labour Productivity in Turkish Manufacturing Industry*

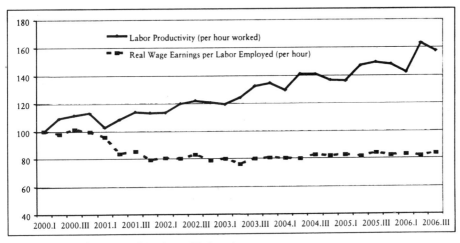

Source: Turkish Statistical Institute (Turkstat).

CHART 7 *Labour Productivity and Hourly Real Wages in US Manufacturing* (1950=100)

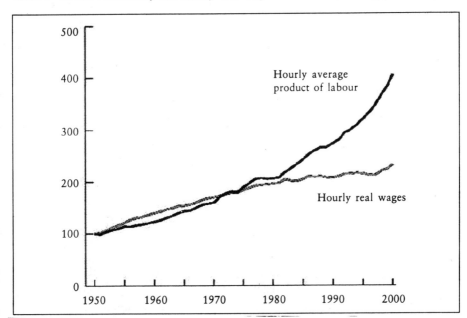

Source: 'The New Face of Capitalism: Slow Growth, Excess Capital and a Mountain of Debt', *Monthly Review,* 2002; www.monthlyreview.org/0402.editr.htm.

and not unique to Turkey either. Capital's assault on labour has, in fact, continued with new forms of industrial organization from the onset of neoliberal globalization in the mid-1970s. With intensified policy changes towards flexibility and privatization, the position of wage labour eroded everywhere. This process was most visible in the US, the hegemonic centre of global capitalism. Chart 7 depicts this

CHART 8 *Labour Productivity and Real Wages in Turkish Manufacturing (1950–2005)*

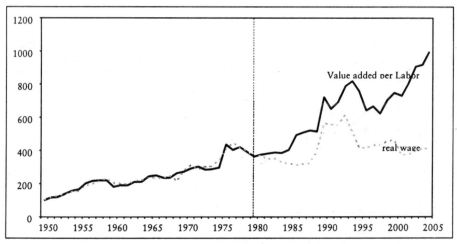

Source: Turkish Statistical Institute (Turkstat), Annual Manufacturing Surveys.

phenomenon by showing the path of real wages and real labour productivity in US manufacturing in the second half of the twentieth century. As clearly visible, the Fordist period under Keynesian policies had been associated with real wages following, to a large extent, the movements in labour productivity, up until the 1970s. The late 1970s, however, reveal the extent of capital's gains against labour. As the real wage rate stagnated, its path remained significantly below the real average product of labour, the gap yielding the increased exploitation of wage labour in the last quarter of the century.[10]

A different facet of this process was at play across the Atlantic as well. Chart 8 contrasts US wage labour's position with that of Turkey. The chart portrays comparable data and the verdict remains exactly the same. Wage rates of Turkish manufacturing labour follow the average real product until 1980. Thereafter, under conditions of military dictatorship during the 1980s, a significant wedge is created between real wage earnings and real labour productivity by way of intensified exploitation of labour.

Clearly, very similar processes had been operational both in the North and South under neoliberal globalization. The end of Fordist technological organization led to the demise of the welfare state, which had enabled a comparatively tolerant attitude towards wage labour. As this delicate balance of mass production for domestic consumption eroded, capital found a new opportunity in financial returns. Overall, this process has led to the demise of the welfare state and an outright hostile attitude against the rights of labour.

As a result, the share of labour in national income fell everywhere. According to Petras and Veltmeyer (2000) and Diwan's (1999) data, the share of wage labour fell from 48 per cent (1970) to 28 per cent (1985) in Chile; from 41 per cent (1970) to 25 per cent (1989) in Argentina; from 37 per cent (1970) to 27 per cent (1989) in Mexico; and from 40 per cent (1970) to 17 per cent (1986) in Peru. Similarly, according to calculations of Yeldan (2001: Chapter III) the share of wage labour in manufacturing value added was reduced from 28 per cent in 1976 to 15 per cent by 1987.

This abrupt shift in the distribution of income against labour coincided with the assault against indigenous strategies for economic development and against the fragile democracies of the South.

Conclusion: From 'Fiscal' to 'Democracy' Deficit

The detrimental consequences of the neoliberal adjustment path on wage labour were not limited to the economic sphere. Labour's position was further curtailed as the developing country governments that were dependent upon foreign capital were conditioned to adopt or maintain contractionary fiscal and monetary policies in order to secure 'investor confidence' and 'international creditworthiness'. Such efforts are directed towards a balanced or surplus government budget, reduction in public expenditure and a relatively contractionary monetary policy with an *ex ante* commitment to high real interest rates. All of these signify reduced policy autonomy in the developing world, in exchange for promises of market access to the industrialized North. This is a bad bargain as far as development is concerned (Rodrik 2001).

In this environment, portfolio investors become the ultimate arbiters of national macroeconomic policy (Cizre-Sakallioglu and Yeldan 2000; Grabel 1996), and any effective public policy is regarded as synonymous with populism and waste. Democratic institutions are put under siege through endless lists of conditionalities set forth by the IMF and the World Bank, and, in the meantime, transnational companies and the international finance institutions (IFIs) become the real governors with an implicit veto power over any economic and/or political decision that is likely to act against the interests of global capital. The IFIs report rating scores in aligning the indigenous economies under the strategic realm of finance capital. Even direct political decisions are under scrutiny.

A critical example here is the rejected war motion by the Turkish parliament, disapproving the request from US troops to utilize Turkish soil in the early days of the invasion of Iraq. In exchange for a total aid of $24 billion, the USA had asked permission from Turkey to use its borders with Iraq. The motion was rejected and chaos ensued, driven by the IFIs and their rating agencies. The following excerpt from 'Morgan Stanley Economic Forum on Turkey' (4 March 2003) is a typical example: 'the latest parliamentary decision to reject the much-debated "war motion" is such a risk that will no doubt disturb the fragile equilibrium . . . [Turkey] is unlikely to get the promised $24 billion that would ease pressure on the domestic debt market. . . .' The report concludes with the stunning question: 'what happens if the parliament does not altogether vote for the economic reforms, arguing that 80 per cent of the Turkish population is against the IMF program?'

Thus the report is not only concerned with the loss of $ 24 billion liquidity for the Turkish financial centres, but is also worried that the people may further exercise their rights over the future of the IMF-led austerity programme in Turkey. To paraphrase the classic words of Diaz-Alejandro (1985): 'Good-bye budget deficits, hello democracy deficit . . .'.

In the words of the 2005 Annual Report of the ISSA, two important consequences of these transformations come to the fore as the basic problem of almost all countries including Turkey. Speaking in broad terms, these are related to the transfer of decisions relating to the public sphere from constitutional institutions of respective countries to 'independent' supreme bodies of regulation working under global rules, and further commercialization of public services and the overall body of public economic activity including decision-making and regulation (ISSA 2006: 4). This process, whose legitimization is presented as 'dissecting politics from economics', enhances the hegemony of global capital and its domestic extensions on society by keeping large sections of the people and working masses far from political processes. Political leaders in all countries where these reforms are being implemented commonly refer to a clumsily working 'old' state and bureaucratic structures lamed by corruption; and the new model is championed by reference to its so-called efficient, strong, rule-abiding and accountable features. Any reader with further interest in a more elaborate and advanced analysis of these reforms and the 'new state' as well as 'the new public sphere', may refer to any website managed by the IMF, WB, OECD or EU.

Increasingly, reports from such organizations containing policy suggestions not only define the necessary measures and arrangements to be adopted, but also go so far as to advise on ways of securing public support in this field. The example below is from an OECD Report (2002: 11), titled 'Regulatory Reforms in Turkey: Important Support to Economic Improvement: Governance':

> . . . It is vital to have open communication channels in order to have continued public support for the reforms. There is a need for dissemination of the targets and the advantages of the regulatory reforms. Another benefit of this approach is to eliminate the widespread public view that the reforms are imposed from abroad. For this reason, the public perception should be treated as an important issue within the communication strategy of the government.

Assessing the processes which the so-called 'emerging market economies' have undergone with the onset of neoliberal globalization, it becomes clear that what has been pursued is not simply a move to 'stabilize' the economic structures, but goes much beyond it to radically alter the social structures of those nations. The executing actors include political circles who shut their ears to reactions coming from different segments of society, justify their stance by repeating 'it is us who decide on policies to be adopted', and maintain these policies at all costs while keeping themselves content with the slogan 'firm commitment is a virtue'. These top-level bureaucrats, whom we can classify as 'global elites', often share the same mode of living and discourse worldwide. Extremely intolerant to any criticism including very innocent ones, these groups may well behave in a manner that is very distant from what can be described as the *sine qua non* of any democracy.

Notes

[1] The underlying elements of the disinflation programme and the succeeding crisis are discussed in detail in Akyuz and Boratav (2003); Ertugrul and Yeldan (2003); Yeldan (2002); Boratav and Yeldan (2006); Alper (2001). See also the GPN Report on Turkey (2005) and the web site of the Independent Social Scientists Alliance (www. bagimsizsosyalbilimciler.org) for further documentation of the crisis conditions.

[2] In fact, many analysts have drawn attention to the timing of the decision to hold early elections in late 2002, only a few months after the three-party coalition government granted no support for the US plans to invade Iraq in summer 2002.

[3] That is, balance on non-interest expenditures and aggregate public revenues. The primary surplus target of the central government budget was set at 5 per cent of GNP.

[4] The target for consumer price inflation was set at 5 per cent for 2006, and 4 per cent for 2007 and 2008.

[5] Measured in 2002 producer prices. If the PPP correction is calculated in 2000 prices, the revised debt to GNP ratio reaches 82.3 per cent.

[6] The ratio of short-term foreign debt to central bank international reserves was 8.47 per cent just before the eruption of the February 2001 crisis.

[7] See also Goldstein (2005) for a recent evaluation of the external fragility across emerging market economies, where Turkey is reportedly found to display above-average fragility indices among comparable economies. See also the IMF's 2006 report on Turkey.

[8] See, for example, UNCTAD, *Trade and Development Report* (2002 and 2003).

[9] See also Yeldan (2006), for a more detailed assessment of labour's position under the post-crisis adjustment of the Turkish economy.

[10] See, for example, Moseley (2001) and the series of reports by the Economic Policy Institute on the position of US labour.

References

Akyüz, Yilmaz and Korkut Boratav (2003), 'The Making of the Turkish Crisis', *World Development*, 31 (9): 1549–66.

Alper, Emre (2001), 'The Turkish Liquidity Crisis of 2000: What Went Wrong?', *Russian and East European Finance and Trade*, Vol. 10, No. 37: 51–71.

Alper, Emre and Ziya Önis (2003), 'Emerging Market Crises and the IMF: Rethinking the Role of the IMF in the Light of Turkey's 2000–2001 Financial Crises', *Canadian Journal of Development Studies*, 24 (2): 255–72.

Anka News Agency, *Daily Economic Report*, 1 September 2006.

Boratav, K. (2006), 'Ilk Dokuz Ayda Sermaye Hareketleri', at SoL Meclis, http://www.sol.org.tr/index.php?yazino=5209.

Boratav, Korkut and Erinc Yeldan (2006), 'Turkey, 1980–2000: Financial Liberalization, Macroeconomic (In)-Stability, and Patterns of Distribution', in Lance Taylor (ed.), *External Liberalization in Asia, Post-Socialist Europe and Brazil* (Oxford University Press).

Cizre Umit and Erinç Yeldan (2005), 'The Turkish Encounter with Neo-Liberalism: Economics and Politics in the 2000/2001 Crises', *Review of International Political Economy*, 12 (3), August: 387–408.

Cizre-Sakallioglu, Umit and Erinç Yeldan (2000), 'Politics, Society and Financial Liberalization: Turkey in the 1990s', *Development and Change*, 31 (1): 481–508.

Diaz-Alejandro, Carlos F. (1985), 'Good-Bye Financial Repression, Hello Financial Crash', *Journal of Development Economics*, 19 (1–2), February: 1–24.

Economic Policy Institute (EPI) (2006), *The State of Working America* (Washington D.C.: The EPI Press).

Ertugrul, Ahmet and Erinç Yeldan (2003), 'On The Structural Weaknesses of the Post-1999 Turkish Dis-Inflation Program', *Turkish Studies Quarterly*, 4 (2), Summer: 53–66.

Goldstein (2005), 'What Might the Next Emerging-Market Financial Crisis Look Like?', Institute for International Economics, Working Paper No. 2005–07, July.

Grabel, Ilene (1995), 'Speculation-Led Economic Development: A Post-Keynesian Interpretation of Financial Liberalization Programmes in the Third World', *International Review of Applied Economics*, 9 (2): 127–249.

—— (1996), 'Marketing the Third World: The Contradictions of Portfolio Investment in the Global Economy', *World Development*, 24 (11): 1761–76.

IMF (2006), 'Staff Report on Turkey', IMF Country Reports, No 06/402, November.

Independent Social Scientists Alliance (ISSA) (2005), *2005 Baþýnda Türkiye'nin Ýktisadi ve Siyasi Yasamý Üzerine Degerlendirmeler*, http://www.bagimsizsosyalbilimciler.org/Yazilar_BSB/BSB2005Mart.pdf.

—— (2006), *Turkey and the IMF: Macroeconomic Policy, Patterns of Growth and Persistent Fragilities* (Penang, Malaysia: Third World Development Network).

Kaminsky, Graciela and Carmen Reinhart (1999), 'The Twin Crises: The Causes of Banking and Balance-of-Payments Problems', *American Economic Review*, 89 (3), June: 473–500.

Moseley, Fred (2001), 'The Rate of Profit and Stagnation in the US Economy', in Baiman, Ron, Boushey, Heather ve Saunders, Dawn (eds), *Political Economy and Contemporary Capitalism* (London and New York: Sharpe).

Petras, James and Henry Veltmeyer (2000), *The Dynamics of Social Change in Latin America* (Palgrave Macmillan).

—— (2001), *Globalization Unmasked: Imperialism in the 21st Century* (London and New York: Zed Books).

Rodrik, Dani (2001), 'The Global Governance of Trade as if Development Really Mattered', paper presented at the UNDP Meetings, New York, 13–14 October 2000.

Rodrik, D. and A. Velasco (1999), 'Short Term Capital Flows', in *Proceedings of the Annual World Bank Conference on Development Economics* (Washington D.C.: The World Bank.

Telli, Cagatay, Ebru Voyvoda and Erinc Yeldan (2006), 'Modeling General Equilibrium for Socially Responsible Macroeconomics: Seeking for the Alternatives to Fight Jobless Growth in Turkey', *METU Studies in Development*, forthcoming.

Voyvoda and Yeldan (2006), 'Macroecoomics of Twin Targeting in Turkey: A General Equilibrium Analysis', June, http://www.bilkent.edu.tr/~yeldane/econmodel/Voyvoda&Yeldan_AltIT-Turkey_2006.pdf.

Yeldan, Erinç (2001), *Küresellesme Sürecinde Türkiye Ekonomisi: Bölü°üm, Birikim, Büyüme*, Istanbul: Ileti°im Publications.

—— (2002), 'On the IMF-Directed Disinflation Program in Turkey: A Program for Stabilization and Austerity or a Recipe for Impoverishment and Financial Chaos?', in N. Balkan and S. Savran (eds), *The Ravages of Neo-Liberalism: Economy, Society and Gender in Turkey* (New York: Nova Science Pub.).

—— (2006), 'Neo-Liberal Global Remedies: From Speculative-led Growth to IMF-led Crisis in Turkey', *Review of Radical Political Economics*, 38 (2), Spring: 193–213.

Recovery and Adjustment after the 1998 Russian Currency Crisis

Vladimir Popov

In most East Asian countries, the recovery after the 1997 crisis was pretty sluggish: investment/GDP (gross domestic product) ratios dropped as compared to the pre-crisis decade; the inflow of foreign investment slowed down; growth rates did not reach the pre-crisis averages. On top of that, the pre-crisis *dirigiste* growth model was partially dismantled: the share of government spending in GDP decreased and interventionist industrial strategy partly yielded place to market liberalism. The notable exception is of course China, which did not have a currency crisis in the first place – the *yuan* was not devalued in response to the devaluation of other East Asian currencies. Nevertheless, China experienced only temporary and marginal decline in exports and production growth rates in 1998–99, but fully recovered afterwards, whereas the share of total and social government spending in GDP increased during 1999–2007.

In Russia the story was very different. One month after the August 1998 currency crisis, the Russian economy started growing (after nearly nine years of output falls during the transformational recession of 1989–98) at about 7 per cent a year; investment increased; and the inflow of foreign investment as well as the share of government spending in GDP, which both fell dramatically during 1989–98, started to rise. Russian post-crisis development resembled that in Argentina after its currency board collapsed in 2002, rather than that in East Asia.

The obvious explanation of differing performance that comes to mind is the dynamics of fuel prices, since oil and gas account for one-half to two-thirds of Russian export revenues. After February 1999, when oil prices reached a quarter-century minimum (less than $10 a barrel in nominal terms), they started to rise, with a positive impact on Russian economic activity. But this was only part of the story. In fact the Russian economy started to recover in October 1998, immediately after the devaluation and half a year before the turnaround in oil prices. Other factors that contributed to the restoration of growth were the end of the transformational recession and the devaluation of the previously overvalued exchange rate. In fact, the crucial difference between Russia (and Argentina) and the East Asian countries was that the reduction of output in Russia (and Argentina) occurred before the devaluation, whereas in East Asia it occurred after devaluation. In both Russia (1995–98) and Argentina (1991–2002), the attempts to maintain an overvalued exchange rate led to the reduction of output, whereas devaluation effectively triggered the growth of output.

Besides, unlike in East Asia, the Russian currency crisis of 1998 led to a strengthening of the state, which had been considerably weakened and virtually 'privatized' in the 1990s. Government revenues and expenditure started to grow faster than GDP, foreign exchange reserves increased from $10 billion in 1998 to over $400 billion in 2007, and state institutions that had collapsed in the 1990s somewhat improved after the crisis. (For example, the murder rate fell in 2002–07.)

This paper argues that: (1) the nature of the Russian 1998 currency crisis was very different from that of the East Asian currency collapses of 1997, which is why devaluation of the currency led to growth of output in Russia, whereas in Asia it led to a decline in output; and (2) the consequences of the currency crisis in Russia were also different from that in East Asia, inasmuch as in Russia the crisis largely discredited the neoliberal economic model of the 1990s, whereas in East Asia the backlash of the currency crises was directed (misguidedly) against the developmental state model.

The Story: Russia's 1998 Financial Collapse[1]

Perhaps the most impressive of all the currency crises that affected the transition economies[2] was the one that broke out in Russia in August 1998. In a matter of days, the exchange rate that had been stable during the preceding three years lost over 60 per cent of its value – more than in all the Latin American and Southeast Asian countries, except for Indonesia (Charts 1, 2). Prices increased by nearly 50 per cent in only two months after the crisis, as compared to less than 1 per cent monthly inflation before the crisis (Charts 3 and 4). Real output fell by

CHART 1   *Exchange Rates in Transition Economies*
(national currencies per $1, January 1997=100%)

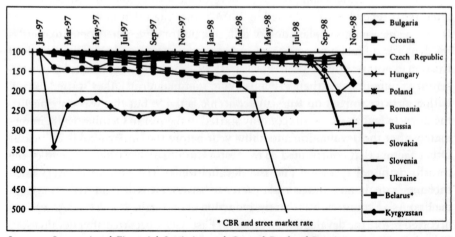

* CBR and street market rate

Source: International Financial Statistics and Central Bank of Russia.

CHART 2 *Exchange Rates in Southeast Asia* (national currencies per $1, January 1997 = 100%) *and in Mexico* (January 1998 = 100%)

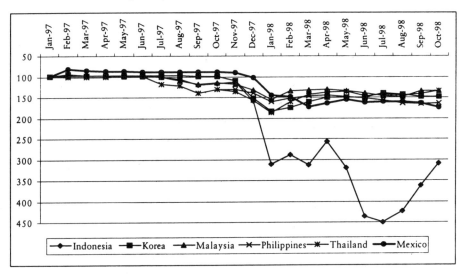

about 6 per cent in 1998 after registering a small increase of 0.6 per cent in 1997 for the first time since 1989 (Chart 3).

Macroeconomic Stabilization of 1995–98

The August 1998 financial collapse in Russia marked the failure of the government programme of macroeconomic stabilization that was pursued for over three years with some degree of success. After experiencing high inflation of several hundred and more per cent a year during the period immediately following the deregulation of prices on 2 January 1992, Russia finally opted for a programme of exchange rate-based stabilization. In mid-1995, the Central Bank of Russia (CBR), after accumulating foreign exchange reserves and managing to maintain the stable rate of the *rouble* for the first half of 1995, introduced a system of the crawling peg – an exchange rate corridor with initially fairly narrow boundaries.

The programme was based on the government's and the CBR's decision to bring down the rates of growth of money supply in order to curb inflation. The key to the programme was to contain within reasonable limits the government budget deficit, and to find non-inflationary ways of financing it. On both fronts, the government stood up to its promises for three long years. It managed not to increase the budget deficit, even though this required drastic expenditure cuts since the budget revenues, despite all efforts to improve tax collection, continued to fall.[3] It also managed to finance the deficit largely without monetizing it, through borrowings. These were partly by means of selling short-term *rouble* denominated treasury bills or GKOs (which were also purchased by foreign investors), and partly by borrowing abroad in hard currency from international financial institutions, western governments and banks, and in the Eurobond market.

CHART 3   *GDP Growth Rates and Inflation* (right axis, log scale) *in Russia (%), 1990–2006*

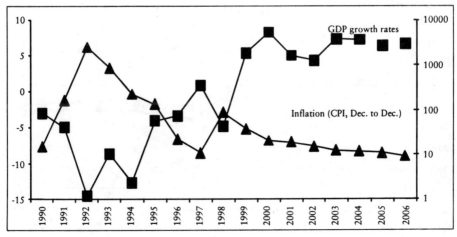

Source: Goskomstat.

Under such conditions, the CBR got the opportunity to ensure the reduction of the rates of growth of money supply and a fall in inflation (Chart 3).

Weak Foundations of the Macroeconomic Stabilization

Thus, macroeconomic stabilization became a reality. Just before the crisis, inflation was running at only 6 per cent per year, the rates of reduction of output in 1997 slowed down, and the country was looking forward to economic growth. The macroeconomic stabilization, however, was based on a weak foundation of an overvalued exchange rate of the *rouble* and on the policy of the CBR to keep the nominal exchange rate intact, that is, despite the ongoing inflation that was markedly higher than in the US although it was falling.

As a result, the 'Dutch disease' developed in Russia from 1995, as the exchange rate of the *rouble* quickly approached 70 per cent of the purchasing power parity (PPP) and continued to increase. The previously high export growth rates slowed down substantially (from 20 per cent in 1995 to 8 per cent in 1996 for total exports, and from 25 per cent to 9 per cent respectively for exports to non-CIS states). In 1997 total exports fell for the first time since 1992. Needless to say, it was Russia's already limited export of manufactured goods that was most affected by the appreciation of the real exchange rate. In 1996, among the economies in transition, Russia (together with Slovenia, by far the richest country experiencing recovery from 1993) had the smallest gap between domestic and international prices.[4]

The decrease in oil prices in the world market in 1997–98 added insult to injury. The decline in exports accelerated in the first half of 1998. Together with still rising imports, this virtually wiped out the trade surplus that in better times (1996) amounted to $20 billion. The current account balance turned negative in the first half of 1998. Given the need to service the debt and the persistence of

CHART 4 *Real Effective Exchange Rate, December 1995 = 100%* (left scale), and *Year End Gross Foreign Exchange Reserves, Including Gold, bln. $* (right log scale)

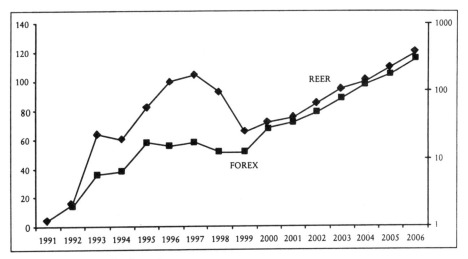

Source: Central Bank of Russia.

CHART 5 *Consolidated Government Revenues and Expenditure, % of GDP*

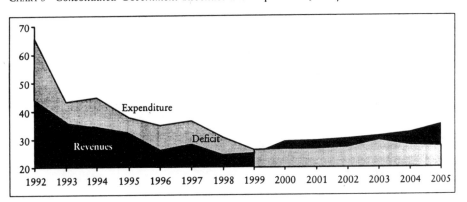

Source: EBRD.

capital flight (which is partly captured in the 'errors and omissions' item in the balance of payments statistics), the negative current account was a sure recipe for disaster.

In fact, under the circumstances, the level of the exchange rate was not sustainable in 1998, since there developed a new vulnerability of the *rouble* with respect to short-term capital flows. After they were allowed by the authorities in 1995, foreign investment into *rouble*-denominated government treasury bills quickly increased to nearly one-third of the $50 billion market for government treasury bills in 1997 (including investment into the GKO through 'grey schemes', that is, through resident intermediaries). From February 1998, the total amount of treasury bills held by non-residents started to exceed the value of the country's foreign exchange reserves.[5]

Foreign investors also started to withdraw from the Russian stock market. They were estimated to control no less than 10 per cent of the shares in the booming Russian stockmarket whose capitalization surpassed $100 billion in the fall of 1997. From that time until mid-1998 – in just about nine months – stock prices in dollar terms fell by over 80 per cent to the lowest level since 1994. The decision of the central bank to expand slightly the width of the exchange rate band from the beginning of 1998 was a cosmetic measure that did not yield much room for manoeuvre. The central bank had to increase the refinancing rate to 150 per cent in May 1998 to prevent capital from fleeing at a rate of about $0.5 billion a week, at a time when foreign exchange reserves were at a level of about

CHART 6   *Goods Export from and Import to Russia, billion $, monthly data*

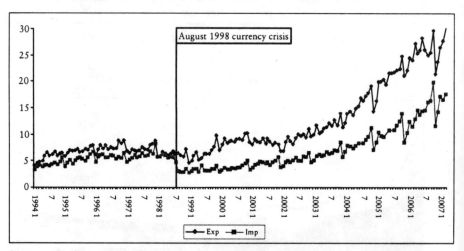

Source: Goskomstat.

CHART 7   *Russia's Balance-of-Payments and Foreign Exchange Reserves*, billion dollars*

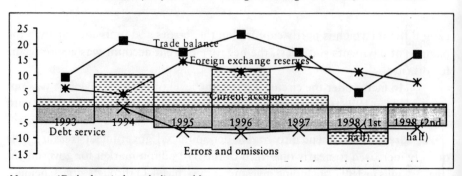

Note: *End of period, excluding gold.
Source: Goskomstat.

$15 billion only. Later the refinancing rate was lowered, but yields on government securities remained at a level of nearly 50 per cent in real terms and then again increased to over 100 per cent in August. The central bank and the government, however, stuck to the policy of a strong *rouble* to the very last moment, maintaining scandalously high interest rates that eliminated all prospects for economic recovery and negotiating a stand-by package with the IMF. In a sense, this was a policy designed to maintain consumption and imports, to avoid export-oriented restructuring and to continue to live beyond the country's means. The IMF finally provided the first instalment ($4 billion) of a $20 billion dollar package that went directly to the CBR to replenish vanishing foreign exchange reserves, but even this did not calm the investors. Public officials' statements about the stability of the *rouble*, including that of Yeltsin made three days before devaluation, had only the opposite effect, if any.

Managing the August 1998 Crisis

Like a number of other economists,[6] I strongly believed before the crisis broke out that the *rouble* was overvalued, arguing that if it is not devalued 'from above' in advance, it is likely to get devalued 'from below' through a currency crisis, with much greater costs (Popov 1996a, 1996b, 1997, 1998b, 1998e).[7]

In a sense, it was not so difficult to predict the crisis and quite a number of scholars did so several months ahead of time. Even Jeffrey Sachs, earlier a strong advocate of exchange rate-based stabilization, in June 1998 spoke out publicly in favour of devaluation (*New York Times*, 4 June 1998).[8]

What virtually nobody was able to predict, however, was the way the Russian government handled the devaluation, that is, by declaring a default on domestic debt and a part of the international debt held by banks and companies.

CHART 8   *Dollar Stock Prices Indices, December 1993 = 100%*

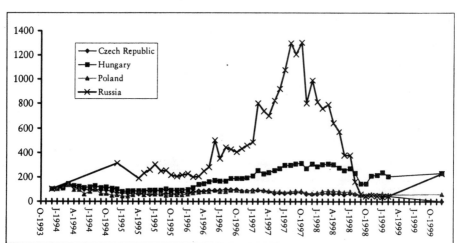

Source: *Economist*. For Russia in 1992–93: author's estimates.

This was by no means necessary since basically there was no debt crisis but only a currency crisis, which was supposed to be handled only by devaluing the *rouble*.

As Chart 9 suggests, the indebtedness of the Russian government in pre-crisis years had been growing, but not that significantly as compared to GDP (since GDP in dollar terms was growing rapidly due to the real appreciation of the *rouble*). In absolute terms, the total government debt by mid-1998 had not even reached the threshold of 60 per cent of GDP. Even when the wage and payment arrears of the Russian government are taken into account, total indebtedness does not increase much: government wage arrears right before the crisis stood at 13 billion *roubles*, or just 0.5 per cent of annual GDP, while total government arrears that were several times higher than just wage arrears were largely offset by tax arrears to the government.

It is true that according to available estimates, government short-term obligations – GKOs, *rouble*-denominated but held by non-residents – exceeded total foreign exchange reserves from early 1998. This was an obvious case of mismanagement and clearly contributed to the crisis. However, the absolute value of the outstanding short-term debt held by foreigners was by no means substantial – only $15–20 billion. The problem, rather, was the negligible amount of reserves, at $15 billion. But even under these circumstances, it would have been possible to continue to service the debt after, say, 50 per cent devaluation (which would immediately reduce debt service payments by half in dollar terms), not to speak of the use of IMF credits.[9]

The mistrust of investors in the first half of 1998 was associated first and foremost with the low credibility of the government strategy of defending the *rouble*, whereas the ability of the government to service its debt was not really put into question. The difference between the rates at which the Russian government borrowed abroad in hard currency (returns on Eurobonds were around 15

CHART 9   *Government Debt, % of GDP*

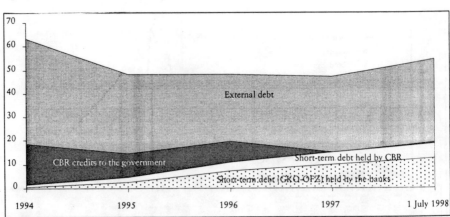

Source: *Russian Economy: The Month in Review*, No. 1, Bank of Finland, Institute for Economies in Transition 1998; Goskomstat.

per cent) and the rates offered to the prime borrowers (7 per cent) was much lower than the gap between returns on *rouble*-denominated bonds (about 100 per cent in real terms) and Eurobonds (15 per cent). Because the first gap is the indicator of country risk (that is, the risk associated with default by the government of this particular country), whereas the second one reflects currency risk (that is, the risk associated with devaluation), it is clear that the anticipation of the market at that time was of devaluation but not of default.

Unfortunately, the default was not the only element of mismanagement in the handling of the crisis. Shortly after the default the CBR, by its clumsy actions, provoked a run on the banks and a banking crisis. Banks already were badly hurt by the devaluation (which was an inevitable cost they were supposed to bear), but also by the default (because they held a considerable portion of their assets in short-term government securities, on which the government defaulted, and also because they lost opportunities for external financing after the government imposed a 90-day moratorium on the servicing of their external debts). To make matters worse, the CBR in early September introduced a scheme to guarantee personal deposits in commercial banks, which implied losses for the depositors, especially for the holders of dollar accounts at private banks.[10] The run on the banks that naturally followed contributed to the developing paralysis of the banking system. In September 1998 banks hardly processed any payments and businesses started to carry out their transactions purely in cash, or through barter and the use of cash substitutes.

After the Crisis

An ailing Russian industry experienced a boom after the August 1998 financial crash, registering high growth rates that were not seen for nearly half a century. By 1995 the transformational recession had largely come to an end, and

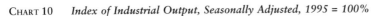

CHART 10   *Index of Industrial Output, Seasonally Adjusted, 1995 = 100%*

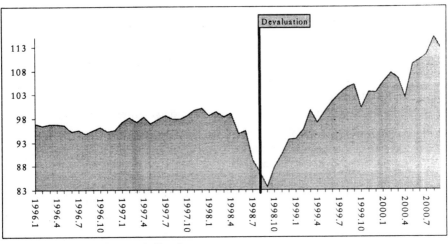

Source: Russian Economic Trends.

CHART 11   *GDP Growth Rates in Selected Southeast Asian Countries and in Russia, %*

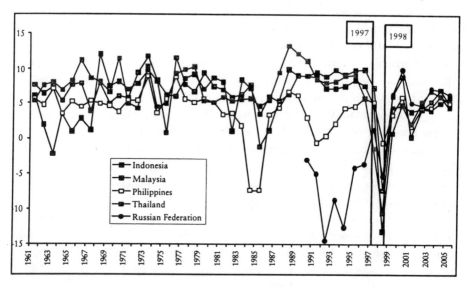

industrial output was more or less stable for the three years 1995–97. But a decline in industrial output had started at the very beginning of 1998 and continued until the August 1998 currency crisis, with the fall totalling 15 per cent. However, after October 1998 industrial output started to recover (Chart 10). Strong growth began not because of, but despite, government policy: whereas before the crisis the overvalued *rouble* was undermining the competitiveness of domestically produced goods, after devaluation domestic producers took advantage of new export opportunities and the shift in demand from foreign to Russian made goods.

In fact, the 1998 recession that occurred before the crisis was artificially manufactured by the poor policy of keeping the exchange rate at an unreasonably high and unsustainable level. The market corrected the mistake of the government and the central bank backed by IMF that defended the unsustainable peg with a persistence that deserved a better application. This is what the August 1998 crisis was all about. Different patterns of decline of output in Russia (before the currency crisis) and in East Asia (after the currency crisis – Chart 11) provide further evidence of the different nature of the currency crashes. Whereas in East Asia devaluation led to a collapse of the previously overextended credit, and this shock (credit crunch) was greater than the regular (Keynesian) stimulating effect of devaluation, in Russia devaluation of the previously overvalued currency did not have much of an impact on the financial system (M2 to annual GDP ratio was only less than 15 per cent in August 1998), but restored the previously lost competitiveness and led to an increase in capacity utilization.[11] Unlike East Asian countries, and very much like the Argentine economy in 2002, the Russian economy experienced a boom after the currency crisis, not a recession.

Alternative Explanations of the Russian Crisis

There are several prevailing – and not mutually exclusive – explanations for the August 1998 currency crisis in Russia. One stresses the unfortunate coincidence of events (Asian virus, a drop in oil prices, political instability, etc.). Yevgeny Yasin (1999), the minister without portfolio in the former Kirienko government and a respected academic economist, said: 'The crisis is not just the result of the evil forces or incompetence, but is caused by the coincidence of circumstances, most of which were against us.' Sergey Kirienko himself believed that even in June 1998 Russia had a chance to get through the bumpy piece of road avoiding the crisis, if only the Duma accepted the tax increases suggested by the government (*Expert*, 18 January 1999). Aslund (1999b) takes a similar stand, noting that by rejecting the government package of sensible policies in July 1998, the Duma pushed the country 'over the brink into a financial abyss'.

Another explanation is that the crisis was caused by budgetary problems in the form of persistent deficits resulting in mounting government debt, or 'the GKO pyramid' ('Russian Economy in 1998', 1999). It is no wonder that the former senior officials of the Central Bank of Russia take this view. 'No doubt, the current financial crisis is mostly of budgetary and debt origin', states Sergey Alexashenko, the then deputy chairman of the CBR (Alexashenko 1999). It is thus the government, not the CBR, that is to be blamed, since the CBR could stick to a restrictive monetary policy only that much and for that long without being supported by the government, which continued to pursue loose fiscal policy. Former government officials, in response, say they knew about the problem but were not able to force the parliament to accept the necessary tough measures to improve tax collection. Hence the scapegoat of last resort is again the red-brown parliament, which, as everyone is supposed to know, is anti-reform-minded.

One variation of these views is that the government debt pyramid was doomed to collapse and eventually collapsed. It is pointed out that the returns on the short-term government bonds (GKOs) were scandalously high, many times higher than in the real sector, and that such a policy was driving away resources from the real sector into purely financial speculation in the market for government debt and the stockmarket (Nekipelov 1998). Financial prosperity that was not based on the foundations of a healthy real economy could not continue for long and finally came to an end in the form of the crisis.

The western explanations of the Russian crisis, at least those that appear outside the area studies field, are generally even more straightforward. The most popular alternative explanations for the Russian crisis are associated one way or another with the crony and criminal nature of Russian capitalism. The government is accused of playing to the interests of 'oligarchs' – heads of large financial–industrial groups in the Russian economy – who have effectively 'privatized' the state and care only about enriching themselves in the short run. The assumption, basically, is that everything is so rotten in Russia that there is no way the exchange rate can be stable.

It seems as if the majority agreed that everything is so rotten in Russia that it would have been strange if the crisis had not happened. It is often stated that funds obtained by the state through domestic and external borrowing were mishandled, if not embezzled or stolen, and that overall, the inefficient and corrupt system of public administration could not ensure any kind of macroeconomic stabilization, be it exchange rate-based or money-based. Oligarchs do not think long-term anyway, and are unable to agree on measures on increasing tax revenues of the state, slowing down capital flight and controlling indebtedness, since, as Paul Krugman puts it, 'there is no honour among the thieves' (Krugman's site, 10 September 1998). This suggests that the IMF–World Bank credits were just wasted, if not stolen, by the short-sighted and *'après nous le deluge'*-minded oligarchs. Aslund (1999a) believes that the August 1998 crash was the outcome of intense competition over the evasive rent that decreased from 15–80 per cent of GDP in 1991–94 to 5–15 per cent in 1995–98.

Some go even further, seeing the root of all Russia's evils in social mis-understanding of the nature of money. References are being made to the Russian national character (described, for instance, in the *Gambler* by F. Dostoyevsky, where Alexei states that Russians are squanderers and like the roulette so much exactly because it allows them to become rich effortlessly in two hours), as well as to 70 years of bolshevism that virtually abolished money as a legal tender of predictable value, making the value of the *rouble* 'something stranger than zero' (*Economist*, 19 December 1998).

These explanations may be journalistically impressive, but to a large extent they miss the point. First, although the role of money and credit in the Soviet centrally planned economy (CPE) was limited, as compared to the market economy, the degree of monetization (M2 / GDP ratio) and credit creation (bank credit outstanding as a per cent of GDP) in the 1980s was much higher than in the Russian market economy of the 1990s (about 50 per cent as compared to less than 15 per cent). So, in a sense, the Soviet CPE was much more monetized than the new Russian market economy. Soviet planners, as a matter of fact, were quite prudent in their macroeconomic policies for four decades: from 1947 (Stalin's confiscatory monetary reform) to 1987 (the beginning of macroeconomic mis-management under Gorbachev) the annual average inflation (open and hidden, that is, the increase in monetary overhang) was only 3 per cent, less than in most countries over this period. Government budget deficits were low or non-existent, government domestic debt was minuscule, external indebtedness was low, and payments were made like clockwork.

To put it differently, the argument about the 'demonetized Russian soul' does not seem to work, just as the argument about a 'difficult Soviet heritage' does not, since neither of the factors prevented Soviet planners from achieving a high degree of macroeconomic stability and solid monetization of the economy.

Second, there is hardly any doubt that Russian state institutions were being degraded in recent years and that the weakening of state institutions is the main *long-term* factor explaining the poor performance of the Russian (and CIS) economy, as compared to China and Vietnam with strong authoritarian institutions, on the one hand, and Central European countries with strong democratic institutions, on the other. As a matter of fact, a recent research study comparing twenty-eight transition economies, including those of China and Vietnam, suggests that it is not the speed of liberalization that should be held responsible for differing performance but the institutional capacity of the state. This factor was overlooked by both schools of transition thought, by shock therapists and gradualists alike (Popov 1998c, 1998d, 2000a, 2007). Such an approach seems to gain more and more support in the framework of the so called 'post-Washington consensus' (Stiglitz 1998, 1999).

Nevertheless, even though institutional weakness is the single most important *long-term* factor that contributed to the extreme magnitude of the Russian recession, it is not linked directly with the collapse of the *rouble* and the failure of the macroeconomic stabilization programme. As was argued earlier, the debt levels of the Russian government and Russian companies were very modest by international standards. Even if the borrowed funds were embezzled, this could not, and did not, lead to the debt and currency crises, since the critical point of really excessive indebtedness was yet to be reached in at least several years. No less important, there was no major change with respect to 'cronyness', corruption and institutional weaknesses in recent years (except, may be, for some stabilization), so references to the criminal nature of Russian capitalism cannot explain much.

Lessons for Transition Economies

Unlike the currency crises in East Asia and the preceding currency crises in Latin America, the recent currency crises in the transition economies seem to be caused not by excessive – private or government – debt accumulation, but by mere excessive appreciation of the exchange rate, undermining the competitiveness of the export sector, leading to deterioration of the current account and, finally, causing the outflow of capital in anticipation of a devaluation. Theories offered to explain the trend towards real exchange rate appreciation in the transition economies proved to be of limited applicability. At the end of the day, in transition economies as well as in other countries, appreciation of the real exchange rate cannot be infinite, and, if it goes too far, inevitably leads to a crisis.

With fixed exchange rates (and even more so with currency board arrangements) that effectively force countries to abandon their independent monetary policy, their economies are forced to adjust to trade shocks, and the inflows and outflows of capital, through real indicators. When the exchange rate is pegged and prices are not completely flexible, changes in the money supply (caused by the fluctuation of reserves) may affect output rather than prices. This kind of real sector adjustment is quite costly. To put it in the simplest form, under a fixed exchange rate regime, neither changes in foreign exchange reserves nor domestic price changes in response to money supply fluctuations provide enough room for manoeuvre for handling trade shocks and international capital flows.

However, the large swings in nominal rates in response to balance of payments shocks are costly because they lead to fluctuations in the real exchange rate and hence to real adjustment. To prevent the appreciation of real exchange rates in cases of positive terms of trade shocks or inflows of capital, it is better to accumulate foreign exchange reserves with sterilization of the resulting growth of money supply. Such a policy is of course possible only with some kind of capital account control.

Besides, the policy of keeping the exchange rate low through the accumulation of reserves seems to be not only prudent, but also conducive to economic growth. For transition economies facing the challenge of export-oriented restructuring, it is highly desirable. The inflationary consequences of such a policy, as the example of the East Asian countries shows, may be dealt with through sterilization operations.

There are two important general policy lessons for transition economies and other similar economies undertaking market reforms which have almost instantly given them access to foreign capital resources. First, they need to avoid real exchange rate appreciation that can lead to currency crises. Second, to the extent that they experience a trend of increasing external indebtedness, they have to draw early lessons from more complex government debt crises (the Latin American countries in the early 1980s and in 1994–95) and private sector debt crises (Southeast Asia in 1997–98) to avoid another episode of currency collapse in the near future. So, capital account control seems to be necessary not only to counter the inflationary consequences of reserve accumulation, but also to regulate increases in private debt.

Post-Crisis Economic Development in Russia
Achievements

After losing 45 per cent of its output in the period 1989–98, the Russian economy started to grow from 1999 (6 per cent in 1999, 10 per cent in 2000, 4–7 per cent in 2001–06). The major push was given by devaluation of the *rouble* in 1998 and by higher world prices for oil and gas later, but the Putin government (Putin became prime minister in 1999 and president in 2000) can at least take the credit for not ruining this growth. Inflation fell from 84 per cent in 1998 (when prices jumped after the August 1998 currency crisis and dramatic devaluation of the *rouble*) to 10–12 per cent in 2004–06.

True, in comparative perspective, the Russian performance is not that impressive. Many other former Soviet republics – Azerbaijan, Belarus, Estonia, Kazakhstan, Latvia, Lithuania, Turkmenistan and Uzbekistan – by 2006 had reached or exceeded their pre-recession (1989) level of output, whereas Russian GDP was still at only 85 per cent of the 1989 level. The Russian Human Development Index (accounting not only for GDP per capita, but also for life expectancy and level of education) is still below the level it had touched in the USSR, and even below that of Cuba which has life expectancy of 77 years against 65 years in Russia. China, with life expectancy of 72 years, is rapidly approaching the Russian level of HDI.

However, there is obviously more stability in Russia today than in the rocky 1990s.[12] Putin tried to limit the all-powerful regions by changing the principles of fiscal federalism, appointing presidential viceroys in seven amalgamated regions, and reforming the Federation Council, the upper chamber of the Russian parliament, which represented the interests of all 89 regions. In 1999, Putin began a second war against Chechnya, refusing to negotiate in any way, shape or form with the separatists, and by today the separatists are largely defeated. He launched court cases against 'oligarchs' while remaining within the limits of the law. They were accused of failing to pay taxes and engaging in financial machinations. Some of them emigrated, others were arrested. The only non-governmental television channel, NTV, was shut down (incidentally, also for totally legitimate reasons, as the 'oligarch'-owner Gusinsky had refused to pay off the debt to the state-owned Gasprom, having apparently decided that freedom of speech was not worth that much money). Another 'oligarch', Mikhail Khodorkovsky, ended up in jail for fraud (taking oil profits to offshore locations via transfer pricing), and his company, Yukos, was bankrupted by the government; its assets were seized to collect the tax arrears due to the state. Another oil company, Sibneft, was purchased in the open market by Gazprom, so the share of the state in the oil industry increased from less than 15 per cent in 2004 to over 30 per cent in 2005.

The government budget moved from deficit to surplus, the decline in the share of state revenues and expenditure stopped, the government debt – both domestic and external – decreased, and the government created a Stabilization Fund to capture the windfall profits from fuel export that stood at over $120 billion by mid-2007. Total foreign exchange reserves, including the Stabilization Fund, increased to over $400 billion by mid-2007, whereas Russian GDP stood at about $1 trillion in 2006 at the official exchange rate.

Even more important was the strengthening of the institutional capacity of the state. A strong and efficient state is one that has the power to enforce its rules and regulations, no matter what these are. Crime and murder rates and the size of the shadow economy are natural measures of the strength of institutions. A strong state may be more or less democratic. Both China and the Central European countries, with murder rates of about 2 per 100,000 inhabitants, have stronger states than Russia, with about 25–30 murders per 100,000 of inhabitants in 2000–05.

The very notion of the state implies that public authorities exercise at least three monopolies: (i) on violence, (ii) on tax collection and (iii) on money emission (coinage). All three monopolies were undermined in Russia during the 1990s to such an extent that the very existence of the state was put into question. Government failure became pervasive and much more visible than market failure.

In 1998, just before the currency crisis, the payment system was on the brink of collapse. Barter deals exceeded 50 per cent of total transactions and enterprises were accumulating non-payments (trade, tax and wage arrears) by delaying payments to their partners, the government and their workers indefinitely. After economic growth resumed in October 1998, the non-payments and barter transactions quickly disappeared, but there is no guarantee that they will not appear again if the monetary authorities resort to a tight monetary policy.

Tax collection, after a dramatic fall during 1992–98, increased slightly, but mostly due to the resumption of growth, not due to better tax compliance. The efficiency of the government in recent years has not improved: different measures of corruption, government effectiveness and rule of law do not register any considerable progress, so low spending levels mean that the state simply cannot provide enough of the public goods.

Worst of all, the criminalization of Russian society has reached an extremely high level. Crime was rising gradually in the Soviet Union since the mid-1960s, but after the collapse of the USSR there was an unprecedented increase – in just a few years in the early 1990s, crime and murder rates doubled and reached one of the highest levels in the world (Chart 12).[13] By the mid-1990s the murder rate stood at over 30 people per 100,000 of inhabitants as against 1–2 persons in Western and Eastern Europe, Canada, China, Japan, Mauritius and Israel. Only two countries in the world (not counting some war-torn collapsed states in the developing countries where there are no reliable statistics anyway) had higher murder rates – South Africa and Colombia – whereas in countries like Brazil and Mexico this rate is two times lower. Even the US murder rate of 6–7 people per 100,000 inhabitants, the highest in the developed world, pales in comparison with the Russian one.

CHART 12   *Crime Rate* (left scale), *Murder Rate and Suicide Rate* (right scale)
per 100,000 Inhabitants

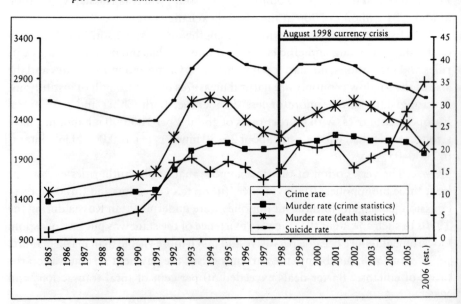

The unprecedented increase in the crime rate in Russia during the 1990s, including shocking murders of famous politicians, businessmen and journalists that went unpunished, de facto bankrupted the law enforcement agencies and brought the Russian state to the point of losing its monopoly on violence. This reasoning has nothing to do with the issue (widely discussed in economics) of the optimal size of the state. The story of the 1990s in Russia and some other former Soviet republics is one of the dismantling of the state in such a short period of time that it was unprecedented in economic history. Simply put, if crime, income inequality, poverty and corruption are on the rise, the state needs more money, not less, to bring these unfavourable developments to a halt.

Hence, the most important achievement of recent years is that the growth of the economy and political stability finally brought about some improvement in social trends: the number of murders reached a peak in 2002 and fell during 2003–06; suicide rates decreased during 2001–06 (Chart 12); the mortality rate stopped rising in 2004 (Chart 13); the birth rate, after reaching a fifty-year minimum in 1999, started to rise; the marriage rate increased and the divorce rate fell. On the other hand, a nearly 50 per cent increase in the crime rate during 2002–05 is most likely the sign of better registration of crimes. True, the improvements are marginal, but at least there is hope, which was completely missing previously.

Nevertheless, despite the important progress during 1999–2007, the macroeconomic policy is still far from being perfect and may be only described as second best – that is, better than before the 1998 currency crisis, but not yet good enough. The important drawbacks include: (1) the inability of the state to

CHART 13   *Mortality Rate (per 1000) and Average Life Expectancy (years)*

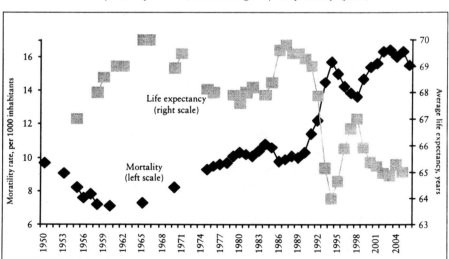

Source: Goskomstat.

restore the provision of public goods even though the increase in oil revenues provides for such a possibility; (2) the presence of an overvalued (Dutch disease level) real exchange rate; (3) the instability of monetary policy and the persistent attempts at monetary tightening in order bring inflation down to single digits; and (4) the premature elimination of capital controls in July 2006.

Government Revenues and Expenditure

Faced with increased oil revenues, the government has chosen to decrease taxes (income tax, corporate tax and the unified social tax). The critics of such measures, including the Moscow office of the IMF, justifiably point out that the current revenues of the budget and the current surpluses are based primarily on high prices for energy sources, and, therefore, if these prices should fall, the government could once again find itself penniless. In addition, it is not the right time to reduce taxes when virtually all government services – health care, education, defence, law and order – are much worse off than the private economy.

Education and health care were free in the Soviet Union, but now these services are provided mostly for a fee, and their quality is way below the Soviet standards. The major reason for such a deterioration in the volume, quality and effectiveness of the provision of government services is the catastrophic reduction of state spending. In the last years of the USSR, expenditure of all levels of government totalled over 50 per cent of GDP and even increased to 65 per cent of GDP in 1992 in Russia, but by 1999 it fell to 34 per cent and in 2005 recovered only slightly to about 40 per cent of GDP (EBRD statistics). Because GDP itself today (after falling in 1989–98 and partly recovering in 1999–2006) has just approached the 1992 level, in real terms state expenditure now is only half of what it used to be in the early 1990s. Hence the state has lower capacity to provide health care and education services, lower ability to fight crime, and no power to cope with corruption.

As a result, as noted above, life expectancy has declined from 70 years in 1987 to 65 years today (as against 73 years in China). Corruption levels have increased significantly according to independent estimates.[14] The shadow economy estimated at 10–15 per cent of GDP in the late 1980s expanded to about 40–50 per cent in the mid-1990s and has not shrunk subsequently.

Exchange Rate

The current real exchange rate of the *rouble* (the ratio of domestic to world prices) is too high. It has been growing since the 1998 crisis and in 2006, exceeded the 1998 pre-crisis level. Given the increase of world fuel prices in recent years, one could have expected an acceleration of economic growth rather than a slowdown, which actually occurred in 2001–06 as compared to 2000. The reason for the slowdown is overvaluation of the real exchange rate – the typical Dutch disease that Russia has developed once again. The first time Russia developed it in 1995–98, it led to the currency crisis of August 1998, and now it seems like history repeats itself. Optimists argue that unlike in 1998, Russia currently has large foreign exchange reserves, but pessimists point out that if oil prices fall and capital starts to flee, reserves will be depleted very quickly. The future devaluation could happen either in the form of a currency crisis or in the form of a 'soft landing', but there is hardly any doubt that eventually it will take place.

Nature of Current Growth

The current upturn is not based on solid foundations: wages and incomes in recent years have been systematically growing faster than productivity (Chart 14), so the share of consumption in GDP has increased at the expense of investment.

CHART 14   *Annual Growth Rates of Real Wages, Real Incomes and Productivity, %*

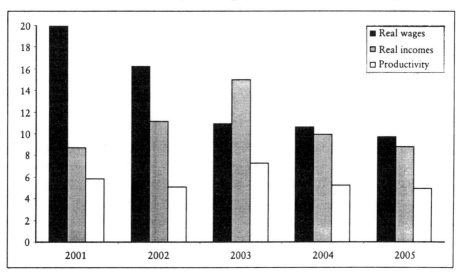

CHART 15   *Growth of Real Investment and Total (private and government) Consumption, 1991 = 100%*

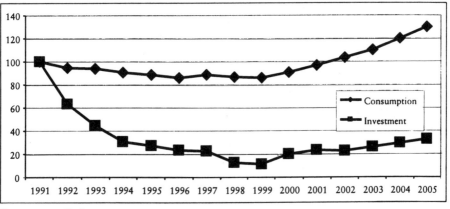

Source: Goskomstat.

As a result, whereas Russian personal and public consumption have already exceeded the pre-recession levels, investment is still less than 40 per cent of what it used to be in the last year of existence of the USSR (Chart 15). Russian gross savings are large – over 30 per cent of GDP – but they are funnelled away via the outflow of private capital and the accumulation of foreign exchange reserves, so gross investment amounts to less than 20 per cent of GDP.

Concluding Comments

It is often said that a crisis opens the window of opportunity for reforms. This is certainly true of the Asian 1997 currency crises, as well as of the Russian 1998 currency crisis. However, the direction of these reforms depends largely on the roots of the crisis itself, or, better to say, on how these roots are viewed by major social groups.

In Russia, as argued earlier, the 1998 currency crisis was associated with overvaluation of the real exchange rate as a result of the policy of exchange rate-based stabilization pursued during 1995–98. More than that, this crisis was largely viewed as a final collapse of the liberal strategy of the 1990s (deregulation, macroeconomic stabilization, downsizing of the government, privatization, opening up of the economy) that led to an unprecedented collapse of output, reduction of living standards and life expectancy, increase in income and wealth inequalities, crime and disorder. Not surprisingly, the reforms that were favoured and introduced after the crisis were mostly of the *dirigiste* type: strengthening the state fiscal and administrative capacity, creation of a Stabilization Fund and accumulation of reserves, some re-nationalization in the oil industry, and restraints on the political influence of the 'oligarchs'.

The argument developed in this paper is that these reforms were not consistent enough (the real exchange rate continued to increase, the institutional capacity of the state was not restored to the pre-transition level) and sometimes were accompanied by measures in the opposite (pro-market) direction (cuts in taxes, elimination of capital account control). Thus, despite some modest progress in recent years, in particular growth of output and income caused mostly by high oil prices, Russia once again developed a Dutch disease (overvaluation of the *rouble*), and did not manage to use the favourable terms of trade for repairing the damage inflicted in the 1990s to public consumption and to the manufacturing industries.

In East Asia the roots of the 1997 crises were different: not overvaluation of the currency but overaccumulation of debt by the private sector. Output contracted after the currency crises despite the stimulative effects of devaluation, and because of the credit crunch that occurred due to non-payments and bankruptcies of private financial and non-financial companies. Therefore, the remedies should have been different as well. There was no need for the devaluation of currencies since they were not overvalued, but there was a need for fiscal and monetary expansion to counter the effects of the credit crunch (new credits from governments and international financial institutions), together with the regulatory measures to prevent excess accumulation of debt by the private sector (tightening prudential standards in the domestic financial system plus capital account controls). What actually happened, however, was the exact opposite – fiscal policy was tightened, new credits were meagre, so the burden of adjustment fell entirely on the exchange rates. The argument at one time was that it did not make sense to issue new credits to the Asian countries until they 'cleaned up the mess' and ensured that the new credits would not be squandered. But, as Stiglitz (2000b) put it, fiscal constraints in the middle of a recession obviously did not make any sense.[15]

What is more, the widespread belief that 'crony capitalism' is to be blamed for the East Asian crisis discredited the idea of industrial policy, which was the pillar of the pre-crisis high growth model. Here again, differences with the Russian situation are striking: whereas in Russia, the post-crisis reforms went in the direction of state-led growth even if not far enough, in East Asia, to an extent, 'the baby was thrown out with the bathwater'.

Notes

[1] The next two sections draw heavily on my articles and papers listed in the References, and on the book by M. Montes and V. Popov, *The Asian Crisis Turns Global* (Singapore: ISEAS, 1999; http://www.iseas.edu.sg/pub.html). An updated Russian edition of the book was published in 1999 under the title *Asian Virus or Dutch Disease: Theory and Evidence of Currency Crises in Russia and Elsewhere* (Delo Publishers).

[2] The Russian crisis of August 1998 was preceded by currency crises in Bulgaria and Romania in 1996–97, in Ukraine and Belarus in 1997–98, and followed by the currency crisis in Kyrghyzstan and Georgia in late 1998 and in Kazakhstan in early 1999.

[3] Russian national statistics on revenues and expenditure of the government budget are somewhat different from the EBRD statistics. Both estimates are presented in Chart 5.

[4] See Popov (1996a, 1996b and 1998b).

[5] This was similar to what occurred in Mexico after June 1994, when the value of dollar-denominated *tesebonos* exceeded total reserves (Griffith-Jones 1997)

[6] See, for instance Illarionov (1998); Shmelev (1998).

[7] This argument was also developed in the newspaper articles. See 'Growth Strategy', *Segodnya*, 14 March 1996 (in Russian); 'The Currency Crisis Is Possible in Russia', *Finansoviye Izvestiya*, 30 October 1997 (in Russian); 'An Emerging Economy's Unaffordable Luxury', *Financial Times*, 11 December 1997; 'What Exchange Rate of the Ruble Is Needed for Russia?', *Nezavisimaya Gazeta*, 21 May 1998 (in Russian); 'Arithmetic of Devaluation: Why Do We Need a Rate of 12 Rubles per Dollar', *Nezavisimaya Gazeta*, June 1998 Supplement (in Russian).

[8] The other major proponent of exchange rate-based stabilization and also the former adviser of the Russian government, Anders Aslund, pretty much like the IMF, continued to deny the need to devalue even in July (see his article 'Don't Devalue the Ruble', *Moscow Times*, 7 July 1998).

[9] This was a sharp contrast to the Mexican situation in the second half of 1994. As in Russia, the value of outstanding short-term government debt exceeded the amount of foreign exchange reserves. But unlike Russian GKOs, Mexican *Tesebonos* were denominated in dollars, not in the national currency, so devaluation of the *peso* could not and did not decrease the dollar value of the debt.

[10] In the state-owned *Sberbank* (Savings Bank) that accounted for 75 per cent of all household deposit savings guaranteed by the state. CBR, while extending the guarantees to personal deposits at commercial banks, asked the depositors to move them to

Sberbank, promising to pay them back only in two months and only in part (dollar deposits, for instance, were supposed to be converted into *roubles* at a 1 September rate of 9.33 *roubles* per dollar, whereas the market rate of the dollar was already about two times higher).

[11] For more details on the differences between the currency crises in Latin America, Southeast Asia and Russia, see Montes (1999); Popov (1999); Popov (2000b).

[12] The victory of 'Yedinstvo', the 'party of power', in the parliamentary elections of 1999 was, among other things, a victory for the have-nots (subsidized regions) over the haves (donor regions), which had joined forces in the Primakov–Luzhkov bloc 'Otechestvo–Vsya Rossiya'.

[13] Crime statistics are usually perceived to be incomparable in different countries because of large variations in the percentage of reported and registered crimes. But murders are registered quite accurately by both criminal statistics and death (demographic) statistics. The first is more restrictive than the second since it registers only illegal murders, whereas the second one registers all murders, including legal ones (capital punishment, and 'collateral damage' during wars, anti-terrorist and other police operations). Both rates skyrocketed in Russia in the beginning of the 1990s and stay at extremely high levels until today. The gap between both indicators widened during the first (1994–96) and second (1999–2002) Chechen wars.

[14] In 1980–85, the Soviet Union was placed in the middle of a list of 54 countries rated according to their level of corruption, with a bureaucracy cleaner than that of Italy, Greece, Portugal, South Korea and practically all the developing countries. In 1996, after the establishment of a market economy and the victory of democracy, according to Transparency International, Russia came 48th in the same 54-country list, between India and Venezuela. In 2005 Russia fell below India.

[15] 'The IMF claimed that all it was asking of the East Asian countries was that they balance their budgets at a time of recession. All? Hadn't the Clinton administration just fought a major battle with Congress to stave off a balanced-budget amendment in this country? And wasn't the administration's key argument that, in the face of recession, a little deficit spending might be necessary? This is what I and most other economists had been teaching our graduate students for 60 years. Quite frankly, a student who turned in the IMF's answer to the test question "What should be the fiscal stance of Thailand, facing an economic downturn?" would have gotten an F' (Stiglitz 2000b).

References

Alexashenko, S. (1999), *The Battle for the Rouble* (in Russian), Alma Mater .

Asian Development Bank (1997), *Asian Development Outlook 1997 and 1998*.

Åslund, A. (1994), 'The Case for Radical Reform', *Journal of Democracy*, Vol. 5, No. 4, October.

—— (1999a), 'Why Has Russia's Economic Transformation Been So Arduous?', World Bank's Annual Bank Conference on Development Economics, Washington D.C., 28–30 April.

—— (1999b), 'Russia's collapse', *Foreign Affairs*, September/October.

Bates, R. and S. Devarajan (1999), 'Framework Paper on the Political Economy of African Growth', mimeo.

Bofinger, P., H. Flassbeck and L. Hoffmann (1997), 'Orthodox Money-Based Stabilization (OMBS) versus Heterodox Exchange Rate-Based Stabilization (HERBS): The Case of Russia, the Ukraine and Kazakhstan', *Economic Systems,* Vol. 21, No. 1, March: 1–33.

Bruno, Michael (1995), 'Does Inflation Really Lower Growth?', *Finance and Development*, September.

Bruno, Michael and William Easterly (1995), 'Inflation Crisis and Long-Run Growth', World Bank, unpublished.

Desai, Padma (1994), 'Aftershock in Russia's Economy', *Current History*, Vol. 93, No. 585, October: 320–23.

Desai, P. (1997), 'Russia', in *Going Global: The Transition From Plan to Market in the World Economy*, edited by P. Desai (Cambridge: MIT Press): 317–51.

—— (1998), 'Macroeconomic Fragility and Exchange Rate Vulnerability: A Cautionary Record of Transition Economies', *Journal of Comparative Economics*, 26 (4): 621–41.

Dollar, D. (1992), 'Outward-oriented developing economies really do grow more rapidly: evidence from 95 LDCs, 1976–1985', *Economic Development and Cultural Change*, 40 (3), April: 523–44.

Dornbush, Rudiger and Sebastian Edwards (1989), 'The Economic Populism Paradigm', NBER Working Paper 2986, Cambridge, Mass.

Easterly, William (1999), 'The Lost Decades: Explaining Developing Countries Stagnation 1980–1998', World Bank.

EBRD (1997), *Transition Report 1997* (London: EBRD).

—— (1998), *Transition Report 1998* (London: EBRD).

—— (1999), *Transition Report 1999* (London: EBRD).

Goskomstat, *Narodnoye Khozyaistvo SSSR* (National Economy of the USSR), *Rossiysky Statistichesky Yezhegodnik* (Russian Statistical Yearbook) and monthly publications for various years, Moscow.

Griffith-Jones, S. (1997), 'Causes and Lessons of the Mexican Peso Crisis', Working Paper No. 132, WIDER/UNU.

Griffith-Jones, Stephany, Manuel F. Montes and Anwar Nasution (2001), *Short-Term Capital Flows and Economic Crises* (Oxford University Press).

Hölscher, J. (1997), 'Economic Dynamism in Transition Economies: Lessons from Germany', *Communist Economies and Economic Transformation*, Vol. 9, No. 2: 173–81.

Illarionov, A. (1998), 'How the Russian Financial Crisis Was Organized' (in Russian), *Voprosy Ekonomiky*, Nos. 11, 12.

IMF, *International Financial Statistics*, Washington, D.C., various years.

Kaufman, Robert R. and Barbara Stallings (1991), 'The Political Economy of Latin American Populism', in *Macroeconomics of Populism in Latin America*, edited by R. Dornbush and S. Edwards (Chicago and London).

Krugman, P. (1979), 'A model of balance of payments crises', *Journal of Money, Credit, and Banking*, 11: 311–25.

—— (1997), 'Currency crises' (prepared for NBER conference, October 1997), http://web.mit.edu/krugman/www/crises.html.

——— (1998), 'What Happened to Asia?', January, http://web.mit.edu/krugman/www/DISINTER.html.

Mau, V. (1998), 'Political Nature and Lessons of Financial Crisis' (in Russian), *Voprosy Economiky*, No. 11.

Montes, M. (1998), *Currency Crisis in Southeast Asia*, updated edition (Singapore: Institute of Southeast Asian Studies).

Montes, M. and V. Popov (1999), *The Asian Crisis Turns Global* (Singapore: Institute of Southeast Asian Studies).

Naughton, B. (1997), 'Economic Reform in China: Macroeconomic and Overall Performance', in *The System Transformation of the Transition Economies: Europe, Asia and North Korea*, edited by D. Lee Yonsei (Seoul: University Press).

Nekipelov, A. (1998), 'The Nature of Russia's Economic Catastrophe: An Alternative Diagnosis', *Transition: The Newsletter About Reforming Economies*, October.

Polterovich, V. and V. Popov (2004), 'Accumulation of Foreign Exchange Reserves and Long Term Economic Growth', in *Slavic Eurasia's Integration into the World Economy*, edited by S. Tabata and A. Iwashita (Slavic Research Center, Hokkaido University, Sapporo). Updated version, 2006, at http://www.nes.ru/per cent7Evpopov/documents/Exchangeper cent20rate-Growth-2006.pdf.

Polterovich, V. and V. Popov (2006), 'Economic Growth, Real Exchange Rate, and Inflation', New Economic School, Research Project 2006–2007, http://www.nes.ru/english/research/projects/proposal/2006–2007/Polterovich-Popov.pdf.

Polterovich, V., V. Popov and A. Tonis (2007), 'Economic Policy, Quality of Institutions, and Mechanisms of Resource Curse', M., Higher School of Economics, 2007, http://www.nes.ru/per cent7Evpopov/documents/Resources-2007-HSE-Polterovich-Popov-Tonis.pdf.

Popov, V. (1996a), 'Inflation During Transition: Is Russia's Case Special', *Acta Slavica Iaponica*, Tomus XIV, Sapporo, Japan: 59–75.

—— (1996b), *A Russian Puzzle: What Makes Russian Economic Transformation a Special Case*, WIDER/UNU, RFA 29.

—— (1997), 'Lessons from Currency Crisis in Southeast Asia' (in Russian), *Voprosy Ekonomiky*, No. 12.

—— (1998a), 'Investment in Transition Economies: Factors of Change and Implications for Performance', *Journal of East-West Business*, Vol. 4, Nos. 1/2.

—— (1998b), 'Preparing Russian Economy for the World Market Integration', in *Recanalization and Globalization in the Modern World Economy*, edited by A. Fernandez Jilberto and Andre Mommen (London: Routledge).

—— (1998c), 'Economic Outcomes of Transformation: The Impact of Initial Conditions and Economic Policy' (in Russian), *Voprosy Ekonomiky*, No. 7.

—— (1998d), 'Institutional Capacity Is More Important than the Speed of Reforms' (in Russian), *Voprosy Ekonomiky*, No. 8.

—— (1998e), 'Will Russia Achieve Fast Economic Growth?', *Communist Economies and Economic Transformation*, No. 4.

—— (1999a), 'The Financial System in Russia as Compared to Other Transition Economies: The Anglo-American versus The German-Japanese Model', *Comparative Economic Studies*, No. 1.

—— (1999b), 'Russia's Financial Collapse', *NIRA Review*, Vol. 6, No. 1, Winter.

—— (1999c), 'Exchange Rates in Developing and Transition Economies' (in Russian), *EKO*, No. 5: 40–52.

—— (1999d), 'Lessons from the Currency Crises in Russia and in Other Countries' (in Russian), *Voprosy Ekonomiky*, No. 6.

—— (2000a), 'Shock Therapy versus Gradualism: The End of the Debate (Explaining the Magnitude of the Transformational Recession)', *Comparative Economic Studies*, Vol. 42, No. 1, Spring: 1–57.

—— (2000b), 'The Currency Crisis in Russia in a Wider Context', *C.D. Howe Institute Commentary*, No. 138, March; http://www.cdhowe.org/eng/PUB/frame.html.

—— (2005), 'Exchange Rate in the Resource Based Economy in the Short Term: The Case of Russia', paper presented at the AAASS Conference in Salt Lake City, November.

—— (2007), 'Shock Therapy versus Gradualism Reconsidered: Lessons from Transition Economies after 15 Years of Reforms', *Comparative Economic Studies*, Vol. 49, Issue 1, March: 1–31.

Prasad, Eswar, Kenneth Rogoff, Shang-Jin Wei and M. Ayhan Kose (2003), 'Effects of Financial Globalization on Developing Countries: Some Empirical Evidence', IMF, 17 March.

Russian European Centre for Economic Policy, *Russian Economic Trends*, various years.

'Russian Economy in 1998: Trends and Prospects' (1999) (in Russian), Institute of Economics of Transition, Vol. 20, March.

Sachs, J. (1994), 'Russia's Struggle with Stabilization: Conceptual Issues and Evidence', paper prepared for the World Bank's Annual Conference on Development Economics, Washington, D.C., 28–29 April.

—— (1995), 'Why Russia Has Failed to Stabilize', Working Paper No. 103, Stockholm Institute of East European Economics.

Sachs, J., A. Tornell and A. Velasco (1996), 'Financial Crises in Emerging Markets: The Lessons from 1995', *Brookings Papers on Economic Activity*, 1: 147–98.

Shmelev, N., 'The Crisis Inside the Crisis', *Voprosy Ekonomiky*, No. 10.

Shmelev, N. and V. Popov, *The Turning Point: Revitalizing the Soviet Economy* (New York: Doubleday).

Singh, Ajit (2002), 'Capital Account Liberalization, Free Long-term Capital flows, Financial Crises and Economic Development', Queens' College, University of Cambridge.

Stiglitz, Joseph (1998), 'More Instruments and Broader Goals: Moving Toward the Post-Washington Consensus', WIDER Annual Lecture, WIDER/UNU.

Stiglitz, J. (1999), 'Whither Reform? Ten Years of Transition', World Bank's Annual Bank Conference on Development Economics, Washington, D.C., 28–30 April.

Stiglitz, Joseph E. (2000a), 'Capital Market Liberalization, Economic Growth, and Instability', *World Development*, Volume 28 (6): 1075–86.

Stiglitz, Joseph (2000b), 'What I Learned at the World Economic Crisis: The Insider', *The New Republic*, 17 April.

UNCTAD (1999), *World Economic Situation and Prospects for 1999* (New York, Geneva).

World Bank (1996), *From Plan to Market. World Development Report* (New York: Oxford University Press).

————— (1997), *The State in A Changing World: World Development Report* (New York: Oxford University Press).

—————, *World Development Indicators*, various years.

Yasin, E. (1999), 'Defeat or Retreat? (Russian Reforms and Financial Crisis)' (in Russian), Report to Economic Club, Moscow, January.

Zettermeyer, J. and D. Citrin (1995), 'Stabilization: fixed versus flexible exchange rates', in *Policy experiences and issues in the Baltics, Russian and other countries of the former Soviet Union* (Washington, D.C.: International Monetary Fund).

Other Asian Experiences

China and Post-Crisis Globalization

Towards a New Developmentalism?

Dic Lo

Introduction

Globalization since the late 1990s, that is, after the East Asian financial and economic crisis, has brought both hope and disappointment for world development. There has been substantial growth on the rebound, worldwide. But there have also been serious obstacles to the translation of the benefits of economic growth into real development. In the light of relevant theories on the political economy of capitalist globalization, these obstacles – deteriorating terms of international trade against developing countries, the pressure on developing countries to accumulate costly foreign exchange reserves, and the phenomena of growing unemployment and rising income inequalities – are intrinsic to the particular nature of the current process of globalization. They are symptomatic of the project of neoliberalism, which aims to prop up profitability in the context of financialization of the world economy. But this project might not be sustainable, both socially and economically. There are social limits to the drive of 'cheapening' labour for the sake of financial interests. Moreover, cheapening labour is likely to reinforce the problem of systemic demand deficiency that financialization tends to bring about, thus threatening to undermine the sustainability of economic growth itself.

Against this background, China's experience of economic and social development since the late 1990s is of general significance. At one level, the country has exhibited the same general phenomena of growth rebound, deteriorating terms of trade, accumulation of reserves, job creation lagging behind the increase in labour supply, and rising income inequality. At another level, however, what seems to be China-specific is the drive to maintain economic growth and translate the benefits of growth into real development, in the face of the above-indicated external and internal constraints. There have been visible and significant state and societal efforts to resist the neoliberal project. It is with respect to these efforts, their characteristics and consequences, that the Chinese experience might turn out to constitute a new model of 'developmentalism' in the era of post-crisis globalization.

Yet, the significance of the Chinese experience might be more than just being a possible new development model. Because of its significant and rising position in the world economy, China's attempt to construct an alternative model of development is bound to have a systemic impact on the future direction of globalization. Specifically, the worldwide cheapening of labour over the past quarter-century and particularly since the early 1990s has been, to a significant measure, associated with the incorporation of China's labour force into the world market. Now that there have emerged strong state and societal efforts in China to resist the pressures to cheapen labour, some fundamental adjustments in world development are likely to occur. Whatever the precise nature of the adjustments, the triumph of neoliberalism is likely to be less complete in the future than in the previous quarter-century. In other words, real development worldwide has a stake in the success or otherwise of China's attempt to construct an alternative to neoliberalism.

Post-Crisis Globalization: Observation and Conceptualization

The very sluggish growth of per capita income across most parts of the developing world over the 1980s and the 1990s, often known as 'the lost decades of development', seems to have been replaced by rapid growth since the turn of the century. The contrast is rather stark. Between 2000 and 2005, the average annual growth rate of per capita real GDP (gross domestic product) for all low- and middle-income economies was 3.7 per cent. This was more than double the average rate of the 1980s and the 1990s, 1.3 and 1.8 per cent, respectively. For both low-income economies and middle-income economies, growth performance

TABLE 1   *Average Annual Growth Rates of Per Capita Real GDP, 1960–2005* (per cent)

	1960–70	1970–80	1980–90	1990–2000	2000–05
China	2.9	3.7	8.8	9.3	8.3
India	1.1	2.3	3.6	4.2	5.3
South Korea	6.0	8.4	7.7	4.7	3.9
Brazil	2.6	6.5	0.7	1.3	1.0
USSR/Russia	4.0	4.7	1.3	-4.7	6.6
Low-income economies (excluding China and India)	2.0	1.8	2.2	1.2	4.2
Middle-income economies	3.5	2.1	1.2	2.2	3.9
Low- and middle-income economies			1.3	1.8	3.7
East Asia and Pacific			5.9	5.7	6.9
Europe and Central Asia			1.2	–1.7	5.2
Latin America and Caribbean			–0.3	1.7	0.9
Middle East and North Africa			–1.1	0.7	2.2
South Asia			3.4	3.7	4.8
Sub Saharan Africa			–1.3	–0.1	2.0
High-income economies			2.7	2.2	1.5

Source: World Bank, *World Development Report* and *World Development Indicators*, various years.

in 2000–05 was also substantially better than that of the 1960s and 1970s, the latter two decades being part of the 'Golden Age' of post-war world development. Finally, the growth rebound in the years 2000–05 was common to all parts of the developing world (except Latin America and the Caribbean region), including countries of the former Soviet bloc which have experienced fully a decade of depression.

It appears as if, finally, the promise of globalization has come true: the growth rebound seems to offer good potential for social and economic development. But such optimism might be premature. There is no certainty that the ongoing economic growth in the developing world reflects a long-term trend of catching-up with the income level of advanced economies, as the neoliberal doctrines of globalization expect, rather than just a recovery from the recession of the second half of the 1990s. For the time being, the promise is better treated as no more

CHART 1 *Foreign Exchange Reserves as Ratios of Average Values of Monthly Imports*

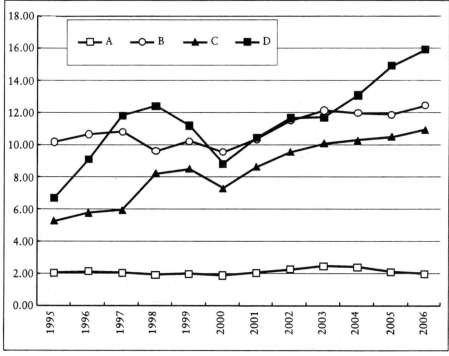

Notes: Data are end-of-year foreign exchange reserves of central bank divided by the monthly average import value of the past 12 months. A = developed countries ('industrial countries' for foreign exchange holding and 'advanced countries' for imports in the IMF categorization); B = developing countries; C = East Asian economies (Mainland China, Hong Kong, Taiwan, South Korea, Singapore, Malaysia, Thailand, Indonesia and the Philippines); D = China (Mainland China not including Hong Kong, Macau and Taiwan).

Source: International Monetary Fund, COFER 2007 and *World Economic Outlook*, April 2007; Asian Development Bank, data bank.

than just a promise. The discussion that follows will tend to conclude that the sustainability of ongoing economic growth is in question, so that the promise of neoliberalism is no less questionable in the future than in the past.

Whatever the nature of the current growth rebound, one point seems clear: that its benefits have not been really translated into economic and social development. For most developing countries, there have been serious constraints on both the external and internal fronts. Three phenomena in the world economy are particularly of note.

First, there has been a conspicuous trend of accumulation of foreign exchange reserves of unprecedented scales in the developing countries, as shown in Chart 1. It is evident that, expressed as a ratio to the monthly average of import values, the official holding of foreign exchange reserves by developing countries has always far exceeded that of developed countries. And the gap between the two groups of countries has now substantially widened. Between 2000 and 2005, the average ratio of reserves to imports for all developing countries increased from 9.53 months to 12.44 months, whereas that for all developed countries

CHART 2 *Net Barter Terms of International Trade* (1980 = 100)

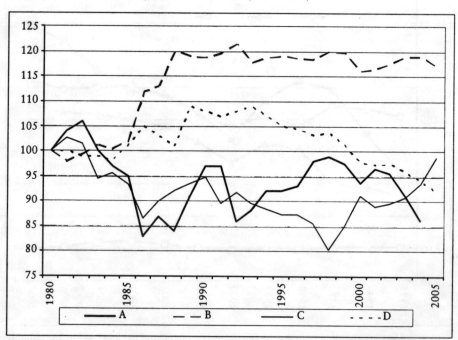

Notes: A = China; B = developed countries ('industrial countries' in the IMF categorization); C = developing countries; D = East Asian newly industrializing economies (i.e. Hong Kong, Taiwan, South Korea and Singapore). East Asian newly industrializing economies' data are terms of trade in goods and services; others are terms of trade in goods.

Source: International Monetary Fund, *World Economic Outlook* and *International Financial Statistics Yearbook*, various issues; World Bank, *World Development Indicators*, various issues.

basically stayed at the level of 2 months. In the face of the pressure arising from the financialization of the world economy, it is understandable that developing countries should accumulate reserves to protect themselves. Yet, given the very low yield of the reserves, the accumulation implies a massive transfer of seigniorage to the developed countries that issue reserve currencies. Meanwhile, also of note from Chart 1 is China's astonishing accumulation of reserves, which, as a ratio to the monthly average of import values, has in recent years far exceeded the average levels of even all developing countries.

Second, there has also been a trend of deteriorating terms of trade against developing countries. This is yet another indication of the outflows of the benefits of economic growth from the developing world. As can be seen from Chart 2, starting with a base level of 100 in the year 1980, the index of net barter terms of trade for all developing countries taken together fell to the level of 91 by the year 2000, whereas that for all developed countries rose to the level of 116. According to the analysis of Ram (2004), until the turn of the century, countries exporting primary products were especially hard-hit. Manufacturing-oriented countries also suffered from a similar trend of deterioration, though this was much less severe than the average of developing countries. The rebound of commodity prices since the late 1990s has reversed the comparison. As shown in Chart 2, whereas the gap between developing countries and developed countries has remained essentially unchanged, China and the broader East Asian region, which are the main manufactured goods exporters, have witnessed a slump in their terms of trade. Conceptually, it was argued early on that the deterioration of the terms of trade against developing countries reflects a situation of systemic demand deficiency in the world economy (Singh 1993). This being the case, what is going on today can be interpreted as reflecting a situation of worldwide excess supply of manufactures and, behind this, an excess supply of labour. This, as explained below, is of fundamental importance in shaping the future direction of globalization.

Third, there has been a worldwide problem of increasing unemployment

TABLE 2 *Average Annual Growth Rate of Real Income, Employment and Labour Force, 1998–2005* (per cent)

	(a) GDP	(b) Employment	(c) Labour force	(a)–(b)	(b)–(c)
China	9.1	1.0	1.1	8.1	−0.1
Hong Kong	5.0	1.2	1.3	3.8	−0.1
Taiwan	3.8	1.0	1.2	2.9	−0.2
South Korea	5.8	2.0	1.5	3.8	0.5
Singapore	5.2	2.8	2.9	2.4	−0.2
Indonesia	3.6	1.1	1.9	2.5	−0.8
Malaysia	5.3	2.2	2.3	3.1	0.0
Philippines	4.5	2.2	2.3	2.3	−0.1
Thailand	4.9	1.8	1.4	3.1	0.3

Source: Asian Development Bank, www.adb.org; Japan Statistical Bureau, www.stat.go.jp.

and casualization of employment in recent years. While global indicators on this may be too scattered and are in any case far from systematic, there is evidence that the problem has occurred even in East Asia, the fastest growing and most rapidly job-absorbing region of the developing world. As can be seen from Table 2, between 1998 and 2005, six out of the nine fast-growing and open economies of East Asia experienced a process of employment expansion lagging behind the growth of the labour force. Even China, which has been the destination of industry and job relocation from the rest of East Asia and beyond, is no exception. Outside the region the situation is most likely to be worse, and there is widespread evidence that employment growth has been slow, labour protection weak, and that the growth of real wages has lagged behind economic growth (Singh and Zammit 2004). Given this situation, it can be further conjectured that there is likely to have been a trend of decreasing shares for labour in national incomes. Associated with this, increasing inequality within and across national economies has been characteristic of world development under globalization (Wade 2004).

Theoretically, the global economic trends summarized above are likely to be interrelated. Accumulation of foreign exchange reserves in developing countries, however costly it is and however unwillingly it is done, is a necessary response to the threats posed by financialization – that is, the rapidly rising predominance of speculative financial activities in the world economy. And, as Robert Wade (2006) has observed, financialization implies a tendency of financial interests dissociating themselves from real investment and the productive process in general. There is thus an intrinsic contradiction associated with financialization: the speculative pursuit of profitability tends to crowd out productive activities, resulting in systemic demand deficiency and undermining the sources of profitability.

This contradiction need not imply that capital accumulation and, with it, economic growth on a world scale must be unsustainable. As David Harvey (1989, 2003) has argued, profitability and therefore capital accumulation in the era of globalization hinge on the balance between the indicated contradiction, on the one hand, and the cheapening of productive inputs, on the other hand. It is in this connection that national and international policies associated with neoliberalism can be seen as essential to the current round of globalization. These policies facilitate the cheapening of productive inputs, labour in particular, and their incorporation into the system of capitalism. Yet, this same process, by expanding the spatial scope of capitalism and creating new centres of accumulation, also tends to reproduce the problem of systemic demand deficiency on expanded scales. The successful achievement, or otherwise, of the balance between these positive and negative factors of profitability will thus remain the central problem of capitalism in the era of globalization.

In terms of the institutional dimension, as Harvey has further argued, financialization necessarily requires flexible production. The rising mobility of capital leads to an inclination towards minimizing fixed investment and maximizing profits via absolute surplus-value production. A central tenet of neoliberalism is precisely to create flexible institutions in the form of casualization of employment, which is made possible through the creation of an 'unlimited supply of labour' and the elimination of arrangements that could undermine the flexible working of the labour market, such as unionization and legislative protection of labour. This appears to be what has actually occurred to date.

Nevertheless, this neoliberal tenet has no prior claim to superiority even in the sense of underpinning the kind of flexible production that is needed for surviving competition in the world market. In line with the literature on techno-economic paradigms, it could be posited that the behavioural flexibility of the productive system could arise from two different, contrasting types of institutional arrangements. One consists of casualization, that is, 'flexible institutions, flexible behaviour', which is based on the principles of detailed division of labour and deskilling of work. The other arrangement involves rigid or long-term-oriented institutions constructed on the basis of the social division of labour – that is, 'rigid institutions, flexible behaviour', where behavioural flexibility arises from collective learning and horizontal coordination. Theoretically, there is no *a priori* reason to believe that one of the two types of arrangements is more competitive than the other (Lo and Smyth 2004). In reality, however, the triumph of neoliberalism, in conjunction with the uncontested drive of financialization, has resulted in the predominance of the 'flexible institutions, flexible behaviour' model across the world. This has been so despite the observation that, in terms of the historical record, the alternative 'rigid institutions, flexible behaviour' model embodies a much higher degree of solidarity, egalitarianism and social justice; and also despite the argument that the alternative model is less prone to produce systemic demand deficiency that could undermine economic growth (Dore 2002).

China as an Exemplar and Its Systemic Impact

In this context, China's development experience and policy efforts since the turn of the century deserve particular attention. In the first place, it is clear that China has been an extreme case with respect to the recent global economic trends. China has registered the fastest economic growth in the developing world, reversing the growth slowdown in the late 1990s from the very high rate of the early 1990s. It has built up an abnormally high level of the ratio of foreign exchange reserves to import needs – abnormal, that is, even relative to the high and still rising level of the average of all developing countries. It has faced a trend of the terms of international trade that is far worse than the average of developing countries. Finally, as is shown in Table 3, unlike its own experience up until the mid-1990s, China's ongoing acceleration of economic growth has not been matched by a comparable pace of employment expansion. This is despite the fact that China has firmly established itself as a 'factory of the world', which implies sucking in manufacturing jobs from the outside world, since the turn of the century.

Yet China is not simply a 'case'. The Chinese experience as depicted above in fact reflects a broader process of economic restructuring in the whole region of East Asia after the 1997–98 financial and economic crises. As indicated

TABLE 3   *Indices of China's Real GDP, Employment and Labour Force*

	(a) Real GDP	(b) Employment	(c) Labour Force	(a)–(b)	(b)–(c)
1978	100.00	100.00	100.00	0.00	0.00
1980	116.00	105.50	105.46	10.50	0.04
1985	192.90	124.21	123.18	68.69	1.03
1990	281.70	161.26	160.57	120.44	0.69
1995	502.30	169.52	169.25	332.78	0.27
2000	759.90	179.53	181.88	580.37	–2.35
2005	1195.50	188.84	191.43	1006.66	–2.58
2006	1323.42	190.28	...	1133.14	...

Source: National Bureau of Statistics, *China Statistical Yearbook 2006*; National Bureau of Statistics, *Statistical Communiqué of National Economic and Social Development in 2006*, www.stats.gov.cn.

in the previous section, similar trends of faster-than-average economic growth, high ratios of foreign exchange reserves to import needs, worse-than-average deteriorating terms of trade, and employment expansion lagging behind labour supply growth, have occurred in most economies of the region. And there is reason to believe that these trends are related to the China-oriented process of regionwide economic integration, which is evident in the rapid increase in the shares of trade with China in the total of foreign trade of the economies.

The impact of China on world development is even likely to be systemic. It could be asserted that one main aspect of globalization is the expansion of the world labour market associated with the incorporation of China into the system. According to the International Monetary Fund (2007), weighing countries' labour force by their export-to-GDP ratio, the effective global labour supply quadrupled between 1980 and 2005, with East Asia contributing about half of the increase. And, as indicated above, over this period, there has been an accelerating trend of massive relocation of industry and jobs from the rest of East Asia and beyond to China. Using the same indicator of employment adjusted by the export-to-GDP ratio, as of 2005 year-end, China's share of the world total of workers producing for the global market reached 25 per cent. No wonder, in addition to its growth performance, the conditions of employment, compensation and work standards in China have increasingly become matters of worldwide concern.

It will be of interest, in this connection, to look at an issue of the world economy that has generated widespread policy concerns: namely, the structural interdependence between the economies of China and the United States of America. At a glance, it might seem strange that China should form an economic relationship with the United States which is conspicuously unequal. The relationship is such that China in effect provides the United States with 'double subsidies': first cheap products (that is, cheaper than what the United States could import from alternative sources), and then cheap credit in the form of holding low-yield US government papers. This phenomenon does not seem to make economic sense, especially when one takes into consideration that China's export earnings and its utilization of foreign direct investment are both very costly (Lo 2005, 2006). Nor does it seem to make political sense, given the very unfavourable response in US political circles towards the country's trade imbalances with China. In fact, China's trade surplus with the United States is by and large the surplus of the rest of the East Asian region – given that China has had trade deficits with its neighbour economies following the regionwide economic restructuring and industrial relocation.

But it might in fact make sense when one takes into consideration the existence of demand deficiency both in China and worldwide. For China, the low returns of both exporting goods and exporting capital might have been compensated by the creation of jobs for its labour force in excess supply, and the utilization of its excess production capacity. Demand deficiency is reflected in the changing composition of China's aggregate expenditure, shown in Chart 3. It can be seen that there has been a trend of secular decline of consumption demand in aggregate expenditure, and, in recent years, the expansion in investment demand has become insufficient to compensate the sluggish growth of consumption. The result is a ballooning trade surplus, which exceeded 7 per cent of GDP in 2006 and is very likely to exceed 10 per cent of GDP in 2007.

CHART 3 *Composition of GDP by Expenditures* (per cent)

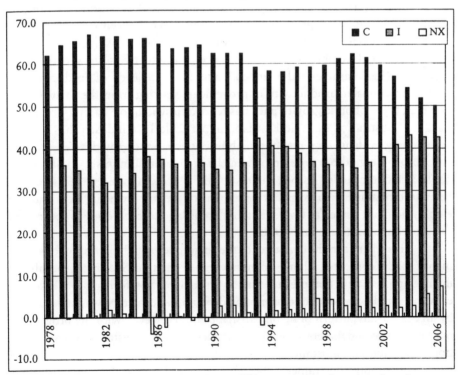

Note: C = final consumption; I = investment; NX = net export of goods and services.
Source: National Bureau of Statistics, *China Statistical Yearbook 2006*; National Bureau of Statistics, *China Statistical Abstract 2007*.

Thus, in the economic sense, the sustainability of China's existing nexus of external transactions and economic growth depends on the match, or otherwise, between the indicated outflows of the benefits of economic growth and the impetus to productivity growth provided by this nexus. Even so, politically, the ballooning trade surplus with the United States might still prove to be unsustainable. Serious trade frictions have erupted not only between the two countries but also between China and a large number of industrialized and semi-industrialized economies. Domestically, even if the ongoing economic growth is maintained, there are still problems of distribution and hence of social development. Further mechanisms, especially in terms of the redistributive and welfare provision function of the state, will be needed.

China's Quest for an Alternative Development Path

It has been a prime target of China's state leadership that economic growth and employment expansion must proceed both smoothly and in tandem. This has been especially true since the turn of the century, when the state leadership emphasized the necessity of correcting the excess in social polarization caused by market reforms, with the objective of 'constructing a harmonious society'.

Yet, the actual path of growth of the Chinese economy in recent years does not seem to have fared well in terms of this objective. It is true that over much of the reform era, especially the first half, China's economic growth was largely labour-intensive, propelled by the absorption of new entrants to employment. More precisely, it was a process of massive transfer of labour from the rural-agricultural sector to industry and services, the latter two sectors (particularly industry) being characterized by much higher absolute levels of productivity as well as much faster productivity improvement. Starting from the early 1990s, however, the economic growth path has tended to switch to a capital-deepening one. The substitution of capital for labour, particularly in industry, has become increasingly evident. As a result, the ability of economic growth to create jobs and absorb new labour to employment has tended to diminish. As shown in Table 3, acceleration of output and productivity growth in recent years has not been accompanied by a comparable expansion in employment. Expansion in employment has tended to lag behind that of the labour force, quite in contrast to the situation prior to the mid-1990s.

The change in the character of the economic growth path should be seen in the broader context of China's economic transformation. Succinctly, the labour-intensive growth path that prevailed in the first half of the reform era was associated with a rapid expansion in consumption demand, which in turn was underpinned by an egalitarian pattern of income distribution. However, with the progress of market reforms and thereby growing unevenness of income distribution, consumption expansion has substantially slowed down and the economy has switched from being supply-constrained to becoming demand-constrained. From the mid-1990s onward, insufficient aggregate demand has prevailed in the economy, and investment has replaced consumption as the driving force behind the expansion in aggregate demand. Consequently, China has tended to follow a growth path characterized by a process of 'producing investment goods for producing investment goods'. That is, it has become increasingly capital-intensive – not only because of normally expanding investment, but also because of the tendency to substitute capital for labour in the production process. This capital-deepening growth path has proved to be capable of generating rapid productivity improvement, but only at the cost of allowing less and less of the expanding labour force to be absorbed into employment.

It is within this broader context that government policies aimed at achieving the twin targets of economic growth and job creation should be assessed. The prevailing path of economic growth might well be efficient, in the sense that it is characterized by fast productivity improvement due to technological progress and dynamic increasing returns. It might even be necessary because of demand constraints, and for the sake of upgrading Chinese industry and enhancing its competitiveness in the world market. But if it does not generate sufficient jobs to alleviate the pressure for employment, it might not be socially sustainable. In this light, government policies in the areas of macro demand management, income redistribution, welfare provision, labour market regulation, as well as those concerning international transactions, all need to be designed in a coherent manner, taking into consideration the broader context. Achievement of the twin targets of sustained rapid economic growth and income-enhancing employment expansion is by no means a straightforward matter. There is no guarantee that maintaining the ongoing growth path, or returning to the previous growth path, will automatically achieve these targets.

Macro Policies

China's economy was already on a downturn on the eve of the East Asian financial and economic crisis. Demand deficiency was the central issue, probably due to the upsurge in market reforms in the early to mid-1990s. In particular, the privatization and downsizing of SOEs (state-owned enterprises) in 1995–97 resulted in mass unemployment, while the complete commercialization of state banks resulted in their behaviour switching from excessive lending to excessively cautious lending.

In the face of the worsening external environment caused by the East Asian crisis, the Chinese state leadership adopted four major categories of anti-crisis policies between 1998 and 2002. These were: (1) several Keynesian-type fiscal packages for expanding investment demand, which were financed by debt issues of unprecedented scales; (2) a range of welfare state policies, which included increasing the benefits for retired or unemployed workers, raising the remuneration of public sector employees and lengthening the paid holidays of workers – all aimed at reversing the trend of stagnant consumption; (3) policy measures to re-vitalize the state sector, including the setting up of four state asset management companies responsible for taking over a substantial share of non-performing loans from state banks and for a programme of debt-equity swaps, which were aimed at improving the financial conditions of SOEs and the balance sheets of state banks; and (4) a cautious approach to reforming the regime of external transactions – in particular, the leadership has in effect shelved the target of liberalizing the country's capital account. These policies, in essence, represent a retreat from the previous stance of pursuing a unidirectional movement towards the idealized, canonical market economy. Thus, while they were designed to be short-term anti-crisis policies, they turned out to be very powerful in shaping the long-term path of economic development.

Consider fiscal stimuli. Initially, the annual budget approved by the National People's Congress in March 1998 maintained that fiscal deficits – which had persisted for every single year since 1982 (except in 1985 when an explosive upsurge in imports generated huge customs revenues for the state budget) – be cut by 10 billion *yuan* from the 1997 level of 58 billion *yuan* (0.78 per cent of GDP). This was already below what was needed to achieve the target, set in the 1994 fiscal system reform, of balancing the budget by the year 2000. Yet, from the second quarter of 1998, the leadership shifted to an active fiscal policy to stimulate economic growth. The actual deficits in that year turned out to be a hefty 92 billion *yuan* (1.18 per cent of GDP). With the continuous use of active fiscal policy, deficits expanded further in subsequent years: 174 billion in 1999, 249 billion in 2000, 252 billion in 2001 and 315 billion in 2002 – i.e. 1.94, 2.51, 2.29 and 2.62 per cent, respectively, of GDP. In the meantime, over the five years 1998–2002, the central government issued a total of 660 billion treasury bills for long-term construction investment. These, together with complementary investment by other economic agents (central ministries, local governments and enterprises), amounted to total public investment of 3200 billion *yuan* (*People's Daily*, 18 March and 10 December 2002).

Viewed from a long-term perspective, the fiscal activism of 1998–2002 represents a shift away from the pursuit of budget balance and minimal government intervention in the economy. This pursuit was clearly discernible in the fiscal system reform of 1994 and was predominant in the design of government economic policies until early 1998. Yet, in the event, budget deficits did not diminish; rather, they expanded very substantially between 1998 and 2002. Budget deficits as a ratio of GDP for the first time approached 2 per cent in 1999 and even exceeded that level in the next four years. Perhaps even more conspicuously, the issue of government debt exceeded 3 per cent of GDP for the first time in 1997, and remained so thereafter. In terms of its impact on the economy, the official analysis states that, in the face of the persistence of deflation caused by sluggish expansion in both domestic and external demand, government investment during 1998–2002 had the effect of contributing to 1.5–2 percentage points of the growth of GDP in each of the five years. Moreover, because the investment was concentrated mainly in infrastructure, it had significant crowding-in effects, in the sense that it paved the way for the subsequent massive expansion in total investment in the economy as a whole from 2001 onwards.

On the whole, it could be argued that the Chinese state leadership was quite successful with its fiscal activism in the period 1998–2002. Central to this activism was the adoption of a range of expansionary fiscal policies to stimulate aggregate demand and therefore economic growth, with the objective of helping enterprises as well as the government to 'grow out of indebtedness'. This was in sharp contrast to the policy recommendation from international financial institutions for East Asian economies as well as for China during these years, which typically argued for balancing government budgets through austerity. In the event, China's actual economic development indicates that the adoption of fiscal activism was justified. Apart from surviving the most difficult years of 1998–2001, from 2002 onwards economic growth reversed the nearly decade-long decelerating trend and even accelerated. Budget deficits, though remaining large in actual amount, have tended to decrease as ratios to GDP.

The same trend has also been evident at the micro level. The reversal of the policy of downsizing and privatization did not result in worsening financial performance of enterprises. Instead, in the context of the rebound in economic growth, the profit rate of enterprises (including SOEs) has risen successively every year since 1998.

The 1998–2002 fiscal activism has had a further, somewhat unexpected, impact on the long-term development of the economy, in the form of strengthening the movement of the growth path towards capital-deepening. Because the government policies were mainly aimed at stimulating investment, the trend of the composition of aggregate expenditure increasingly skewing in favour of investment has not been reversed but has accelerated (as is clearly indicated in Chart 3). This, while being helpful to the efficiency and sustainability of economic growth, has had serious deficiency in terms of employment growth. Moreover, it appears that even the investment expansion subsequent to the fiscal activism has been insufficient to compensate for the sluggish growth in consumption demand. The enlarging deficiency in aggregate demand is clearly evident in the massive expansion in the surplus of foreign trade in goods and services, which reached an astonishing high level of 7.3 per cent of GDP in 2006.

Labour Market Policies

Essential to the Chinese state leadership's pursuit of 'constructing a harmonious society' is the emphasis that the trend of increasing social polarization must not be left unchecked. And an important aspect of social polarization is the fact that, until the turn of the century, labour's compensation had experienced very sluggish growth – quite in contrast to the sustained rapid growth of the economy. Indeed there have been widespread reports that outside the formal, mainly state-related, sector, the wage rate had been almost frozen for fully twenty years since the onset of reform. This was especially true in the labour-intensive, export-oriented industries in the coastal provinces, because of the almost unlimited supply of unprotected, un-unionized labour from the rural areas of inland provinces.

Even in the formal sector, the trend of evolution of the wage rate has seriously deviated from that of per capita GDP. As can been seen from Chart 4,

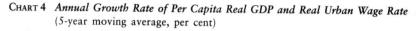

CHART 4 *Annual Growth Rate of Per Capita Real GDP and Real Urban Wage Rate*
(5-year moving average, per cent)

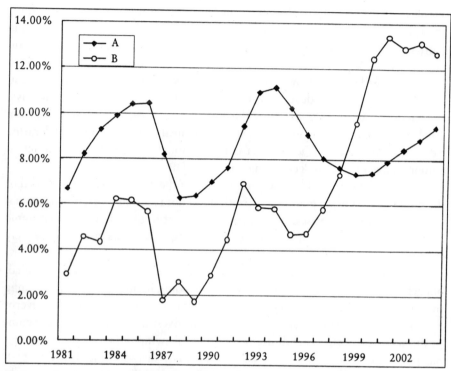

Note: A = per capita real GDP; B = urban real wage rate.
Source: National Bureau of Statistics, *China Statistical Yearbook 2006*; National Bureau of
Statistics, *China Statistical Abstract 2007*.

before the turn of the century, growth of the real urban wage rate persistently lagged behind that of per capita real GDP. Moreover, in the years of enterprise downsizing and mass unemployment in the 1990s, the two indicators moved in opposite directions: the growth of the real wage rate slowed down even as the growth of per capita GDP accelerated. It is basically from the turn of the century onwards that the situation has been reversed. In recent years, the growth of the real wage rate has substantially exceeded that of per capita GDP, although both have been increasing. It is likely that government policies have played an important role in this reversal.

It would not be much off the mark to assert that before the turn of the century, the government had basically adopted a *laissez-faire* approach toward labour conditions outside the state sector. This is particularly evident in the declining influence of the only existing official trade union, the All China Federation of Trade Unions. Union members as a proportion of total employees in the secondary and tertiary sectors decreased from 49 per cent in 1981 to 29 per cent in 2000 (Chart 5). In recent years, however, union membership has had a substantial rebound: as a proportion of total employees in the secondary and tertiary sectors,

CHART 5 *Proportion of Unionized Workers* (per cent)

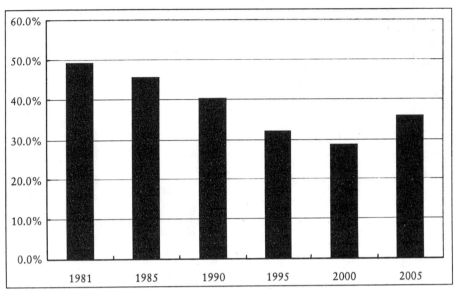

Note: Figures are the number of members of All China Federation of Trade Unions divided
         by the total number of employees in the Secondary and Tertiary sectors.
Source: National Bureau of Statistics, *China Statistical Yearbook 2006*; All China Federation
         of Trade Unions, *China Statistical Yearbook of Trade Unions*, various issues.

it climbed back to a level of 36 per cent in 2005. This owes much to the enforcement
by the central government of the stipulation that enterprises of all types of ownership are required to allow for the setting up of unions or for workers joining
unions. This requirement has for a long time been sternly resisted by local governments, private employers and, most notably, foreign capital-funded enterprises
(particularly multinational corporations). Yet, from the point of view of the state
leadership, this is essential to the promotion of collective bargaining over labour
compensation. And collective bargaining, in turn, is considered to be indispensable
for reversing the decreasing trend of labour's share in national income.

　　Notwithstanding this, there is no sign that China's enterprise system is
returning to the pattern in the formal sector during the first half of the reform era,
where workers as a collective had a powerful influence over their compensation
as well as over the division of enterprise surplus as a whole. The withering of
public firms as a proportion of the corporate sector simply makes this impossible.
Even in the public firms that remain and in large-scale SOEs (which are traditionally the core of the public sector), the bargaining power of workers vis-à-vis the
management is minimal nowadays. This is because the employment relationship
has already been fully marketized. The traditional system of lifetime employment,
which was characteristic of China's socialist system pre-reform, is now history.
Instead, the employment relationship is now governed by market-determined
contracts. As can be seen from Chart 6, it was still the case in 1995 that labour

CHART 6   *Proportion of Urban Employment Covered by Employment Contracts* (per cent)

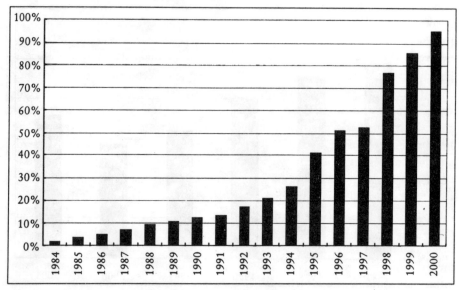

Source: National Bureau of Statistics, *China Statistical Yearbook 2006*; All China Federation of Trade Unions, *China Statistical Yearbook of Trade Unions*, various issues.

contracts covered only 41 per cent of total urban employment. By 2000, however, the proportion reached 95 per cent.

The trend of rebound in wage rate growth in recent years can also be ascribed to a variety of other factors. In addition to increased unionization, government protection of labour rights in the drafting and enforcement of employment contracts is reportedly of increasing significance. And the acceleration of economic growth, together with its capital-deepening orientation, has also resulted in very rapid growth in labour productivity, thereby contributing to the wage rate growth. It seems that the twin targets of sustained rapid economic growth and compensation-enhancing employment expansion have been achieved thanks to the concerted working of the economic growth path itself and appropriate government policies.

But there is an intrinsic problem with this economic condition – namely, the problem of unemployment. The very fast wage growth since the turn of the century, shown in Chart 4, has not resulted in a rebound in the growth of consumption. Instead, as shown in Chart 3, the decline of consumption as a proportion of aggregate expenditure has accelerated precisely during this period. And the deficiency in aggregate demand has tended to worsen, as is also shown in Chart 3. The sustainability of the ongoing economic growth path and employment expansion, at least in the social (if not economic) sense, is thus still in question.

Assessment

By design or by default, it appears that the government policies detailed above – together with other related policies such as the increased protection of labour rights, the enforcement of minimum-wage legislation, the emphasis on income redistribution to avoid further worsening social polarization, the expansion in social welfare provision, as well as the ongoing attempts to reconstruct a government-funded health-care system – do have a coherence. They are all conducive to the pursuit of compensation-enhancing employment. They are also consistent with, if not also conducive to, the prevailing capital-deepening path of economic growth. The hoped-for employment expansion thus ultimately rests on the labour-absorption capability of the services sector, as has been emphasized by the government. In other words, the sustainability of the pattern of economic growth and employment expansion, and therefore of the relevant government policies, depends on whether the fast productivity gains in industry can be effectively channelled to the development of the labour-absorption capability of services.

A question naturally arises as to why wouldn't (or shouldn't) the Chinese state leadership adopt an alternative policy line – of a return to the labour-intensive path of economic growth that prevailed in the first half of the reform era. This alternative clearly fits better into principles of the market, particularly the principle of comparative advantage. And it has widespread support from influential Chinese economists. It has been argued that this alternative growth path is not only allocatively efficient but also equitable, in the sense that it would create more jobs and thus its immediate benefits would be spread to a larger proportion of the population. In so far as it would result in a negative impact on labour compensation, the argument goes, this could be offset by redistributive government policies and the system of social welfare provision.

The assessment of the prevailing policy line thus needs to take into consideration its costs and benefits relative to alternative strategies. Note that, even in principle, this is in no sense a straightforward matter of judging which of the two policy lines is better or easier to pursue. Yet, for the sake of argument, the assessment could be carried out in the following way. Consider growth. The productive efficiency associated with capital-deepening growth should be weighed against the allocative efficiency associated with labour-intensive growth. The net outcome of this trade-off is necessarily an empirical issue, and, as has been indicated earlier, the productivity and output growth of the Chinese economy in the second half of the reform era appears to have out-performed that of the first half. In the context of a demand-constrained economy where scarcity of resources is not necessarily a binding constraint, it can be further argued that allocative efficiency is likely to be less important than productive efficiency in underpinning economic growth. Again, as indicated, it is evident that China has been in a state of serious and worsening deficiency in macroeconomic demand since the mid-1990s.

Turn to employment. It seems straightforward that a labour-intensive growth path must create more jobs than a capital-deepening one. Yet this is not necessarily the case in a demand-constrained economy, i.e. when aggregate expenditure is less than the full-employment output level. If such a situation is caused by factors unrelated to the wage rate being too high, as has been elaborated in the preceding sections, a fall in the wage rate (for inducing the substitution of labour for capital) would not necessarily result in an increase in employment. Everything depends on, first, the net impact on labour's share in national income and thereby on macroeconomic demand; and, second, the balance between the distribution-induced impact on macroeconomic demand and the wage-induced impact on capital–labour substitution.

At this point, the issue of demand also raises the question of the feasibility of a return to the previous, labour-intensive growth path. Note that the trend of China's aggregate expenditure skewing to investment rather than consumption has accelerated in recent years, despite all the redistributive and labour compensation-enhancing government policies. There is indeed a serious question, on the domestic front, as to what would be the sources of demand for the increased labour-intensive, mostly consumer, goods. Exporting might be a viable alternative. This has been witnessed in the ballooning trade surplus in recent years, and the fact that made-in-China labour-intensive manufactures are now flooding the world market. The consideration of market outlets, and thereby job creation, might even be an important reason behind China's willingness to maintain an anomalous economic relationship with the United States in recent years. Yet trade frictions and the pressure on China to contribute more demand to the world economy have become the norm in China's economic relationship with the USA and other major trade partners. Given all these hurdles on both the domestic and external fronts, the question of the feasibility of the labour-intensive growth path appears to be at least no less serious than that of the capital-deepening growth path.

Conclusions

In the context of the opportunities for and challenge to development under globalization, it is of general importance to clarify the dynamics, achievements and limitations of the ongoing Chinese development experience. This paper has undertaken such an exercise, with three central propositions. First, the prevailing economic growth path is in the main efficient, and is potentially capable of increasing labour's compensation and solving the problem of sluggish growth in employment. Second, the economic growth path, which is capital-deepening in character, is the result partly of the marketized economic system, and partly of the anti-market social and economic policies that arise in response to the excess of marketization before the turn of the century. Third, the sustainability of the prevailing pattern of social and economic development depends, ultimately, on the match between the two main aspects of the existing nexus of external relations and economic growth: on the one hand, the negative impact of economic surplus outflows similar to the rest of the developing world, and, on the other hand, the positive impact of fast productivity growth.

Granting that the prevailing pattern of China's economic transformation is sustainable, whether or not it represents a new model of developmentalism in the context of globalization after the 1997–98 East Asian crisis is a question with far-reaching policy implications. The analysis and discussion in this paper might offer some thoughts on this.

References

Acemoglu, Daron and Jaume Ventura (2002), 'The world income distribution', *Quarterly Journal of Economics*, 117 (2): 659–94.

Christopherson, Susan (2002), 'Why do national labor market practices continue to diverge in the global economy? The "missing link" of investment rules', *Economic Geography*, 78 (1): 1–20.

Dore, Ronald (2002), 'Stock market capitalism and its diffusion', *New Political Economy*, 7 (1): 115–27.

Fine, Ben (2004), 'Examining the ideas of globalization and development critically: what role for political economy?', *New Political Economy*, 9 (2): 213–31.

Harvey, David (1989), *The Condition of Postmodernity: An Enquiry into the Origin of Cultural Change* (Oxford: Blackwell).

—— (2003), *The New Imperialism* (Oxford: Clarendon).

International Monetary Fund (IMF) (2007), *World Economic Outlook*, Washington, D.C.: International Monetary Fund, April.

Lo, Dic and Guicai Li (2006), 'China's economic growth, 1978–2005: structural change and institutional attributes', Department of Economics working paper no.150, School of Oriental and African Studies, University of London, www.soas.ac.uk/departments/departmentinfo.cfm?navid=437.

Lo, Dic and Russell Smyth (2004), 'Towards a re-interpretation of the economics of feasible socialism', *Cambridge Journal of Economics*, 28 (6): 791–808.

Ram, Rati (2004), 'Trends in developing countries' commodity terms-of-trade since 1970', *Review of Radical Political Economics*, 36 (2): 241–53.

Singh, Ajit (1993), 'Asian economic success and Latin American failure in the 1980s: new analyses and future policy implications', *International Review of Applied Economics*, 7 (3): 267–89.

Singh, Ajit and Ann Zammit (2004), 'Labour standards and the "race to the bottom": rethinking globalization and workers' rights from developmental and solidaristic perspectives', *Oxford Review of Economic Policy*, 20 (1): 85–104.

Wade, Robert (2004), 'On the causes of increasing world poverty and inequality, or why the Matthew effect prevails', *New Political Economy*, 9 (2): 163–88.

—— (2006), 'Choking the South', *New Left Review*, No. 38: 115–27.

Vietnam and the Experience of the Asian Crisis

Pietro Paolo Masina

The Vietnamese Transition

In 1975 the 'Vietnam war'[1] ended with the collapse of the pro-American regime in the South. The country was reunified under the political institutions of the North, and the economy was reorganized through the extension of central planning and agricultural communes to the South. The reunification brought peace to a country that had been devastated by decades of war, but the new policies further strained an economy already in dire conditions. Within a few years Vietnam was facing a 'systemic crisis'. The imposition of collectivization measures was resisted in the South and contributed to the 'boat people' crisis. At the same time, Vietnam was again engulfed in a war when it decided to invade Cambodia in response to the military operations of the Khmer Rouge regime against its borders. The 'boat people' crisis and the war in Cambodia exposed Hanoi to an international outcry that further led to a contraction of aid flows, which had been already strongly reduced after the end of the war (Beresford and Dang 2000). Agricultural production was below the national requirement, resulting in chronic food shortage and insecurity for a large part of the population. Eventually, the 'systemic crisis' made apparent the need for economic reforms, initially introduced with local 'fence-breaking' activities at the local level and then with national experiments.[2]

The *doi moi* (renovation) process was launched officially at the end of 1986. Contrary to other transitional economies, the reforms were not carried out through 'shock therapy' but with a gradual approach, which allowed the society and the economy to adjust to market mechanisms. The first trials with limited pro-market reforms were attempted locally from the late 1970s and nationally from the early 1980s. After the adoption of *doi moi*, new policies were introduced and implemented step by step. An acceleration in the reform process occurred between 1989 and 1991 – but at that point the Vietnamese economy was ready to operate on the basis of market principles. Having put in place adequate foundations in the initial phase of the reform process, the economic transformation promoted during the 1990s and 2000s did not imply the displacement and destruction experienced by many transitional European countries.

Systemic change in Vietnam was obviously less complicated than in other transitional countries because here central planning was never extended to all the economic sectors and, conspicuously, did not extend to agriculture. The role of agriculture was (and still is) paramount in Vietnam, as the wide majority of the population was and still is employed in agriculture, and resides in rural areas. It is possible to argue that the *doi moi* was particularly successful because it started by reforming the agricultural sector and thus created the basis for a significant national market.[3] The substantially egalitarian redistribution of farm-lands to rural households allowed for a strong recovery of agriculture. By 1991, not only was food sufficiency achieved but Vietnam also became one of the lar-gest rice exporters worldwide. Subsequently, agricultural diversification and the (still embryonic) creation of non-farm activities in rural areas accounted for the largest contribution to poverty reduction.

By the early 1990s, Vietnam had become one of the most dynamic econo-mies of East Asia, although starting from very low levels of GDP (gross domestic product) per capita. In the first part of the 1990s, before the outbreak of the regional economic crisis, economic growth was consistently between 8 and 9 per cent per year. As is evident from Chart 1, Vietnam did pay a price for the regional crisis with a deceleration of growth, but it was much less affected than the other countries of the region. Recovery was also faster and more balanced than in the rest of East Asia, and by the mid-2000s, the economy was growing once again at more than 8 per cent per year.

The most striking indicator that Vietnam had successfully completed its transition towards a rather balanced market economy was not so much growth

CHART 1   *GDP Growth Rate, 1986–2006 Trend Line*

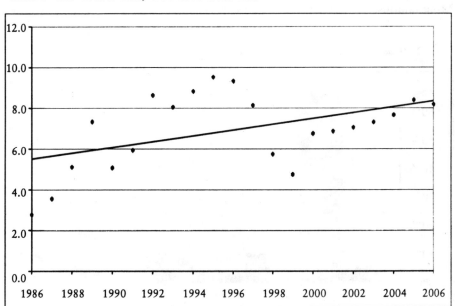

Source: World Bank, *World Development Indicators Online*, 2007.

as poverty reduction. While periods of rapid economic growth may, and often do, result in a deterioration of living conditions for the lower strata of the population, the case of Vietnam was remarkable for its inclusive distribution of gains. No other country in the world succeeded in reducing poverty so much and so fast as Vietnam did in the period 1993–2004: the number of households living below the national poverty line declined from 58 per cent to 18 per cent. A number of studies indicate that this impressive dimension of poverty reduction is confirmed even when assuming different poverty lines (for example, food sufficiency, one or two dollars per day, etc.) or qualitative indicators (such as the Participatory Poverty Assessments, World Bank 1999b and 1999c). Even the depth of poverty – the distance from the poverty line – was reduced for a large part of poor households. Research on marginal groups, such as migrant workers and street children, further confirms that living conditions improved even for those who are typically left out in periods of rapid economic transitions (Gallina and Masina 2002; Masina forthcoming). In this regard, Vietnam scored much better than China and many other Southeast Asian countries.

Poverty reduction remains a major concern for Vietnam, for various reasons. First, the country is still poor by international standards although GDP per capita is growing fast. If the gains from growth do not continue to be distributed among different sections of the population, there is a risk that the remarkable results achieved so far could be reversed, if not in absolute terms (income level measured by international indicators) then at least in relative terms (national poverty lines). Second, in some areas of the country, poverty reduction efforts have not resulted in a significant improvement of living conditions – this is particularly evident in areas inhabited by ethnic minorities such as the Northern Mountainous Regions and the Central Highlands. Third, the country is now

CHART 2 *Households Living Below the Government Poverty Line* (percentage)

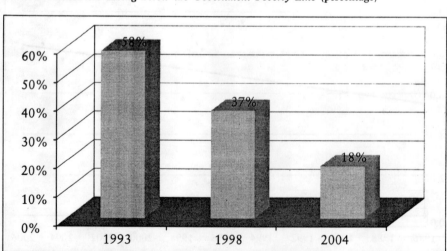

Source: GSO, *Living Standard Surveys*, 1993, 1998 and 2004.

facing massive transitions of industrialization and urbanization, with connected phenomena of displacement. The mechanization of agriculture will eventually make redundant large numbers of farmers in areas where underemployment or hidden unemployment are already apparent. Thus, a very large number of jobs need to be created in the urban and industrial sector to prevent the impoverishment of millions of households.

In broader terms, preserving and furthering poverty reduction requires keeping under control the growing inequality between rural and urban areas, and among different segments of the population. This is one of the main challenges facing the Vietnamese authorities. To a large extent, the poverty reduction results were achieved through the development of market forces, which could build upon the positive preconditions inherited from the pre-reform period: educational and health systems that were quite efficient even though they were strained by the lack of financial resources; a capable administration; a substantially egalitarian social structure. Once the opportunities were created, in both rural and urban areas, a large part of the Vietnamese population was fast and skilful in making use of them. The increasing inequality is a result of the operation of the same market forces that have lifted many households out of poverty. At the time of growing prosperity, the most vulnerable sections of the populations are not able to benefit from the new opportunities and risk being further marginalized. Therefore, to include these sections, there is a need for more effective income redistribution measures and stronger safety nets.

CHART 3 *Gini Index, Selected Asian Countries (2002–04)*

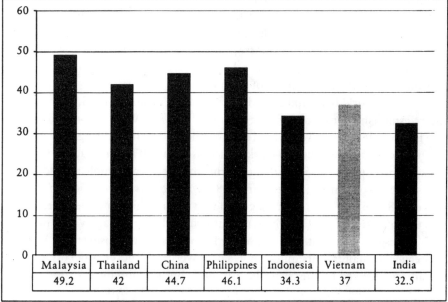

Malaysia	Thailand	China	Philippines	Indonesia	Vietnam	India
49.2	42	44.7	46.1	34.3	37	32.5

Source: UNDP (2006) *Human Development Report,* New York: United Nations Development Program.

Current data indicate that since the implementation of *doi moi*, income inequality has increased substantially, but less than in other Asian countries. While India and Indonesia score better than Vietnam in terms of equitable income distribution, many other Asian countries appear to have more unbalanced social structures. It is noteworthy that China, whose reform process shares several features with Vietnam, is experiencing a much higher level of income polarization: the income ratio of the richest 10 per cent of the population to the poorest 10 per cent is practically two times higher in China than in Vietnam (UNDP 2006).

The risk of an increase in inequality is greater because of international trends in the developing and developed countries. The Vietnamese leadership is aware that higher inequality may have a destabilizing role on the political system, but it seems that this concern is only partially translated into policies that support income redistribution. As the country becomes more economically developed, the creation of formal safety nets and stronger support to public services in education and health are expected to occupy a central position in the development agenda. While, for the moment, attention is concentrated on the positive results achieved, policy-making should not neglect the impending risks of further increases in inequality.

By 2010 Vietnam aims at achieving the status of a middle-income developing country. This target is also considered realistic by the World Bank. At the same time, the country is fully on schedule for fulfilling the Millennium Development Goals. Vietnam is now often presented as a 'role model' for other developing countries, with agencies such the World Bank attempting to take credit for their work in the country. However, looking back at the relations between the international financial institutions (IFIs) and Hanoi in the period from the early 1990s to the mid-2000s, it is evident that the story is more complex than it is often presented.[4] As elaborated below, the International Monetary Fund (IMF) expressed its discontent several times by interrupting its concessional lending. The World Bank alternated between criticism and praise, threats and encouragement – and eventually tried to claim a share of the Vietnamese success.

The World Bank and the IMF returned to Vietnam in 1993, a little before the re-establishment of diplomatic relations between Washington and Hanoi. The first couple of years were a kind of honeymoon. The IFIs had big expectations. Vietnam was implementing pro-market reforms and the IFIs were ready to welcome back the prodigal child. Since the government had already implemented a hard adjustment programme in the years 1989–91, the IFIs proved benign in their requests. Some observers even suggested that behind this benevolent behaviour was the influence of the US, which probably hoped to re-engage Vietnam for an anti-Chinese containment. In any case, the IFIs were soon disillusioned for Vietnam was eager to maintain its autonomy. The government never officially rejected the advice received by the 'sister institutions', but it maintained strong control over choosing the timing and sequencing of reforms. The IMF responded by cutting its lending agreed upon through the structural adjustment programme (SAP). The World Bank continued to lend, but by 1996 started to voice strong criticism.

As we will see in the next section, these complaints reached a climax just ahead of the Asian crisis and continued for some time after the crisis had unfolded. Vietnam was accused of being too slow in implementing reforms in key sectors: privatization of SOEs (state-owned enterprises), liberalization of foreign trade, reform of the financial sector and strengthening the role of the private sector. Once the crisis started to cast its heavy shadow over the region, the World Bank even suggested that Vietnam would face the risk of being left out of the recovery. As is often the case, the IFIs were trying to fulfil their political agenda rather than provide unbiased policy advice. Eventually Vietnam proved that its step-by-step attitude was the best suited to achieve balanced and inclusive economic growth.

After the regional crisis, the Vietnamese performance was so remarkable that the IFIs attempted to present Vietnam's success as their own success. Hanoi was presented as a good pupil of the new development orthodoxy, which could be named as the post-Washington Consensus. But some inconsistencies remained in the attitude of the IFIs. For instance, while the World Bank internationally presented Vietnam as a success story, locally it continued to pressurize Hanoi to adopt a more orthodox economic policy. These inconsistencies partially reflected the increasing difficulty for the IFIs to maintain coherence for their strategies after the loss of credibility in the Asian crisis and the ignominious demise of the structural adjustment programme in the late 1990s.

Resilience during the Asian Crisis

Officially, the Asian crisis started on 2 July 1997. On that day, the Central Bank of Thailand refused to defend the peg of the Thai *baht* against the US dollar, unleashing a free attack on a number of Asian currencies. This did not come as a surprise to most experts – with the possible exclusion of those working for the IMF. Already, in December 1996, the prospect of an economic crisis in Asia had occupied the front page of *Business Week*. Financial liberalization had exposed many Asian countries to unregulated inflows of speculative capital. In the case of Thailand, such speculative capital supported the creation of a real estate bubble. In South Korea, short-term investments encouraged the excessive expansion of productive capacity in industrial sectors in which a tendency towards overproduction was already apparent.

The economic malaise in the region revealed its symptoms in Vietnam from late 1996, at a time when the World Bank and mainstream economists were trying to force Vietnam to implement bolder market-oriented reforms. In 1997 economic growth in Vietnam decelerated to 8.2 per cent, from 9.3 in the previous year. The deceleration was explained as a sign that the reforms were losing momentum, and used to argue that there was a need for a *doi moi* 2 that could deepen the work of the first phase. This interpretation was further motivated by an alleged contraction of FDI (foreign direct invetsment) commitment and disbursement to the country in the months ahead of the regional crisis. Mainstream pundits stated that the FDI contraction was due essentially to national causes: because foreign entrepreneurs were unsatisfied by the excessive corruption, red tape and obstacles for doing business. The linkage between the unfolding of a major crisis in the neighbouring countries and a decline in FDI flows to Vietnam was concealed even once the crisis had unfolded, although over 60 per cent of FDI disbursement had previously originated from the countries hit by the crisis. A critical review of the data reveals that if the economic distress in the region is taken into account, and particularly the bursting of the real estate bubble, the alleged FDI contractions are easily explained. FDI commitments declined from $7,702 million in 1996 to $4,456 million in 1997, and this decline was due almost entirely to a contraction of $3,000 million in the real estate sector. Data on disbursement reveal that inflows in 1997 were actually higher than in 1996, and that a contraction occurred only in 1998 as a consequence of the regional crisis (Masina 2002b).

Contrary to the bleak predictions of mainstream economists, Vietnam remained conspicuously resilient during the regional crisis. Since the *dong* was not convertible, the country was protected from speculative attacks against the national currency. Financial contagion could not enter via short-term financial flows because they were strictly regulated. In neighbouring Thailand, a real estate bubble had been fuelled by hot money pouring into the country. In Vietnam, a similar tendency towards overinvestment in the real estate sector was visible in FDI flows, but its demise had much less serious consequences than in the rest of the region.

In the midst of a very dramatic financial crisis in the region, Vietnam was able to avoid being submerged. Its currency did not depreciate – actually it appreciated against most other Asian currencies except for the Chinese *yuan*. The financial sector was basically untouched by the storm, also due to very prudent macroeconomic management. The government set strict controls on trade flows and succeeded in balancing imports and exports to avoid creating a condition of vulnerability.[5] Unlike China, Vietnam could not afford to launch an anti-cyclical economic policy through state investment in infrastructure to keep the economy growing fast notwithstanding the regional depression. However, Vietnam managed to keep the economy afloat enough to consolidate the reform process and to further contribute to poverty reduction.

Interestingly, there was one area in which the Vietnamese state was able to channel resources and, eventually, to create an anti-cyclical stimulus to the economy: agriculture and rural development. Strengthening the rural sector was decided as a high priority by the Communist Party and by the government as soon as the effects of the crisis became visible in the region. Eventually, this produced two positive results. First, while in industry and services the regional crisis corresponded to a severe deceleration of growth, in agriculture the period from 1997 to 2001 saw a jump in growth rates contributing to a more resilient GDP growth. Second, in a regional context of crisis, the strength of the agricultural sector sheltered a part of the population that was temporarily prevented from finding job opportunities in the industrial sector. This counter-cyclical role played by agriculture made it possible to continue reducing poverty rates in Vietnam

CHART 4 *GDP Growth by Sector, 1996–2005*

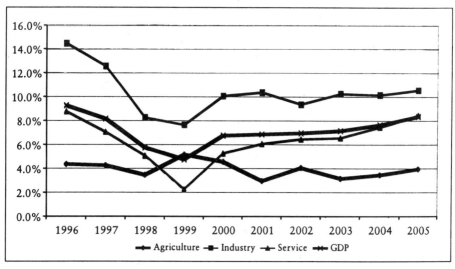

Source: World Bank, *World Development Indicators Online*, 2007.

during a period when other countries in the region such as Indonesia and Thailand saw a painful reversal of past achievements.

It is now well known that the regional crisis was used by neoliberal forces to impose on Asian countries economic reforms that these countries had resisted until they were forced to seek a bail-out from the IMF (see Bullard *et al.* 1998; Bullard 2002; Jomo 1998; Masina 2002a). The case of Vietnam was not different. The regional crisis presented an opportunity to the World Bank to ask for bolder pro-market reforms in order to allow the country to reduce the pain from the crisis, and to facilitate recovery once the crisis had receded. As usual, Vietnam did not openly oppose the recipes presented by the World Bank, but it maintained its cautious attitude. The government did introduce a number of reforms to enable a more favourable environment for the national private sector, but the privatization of SOEs and reform of the financial sector proceeded very slowly. By the end of the century it became clear that the advice promoted by economists working for the IMF and the World Bank to deal with the Asian crisis had failed substantially. In Indonesia, the IMF contributed to transform a financial crisis into a severe economic depression and then a collapse of the political system. In Thailand and South Korea, the IMF recipes had to be renegotiated several times as it was clear that these were aggravating the economic conditions and becoming increasingly unpopular (Chandrasekhar and Ghosh 2002). Among the countries that had been hit severely by the crisis, one of the first to recover was Malaysia, which did not accept the IMF bail-out and reintroduced state control on short-term capital flows, thereby reversing the liberalization measures that had been at the core of the IFIs' agenda.

In this context, it is no surprise that Vietnam tried to resist the pressure of

CHART 5   *GDP Growth, 1991–2006 (ASEAN 6)*

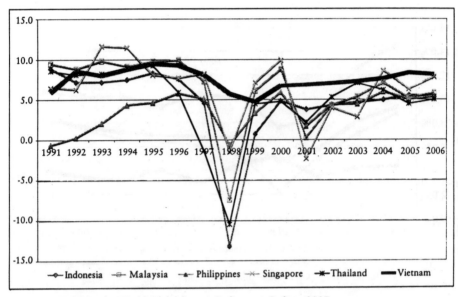

Source: World Bank, *World Development Indicators Online*, 2007.

the 'sister institutions' for a more orthodox and rapid implementation of Washington prescriptions (see World Bank 1997 and 1999a). By the end of the 1990s and early 2000s, however, it was clear that the IFIs had little space for manoeuvre to keep pushing Hanoi: Vietnam was the best performing among the six largest ASEAN economies. Not only did the Vietnamese economy grow faster than most others in each single year from 1991 to 2006, but its growth was much more stable and reliable.

We have already seen that an alleged decline of FDI to Vietnam was identified by neoliberal economists and by the World Bank (1997) as a sign of structural deficiencies in the national economic system. Difficulties in doing business were supposedly motivating foreign investors to look for alternative locations. These criticisms contain a grain of truth because in the late 1990s the Vietnamese business sector was suffering from an excess of bureaucratic controls that represented a real burden for the business sector (both national and foreign-invested). However, a comparative review of FDI flows to Vietnam and to the other four largest ASEAN economies (excluding Singapore) in the twenty years from 1986 to 2005 reveals a story different from the one usually told. Inflows to Vietnam suffered from a moderate contraction as the regional crisis unfolded (due to a decline in the real estate sector, as noted above), but overall there was a positive trend.

When compared with the other ASEAN economies, the Vietnamese pattern reveals interesting features:

- Flows to Vietnam remained low until the early 1990s, when the *doi moi* made this country more attractive.

- Vietnam did not attract a major FDI surge ahead of the regional crisis, and neither did it suffer from a major decline after the crisis. The investment curves were broadly the same as those of the other economies, but the changes are quite limited.
- By the mid-2000s FDI flows returned to the pre-crisis levels. Indeed, a further increase is expected with admission into the WTO (World Trade Organization).
- In any case, Vietnam was less afflicted by the speculative tendencies present in the region in the mid-1990s and therefore suffered less from the regional economic debacle.

Another major feature of FDI flows to Vietnam is often neglected. In the years ahead of the regional crisis, Vietnam succeeded in attracting a very high level of foreign investment in relation to the size of the economy. The trend was confirmed after the crisis. Net inflows of FDI as a percentage of the GDP have been among the highest in the region: higher than in China and several times higher than in India, Thailand and the Philippines. The percentage of GDP represented by FDI in Vietnam is very close to that in Malaysia, a country well known for its large foreign-invested industrial sector. The impact of FDI as a major source for industrial investment is still debated in the economic literature, and indeed the high level of FDI dependence may eventually reduce Vietnam's national autonomy in deciding upon its economic policy. In any case, the argument that Vietnam had to further liberalize its economic structure in order to attract more investment is clearly unsubstantiated by the data.

CHART 6   *FDI Inflows, 1986–2005*

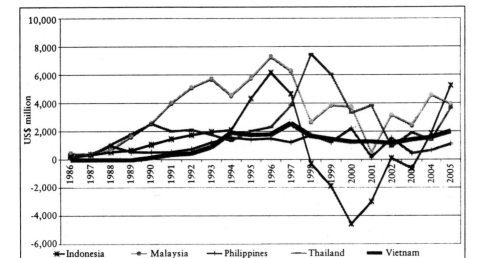

Source: UNCTAD, *World Investment Directory Online*, 2007.

CHART 7 *Net FDI Inflows, 2004* (percentage of GDP)

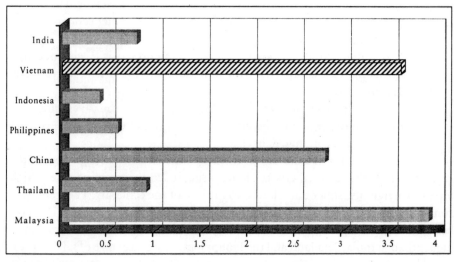

Source: UNDP, *Human Development Indicators Online,* 2007

Economic Policy

By the mid-1990s, the Vietnamese 'transition' had achieved major results. The country had evolved from a command economy to an economy based on market institutions. This was done without suffering the dislocation experienced by the transitional countries which had adopted IMF-inspired shock therapies. In the years immediately before the regional crisis, the first phase of *doi moi* had been completed. The second phase focused on the creation of a coherent system of rules and institutions to reduce distortions, promote further economic development and facilitate integration into the world economy. The main option for this second phase was the adoption of a neoliberal agenda, which, during the 1990s, had become more prominent in neighbouring countries. This option was supported by the IFIs, international economic advisors, and a few Vietnamese scholars and policy makers. Alternative views were much less visible in the policy debate, but it was clear that the political leadership resisted full-fledged liberalization. By the mid-1990s some observers denounced an apparent impasse in Vietnamese policy-making, suggesting that the national authorities had lost interest in deeper reforms once the economic conditions of the country had become more favourable. This sense of impasse was reinforced by the 8th Congress of the Communist Party in May 1996, which apparently did not produce any major decision for furthering of the reform process (see debate in Masina 2006). A few months thereafter, however, the Asian crisis unfolded. It sounded as a wake-up call because it unveiled the destructive potential of unregulated capitalist forces. The crisis confirmed the fears that too hasty an adoption of radical market reforms could destabilize the country both economically and politically. Once again, Vietnamese pragmatism prevailed. The government officially did not oppose the agenda promoted by the

IFIs, but it proceeded 'step-by-step', that is, by *de facto* resisting a number of measures, and deciding upon the timing and phasing in the implementation of reforms.

The adoption of a gradual and prudent strategy did not imply immobility. Important legislation was approved in key areas: simplifying and strengthening the regulation for private enterprises, the financial sector, the judicial system, etc. Among these reforms was progressive liberalization of foreign trade, with the ultimate goal of obtaining admission into the WTO. Eventually Vietnam was admitted into the WTO at the end of 2006, although the price paid during the negotiation was quite high. Vietnam, like every new entrant into the trade organization, had not only to accept the conditions applied on all member countries, but also the special 'WTO plus' concessions requested by the negotiating partners (the US, the European Union, etc.) in order to obtain their favourable vote.

The Vietnamese leadership has normally avoided formulating a rigorous development agenda. Officially, the only divergence between international agencies like the World Bank and the Vietnamese government is in the timing of the reform process, with Hanoi cautiously sticking to the 'step-by-step' model that also implies an element of learning-by-doing. However, a review of twenty years of *doi moi* implementation suggests that Vietnam may have a more fundamental disagreement with the post-Washington Consensus recipes. It is quite evident that Vietnam continues to believe that the leading role of the state in the economy should be preserved. The experience of the Asian crisis has probably confirmed this view. Those countries that moved away from the 'East Asian developmental state' model, like South Korea in the 1990s through the liberalization of short-term capital flows, paid a dear price for it. On the contrary, those who maintained a closer state control on the financial sector were more successfully insulated. Although there is only limited evidence to suggest that Vietnamese policy-making is strongly and coherently inspired by the regional 'developmental state' experiences, a number of indicators seem to point in that direction.

Particularly striking is the share of GDP represented by the state sector after twenty years of market-oriented reforms. Interestingly, the SOEs increased their economic importance in the first phase of *doi moi*. Acceleration in the privatization process in the mid-2000s has made the SOEs sector represent about 30 per cent of the national GDP, and it is unlikely that this figure will decrease in the near future. The SOEs still maintain a dominant role in strategic sectors (from steel production to export of cash crops like coffees, from ship-building to the banking system). While the national private sector is becoming stronger and has a fundamental role in the provision of new jobs, the state sector remains mainly responsibile for the modernization of national industry, investing in more technology- and skill-intensive sectors. The SOEs are also major attractors of FDI, as they can guarantee easier access to the Vietnamese market in exchange for access to new technologies and new markets overseas. It is noteworthy that the strong role of the SOEs in the economy was denounced by the IFIs already before the Asian crisis, and that this remains a contentious issue ten years after the crisis.

CHART 8   *GDP by Ownership*

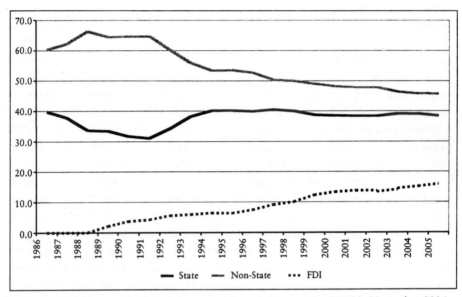

Source: IMF, *Vietnam Statistical Appendix*, Country Report No. 06/423, November 2006.

CHART 9   *Savings and Investment* (percentage of GDP)

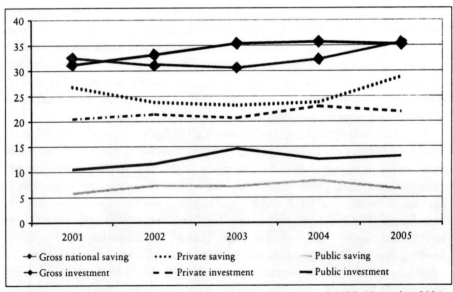

Source: IMF, *Vietnam Statistical Appendix*, Country Report No. 06/423, November 2006.

Another area in which Vietnamese economic policy appears quite distant from neoliberal principles is in the stimulus to growth through a high level of public investment. While private investment tends to be lower than private savings, state investment is constantly higher than public savings.

The high level of public investment is financed through two channels. The first is the normal budget expenditure, which increased from 24.4 per cent of GDP in 2001 to 27.1 per cent in 2005. Within this, a notable change in the current expenditure is represented by an increase in social services spending from 7.8 per cent of GDP in 2001 to 9.2 per cent in 2005. Such government expenditure resulted in a limited budget deficit, from –2.8 per cent of GDP in 2001 to –1.2 per cent in 2005. The second contribution to investment spending comes from off-budget expenditure, which include subsidies to SOEs, infrastructure bonds, education bonds, reform bonds, etc. The sum of budget and off-budget expenditure brought the overall fiscal balance (according to the IMF definition) to a much higher deficit: from –5.0 per cent of GDP in 2001 to –5.9 per cent in 2005 (IMF 2006).

These figures reveal not only a very active role on the part of the government in supporting public investment, but also a clear departure from the prevailing development orthodoxy. It should be noted that after the hard experience of the Asian crisis, most countries in the region have opted for a much more cautious approach. This may explain the difference in growth rates between Vietnam and most of its neighbours.

CHART 10   *Government Expenditure and Budget Balance*

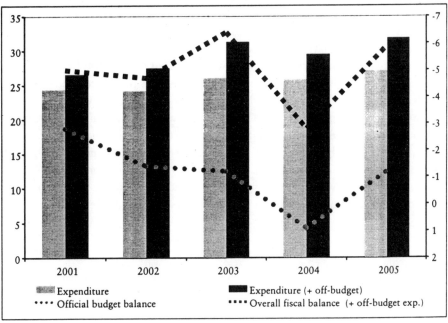

Source: IMF, *Vietnam Statistical Appendix*, Country Report No. 06/423, November 2006.

CHART 11   *External Debt* (percentage of GDP)

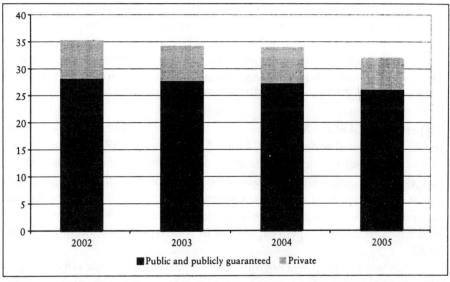

Source: IMF, *Vietnam Statistical Appendix*, Country Report No. 06/423, November 2006.

In the long run, large fiscal deficits may create a debt problem and force the government to adopt a tighter fiscal policy. By the mid-2000s, however, Vietnam had a rather sound position, and both domestic debt and external debt appeared to be sustainable. Public and publicly guaranteed debt amounted to 38.2 per cent of the GDP in 2002 and 44.0 per cent in 2005. Of this, domestic debt increased from 10.1 per cent in 2002 to 17.4 per cent in 2005. Public external debt saw a decline, instead, from 28.1 per cent to 26.6 per cent. In the same period, private external debt also declined slightly, from 7.0 to 5.9 per cent.

There is some irony in the news circulated in late 2007 that Vietnam was considering a diversification of its foreign reserves to reduce exposure to the US dollar. Although this move of the Vietnamese Central Bank was not expected to have *per se* a strong impact on the dollar, it would contribute to making the American currency even more volatile. In other words, by the mid-2000s Vietnam was on its way to become a new Asian tiger, coupling high economic growth with very positive social indicators. Through two decades of reforms and eventually accession to the WTO, Vietnam has completed its transition towards market-economy status. However, Hanoi has not lost its independence.

Notes

[1] 'Vietnam war' is obviously the term used by western sources. The Vietnamese refer to the conflict from 1965 to 1975 as the 'American war'.

[2] 'Fence-breaking' activities occurred through bottom-up pressures, but also through the initiatives of local cadres. For an analysis of the first phase of the reform process, see Fford and Sde Vylder (1996), Beresford and Tran (2004), Masina (2006).

[3] Vietnam managed to create those *virtuous circles* indicated by Gunnar Myrdal as a

condition for leading a country out of underdevelopment. It is possible that Myrdal's ideas influenced Vietnamese policy-making as Sweden was a major economic supporter of the country even during the war period.

[4] For a wider review, see Masina (2006).

[5] The trade balance was slightly negative in 1998 and had a deficit of only 100 million US dollars in 1999 (Masina 2006: 84).

References

Beresford, Melanie and Dang Phong (2000), *Economic Transition in Vietnam: Trade and Aid in the Demised of a Centrally Planned Economy* (Cheltenham: Edward Elgar).

Beresford, Melanie and Tran Ngoc Angie (eds) (2004), *Reaching for the Dream* (Copenhagen: NIAS Press).

Bullard, Nicola (2002), 'Taming the IMF: How the Asian Crisis Cracked the Washington Consensus', in P.P. Masina (ed.), *Rethinking Development in East Asia: from Illusory Miracle to Economic Crisis* (Richmond: Curzon Press).

Bullard, Nicola, Walden Bello and Kamal Malhotra (1998), 'Taming the tigers: the IMF and the Asian crisis', in Jomo K.S. (ed), *Tigers in Trouble: Financial governance, liberalization and crises in East Asia* (London: Zed Books).

Chandrasekhar, C.P. and Jayati Ghosh (2002), 'Finance and the Elusive Recovery: Lessons for Emerging Markets from South Korea and Thailand', in P.P. Masina (ed.), *Rethinking Development in East Asia: from Illusory Miracle to Economic Crisis* (Richmond: Curzon Press).

Fforde, Adam and Stefan de Vylder (1996), *From Plan to Market: The Economic Transition in Vietnam* (Boulder, Colorado: Westview Press).

Gallina, Andrea and Pietro P. Masina (2002), *Street Children in Vietnam: An Enquiry into the Roots of Poverty and Survival Livelihoods Strategies*, Federico Caffé Centre Research Report 3, Roskilde University.

Gainsborough, Martin (2004), 'Key Issues in the Political Economy of post-*Doi Moi* Vietnam', in Duncan McCargo (ed.), *Rethinking Vietnam* (London: Routledge).

Jomo K.S. (ed.) (1998), *Tigers in Trouble. Financial Governance, Liberalization and Crises in East Asia* (London: Zed Books).

Masina, Pietro P. (2002a) (ed.), *Rethinking Development in East Asia: From Illusory Miracle to Economic Crisis* (Richmond: Curzon Press).

—— (2002b), 'Vietnam and the regional crisis: the case of a "late late-comer"', *European Journal of East Asian Studies*, 1 (2).

—— (2006), *Vietnam's Development Strategies* (London and New York: Routledge).

—— (forthcoming), 'Street Children in Vietnam', in Hugh D. Hindman (ed.), *Child Labor Word Atlas: A Reference Encyclopaedia* (Armonk, New York: M.E. Sharpe Inc.).

Painter, Martin (2003), 'The Politics of Economic Restructuring in Vietnam: The Case of State-Owned Enterprise "Reform"', *Contemporary Southeast Asia*, Vol. 25, No. 1.

—— (2005), 'The Politics of State Sector Reforms in Vietnam: Contested Agendas and Uncertain Trajectories', *Journal of Development Studies*, Vol. 41, No 2.

Van Arkadie, Brian and Raymond Mallon (2003), *Viet Nam: A Transition Tiger?* (Canberra: Asia Pacific Press).

UNDP (2006), *Human Development Report* (New York: United Nations Development Program).

World Bank (1997), *Vietnam: Deepening Reforms for Growth* (Hanoi: World Bank).

—— (1999a), *Vietnam: Preparing for Take-off?* (Hanoi: World Bank).

—— (1999b), *Vietnam Development Report 2000: Attacking Poverty*, Hanoi: World Bank.

—— (1999c), *Voices of the Poor in Vietnam: Synthesis Report of Participatory Poverty Assessments* (Hanoi: World Bank).

Index

accumulated costs, 73–79, 80
  see also cost recovery
adjustment, 1–4, 10–11, 25, 53, 55, 57, 59, 61, 63, 65, 118, 215, 225, 237–39, 245
  path, 235
  strategies, 1, 10–11
age of finance, 225, 227, 229, 231, 233, 235, 237, 239, 241
aggregate demand, 13, 27–28, 126, 211, 283, 285, 288
aggregate expenditure, 281, 285, 288–89
agriculture, 11, 14–15, 24, 103, 108, 140, 167, 194–95, 225, 236, 293, 295, 298
anti-crisis policies, 13, 283
  short-term, 14, 284
Argentina, 2, 11–12, 36, 38, 55–56, 210, 214–16, 220–11, 240, 245
ASEAN economies, 300
Asia, 2, 11, 37–40, 47, 58, 89, 91, 118, 129, 182, 209, 213, 217, 246
  development outlook, 70–72, 74–75, 77–78, 80
Asian
  countries, 37, 58, 120, 128, 296–97, 299
  crisis, 1, 4, 9–10, 14, 32, 56, 69, 71, 73, 75, 77, 79, 81, 83, 85–89, 91, 93, 191, 194–95, 197, 199–201, 204, 233, 292–93, 297, 299, 302–03
  financial crisis, 5, 44, 56, 168
  markets, 139
  miracle economies, 73, 76
assemblers, 95
asset / assets, 2, 19, 21–26, 30, 34, 40, 43, 45–47, 100, 135, 158, 253, 259
  bubbles, 135
  markets, 20, 23, 227
  prices, 20–21, 29, 33, 135, 140

baht, 97, 116–17
bail-out, 46, 299
balance of payments (BoP), 9, 58, 77, 132, 180, 197, 199, 211, 215, 226, 230–34, 249, 258
balance sheets, 91–92
Bank Central Asia (BCA), 130
Bank Indonesia, 7, 121, 123, 130–31, 136
Bank of International Settlements, 33–34, 180
Bank of South Korea, 143, 146–48, 150–52, 154–55, 159, 161
Bank of Thailand, 92–94, 104, 118
Bank Management Statistics of Financial Supervisory Service, 157–58
banking
  crisis, 120, 181, 234, 253
  sector, 43, 101, 121, 137, 155, 231, 234
bank / banks, 4, 29–30, 33–35, 37, 43–47, 91–94, 105, 120–21, 127, 129, 143–45, 155–57, 169, 180, 232, 253
  compounded, 156–57
  merchant, 46, 145
  profitability, 8, 29, 142, 155, 158, 211, 216, 273, 278
  troubled, 144–45
Berkeley mafia, 7, 126–27
  myths put forward by, 130, 132
bond market, 24, 36
boom–bust cycles, 9, 32–33, 191
Brady plan, 209–11, 213, 220
Brazil, 2, 11, 38, 209–10, 215–18, 220, 260, 274
  exchange rate crisis, 209
business groups, 97–100, 106–05

capital
  account, 143, 153–54
   control, 258
   liberalization, 142, 153, 162, 182–83, 187, 198–99, 211
  accumulation, 114, 278
  and capitalism, 1, 23–24, 27–28, 30, 32, 108, 118, 239, 278
  in Thailand, 108–09, 111, 113, 115, 117

controls, 8–9, 80, 82, 153, 180–89, 262
    measures, 9, 182, 184, 186–87, 189
    regime, 184, 189
-deepening growth path, 13, 283, 290
flows, 17, 19, 21, 23, 25, 27, 29, 33, 35–
    36, 41, 65, 83, 138, 181, 211
    to developing countries, 35
    volatility, 153
formation, 91
inflows
    external, 209, 213, 216
    private, 131, 214
market, 9, 91, 142, 162, 181
    bank-based, 92–93, 103
multinational, 95, 98, 106–05
originating, 233
productivity of, 110–11, 118
restrictions, 93, 97–98
reversals, 10, 180, 209
shares, 109–11
stock, 110, 113–14, 118
    growth, 114
    see also banks
capitalist power, 28
Central Bank of Russia (CBR), 246–49, 251,
    253, 255
Central Bank of Thailand, 297
central banks
    independent, 227, 235
    intervention, 4, 22–23, 26, 28–29
Central European countries, 257, 259
centrally planned economy, 256
chaebol, 57, 165, 168
China, 10, 12–14, 27, 38, 58, 89, 118, 245,
    257, 259–60, 274–77, 279–83, 285, 289,
    296
    Federation of Trade Unions, 286–88
    and post-crisis globalization, 271, 273, 275,
        277, 279, 281, 283, 285, 287, 289
    state leadership, 13, 283–84, 289
    Statistical Yearbook, 280–81, 286–88
    see also Asia
citizenship, 165–68, 173
civilian employment, 236
commercial banks, 8, 91, 143, 145, 151, 155–
    58, 160, 253
    see also banks
compensation, 111
consumption of fixed capital, 118
contagion effects, 55, 152
cooperation, regional, 189
corporate
    management, 175
    sector, 120, 126, 142–45, 147, 162
cost / costs, 78, 81, 83, 85
    recovery, 81
countries

Country Report, 304–06
five, 5, 55, 57–59, 62
industrial, 33, 275–76
member, 238, 303
neighbouring, 298, 302
transitional, 293, 302
western, 175, 198
credit, 29, 44–46, 92–93, 103, 105, 121, 131,
    161, 187, 203, 212, 256, 258, 296
    and creditors, 40, 42–43, 99, 126, 131–32,
        220–21
    private, 42, 221
    derivatives, 43–44
    domestic, 200, 212
    government policy of, 160
    growth, 137
crime, 259–61, 264
crisis, 1–12, 55–59, 69–74, 81–85, 93–103,
    105–09, 111–14, 116–18, 123–29, 142–
    44, 146–50, 152–60, 162, 180–91, 251–
    57, 297–99
-affected countries, 55, 56, 59, 70–71, 99,
    181, 183
-affected economies, 5, 12, 69, 70–71, 72–
    73, 77, 81–82, 84–85, 181
    Indonesia, 125
    Malaysia, 75
    South Korea, 78
    Thailand, 80
boat people, 292
confidence, 124
currency, 12, 41, 123, 162, 229, 233, 245–
    46, 251–52, 254–55, 257–59, 261–64
economies, 2
fiscal, 10, 198, 200–01, 203
free capitalism, 27
    financial, 24
government debt, 258
political, 81, 225
prevention of, 23, 27
proletarian, 166, 168, 175
resolution policy, 220
systemic, 292
currency, 1, 9, 24, 27–28, 33, 57, 65, 91, 102,
    116, 123–24, 132, 189, 210–11, 225,
    264
    regional, 184–85
current account
    balance, 150, 198, 214, 228, 230–31, 233,
        248
    deficit, 9, 28, 117, 121–23, 144, 149–50,
        180, 197, 204, 214, 216, 231–32

debt, 7, 9, 34, 36, 42, 44–45, 92, 99, 114, 126,
    128–30, 180–81, 221, 252, 264
    crisis, 35, 201, 209, 252
    equity ratios, 143, 145–46

outstanding, 210, 212, 214
   service payments, 122, 129–30, 214–15, 252
   short-term, 36, 180, 233, 252
decumulation reserve, 26–28
deficits, 64, 121, 130, 133, 201, 213–14, 218, 230, 241, 247, 259, 284, 305
   domestic, 218–19
   external, 210–11, 214, 216
demand deficiency, 13, 281, 283
   systemic, 273, 277–79
democracy, 241
Department of Finance, Central Bank of Philippines, 201–03
deposit rate, 22–23, 200
developed countries, 32–33, 35, 39–40, 44, 64, 118, 214, 275–57, 296
developing countries, financial crises in, 17
domestic
   absorption, 27–28
   equity markets, 210–11
   producers, 212, 254

East Asia, 2, 12–14, 32–33, 35, 37, 39, 41–43, 55–56, 90, 152–53, 180, 182, 245–46, 254, 256–57, 275–80, 283, 293
   crisis-affected economies, 8, 181, 182, 187
   dynamic economies of, 14, 293
ECONIT advisory group, 121–25
economic activity, 64–65, 118, 218, 222, 225, 245
economic conditions, 57, 128, 288, 299, 302
economic costs, 87
economic crisis, 8, 11, 15, 76, 118, 120, 123, 127, 138, 140, 165, 168, 176
   national, 166, 175
   regional, 14, 293
economic development, 108, 241, 275, 285, 290, 302
   long-term path of, 14, 284
economic environment, stable, 5, 69
economic expansion, 5, 70–71, 73, 75–83
   broad-based, 73, 84
economic front, 136, 167
economic fundamentals, 72, 123, 125, 135, 137
economic growth, 9, 13–14, 64, 70, 75, 77–85, 120–21, 125, 127, 130, 134, 166, 275–76, 278–80, 282–85, 289
   acceleration of, 262, 288
   benefits of, 273, 277, 282
   capital-deepening path of, 14, 289
   fastest, 279
   high, 306
   inclusive, 297
   moderates, 85
   rapid, 294

recorded, 128
robust, 5, 76, 78–81
slow, 76
sustainability of, 273, 285
sustained, 165, 167
   targets of, 283, 288
trajectory, 69
   basic, 56
   lower, 70
economic instabilities, 121, 200
economic integration, 55, 280
economic model, 12, 246
economic outlook, 123
economic performance, 5, 7–8, 10, 69–73, 75–77, 79, 81, 83, 85–87, 167, 194, 207
economic plans, 82–83
economic policies, 5, 15, 69, 83, 124, 173, 204, 214, 220, 284, 290, 301–02, 305
economic recovery, 56, 74, 76, 82, 128, 183, 185, 201, 251
   rapid, 171
economic reform, 241, 292, 299
economic relationship, 280, 290
economic sectors, 91, 194, 293
economic sense, 280, 282
economic stability, 85
   endangered national, 121–22
   and growth, 30
economic stagnation, 70
economic strategies, 56, 65, 189
economic structures, 242, 301
economic team, 140
economic transformation, 282, 290, 292
economic vulnerability, 120–21
economic welfare, 83
economics
   and depression, 7, 299
   anti-cyclical, 14, 298
economists, mainstream, 297–98
economy / economies
   advanced, 89, 275
   demand-constrained, 289
   developing, 10, 237
   domestic, 84, 203, 212, 231, 233, 235
   five, 57, 59, 62
   global, 1, 37
   informal, 108, 118
   leading, 143–45
   low-income, 274
   national, 120–21, 162, 165, 168, 176, 278
   open, 9, 14, 188, 278
   post-crisis, 3
      South Korean, 8, 169
   reserve-accumulating, 27–28
   shadow, 259, 262
emerging market economies (EMEs), 28, 37–38, 229, 232, 242

emerging markets, 10, 33, 35, 40–41, 44, 47, 207, 209
employment, 2–3, 13, 25, 30, 33, 47, 63, 66, 108, 116, 166–67, 217–18, 236–37, 280, 282–83, 289–90
  contracts, 288
  expansion, 14, 278–80, 282, 288–89
  growth, 195, 237, 278, 285
  growth aggregate, 5, 65
  rates, 195
  relationship, 287
enterprises, 63, 99, 232, 234, 260, 284–85, 287
  financial, 168, 232
equilibrium, 19–20, 22–26
equity
  markets, domestic, 210–11
  private, 40
Europe and Central Asia, 43, 274
exchange markets, foreign, 20, 22, 25, 34–35, 162, 229
exchange rate, 3, 6–7, 22–23, 25–29, 122, 143–44, 149, 155, 162, 199, 209–12, 216, 248–49, 254–55, 257–58
  band, 216–17, 250
  crisis, 120, 123
    and recovery, 216
  equilibrium, 25
  fixed, 121–22, 144, 257
  overvalued, 11–12, 123, 245–46, 248
  policies, 11, 216–17
  real effective, 116–17, 249
  stability, 212–13
  stabilization, 26, 210
exports, 9, 12, 14, 56–58, 65, 90, 93, 95–96, 102, 136, 188, 205, 215, 218, 230–31, 248
  automotive, 95–96
  export-to-GDP ratio, 280
  growth of, 5, 66, 136, 218
    rates of, 57–58
  non-oil, 218
  performance of, 57–58, 80
  total, 102, 248
external account, 11, 198, 211–12, 214
external balances, 209, 214–16, 221
external debt, 7, 42, 99, 226, 228, 230, 232–34, 253, 306
  stock, 232
  see also debt
external sector and economic crisis, 197

finance
  consolidation of, 4, 37, 41
  international, 36, 105, 204
finance capital, 32–33, 41, 99, 241
  in developing countries, 32

foreign, 227, 229
financial
  centres, 105, 242
  crisis, 1–7, 10, 12, 15, 17, 19–29, 33, 35–36, 55–57, 63–64, 67, 118, 142, 150–52, 162, 209
    domestic, 3, 26
    and recovery in South Korea, 142
  firms, 32–35, 37
  flows, 5, 19, 22, 26, 32, 35, 47, 69
  institutions, 4, 7, 35, 37, 39, 92, 121, 145, 149, 151–53, 158, 169, 201
  instruments, 135
  investors, 32, 40–41
  liberalization, 1, 3–4, 10, 32, 37, 39, 41, 55, 72, 76, 83, 180–81, 183, 185, 187
  markets, 4, 10–11, 44, 55, 57, 118, 135, 152, 159, 214–16, 229
    deregulation of, 211–13
  resources, 209, 295
  sector, 2–3, 7, 33, 37, 41, 47, 56, 121, 133, 140, 142–45, 147, 149, 158, 297–99, 303
  structures, corporate, 123
  systems
    global, 4, 36, 39, 46
    international, 2, 4–5, 35, 37, 69, 189
Financial Supervisory Commission (FSC), 145
Financial Supervisory Service (FSS), 145
firms, 37, 40–41, 45–47, 91–93, 95–97, 99, 126, 146, 165, 169
  foreign, 2–3, 98
  listed, 105, 145
first world assets, 21–23
first world wealth-holders, 19–24, 30
fiscal activism, 284–85
fiscal policies, 5, 11, 56, 63, 79, 128, 133, 162, 182, 216, 218, 221, 225, 235, 255, 284
fixed capital, 118
fixed exchange rate system, 162
foregone output per capita, 74–80
foreign banks, 156–57, 159–60
foreign capital, 7–8, 98, 142–43, 145, 147, 149–55, 157–62, 226, 233, 241
  inflow of, 2, 7, 62, 98, 142–43, 149–50, 154–55, 158, 180, 211–12, 234
foreign debt, 91, 120, 122, 129, 210, 231–32, 234
foreign direct investment (FDI), 37, 91, 94, 116, 136, 149, 154, 162, 183–84, 188, 216, 231, 281, 300–01
foreign exchange, 24–25, 56, 65, 122, 125–26, 148, 211, 215, 229, 231, 275
  markets, 20, 22, 25, 34–35, 162, 229
  reserves, 7, 22, 24–26, 29, 64–65, 135–36, 143–44, 152, 154–55, 185, 246–47, 250, 257–58, 264, 275–76, 278–80

foreign institutional investment (FII), 40
foreign investment, 6, 11, 41, 56, 62, 95, 97,
     102, 215, 249, 301
  inflow of, 12, 245
foreign investors, 2, 8, 39, 135, 150, 159–60,
     169, 181, 186, 199, 209, 217, 247, 250,
     300
foreign portfolio investment, 94, 151

global capital, 12, 39, 241–42
global economic performance, 76, 78, 83
global economic trends, 278–79
global markets, 6, 102, 139
globalization, 15, 32, 89, 183, 273, 275, 278,
     280, 290
government, 39, 63–65, 78–80, 82–85, 92–
     93, 126–30, 140, 147–48, 166–69, 203–
     05, 217–27, 251–57, 259–60, 262–64,
     284–87
  budget, 128–30, 214, 259
     deficits, 63, 247, 256
  debt, 214–15, 252, 255, 259, 284
  developmentalist, 165–66
  efforts, 23, 185
  expenditure, 213, 215, 218–19, 305
  failure, 205, 259
  intervention, 23–24, 180
  local, 284, 287
  officials, 175, 255
  policies, 103, 188–89, 254, 283, 285–86,
     288–89
  poor track record in reducing economic fluc-
     tuations, 138
  programme, 220, 247
  revenue, 202–03, 218, 246
  sector, 142, 144
  securities, 29, 201, 251
  services, 262
  set, 14, 298
  spending, 12, 245
  three-party coalition, 235
gross domestic product (GDP), 29, 34–35, 64,
     81, 85, 101–03, 108–10, 114–16, 118–
     20, 191–94, 198–203, 245–46, 252,
     262–64, 284–301, 285–306
  deflator, 116
  growth, 59–61, 114, 195, 299–300
  per capita, 14, 70–82, 85, 103, 195, 258,
     285–86, 294
     growth, 74–75
  Southeast Asian countries, growth rates in,
     254
gross investments, 137, 193
  gross domestic savings and, 193
gross national product (GNP), 191–92, 228,
     230, 232, 235
growth, 5, 10–13, 15, 30, 55, 57–59, 61–63,

102–04, 113–14, 118, 191–92, 194–95,
     210–11, 215–18, 226–27, 286
  acceleration, 73, 79, 81
  engine of, 56–57, 65
  financed, 11, 216
  path, 283, 285, 289
     economic, 282, 288, 290
     labour-intensive, 13, 282, 289–90
  rates, 59, 65, 67, 103, 111, 113, 118, 191–
     92, 216, 218, 245, 247–48, 298, 305
     high, 58, 191–92, 253
  rebound, 273, 275–76
  trajectories, 70
  wage rate, 288

Hanoi, 296–97, 303, 306
hedge funds, 4, 34, 39–40, 43–44, 46, 139,
     200
Hong Kong, 38, 275–77
hot money, 7, 135–36, 138, 140, 231, 234
households, 10, 103, 137, 160, 172, 174–75,
     294–95
  loans, 8, 160
human capital, 162
hyperinflation, 11, 209–10, 212, 214–15
Hyundai Motors workers' complaints, 170,
     176

income
  distribution, 13, 63, 238, 282, 296
  median, 175
  share, 109–11, 116
Independent Social Scientists Alliance (ISSA),
     226, 242
India, 27, 29–30, 57, 89, 118, 296, 301
Indonesia
  and South Korea, 182
  economic crisis, 127, 135, 140–41
  GDP per capita, 73–74
  government recovery policies, 7
  left, 131, 133
  post-crisis recovery, 128
  slow recovery, 7
inelastic price expectations, 20, 22–23
  see also prices
inequality, 23, 32, 165–66, 261, 273, 278, 295–
     96
initial public offers (IPOs), 36
interest rates, real, 211–12, 229, 235, 238, 241
international capital markets, 76, 210, 213,
     220, 223
international finance, 36, 105, 204
international financial institutions (IFIs), 225,
     241, 296–97, 299–300, 302–03
International Monetary Fund (IMF), 2, 7, 11,
     36, 56, 69, 81–82, 84, 91–92, 114, 123–
     33, 140, 144, 150, 153, 155, 165, 168–

69, 173, 182–83, 187, 203–04, 216–17, 220–22, 225–26, 234–35, 241–42, 251–52, 254, 256, 262, 265–66, 296–97, 299, 302
loans, 125–26, 128, 131–32
programmes, 125, 130–32
recommendations, 7, 127–29
investment
goods, 227, 235, 283
rates, 5–6, 9–11, 59, 62–63, 133, 192, 194, 209
investment banks, 39, 41, 123

Jakarta Stock Exchange (JSX), 133, 135, 137–39
index, 133, 135, 137–39
Japanese banks, 150–52
jobless growth, 8, 195, 206, 226–27, 236–37
jobs, 8, 82, 120, 148, 165, 167, 171, 176, 188, 236, 279–83, 289, 295, 303
Justice and Development Party (AKP), 225–28, 256
and government, 225–27, 235

labour
activism, 176
business–government committee, 175, 177
cheapening, 273–74
costs, 116, 163, 213
income share, 111, 116
leaders, 175
markets, 166, 176, 226
participation rates, 238
productivity, 6, 82, 108, 111–12, 116, 118, 195, 238, 240, 288
relations, 8, 169, 171, 175
rights, 14, 288–89
share, 109, 116, 118–19
unions, 147, 175–77
wage, 108, 226, 238–41
Latin America, 107, 201, 209–11, 213, 246, 258
letter of intent (LoI), 127
life expectancy, 258–59, 262, 264
liquidity, 2, 4, 7, 9, 22, 30, 33, 35, 44–47, 120, 123–24, 126, 129–30, 138–39, 153, 180, 187, 204, 206, 241
crisis, 120, 123, 129, 138
loans
commercial, 149–50
sub-prime, 45, 137, 139, 200
local assets, 22–23, 26, 33
local currency, 22–26, 29, 92, 213
assets, 22–26, 29
low-income economies, growth performance, 274–75

macroeconomics
demand, 289–90
fundamentals, 11, 211–12
policies, 2, 55, 256
Malaysia / Malaysian
authorities, 181–83, 185–88
government, capital controls regime, 184
rates, 183
recovery, 128, 132, 183–84, 299
market
domestic, 28, 95, 98, 181, 218
forces, 183, 211, 289, 295
reforms, 13, 258, 282–83, 292, 296, 299, 302
sub-prime, 46
medium term economic expansion, 76, 79–80, 188
merger and acquisition (M&A), 37, 39–40, 159–60, 162
hostile, 159–60, 162
Mexican crisis, 39, 150, 217
middle-income economies, growth performance, 274–75
mismanagement, economic, 7, 91, 151–53, 252–53, 256
monetary authorities, 121–24, 133, 260
monetary crisis, 123–24, 126
monetary policies, 124, 129, 229, 241
super-tight, 211–12
money supply, 29, 124, 186, 210–11, 214, 247–48, 257–58
moral hazard, 32, 85, 220–21
mortgages, 45, 137, 139
sub-prime, 45, 139
multinational companies, 98, 106, 116
murder rates, 260

national income and product accounts (NIPA), 109
neoliberalism, 175, 187, 273–74, 276, 278–79
and neoliberal economists, 9, 300
new order economic mafia, 130, 132
newly industrializing countries (NICs), 28, 64

oil industry, 12, 218, 259, 264
oil prices, 12, 80, 200, 219, 245, 248, 255, 263–64
open unemployment, 66–67, 133, 227, 236
operating surplus of private unincorporated enterprises (OSPUE), 109
opportunity cost per capita, 73–80
Organization for Economic Cooperation and Development (OECD), 34, 142–43, 152–53, 242
organized labour, 166, 175–76
output growth, 13, 57, 62, 67, 237, 289

pension funds, 32, 34, 44–47
Philippines and South Korea, 71, 81
portfolios, 19, 46, 93, 138, 206
    investments, 198, 231
post-crisis, 2–3, 6, 8, 10–11, 57, 63, 66, 70, 77,
    81, 94–95, 117, 128, 153, 169, 173, 210,
    216, 225–26, 229, 231, 234–35, 237,
    245, 258, 265, 273–75; *see also* crisis
    adjustment, 11, 210, 226, 231, 234–35, 237
        path, 235, 237
        policies, 210
    characteristics of growth, 226–27
    decade, 81, 94
    era, 94, 226
    experience, 2, 57
    globalization, 73–75
    growth
        performance, 70–73
        trajectories, 10
    period, 70, 77, 81, 229
    recovery, 8, 128, 153, 216
    see also crisis
post-crisis economic development in Russia
    achievements, 258–62
    government revenues and expenditure,
    262
    nature of current growth, 263–64
    real exchange rate of, 262–63
post-crisis experience in Brazil, 216
poverty rate, 172, 175
poverty reduction, 14, 206, 293–95, 298
pre-crisis
    dirigiste growth, 245
    era, 103
    high growth, 265
    levels, 6, 67, 155, 225, 301
    performance, 5, 69
    period, 6, 62, 76, 223
    see also crisis
price / prices
    basic commodities, 138
    expectations
        elastic, 20
        inelastic, 20, 22–23
    expected, 226, 229
    relative, 192
private capital, 5, 31–32, 214, 264
private equity funds (PEFs), 4, 34, 39–41, 158–
    59
private investment, 63, 114–16, 305
privatization, 7, 11, 13, 106, 148, 210, 226,
    231, 239, 264, 283, 285, 297, 303
productivity
    gains, 14, 111–13, 289
    growth, 111, 282, 290
profit rate, 6, 110–11, 113–14, 118, 285

property sector, 137–38, 204
public
    debt, 7, 128–29, 203, 205
    investment, 6, 103, 284, 305
    sector, 11, 13, 120, 122, 129, 148, 223–26,
        232, 234–36, 283, 287

rates of growth of money supply, 247
rating agencies, 46–47, 82, 200, 203, 241
real economy, 1, 3, 32, 133, 135, 137–38, 140,
    255
real estate
    bubble, 297–98
    sector, 298, 300
real exchange rate, 11–12, 56, 210, 212, 216,
    229, 232, 248, 257–58, 262, 264
real wages, 112, 218, 224–25, 238, 240, 278
recession, transformational, 12, 245, 253
recovery
    of investment, 6, 114
    period, 76, 109
    process, 82, 153
    slow, 128–29
refinance, 210–13
    rate, 250–51
reform process, 225–26, 292–93, 296, 298,
    302–03
regional crisis, 14–15, 293, 297–302
reserve accumulation, 27, 258
Reserve Bank, 29–30, 185
restrictive policy, 216, 222
Russia / Russian
    capitalism, criminal nature of, 255
    crime rate in, 261
    crisis, 255, 265
    currency crisis, 246–65
    economy, 12, 245, 254–55, 258
    government, 251–52, 257
    market economy, 256

savings rates, 5–6, 59, 62
secondary and tertiary sectors, 286–87
shareholder
    foreign, 157
    largest, 157, 159
short-term bank debt, rapid growth of, 180
Singapore, 94, 181
slow growth, 113, 116, 137, 239
slow recovery, 128–29
social
    citizenship, 165–68, 173
    costs, 73, 88, 127
    development, 118, 273, 276, 282
    policies, 10, 206
South Korea / South Korean
    crisis, 8, 152

economic restructuring and social displace-
    ment, post-crisis, 165
economies, post-crisis, 8, 169
financial crisis and recovery, 142
firms, 7–8, 143–46, 149, 151, 159–60, 162,
    165
grassroots, 166
performance of commercial banks in, 156
post-crisis, 4, 8, 57
stockmarket, 149–51, 154–56, 160
    see also Asia
Southeast Asia, pre-crisis, 57
    see also Asia
speculative capital, 64, 204, 297
state-owned enterprises (SOEs), 13–14, 148,
    210–11, 283, 297
stock equilibria, 20–21, 26
stockmarket boom, 29
strong governments, 84
structural adjustment policies, 209, 211–12
structural adjustment programme (SAP), 226,
    296–97
sub-prime crisis, 46, 198, 200, 204
    lending, 4, 138
    loan, 10, 139
sustained economic growth, 211, 220–21, 227,
    283, 288

Taiwan, 94
tax / taxes, 12, 118, 130, 141, 205, 218, 259,
    262, 264
    collection, 10, 205–06, 247, 255, 259–60
    effort, 201, 203
Thailand, 93, 96–98, 101–03, 105–08, 112,
    114, 117, 151, 182–83, 297
    capital, 6, 91
    capitalism, 108–09, 111, 113, 115, 117
    cost recovery in, 79
    economy, 6, 97, 103, 108
    and South Korea, 128, 299
    stockmarket, 105–06
    Thailand Research Fund, 107
    Thaksin government, 6, 103, 106, 132
third world assets, 3, 19, 21–22, 24, 30

third world economy, 21–22, 24
Tim Indonesia Bangkit (TIB), 130, 135
transition economies, 180, 257–58
Turkey
    labour market, 236–37
    Turkish government, 11, 227
    Turkish *lira* (TL), 29–30, 32, 229–30, 232
    Turkstat data, 227, 236

unemployment
    payments, 175
    rates, 65–67, 138, 195
        open, 66–67
United Nations Economic and Social Council
    for Asia and the Pacific (UNESCAP),
    69
unit labour cost, 116–17
    measure, 119
unorthodox crisis management measures, 9,
    189

Vietnam, 10, 12, 14–15, 257, 292–94, 296–
    301, 303, 305–06
    FDI flows, 298, 300–01
    and Vietnamese, 14, 292, 295–98, 300,
    302–03, 305–07
    Vietnamese Central Bank, 306

wage / wages, 32, 109, 112, 171, 177, 213–
    15, 218, 223–24, 238, 240, 263, 278
    earners, 108–109, 118
Wall Street, 45–46
wealth-holders, 19–20
wholesale price inflation (WPI), 225
work participation, 227, 238, 266
workers
    informal, 109, 119
    non-regular, 171, 176, 178
    overseas, 77, 191, 205–06
    population rates, 65–66
World Trade Organization (WTO), 301, 303,
    306
worldwide suppliers, 95